P9-AFA-417

WITHDRAWN

FRANCES
FULLER
VICTOR

Dedicated
with thanks and esteem
from

Hazel Mills & Constance Bordwell

to

Prof. Randall Mills & Douglas Bordwell

and with much appreciation

to

historians

EAP Crownhart-Vaughan ◆ Nellie Pipes McArthur
Jean Bell ◆ Alice Smith LLD ◆ Dorothy Sonneman
Rebecca Tarshish ◆ E.G.R. Remington-Dunhill
Virginia Guest Ferriday ◆ Rev. Irene E. Martin
Barbara W. Tuchman LLD ◆ Marie Sandoz LLD
Helen Wallis O.B.E. ◆ C.V. Wedgewood D.B.E.
Gladys Seufert ◆ Dorothy O. Johansen PHD
Dorothy N. Morrison ◆ Caroline P. Stoel
Barbara Elliott Davies ◆ Susan K. Seyl
Virginia Errutia ◆ Priscilla Knuth

FRANCES FULLER VICTOR

THE WITNESS TO AMERICA'S WESTERINGS

Hazel Mills &
Constance Bordwell

Edited by
Thomas Vaughan &
Marguerite Wright

PEREGRINE PRODUCTIONS
for the
OREGON HISTORICAL
SOCIETY PRESS

Frontis: Frances Fuller Victor
ORHI 5463 NO. 1080

Copyright © 2002
Peregrine Productions
Portland, Oregon
for the
Oregon Historical Society Press

ISBN: 0-9726948-0-3

Design and production
Bruce Taylor Hamilton
Santa Fe, New Mexico

Printed in Canada

CONTENTS

FOREWORD

Reflections on the Eve
of the 200th Anniversary
of the Lewis & Clark
Expedition

O NE HUNDRED AND FORTY YEARS AGO, in the formative years of
the Society, there were countless reassuring stories and examples of
some basics in human conduct. These memories have been preserved by
this old and vigorous institution devoted to learning. And they reinforce
that we know: We do want to learn, we do want to remember, and most
of us want to know and review the past. The question persists: What
really happened?

In most cases we prefer reality first and myths and their endless and
assorted cousins as dim seconds. Fortunately, in this absorbing story at
last completed, Frances Fuller Victor saw it that way. As we shall see, it
was seldom to her advantage to do so. Throughout her brilliant, star-
crossed life, this early Oregon historian of the Northwest announced
that she was looking for the truth in events. That pursuit was not always
beneficial to her career.

In their seemingly endless saga, namely the writing of this long
delayed biography of Mrs. Victor, my colleagues have turned up no mention of a near contemporary of hers in Europe, the renowned German
historian Leopold von Ranke. Yet in somewhat unlike works in different
languages they each expressed the basic need, to tell as nearly as possible
what actually happened. Their emphasis on "truth" indeed was as perva-
sive as Sir Edward Coke's focus on "reason" when England's supreme six-
teenth century legal mind declared that "reason is the life of the law, nay
the common law itself is nothing else but reason."

The history professor, deep in his Berlin library surrounded by students, and the "lady correspondent" strolling the foam-flicked sands of a Clatsop beach in Oregon near Lewis and Clark's abandoned salt works, were both in pursuit of the truth of things.

It would appear that, in part, this pursuit of truth was easier for Mrs. Victor. In her later career she was moving up and down the north Pacific coast, from San Francisco to Victoria by wagon, stage, steamers, and, in time, by train. She was listening and recording the secrets and stories of the first generation of Oregon and Western pioneers, men (mostly) rapidly vanishing from the farms, flumes and forest clearings.

But, in another aspect, her tireless drive and industry and acute insights were dangerous to legend and lore, often controversial, and possibly explosive. And Mrs. Victor, always short of cash, was never short of vital projects to be done and the courage to follow them through to completion. Together, with these qualities she was also fearless and enormously talented. Who knew, Judge Matthew Deady and H. H. Bancroft possibly excepted, what pioneer recollections might be produced and pulverized next?

Nor should we forget, our heroine was researching and writing in the last half of a socially straightjacketed century; she was, in effect, twice scarred as a Civil War military widow. Frances Fuller Victor was a highly intelligent writer, living by her wits and her pen, often around wary, sober-sided sages. And, for obvious reasons, she alarmed women as well as men, possibly more. Who knew what she might decide to publish next?

What we know a century after her almost destitute death on a lonely winter night in Portland, Oregon, is that her reputation as a Western historian and writer rises ever higher. Hers was a singular achievement we proudly recognize that Mrs. Victor was now a unique frontiers historian and one of America's greatest chroniclers of nineteenth-century history.

The Oregon Historical Society is proud of our century-old association with so great a personage. I wish to extend the Society's thanks to Mrs. Hazel Mills, Lt. Commander Constance Bordwell, USNR, and to their associate Priscilla Knuth, and to editors Thomas Vaughan, Oregon

Historian Laureate, and his principal associate Marguerite Wright for this special contribution to knowledge in North America, and for returning Frances Fuller Victor to life.

Norma Paulus
Executive Director
Oregon Historical Society
November 2002

INTRODUCTION

FRANCES FULLER VICTOR: for more than half a century this force of nature roamed the western frontiers of nineteenth-century America. Chronicler, historian-poet, journalist and oral historian; she was a puzzle then and she is now, demanding much reflection. In part the problem is how very direct Victor was, usually. Almost always she said or wrote what she meant, recording factually what she observed. We are all recipients of her special endowments as an observer on our several western frontiers.

Most important for our era is the huge mass of information she acquired on her endless trawls. There is still much to consider in all she saved for us in the essentially unprocessed, uninterpreted information concerning those uncharted landscapes Victor visited from the Isthmus of Panama north to Alaska. How much she has provided, not only for us in the Far West, but as well for historians of the Erie Canal and upper New York State districts, and the early Michigan, Illinois and Nebraska frontiers. With cool confidence and curiosity born of Puritan New England genes running back to "good King Egbert," we can be grateful that she spent far more time recording and preserving rather than interpreting her bountiful catch.

Francis Fuller was born in the township of Rome, Oneida County, New York, on May 23, 1826. In the years that followed, "Frank," as her parents and sisters and brother always called her, alluded to her taproots in 17th century New England. This gave her association with old Puritan stock and an identity with notables of earlier times. Where it suited her, "Frank" would on rare occasions reveal her lineage back into the mists to King Egbert—a most successful Wessex contemporary of Emperor Charlemagne. These signs of grace and favor in later years, especially with all the bad luck she suffered with her two willful if not wayward husbands, were sources of strength. And certainly the unexpected turns and turbulence Frances experienced, as the eldest in the large family of a robust innkeeper on the canals, early railroads, and turnpikes of an expanding America, would have on occasion demanded any kind of reassurance.

Fortunately for Frances, her mother Lucy Williams, a descendant of the famous Puritan reformer and founder of Rhode Island, Roger Williams, and her younger sister Metta were very supportive allies who dreamed her dreams.

The extensive family was always on the move, generally west, looking for the "main chance." Her father, Adonijah Fuller, also descended from Plymouth Colony stock, was scarcely twenty when he married his sixteen-year-old bride and moved to a stop on the Erie Canal. From there they pushed on in a few years to a larger coaching inn in Wooster, Ohio, one of the countless new villages with important crossroads and larger prospects. It was there, in a newly established female academy, that the Fuller daughters received the little formal education they experienced. And it was there that Frances published her first poetry in the local newspapers and for the *Home Journal* in New York City. At twenty-two Frances published a romance in Boston, *Anzietta, the Guajua or The Creole of Cuba: A Romance of the Spanish Isles*.

It is remarkable even today to read that youthful Frances and Metta Fuller were published in New York, and were familiar with many editors and writers including Edgar Allen Poe, and that Rufus Griswold included Frances in *The Female Poets of America* (1849). The following year Poe included her in a quartet of "most imaginative female poets in the United States." In 1851, Griswold published a collection of poems by Frances and Metta. During this heady time Frances also was planning a trip to Europe, but she was called home to Ohio by her father's illness and death. "Frank" was suddenly singled out with the help of Metta as the Fuller family supporter. They became assistant editors of the monthly *Hesperian* and the *Odd-Fellows Literary Magazine,* an aspiring monthly in Detroit, Michigan. They were associated with this publication until 1853 and in June of that year Frances married Jackson Barritt in the Congregational Church in St. Clair, Michigan, the Fuller family sanctuary.

The Barritt family had also migrated to southern Michigan from upper New York State, where the father Hiram established himself as a farmer-surveyor, justice of the peace and framer of the constitution in the 1846 Michigan legislature.

In the spirit of pioneering, Jackson and Frances soon moved west to Omaha, Nebraska Territory. Frances wrote some very accomplished and telling articles during this interlude especially pertaining to the harsh realities of western farm life.

For reasons undefined their marriage did not flourish. In the meantime Frances' sister Metta had married her literary agent Orville J. Victor and in 1858 relocated in New York, where Orville had joined the *United States Journal* as editor. Metta, now an established author of successful romances, joined *Beadles' Home Monthly* as an editor. Very soon both husband and wife were writing for Beadle, especially for the Dime Library Series and he for the Biographical Library. In 1861 Beadle Company employed Orville as editor. Frances now moved east to join them in Manhattan.

She re-established her literary career, writing for *Godey's Ladies Book* as well as two Beadle Dime Novels concerning the Nebraska frontier. "Frank" was in fact, grounding herself in historical writers such as Washington Irving and earlier romantic chapters of the American frontier experience. As she later wrote in her preface to the *River of the West*:

> reading and musing over Astoria and Bonneville [Washington Irving] in the cozy quiet of a New York study no prescient motion of the mind ever gave prophetic indication of that personal acquaintance which has since been formed with the scenes, and even with some of the characters which figure in the works just referred to.

She could not know then the range of living legends waiting for her in the Far West.

Before moving away from Barritt-Victor's somewhat mysterious interlude in the Nebraska frontier I wish to mention a review of this experience which I years ago discussed at length with Alice Smith and Mari Sandoz, two profound students of the middle frontier. They revealed how profoundly important this experience of hard frontier farm life would have been; and that her very telling descriptions of the Nebraska years would not have been born of a fecund imagination but from seasons of harsh reality. Mr. Barritt also drank hard.

It should be mentioned here as well that Jackson Barritt the former husband returned to Michigan and enlisted as a thirty-four-year-old volunteer private in Company G, Ninth Cavalry on March 16, 1863. On April 14 he was mustered in and soon rose to sergeant. In October of the following year he was killed on picket duty near Stone Mountain, outside Atlanta, Georgia. It would seem that she never mentioned this except in her later pension application.

In Manhattan she wrote constantly, including *East and West: The Beauty of Willard's Mill* (1862) as well as *The Land Claim* (1862). Meeting members of New York literati, especially in company with Metta and writers Alice and Phoebe Gary, Frances would years later in San Francisco refer to Horace Greeley, Robert Dale Owen, John Greenleaf Whittier, Whitelaw Reid, Ole Bull the violinist, and feminine writers and editors such as Mary Booth, Kate Field and Marcy Dodge. It was in Metta Victor's home that she was introduced by Orville to his younger brother Henry. He was a native of Pennsylvania born October 11, 1828 and raised and educated in Sandusky, Ohio, a town well known to Frances. Henry Clay Victor had gone on to further study in Norwalk and then into marine engineering. In August, 1855 he was commissioned third assistant engineer in the United States Navy and sent to the U.S.S. *San Jacinto* on patrol in Chinese waters during the Opium Wars. This tour was followed by service off the African coast where he contracted a debilitating fever which put him in the naval hospital in Brooklyn.

As second assistant engineer he served on the *Michigan* and was then promoted to First Engineer serving from June, 1862 aboard the *Canandiagra* on Civil War blockade duty off Charleston harbor, South Carolina. It was in this sector that the U.S.S. *Unadilla* captured a British-owned iron screw steamer *Princess Royal*, filled with valuable military supplies for the southern armies. Henry Victor was part of the prize crew that brought the important capture into Philadelphia Navy Yard. Some time during this period Henry, a widower, received news of his award of prize money from this capture. Subsequently he paid serious attention to Metta's older sister.

In the midst of this time of war stress and excitement Henry and Frances planned to wed. The decision to marry this career sailor two-and-a-half years her junior would bring our romantically inclined historian moments of happiness intermixed with a dozen years of grief and humiliation. In the parlance of the day it would appear that Henry was an officer but not a gentleman, a good engineer but a financially irresponsible sot. At the onset Metta and Orville wished them well. Henry had his order to join the U.S.S. *Narragansett* in the Pacific squadron and Frances had joined her hero on the steamship *America* bound for the Isthmus of Panama. It must have seemed to Frances that, once they crossed the Isthmus, a whole new life lay ahead filled with bliss and opportunity. The Golden State and San Francisco lay ahead. As with so many sojourners before and after, this was a new start, one filled with promise.

Thomas Vaughan
Oregon Historian Laureate

CHAPTER I

VOYAGE TO THE GOLDEN GATE

(1863)

FRANCES FULLER VICTOR could have been the dashing and desirable heroine of one of the orange paper-covered novels so popular with American readers in the 1850s. With her luxuriant auburn hair and challenging hazel eyes, did she not wear that incredible dream of a dress that captured the Russian admiral's attention at the grand ball in San Francisco in 1863?

And was she not the gently-reared descendant, on her mother's side, of England's first king, Egbert, and, on her father's side, of ancestors who were early settlers of Plymouth, Massachusetts?

Yes, all of that, and more, would have enraptured Victorian audiences from New York State, where she was born in 1826, to Portland, Oregon, where she died in 1902. She was buried in a grave unmarked until the Daughters of the American Revolution eventually installed a suitable plaque in Portland's Riverview Cemetery in 1947.

Instead of starring as a heroine in the Penny Press, Frances Fuller Victor's role was to serve as one of the least recognized and possibly most prolific chroniclers of one of the most exciting periods of American history. She began writing as a child poet who developed into a teenage short story writer published in popular magazines. She did, indeed, write Dime Novels and other fiction, newspaper columns and commentary, and factual reports based on personal experiences and observations, published in newspapers and magazines from coast to coast. Finally, her massive historical accounts earned her the honorific title, "Mother of Oregon History," and a hallowed position on the north face of the the state capitol's senate chamber in Salem.

Born the first of five daughters of Adonigh and Lucy Williams Fuller, Frances was four when the family moved from Rome, New York to Pennsylvania and then to Ohio where she attended a girls' school. She began submitting poems and stories to local editors, was published in Sandusky and Cleveland newspapers, and inspired her younger sister, Metta, to follow in her footsteps. Both sisters won recognition as talented writers among celebrated denizens of New York publishing circles. *The Home Journal*, which featured such distinguished authors as Henry Wadsworth Longfellow, Charles Dickens, James Fenimore Cooper, and Herman Melville, also listed both Fuller sisters as contributors. Edgar Allen Poe included Frances in a list of leading poetesses, and she and Metta were often seen in New York literary salons in 1848–49. Then, in 1850, their father died, and the young ladies were required to return to the Midwest to help support the family. By July, they were working as assistant editors of the *Monthly Hesperian* and *Odd-Fellows Literary Magazine* in Detroit.

In 1853, Frances married Jackson Barritt of Pontiac, Michigan, the son of Hiram Barritt, a former state legislator, farmer, and surveyor. In 1855, the young couple began pioneer life on a land claim near Omaha, Nebraska. Her sister, Metta, married Orville James Victor, editor of the *Sandusky* (Ohio) *Daily Register*, in 1856. The next year Orville and Metta moved to New York where he became editor of a number of publications at various times. Meanwhile, for the Barritts neither homesteading nor marriage was successful, and Frances returned to New York in 1859 to resume her writing career. Her production included Dime Novels as well as stories published by *The Home Magazine*, now being edited by Metta. In March, 1862, Frances was granted a divorce on grounds of desertion. In May, 1862, she married Henry Clay Victor, brother of Metta's husband, Orville.

Scarcely a year later, during the five weeks between March 11 and April 18, 1863, profound changes in the life of Frances Fuller Victor—in her sense of place, her identity as a married woman, and her determination to launch a new literary career in San Francisco—began. At 36, at the height of her physical vigor and creative powers, attractive, auburn-haired Frances realized that her voyage to the Golden Gate constituted a point of no return for her as a family member and writer.

Her restless second husband, now First Assistant Engineer Henry C. Victor, U.S.N., was scheduled to join the U.S.S. *Narragansett*, attached to the Navy's Pacific Squadron, in Acapulco, Mexico. The couple planned to travel together to Acapulco, and then Frances would proceed alone to San Francisco. They would sail from New York aboard the Vanderbilt Line's wooden side-wheeler, *Northern Light*,[1] for Aspinwall, now Colon, on the Caribbean side of the Isthmus of Panama.

Frances would vividly recall their departure on that chilly March morning. They were accompanied to the North River dock of the Vanderbilt Line by Metta's husband Orville, who had chronicled the December disaster of the Battle of Fredricksburg that had cast a pall of gloom over the Union cause. Also, the mission of the *Narragansett* on the Pacific Coast was a wartime secret. In describing the scene, Frances reported: "There was noise and jostling . . . . people fell into each other's arms and wept . . . . Then the bell was rung to warn loiterers ashore, and the leviathan began to tremble and chafe at her moorings." As the cheering died away, the *Northern Light*, her decks jammed with passengers, churned down the Hudson River channel. When the ship passed the Battery and steamed through the Narrows to Lower New York Bay, Frances felt a resurgence of the enthusiasm for the magnificent "eastern village" that she had entertained since her girlhood days in Ohio.

In the meantime, Henry had secured first-class accommodations for himself and Frances. Fares for passage and food between New York City and San Francisco were surprisingly reasonable: $200, first-class; $156, second class; $100, steerage. Brigantine-rigged, with three masts, the steamer had three decks. When crowded, as it was during the Civil War, it transported over 1,200 passengers. On this sailing there were more passengers than the ship could accommodate. A mad scramble ensued as each tried to preempt the space for which he had paid, though the press had warned that after the outbreak of the war Vanderbilt ships had been turned into "floating pigsties," overloaded, undermanned, and often without sufficient food on board.[2]

Since 1860, Vanderbilt had shared a profitable monopoly of the vital steamship operations between New York and San Francisco with the Pacific Mail Steamship Company. Vanderbilt ships ran the two thousand miles between New York City and Aspinwall and return on the Atlantic; Pacific Mail steamers traveled from Panama City to San Francisco and return on the Pacific. Three steamers a month cleared in both New York City and San Francisco, transporting mail, passengers—both military and civilian—and supplies, via the Isthmus. In addition, Pacific Mail steamers carried California gold and Nevada silver, which helped to finance the war to preserve the Union. Ships on both runs, especially those carrying bullion, were targets for the Confederate fleet on the Atlantic and for Confederate privateers on the Pacific side of the war-torn continent.

Only a week earlier, the north-bound *Northern Light* had been pursued off the Florida coast by an unknown vessel, which had been driven off by a unit of the Union Blockading Squadron. Now the south-bound *Northern Light* was relatively safe, as she followed the route that the Union Navy prescribed for all Vanderbilt steamers: five days due south in the open Atlantic, then through the Mayaguana Passage in the Bahamas and the Windward Passage between Cuba and Haiti, thence southwesterly across the Caribbean to Aspinwall.

During the first leg of the voyage, the Victors explored the vessel, measuring over 250 feet in length. They discovered that the first- and second-class cabins occupied the entire first deck from stem to stern. Their cabin opened into an elegant dining salon and other public rooms located amidships. In warm latitudes, they joined fellow passengers on deck by day to sympathize with invalids, to grumble about shipboard conditions, and to exclaim at the antics of flying fish and porpoises. At night they paraded the starlit decks if they were not playing cards, according to Frances.

Early in the morning of March 21, the *Northern Light* docked at Aspinwall. Here Frances and others bought oranges and sea shells from smiling native women while Henry learned that the *Narragansett*, which he had been ordered to board at Panama City, had gone up the coast to Acapulco, Mexico. Two hours later, they were summoned to board a car of the

Pacific Mail Steamship Co.

FROM NEW YORK TO CHINA,

VIA

Isthmus of Panama, San Francisco and Japan, and vice versa.

Making trips from New York to San Francisco in 22 days;
From New York to Hong Kong in 51 days;
From Hong Kong to New York in 49 days, and from San Francisco
to New York in 20 days.

STEAMERS LEAVE NEW YORK THE 1st, 11th AND 21st OF EACH MONTH; LEAVE SAN FRANCISCO 10th, 19th AND 30th.

The Steamer of the 11th of each month from New York connects at San Francisco with the Steamer for China on the 3d of month following. Passengers from China for New York leave San Francisco by the Steamer of 19th of each month.

This Company sells Tickets in connection with Steamers for Central and South America, Australia, France and England, by all the different routes.

Steamers on the route from New York to Aspinwall.	Steamers on the route from San Francisco to Panama.	Steamers on the route from San Francisco to China.
Henry Chauncey,	*Golden City,*	*Colorado,*
Arizona,	*Constitution,*	*Great Republic,*
Ocean Queen,	*Sacramento,*	*Celestial Empire,*
Rising Star,	*Montana,*	*Niphon,* } Building.
New York,	*Golden Age,*	*America.* }

OFFICERS:

Allan McLane, Pres't, New York;   Oliver Eldridge, Agent, San Francisco;

F. R. Baby, Agent,   "   S. L. Phelps, Agent, Hong Kong;

D. M. Corwine, "   Panama;   J. H. Phinney, Agent, Yokohama.

Advertisement for the Pacific Mail Steamship Line.

American-built Panama Railroad at its passenger depot on a wharf that extended into Navy Bay.

After seven miles through a swampy tropical jungle to the first station on the bank of the Chagres River, Henry got out his sketch pad and Frances began jotting down word pictures of that "delightful ride! I don't remember the fellow of it in all my many experiences of travel," she wrote. The luxuriance of the vegetation along the way, the glimpses of planters' houses nestled in beds of bloom, curious crowds of natives in holiday dress at every station; the clear, fine atmosphere; the violet haze hanging over the Andean ridge that connected the two continents—all this and more intoxicated her senses.[3]

A few months later, when Frances introduced herself to California readers under the pen name of "Florence Fane," she confessed that on that memorable ride she had shed her loyalty to New York City and become a Californian about the time she reached "the highest grade of the Panama Railroad." She did not know how to account for it: Was it the landscape—the forests, the vines, the gaudy flowers—or was it the native women in flounced skirts "with red flowers in their hair, and baskets of yellow oranges on their heads, their white teeth, and saucy laughter . . . ?" She posed this question to "Will," her traveling companion (a stand-in for Henry), whom she cast as a much-traveled older brother in her weekly column. He had simply scowled, "as older brothers often do," and stroked away at his sketch, but his sketches made plain that he was not "thinking of New York nor the girl he left behind him."

Then she invited her readers to remember how they, too, had "changed from New Yorkers, Chicagoans, Bostonians, and Cosmopolitans into Californians, about five miles from Panama City." In "The Panama Railroad,"[4] Otis described the steep descent from the summit to Panama City with Mount Anson looming over all. The long metallic roof of the railroad's Pacific terminal, the cathedral towers, the high, tiled roofs and decaying fortifications came into view. Leaving the depot, passengers caught their first glimpse of the Gulf of Panama with its sweeping, white beaches. To their left were the company's warehouses and covered wharf, where small steamers, lighters, and tugs wait to transfer passengers and freight to the Pacific Mail steamer, *Golden Age*, and other ships anchored in the harbor. Among them, Frances wrote, was a depot ship to which Henry reported to get orders to proceed to Acapulco to board the U.S.S. *Narragansett*.[5]

Frances longed to explore the high-walled, turreted city on the rocky peninsula that extended from the foot of Mount Ancon into the Gulf. But she had to transfer their considerable baggage to the *Golden* Age by means of a stifling, overcrowded lighter. After a two-hour wait, she boarded to find another scramble for accommodations underway. Since Henry was delayed in boarding, she went supperless to bed, consoled by the fact that he would accompany her as far as Acapulco.

The next morning, affairs took on a more cheerful aspect. The *Golden Age* proved to be roomy and clean, their breakfast was good, and "the sea—oh, the Pacific in the tropics is mildness and serenity itself, compared with the Atlantic . . . ." The *Golden Age*, they learned, was one of four steamers operated by the Pacific Mail that made connections with the steamers of the Vanderbilt Line by way of the Panama Railroad. They sailed the northwesterly course between Panama City and San Francisco with stops at Acapulco and Manzanillo in 12 days or more.[6]

During the days that the Victors spent aboard the *Golden Age*, they found that the Pacific Mail steamers were rightfully renowned for the ability of their officers and the excellence of their accommodations. Further, they agreed that if Henry's ship was not in port when the *Golden Age* took on coal at Acapulco, Frances would disembark to await the *Narragansett's* arrival and Henry's departure. Then, alone, she would take the next north-bound Pacific Mail steamer.

Upon entering the ancient port at 10 o'clock one evening, they learned that the *Narragansett* had not yet arrived. So the Victors disembarked with their luggage for a memorable sojourn. Here Henry learned about the secret maneuvers of the Navy's Pacific Squadron and more about the prize money he expected for his part in the capture of a British ship caught when trying to run the Union blockade of Charleston in 1863. And here, too, Frances found material for her ever-ready pen.

In her "A Short Stay in Acapulco," Frances reported that at the Custom House a seasoned Californian had offered to "chaperone" them to a good hotel. People, accompanied by a canine chorus, were astir, selling flowers, fruit, and shells at the ship's dock, but she looked for a bandit in every shadow as they traversed the moonlit streets of "decayed old Acapulco." At length they found themselves at a bar, lit by a single tallow dip, in one corner of a large room with an earthen floor in a long, adobe building. They were greeted by a short, stout person with cropped hair and in male attire: Madame Moreno, the French wife of "old John," Spanish by name, but French, Frances speculated, should the army of Maximilian occupy Mexico. This accommodating couple had come from New Orleans some time since.

When the Victors indicated they were seeking room and board, John led them down an outside corridor that faced a walled garden, through a mahogany doorway, and into a slightly elevated room. This shadowy cavern was filled with a row of hospital-like cots, each with a mattress, two sheets, a pillow, and with a strip of matting beside it on the floor. "I shivered secretly," Frances recalled. But when they returned to the bar to bid farewell to fellow passengers and Henry suggested that she return to the ship with them, she protested: "You will have to live here until the *Narragansett* returns. I can live here, if you can."

It was well after midnight when they returned to their quarters and selected beds near the door, left ajar for ventilation. Along the wall, Frances spied a tin wash basin and stone water jug on a pine table. Above it, through a large, square opening, she glimpsed the night sky. While inspecting their baggage piled against a wall, she disturbed "an immense spider" that left her uneasy until she fell asleep from sheer exhaustion.

The terrors of the night vanished at daybreak. Remembering the change that "a sudden burst of clear, bright day" had wrought, she philosophized: "Our first impressions are by no means reliable. Our most distasteful experiences are good for us; all knowledge, however acquired, is for our advancement . . . . [L]et me testify that I never had a more delightful waking." Soon she and Henry, clad in night robes and sandals, were savoring Madame Moreno's early morning French coffee and hot cakes as they lounged in camp chairs in their "sitting room" in the outside corridor. Here they looked out on a garden, bright with flowers and lime trees, and beyond the wall to a fine specimen of lordly coconut palm.

FRANCIS FULLER VICTOR

After a ten o'clock breakfast of fowl, vegetables, and fruit, Henry paid his respects to the American consul, who introduced him to the agent of the Pacific Mail Steamship Company and others. Most came to call on Frances and to acquaint her with local customs and the "glorious' and often troubled history of the palm-fringed bay of Acapulco. [7]

During the heyday of New Spain in the Pacific, Acapulco had been the great port and trade center of Mexico's west coast. As early as 1591, Spanish galleons had sailed across the Pacific from Manila in the Philippines to anchor here and offload cargoes of Chinese goods—silks, cotton fabrics, earthenware, and wax—to be displayed at the annual fair. From all over New Spain as far away as Peru, merchants flocked to the fair to compete for the precious imports, and to gamble and dance the fandango.

As Frances explored contemporary Acapulco, alone or with Henry, she saw that its storybook past had all but been obliterated by earthquakes, attacks by buccaneers like Sir Francis Drake, frequent civil wars, and more recently, by foreign invasion. [8] The most recent attempt was on the tenth of last January when a squadron of the French fleet had bombarded the city for 12 hours and fired on the old Spanish fort for two days in an effort to take the port. Though the attempt failed, the American consul predicted that, if Maximilian's army were successful, France could control Mexico by blockading major ports like Acapulco and Manzanillo.

After the first day of what was to be a 12-day stay for Frances, she saw the necessity of using the early morning and evening hours for sightseeing, as the hours between the ten o'clock outsized breakfast and the tasty four o'clock dinner were scorching. On her morning walks, which she took alone as Henry was usually otherwise engaged, she picked her way through many of the male population who had spent the night on the earthen pavements. By the time she arrived, they were breakfasting on coffee, fruit, and tortillas, dispensed by obliging market women. Her favorite haunt was a coconut grove on the bay, cathedral-like in its "stillness and grandeur." Here a native family entertained her by harvesting a fresh coconut and serving her a glass of its milk, which she found too raw for her taste. On these friendly forays she came to regard the "princely" palm as a union of sun and sea, and she singled out "the solitary one" beyond the garden wall whose top she could see at night as she lay in her cot "with one great star shining through its branches as they moved in the night breeze."[9]

During the oppressive heat of the day, she sipped sweetened lime juice that she made from limes in the garden, entertained a visitor, or read or wrote at a small pine table in the corridor, while keeping an eye on the "impertinent" gray lizards on the wall. The scorpion, which she learned to call *alacran*, she instinctively pursued, crushing one to death under a piece of matting with her slipper.

Her evening walks with Henry after dinner were longer and more daring. On one occasion, they counted the marks made by French cannon on the sea side of the fort—the only "memento" left of "proud, violent, aggressive Spain" in "miserable and dilapidated Acapulco." They never visited the fort. "Sluggish, uniformless, and hatless" Mexican soldiers saw to that. Yet Frances credited them with having taught the French "to respect their fighting qualities." However, Henry, who understood the strategy of a naval blockade, reminded her of the consequences of a French naval blockade of Acapulco.

This possibility deprived her of the opportunity to tour the interior mountains and visit the ancient city of Oaxaca, some 70 miles southeast of Acapulco. An invitation to do so had been tendered her by an American family whom the Victors met upon their arrival. The husband, a sea-going trader who regularly made trips into the interior by mules, wanted to take his consumptive wife on the journey, with a view to improving her health, but not "without a lady to accompany her . . . . The scheme suited me well," Frances noted in her account. She had been willing to brave *banditti* to satisfy her curiosity about a place "out of the line of travel" and where she had the expectation of being "lionized by the inhabitants." But she yielded to her husband's objection that the French might blockade Acapulco during her absence.

All too soon, the *Narraganset* arrived to take on coal and First Assistant Engineer Henry C. Victor. Frances reported that she enjoyed being "seated in the commander's gig. . .and being rowed over shining waters . .

. to the rhythmical plash of three sets of oars." But left by herself most of the day, she must have felt stranded. In her corridor "sitting room" she composed the first of two poems she wrote on the voyage. Inspired by the life-giving palm and her upcoming separation from Henry, it is titled "Palma" and reads, in part:[10]

> *What telleth thou to heaven,*
> *Thou royal tropic tree,*
> *Morn, or noon, or even,*
> *Proud dweller by the sea. . . .*

The Victors spent their last evenings together, sometimes bathing among the rocks, where the sharks dare not risk their tender skins. Sometimes wandering about the city, they were invited to enter when "pausing to listen to the music of the 'light guitar'." On some occasions, they caught glimpses of Mexican ladies clad in black with beautiful lace mantillas on their heads, such as they observed also at church or in religious processions. Remembering these romantic moments with Henry, Frances later regarded Acapulco "with a certain tenderness." This she attributed to her awareness of past glories and present helplessness, but she had not taken kindly to the climate, and except for leaving Henry, perhaps to suffer a recurrence of the fever had contracted off the coast of Africa, she was ready to depart when the Pacific Mail steamer *Sonora* arrived from Panama City to recoal and embark a few passengers like herself.

As the vessel steamed northwesterly for the port of Manzanillo, talk was inevitable of the pending French invasion of Mexico. There also were fears that confederate privateers might seize south-bound Pacific Mail steamers transporting gold and silver to the Panama Railroad and would attempt, with the aid of Confederate sympathizers, to destroy the defenses of San Francisco and take over the state of California, if not the entire Pacific Coast. In these lines from her second poem, "Palo Santo," penned on her voyage to the Golden Gate, there is a note of uncertainty:

> *In these deep tropic woods there grows*
> *A tree, whose tall and silvery bole*
> *Above the dusky forest shows*
> *Among the souls of sinful men . . . .*

How do we all in life's wild ways,
Which oft we traverse lost and lone,
Need that which heavenward draws our gaze,
Some Palo Santo of our own!

Except for such soul-searching, Frances Fuller Victor's days aboard the *Sonora* were delightful. She watched great whales spout and dive alongside the ship, and clouds of seagulls hover overhead when it neared land. Beyond Point Conception, north of Santa Barbara, she exulted in views of the Coast Range as the steamer rolled through rough seas off the central California coast.[11]

On the morning of April 18, word was passed that they were approaching the Golden Gate. Frances was among those who lined the railing for their first glimpse of the entrance to San Francisco Bay, and the city that gold and silver built on the sandy hills within. By afternoon, the *Sonora* had rounded west-jutting Point Lobos and was crossing the bar into San Francisco Bay by way of a strait, named the Golden Gate by the American explorer and politician, John C. Fremont, in 1846. Frances was familiar with his *Geographical Memoir Upon Upper California.*[12] It had foreseen that the wealth of the Orient was destined to flow through the natural gateway to a flourishing village, then called Yerba Buena, on the south side of the spacious bay. During the Gold Rush, the term became increasingly appropriate and gained world-wide currency.

The strait—the drowned mouth of the unified Sacramento and San Joaquin rivers—was some four miles long and a mile or two wide. Hidden from view from the sea by the mountainous coastline, passage through it was fraught with surprises. At the narrowest point on the south side of the strait was Fort Point. Perched on a rocky height near the beach, it had been built in 1857 by the U.S. Army, after the model of Fort Sumpter.[13] Now, its batteries were San Francisco's first line of defense against Confederate privateers and other armed vessels. Before the Civil War, between Fort Point and Black Point, two miles further inland, Fremont had built a charming cottage with a sweeping view of the San Francisco peninsula for some 20 miles.

Though prepared by travel writers like Horace Greeley and Bayard Taylor, both of whom she knew and had read, Frances was dismayed at the seemingly endless sandhills.[14] However, she was somewhat reassured as the *Sonora* steamed toward heavily fortified Alcatraz Island. Its three sets of batteries, she learned, faced in three different directions. Nineteen cannon were directed at the Golden Gate; 35 faced the hillside city of San Francisco and the new Presidio on the site of the old Spanish Presidio; and 40 pointed toward the settlement of Sausalito to the north.[15]

Only a month before Frances' arrival, authorities had uncovered a conspiracy by a local secret association of Secessionists to capture the fortifications of San Francisco Bay and declare California a Confederate state. The unlikely plot anticipated the capture of treasure-laden Pacific Mail steamers that would then proceed to Victoria, B.C. to divide the spoils.[16]

This failed attempt, which resulted in a capture of contraband cannon and ammunition and a number of armed plotters, and another plot to capture Mare Island Navy Yard, prompted the erection of gun batteries on Angel Island and the construction of Fort Mason on Black Point. The Fremont property was confiscated and a battery of artillery installed on the site of the family cottage.[17] In any event, at Frances' arrival and during the rest of 1863, she was aware of real and rumored Confederate threats and felt closer to Secessionists than she had in New Jersey.

By late afternoon when the *Sonora* passed the foot of Telegraph Hill, Frances saw the glittering, well-protected hillside that constituted the heart of San Francisco, a city she had adopted unseen. Gone was the Mexican village of Yerba Buena and its anchorages so colorfully described by earlier travelers. They had been filled in with tons of sand gouged from the nearby hillsides. The city now had a handsome waterfront with a number of wharves extending into the bay, along which a variety of ferries, sailing ships, and steamers were docked. It was seven o'clock and getting dark when the *Sonora*, 16 days out of Panama City, dropped anchor at the Pacific Mail dock at the foot of Folsom Street, and Frances joined in the usual confusion of the docking of a steamer.

No one met her. But Frances was an experienced traveler and, armed with letters of introduction penned by influential New Yorkers, made her way with her luggage to the Russ House on Montgomery Street between Bush and Pine, one of three recently-built first class hotels, the others being the near-by Occidental Hotel and the Lick House.[18]

The Russ House, which provided her with a prestigious address, was a convenient listening post while Frances acquainted herself with the city and surveyed possibilities for earning money by her pen to supplement Henry's Navy pay of $150 per month while at sea.[19] Her arrival in San Francisco in the spring of 1863, just as the city was burgeoning culturally, was fortunate indeed. It opened up writing opportunities for her, first as a poet and journalist

A day or two after her arrival with her unpublished poems and letters of introduction in hand, she called on James Nesbit, editor of the *Evening Bulletin,* located within three blocks of the Russ House. Her foray was successful. On April 27, her poem, "Palma," was published in the "Poet's Corner" of the *Bulletin.* It marked the beginning of a professional connection that lasted several years. She continued to publish in the "Poet's Corner" and became one of the *Bulletin's* "lady correspondents." Since such correspondence was often unsigned, not all of her contributions to the *Bulletin* in 1863–64 have been identified. However, in an autobiographical sketch published in Salem, Oregon many years later, Frances stated: "When I was in San Francisco, I wrote for the *Evening Bulletin* quite regularly on inside and outside matters. Mr. James Nisbet. . . editor-in-chief at the time . . .was a noble man, and his loss by the sinking of the *Brother Jonathan* off Crescent City (California) made many hearts sad. . . . [T]o me, he acted like an older brother during my connection with the *Bulletin.*"[20]

Nisbet, a bachelor some ten years Frances' senior, had also come to San Francisco in search of a literary career.[21] A native of Glasgow, Scotland, he had traveled throughout Europe and, after a financial reversal, had migrated to Australia before trying his fortune in San Francisco in 1853. The *California Chronicle* had just published a prospectus for the *Annals of San Francisco,* for which had been gathered an immense amount of data that needed to be woven into narrative form. When Nisbet applied for a position, he had been handed this assignment. His literary skills had earned him a place on the editorial staff. Two years later, he had been offered the editorship of the *Evening Bulletin.*

If, on Frances' first visit, Nisbet gave her a copy of the *Annals* it would have provided valuable background material for her subsequent explorations of the city and state. Through him she became acquainted with prominent residents such as the Unitarian minister, Thomas Starr King, and his wife Julia, who were about Frances' age and whose religious persuasion she shared. King, a dedicated Unionist, also lectured on American literature and encouraged local and eastern writers by introducing them to San Francisco publishers and editors, like Col. Joseph Lawrence, co-owner and editor of the *Golden Era*, the leading literary journal of the region.

Another new arrival in San Francisco who helped shape Frances' literary fortunes was Charles Henry Webb, who came to the city just two days after she unpacked her trunk at the Russ House. Webb, the newly appointed San Francisco correspondent for the *New York Times*, took up residence in the nearby Occidental Hotel and approached Nisbet of the *Evening Bulletin* with a travelogue in hand. On April 23 Webb's amusing account of his journey from New York City to San Francisco by way of Nicaragua and his first impressions of the city appeared in the *Bulletin*.[22]

In New York City, Webb had been a member of a bohemian literary group, the Pfaffians, who met at a tavern of that name, as well as a columnist and literary editor for the *New York Times*. At the outbreak of the Civil War, the newspaper had dispatched him to the front to cover the first battle of Bull Run and the Shenandoah Valley campaign. After that experience, he had gladly accepted an offer of a transfer to San Francisco. Here he was soon working for the *Bulletin* as reporter and literary editor. Given her penchant for making literary connections, Frances took an interest in the witty, red-headed bachelor. Later events indicate that Webb was attracted to the vivacious and safely married Frances.

During her first month in the city, a stranger there living alone in a downtown hotel but under the guidance of the brotherly Nisbet, the influential Kings, and the ubiquitous Webb, Frances came to appreciate the city's seasonless climate and its spectacular growth. Like them, she saw that after the Civil War and the completion of the transcontinental railroad, San Francisco would become the "Queen City" of the Pacific coast.

From the outset, Frances took the measure of other lady guests at the Russ House.[23] As the wife of a Union naval officer, she kept her own counsel, especially after the Union defeat at Chancellorsville, Virginia, in early May brought out a chorus of Confederate sympathizers, who were not impressed with her New York and Boston connections. Fortunately, she found a more receptive class of ladies living in the hotels on Montgomery Street. Like her, they were temporary "widows" while their husbands were engaged in mining silver in Nevada. To acquaint herself with the gold mines in the Sierras and the silver mines of Washoe, Frances in June boarded a steamer for Sacramento, gateway to the mining regions. She made this trip in the company of Julia King, who had previously visited the area with her husband to raise funds for the U.S. Sanitary Commission, the Civil War forerunner of the American Red Cross.

Much as she had done in New York City, Frances also explored the cultural diversity and resources of San Francisco. In 1863, the city's population of some 112,000 had fascinating pockets of Mexican, Chinese, German, and other ethnic groups, as well as thousands of Americans from the East and the South, who had come west to speculate in land or mines, or to escape the ravages of the Civil War.

None of this as lost on Frances as, with long skirts gathered in one hand, she negotiated the crowded planked sidewalks, watchful for crevices and spikes, or jolted over planked thoroughfares on street-car lines, all horse-drawn except for the steam-powered Market Street line. Confederate interference with the trade around Cape Horn and across the Isthmus of Panama was forcing construction of local factories. Enterprising San Franciscans, who were developing silver mines in Nevada, were extending and rebuilding the city. Everywhere, laborers were stirring up the gritty, yellow sand as they literally moved hills and regraded or affixed planked sidewalks to existing streets or opened new ones. In many parts of the city, the wooden buildings of the 1850s were being replaced with brick and stone structures. During the year of 1863, some two thousand buildings, including houses, were erected. [24]

The first main thoroughfare Frances explored was Montgomery Street. South of California, it was lined with the finest hotels and other multi-story brick buildings. Most had rooms or offices on the upper floors with street-level shops that displayed their colorful wares on the sidewalks. The office of the *Evening Bulletin* was at 622 Montgomery. Around the corner at 543 Clay was that of the *Golden Era*, which served as a literary club for local and visiting authors, many of whom stayed at the nearby Occidental Hotel or Lick House.

The financial and commercial center of the Pacific Coast was also located on Montgomery between California and Washington Streets. But the most fashionable shopping area was on Kearney, just a block off Montgomery. Frances also visited the ever-expanding book and stationery store of H.H. Bancroft and Company at Montgomery and Market, which Bancroft, a young Ohio-born bookseller, had established in 1856.[25] Not far removed were the city's leading churches. Two blocks from Montgomery at the corner of Grant and California, St. Mary's Church towered skyward. The block beyond was dominated by Grace Cathedral, founded earlier that year by the Episcopal bishop, William L. Kipp, a friendly rival of Thomas Starr King, whose Unitarian Church of the Pilgrims, then under construction on Geary Street, faced Union Square.

Of enduring fascination for those who relished San Francisco's ambiance were the developers and preservers of the city's cultural life— theaters, musical societies, literary publications, and scientific associations, as well as public and private schools and colleges.[26] In 1863, chief of the four theaters was Maguire's Opera House. Maguire, who dominated the theater scene in San Francisco for 30 years, imported French, Italian, and English opera troupes that performed at popular prices. The San Francisco Philharmonic Society, the German Turnverein Choral Society, and the Handel and Haydn Society provided classical music for the city's elite. Library associations included those of the California Academy of Sciences, the Mechanics Institute, and the Odd Fellows. The Mercantile Library, with a book collection of over 33,000, provided a much-needed service for authors and journalists.[27] Frances could have been expected to spend many hours here, reading in the section reserved for ladies.

Once she mastered the transportation system, Frances ventured farther afield. Some of these trips later served as grist for her literary mill. On one such occasion, with sketch book and lunch basket in hand, she boarded a horsecar of the Omnibus Railroad Company line that ran from Portsmouth Square to South Park in an upper-class residential area of the same name. She was vexed to find the so-called park to be a fenced-in "garden plot," around which she walked once or twice while reflecting that until San Francisco had a sizable park like New York City's, it could not call itself a city. On another occasion she boarded a car of the Central Railroad Company and traveled out Post Street to the cemetery on the lower slopes of Lone Mountain at the end of the line. Later she wrote that she grieved for the young wanderers, mostly disappointed miners, who slept on these slopes. After reading their epitaphs, she resolved to improve the genre by writing one of her own, and asked other poets to follow suit. [28]

In early July, Frances and other Unionists in San Francisco breathed a vast sigh of relief. The Union Army had prevailed at the Battle of Gettysburg, fought during the first three days of the month. In the West, Union troops had also captured the last two Confederate strongholds on the Mississippi River: Vicksburg on the Fourth of July and Fort Huron, 200 miles south, five days later. Now the entire river was under Union control.

A month later, on August 6, San Francisco Unionists, under the leadership of Thomas Starr King, staged a day-long celebration to honor these July victories. Frances, the only woman columnist on the Golden Era at the time, later reported that she was among those who witnessed the morning parade down Montgomery Street. [29]

Three days later, on Sunday, August 3, the editor announced: "The first effusion of 'Florence Fane in San Francisco' appears on the fifth page. It is piquant, picturesque, and pleasant, and will at once place the new contributor in the front rank of popularity with readers of the Golden Era . . . ." So, only five months after departing New York City, Frances Fuller Victor had secured a highly visible corner of her own in the competitive San Francisco literary scene.

CHAPTER 2

FLORENCE FANE
IN SAN FRANCISCO
(1863-64)

CHARLES H. WEBB, New York Bohemian and *bon vivant*, paved the way for Frances Fuller Victor when he joined the staff of San Francisco's Sunday journal, *Golden Era*. His weekly column, "Things," signed Inigo, first appeared in the July 28, 1863 issue of the *Era*, just two weeks prior to the appearance of her column. Either at his suggestion or on her own initiative, she approached the editor of the *Era*, who was then negotiating with Mark Twain of the *Territorial Enterprise* in Virginia City, Nevada. She offered to write a column under the pseudonym of "Florence Fane," derived from "Florence Vane," subject of a doleful love poem, written by Philip P. Cooke about 1830.[1]

Several months after the fact, in an account of how she had "fixed on *Era*" to publish her notes on "people and things," Florence Fane indicated that her friend "Brown," a stand-in for Webb, had influenced her decision to approach the *Era*.[2] When Florence Fane told Brown that she intended to get an introduction to the *Era*, he had argued that the publication was "not grounded on the great fundamental principles of humanitarian philosophy," and that, being possessed of a "subtle and analytical mind," she should expend her efforts "on the great, lofty, noble, and profound work to be done here in California," which only Starr King was doing. When Florence Fane asked who would publish such moral work, Brown answered that no such journal now existed, but that he hoped to start one within a year or two. When Florence presented the editors of *Era* with a series of essays on "social sins," they had been polite, but were not about to let a correspondent do anything so disagreeable as to advocate good morals. Glancing at the headline, she saw "sure enough, it was just 'Things' . . . signed Inigo." She told the editors that nothing could be easier than writing "that sort of matter," but they could not expect Florence Fane to compete with Inigo, "a lordly male."

By the time Frances offered this explanation, Florence Fane had already competed with Inigo and other lordly males such as Bret Harte and Mark Twain to the satisfaction of *Era*'s editor, Colonel Joseph Lawrence, and his partner, James Brooks, who had acquired the Sunday journal late in 1860.[3]

Founded in 1870 by Rollin M. Daggett and his partner, J. McDonough Ford, as a frontier periodical with a newspaper format, it had appealed to farmers and miners as well as San Franciscans. From the outset, it had featured fiction, poetry, columnists' comments, and signed articles, as well as news summaries and editorials. After its sale, Daggett had joined the staff of the *Territorial Enterprise*, thereby establishing a relationship between the Washoe, Nevada, newspaper, which published Samuel Clemens' first contribution signed "Mark Twain" in February, 1863, and the *Golden Era*.

Lawrence was suited by experience and disposition to redirect the fortunes of the *Golden Era*. A native of Long Island, New York, he had worked as a newspaperman since his arrival in California in 1849. Blessed with great energy and a keen business sense, he doubled the size of the weekly journal from four to six-column pages. He retained the original flavor and sought to appeal to a growing number of San Franciscans interested in local social and cultural events. To this end, he recruited staff members who could write on a variety of subjects, ranging from operas, plays, lectures, and books to natural wonders like Yosemite Valley and the Big Trees, or redwoods.

He also solicited material from distinguished visitors. These he often entertained at the nearby Lick Hotel. Charles Webb, alias Inigo, may have been so recruited. The case of Frances Fuller Victor was somewhat different. Lawrence engaged her on a trial basis after Mark Twain declined to become a regular correspondent, only contributing occasional essays when he visited San Francisco.[4] If Webb had been Fane's rival, it was Francis Bret Harte who influenced her literary aspirations. A decade her junior, he had been associated with the *Era* since March, 1860—some five years after he arrived in California from New York to join his mother and stepfather in Oakland.[5]

Largely self-educated, Harte had always felt an urge to write. In 1858–59 when he worked as an expressman and miner in the gold country, he submitted verse and an article or two to the *Era*. However, it was in Uniontown (Arcata) in northern California, where he was living with a married sister, that he got his first taste of frontier journalism—first as a printer, then as a reporter and editor for the *Northern Californian*. On February 26, 1860, during the editor's absence; he wrote and published an editorial on the massacre of some 60 peaceful Mad River Indians, mostly women and children, on an island in Humboldt Bay. In it, he charged local figures with the carnage. Soon after, he fled the region by steamboat to escape lynching by an angry mob of miners and rowdies. In San Francisco he turned up at the office of the *Golden Era*. Fastidiously dressed, of medium height and slender build, with a handsome, sensitive face, silky mustache, and dark, wavy hair, he looked every inch the stereotypical poet of the day. He was hired as a typesetter, the only position open, and began contributing sketches and stories. In December, after Lawrence and Brooks purchased the *Era*, Harte submitted an arresting story. Titled, "The Work on Red Mountain," it was based on his March editorial. Signed Bret, its publication would change the course of his life.

Before long, Bret Harte was writing a column. First titled "Town and Table Talk," the following year it became "The Bohemian Feuilleton," perhaps at the suggestion of Jessie Benton Fremont, a San Francisco social leader. Daughter of Missouri Senator Thomas Hart Benton, she was the wife of the celebrated western explorer and surveyor, California Senator John C. Fremont, who later became a Civil War general and Arizona Territorial governor. Jessie Fremont had been impressed by an article in the *Era* signed Bret and, after querying the editor about Bret's identity, she invited the young writer to Sunday dinners at the Black Point cottage that her husband had built for her, overlooking San Francisco Bay. Here she envisioned establishing a literary salon with the help of Starr King. In this scenic setting, Bret Harte became a protégé of King, who, along with Mrs. Fremont and her daughter Elizabeth, encouraged Harte to read his manuscripts aloud. They offered constructive criticism, which he needed and welcomed.

At the outbreak of the Civil War early in 1861, before Fremont was called East to serve as a general in the Union Army, Jessie Fremont secured Harte a position as clerk in the San Francisco office of the surveyor general. Now able to give up his job as a typesetter, Harte continued to write for the *Era*. He was known for his Civil War poems, which King read aloud at meetings and rallies, as Harte was too shy to do so. Through one of his parishioners, King found a better position for Harte as clerk to the superintendent of the U.S. Mint at $180 a month. When Frances Fuller Victor and Charles Webb arrived in San Francisco in the spring of 1863, Harte, now a married man, was a senior staff member at the *Era*. As such, he would play influential, though different, roles in their literary careers.

While Frances planned her debut as Florence Fane, several well-known personages arrived in San Francisco, where they were welcomed by Colonel Lawrence. In July, Fitz Hugh Ludlow, the bohemian author of the sensational book, *The Hasheesh Eater*, and his friend, Albert Bierstadt, whose studio was in New York City, arrived after a three-month overland journey across the continent. On the way, Bierstadt sketched and painted while Ludlow collected notes for a series of *Atlantic Monthly* articles, which he later published in book format.[6] On August 1, they departed for Yosemite Valley with two local artists and a scientist. Late in September they returned to San Francisco. During this time, Bierstadt designed a new masthead for the *Golden Era* and Ludlow contributed several articles.

As Florence Fane, Frances Fuller Victor met these gentlemen at the office of the *Golden Era* before they set out, first on a Sacramento River steamboat to the head of navigation and then, by horseback, to the Columbia River in Oregon.[7] On August 7, the *Pacific Mail* brought other distinguished visitors. Irish-born J. Ross Browne, a government agent, world traveler, author, and part-time resident of Oakland, California, arrived to lecture on Ireland, which he had recently visited. In her column in the *Era* of August 10, 1863, Florence Fane noted that, on the same ship were the Civil War satirist, Orpheus C. Kerr (Robert Henry Newell) and his sensational actress-wife, Adah Isaacs Menken. She was scheduled to make her San Francisco debut at Maguire's Opera House later that month.[8] Bohemians like Webb, they joined the bohemian writers at the *Era*. Lawrence reprinted some of Kerr's published comments, and during Miss Menken's nine-month stay, he published some of her free verse written in the style of Walt Whitman, whom she had met in New York City.

Miss Menken, however, achieved her greatest notoriety as the first female to perform in the male lead in the play based on Byron's *Mazeppa*, written in 1819. As Florence Fane, Frances reported on the performance in which Miss Menken's beautiful figure had been clad only in flesh-colored tights as she played the role of the youthful hero who had been "bound naked to a wild horse and driven off into the desert to perish." When Florence looked at her male escorts, "Brown" and "Will," to see their reactions, the latter said, "Plump as a partridge." The former gasped, "Lord! How pretty!" Florence exclaimed, "Barbarous!" and hoped that "some good Samaritan stopped that runaway horse."

At the office of the *Era* that fall, Frances also met less distinguished contributors, like the mysterious 22-year-old poet, Ina Coolbrith, and the even younger Charles Warren Stoddard, who had just come out from behind his literary mask, "Pip Pepperpod."[9] During the summer and fall of 1863, 24-year-old Cincinnatus Hiner Miller and his dark-eyed bride, Minnie Myrtle, from Oregon haunted the office of the *Era*. Lawrence published some of Minnie Myrtle's poems, but he gave her husband short shrift. Unable to make a living by writing, the couple departed San Francisco. Minnie Myrtle returned temporarily to her family home on the Oregon coast, and Miller traveled the road to fame as "Joaquin Miller, Poet of the Sierras" without her.[10]

The older and more experienced Frances Fuller Victor was more fortunate. During 1863–64, she wrote 38 weekly "Florence Fane in San Francisco" columns for the *Golden Era*. In the first 15, published between August 9 and December 6, 1863, she referred to her fellow columnists, Charles Henry Webb and Francis Bret Harte, as "Inigo" and "Bret," as well as Florence Fane's personal friends, "Brown" and "the Poet." As such, they were members of a small set of characters, who provided continuity and bound together the random subject matter of the Florence Fane sketches. The character who provided the most continuity was "Will," Florence Fane's "older brother," to whom she deferred—apparently as a stand-in for her husband, Henry Victor, while he was at sea on the U.S.S. *Narragansett.*

By the end of August, Florence Fane's circle of friends included "the Poet," whom she had met on Telegraph Hill. Her "brother Will" had been sketching the bay below with Frances in the foreground when a handsome young man strolled by. Florence explained to him that she was holding her pose on orders from the artist, whereupon the young man had assumed "a graceful attitude," and Will had included him in the drawing. After learning that he was a poet, Frances invited him to dinner at the "Accidental Hotel," with Browne and others. Here she had prevailed upon the Poet to read some of his verses. Reportedly, the Poet included in the reading Frances Fuller Victor's published poem, "Love's Footsteps," which he had brought along for the occasion.

Two women characters were also featured in Florence Fane's columns. One was Florence's beautiful friend, Belle Jones, an outrageous flirt who doted on fine clothes. The other was "the Princess," an aristocratic Southern lady who defended her Secessionist convictions and owned a troublesome dog named Beauregard after a Confederate general. In her first Florence Fane column, Frances introduced the Princess as a fellow boarder at the "aristrocratic" hotel, where all the ladies but two supported the Confederacy. As Florence Fane, Frances admitted that she supported the Union cause but maintained a tolerant attitude toward the city's Southern minority, thus reflecting the tolerance of San Francisco's socially elite.[11]

After paying her respects to San Francisco's "happy combination of climate, enterprise, and taste," and revealing her Union sympathies, Florence Fane was more discreet about her religious views. "Where do you attend divine service, my dear *Era?*" she asked. Then she reported that her friend Brown was "divided between Bishop K-p and S-arr King."

During the rest of August, Frances rounded out Florence Fane's character and beliefs and found pretexts for including previously published poems in her column. In her August 16 column, responding to the charge that many women loved misery, she noted that, not being a "Woman's Rights woman," she asked only to be allowed to enjoy the common privileges of life as "so many favors at the hands of Creation's Lords." If that did not show a "talent for happiness," she did not know what did, though she sometimes suffered from "the womanly malady of homesickness, second only to heartbreak."

In her September 6 column, Florence Fane reaffirmed that she was "not a Rights woman, nor a Bloomer, nor a Free Lover, nor a spiritualist," like many literary women of the day. Nor did she long to define her position with regard to "the suffering afflicted on womankind by their natural enemy, man." In describing the behavior of a party of ladies who had met in her rooms to discuss the merits of the play "Mazeppa" and how they were going to make their new dresses, Florence stated that it was just as well that they were not allowed to vote. After they had discussed Brown, admired the Poet, and inquired about Inigo, Florence, rather than divulge "professional secrets," had steered the subject to politics. The ladies, she reported, knew all about the candidates on the various tickets, and most preferred the handsomest. Though disappointed in their responses, Florence supposed that a vote won by "bright eyes" was as good as one "bought with money and poor whisky."

In September, Florence Fane parodied other civic practices. She had not been invited to the Pioneer Ball, at which the thirteenth birthday of Miss California was celebrated, because she was not "personally acquainted with the managers," clearly their misfortune. However, she and her circle were serving the cause of the "Washoe widows," and had moved that they form the "Washoe and Reese River Widows' Association," complete with constitution, by-laws, trustees, and a secretary. The Association would hold a monthly soiree, an anniversary ball, and a farewell benefit on the second marriage of any member in good standing. Spinsters like Florence were not eligible for membership until they became Washoe widows and could present suitable references to the trustees. At the first meeting, Will, who was usually afraid of ladies, volunteered to serve as trustee, and Florence was elected corresponding secretary *pro tem*. This elaborate farce provoked chuckles, especially in the mining regions, as Frances later learned.

At times the U.S. Navy dock at Mare Island just up the shore from San Fransico offered anchorage for errant Henry Victor, having been an engineer officer on Commodor Perry's famed *San Jacinto* in the 1850s.

ORHI 104225

Still thinking of herself as a poet and short story writer, she sought the criticism of her colleagues, especially Bret Harte. In the column in which she reprinted her poem, "To Edith," she noted that the "cold-water treatment is very much esteemed for poetry on the brain." On September 20, she prevailed upon the editor to replace her column with her short story, "The Challenge of Fate; or, Imogene's Dream." An overly sentimental love story, it was typical of the stories being written by her sister Metta and published in the East. It was the only short story Frances published in the *Era*. She was silenced by Bret Harte's "The Story of M'liss." A revision of his classic, "The Work on Red Mountain," published in the *Era* in 1860, it appeared in serial form in the Octo-

ber, 1863 numbers, and was praised by Florence Fane. It would be years before Frances Fuller Victor published her first Western short story in the *Overland Monthly*, edited by Bret Harte.

In October, 1863, Florence Fane was back in her own "hired corner," to acknowledge the criticism of her poetry that she had received, and through "Mr. Era," to warn the city fathers, to whom she had not been introduced, that San Francisco would die from consumption for lack of "a huge pair of lungs." It needed a forested park. The "poor little flower pot" of South Park would not longer do. She suggested trees like the elm and the maple that put out pink buds in the spring and scatter colorful leaves in the fall as well as "the lofty palm that loves the sun and the sea."

She longed for a place where young ladies could canter their horses, invalids could breathe fresh air, and children could play. A lifelong lover of trees, Frances ended her plea with a challenge: "Don't tell me that trees won't grow in California. You haven't tried them." Her challenge would trigger an interest in developing a park system, unrivalled on the Pacific Coast.

In the same forthright spirit, Florence Fane closed with a poem on autumn, which she challenged Inigo to unravel "webb and woof." This spirited rivalry between staff members was encouraged by editor Lawrence. Many years later Frances recalled: "Webb and I wrote our articles in a half-mirthful, half-satiric vein. . . We reached for precedence in the public favor with the result that most people said the two were one— for, as usual, they declared that no woman could be as 'smart' as a man who was an acknowledged wit."[12]

A close reading of the October 4, 1863 Florence Fane column indicated that Frances knew that within the month the U.S.S. *Narragansett* would undergo overhaul at the dry dock of the Mare Island Navy Yard. The U.S.S. *Lancaster*, flag ship of the Pacific Squadron, under the command of Admiral Bell, was in port to welcome the six-ship Russian Colonial Squadron, which was undergoing overhaul at the invitation of President Lincoln. At the beginning of the column, Florence Fane noted that she had received a confidential letter from Will in Washoe, Nevada, where he had gone to investigate the behavior of a husband of a member of the Washoe and Reese River Widows' Association. Will's letter may have represented a letter from Henry Victor off the coast of Mexico, for later in the column Florence Fane boasted that she might be holding her own "Feast of the Roses" aboard the *Lancaster*, which quartered the crew of the *Narraganett* during its overhaul.

In the next columns there is no reference to Will except for a three-stanza love poem, which Florence Fane attributed to a secret admirer in Acapulco.[13] Her October 25 column was primarily devoted to explaining why on occasion she wished to be a man. After comparing "The Disadvantages of Being a Woman" with "The Advantages of Being a Man," she concluded that "a man can do what he pleases." The column closed by comparing the "pluck" and "gallantry" of men on American ships to the lack of these qualities on French ships in Mexican waters.

What Henry made of Florence Fane when he was granted shore leave after his transfer to the *Lancaster* with the rest of the *Narragansett* crew can only be imagined. However, a number of prominent San Franciscans honored Henry's commanding officer, Commander Selim E. Woodworth, U.S.N., at an elaborate dinner at the Occidental Hotel to celebrate his return to San Francisco, where he lived prior to joining the Union Navy in 1861. Admiral Bell and officers of both ships also were present. Among civilians in attendance was the Rev. Starr King. Frances Fuller Victor would have been an enthusiastic participant, but Florence Fane's comments on the event were slight, although complimentary of Henry's commanding officer and friend. Then, on November 19, Henry applied through the proper chain of command for permission to resign his commission as senior engineer—presumably for reasons of health but more likely because he knew that the *Narraganett* was scheduled to return to Boston via the Horn after its overhaul. His resignation was officially accepted on December 12, 1863.

During this time of uncertainty, Frances had other things on her mind, too. In her November 1 column, Florence Fane made a startling proposal. Addressing her colleague, Inigo, she charged: "The editors of *Era* don't know how to edit a Sunday paper. You and I could do better." Then she recalled how, months ago, her friend Brown had advised her against writing for the *Era* and had outlined a plan for a journal of his own. She had ignored Brown's advice and made a fair bargain with the *Era*. This she had fulfilled "with distinction." Now she believed that she and Inigo, ". . . the most barbarously used . . . of all the correspondents, could separately or together make a better paper . . ." After announcing her resignation as secretary of the Washoe and Reese River Widows Association, she issued this invitation to Inigo: "If you think well of crushing the *Golden Era*, and starting a responsible journal somewhat on Brown's plan, chiefly on our own, I shall be happy to have your cooperation."

In his November 8 *Era* column, apparently with editor Lawrence's consent, Inigo approved of Florence Fane's plan, which was to be carried out immediately. He and Bret had determined to start the new journal.

Bret would write "all the clever things," and Inigo would get all the credit. Any author expecting to be paid would be kicked down the stairs by the Washoe giant (Mark Twain), employed for that purpose. Inigo would attend to all the young and pretty authoresses. Older lady correspondents would be turned over to Bret, who had "a good moral tendency." Florence Fane would do all the clippings, write the leaders and furnish the money."[14]

In her November 15 column, Florence Fane denounced Inigo's response and renounced her "former secession." She left it to the editors to make her "an example of refractory correspondents," but thought it only fair that Inigo suffer similar punishment for his part in "the paper conspiracy." She further stated that she had visited the U.S. Mint to advise Bret that she would not join Inigo's conspiracy. He had been "invisible," but she and her escorts had learned something about the "mysteries of making money."

In the same column, Florence Fane reported on the literary sensation of the month—a lecture billed as "Babes in the Woods," delivered at Platt's Hall on November 13 by Charles Farrar Browne, author of the nationally popular "Artemus Ward—His Book." Mark Twain welcomed the lecturer with "Greetings to Artemus Ward" in the *Era*. When Starr King had sat on the lecture platform Inigo, a fellow Bohemian, praised him in his column, "Things."[15] In a lengthy essay, Bret pointed out that Ward's humor was "exaggerated and purely American." Meanwhile, editor Lawrence appointed Ward a temporary correspondent. Florence Fane's comments were more laconic: "A. Ward's Babes got lost in the wood Friday night—very."

Of far greater interest to Florence Fane were preparations by San Francisco's elite "City Guard" for a magnificent civil and military banquet and ball at Union Hall. There honored guests would be officers of the six-ship Russian Colonial Squadron being overhauled at the Mare Island Navy Yard. About the same time, another fleet of Russian warships was in New York Harbor for a three-month visit. Czar Alexander II had sent the fleet as an expression of Russian pro-Union sympathy, and New Yorkers had feted the Russians at a lavish ball at the Academy of Music.[16]

San Franciscans were not to be outdone! Tickets costing $100 and more were offered to army officers at the Presidio, naval officers on Union warships in the Bay, as well as social leaders like Starr and Julia King, and city and state officials, including Governor Leland Stanford. The Nov. 18 issue of the *Evening Bulletin* covered the ball the night before in detail. Police shepherded the orderly crowd milling about outside Union Hall. Its interior was decked with arches of evergreens and banners. From the gallery a portrait of George Washington looked down on those of Czar Alexander II and the Czarina in an appropriate place of honor. The music was loud enough for a battlefield. French champagne flowed freely to accompany a gourmet banquet consisting of more than 100 courses, ranging from oysters in a variety of forms to a rich array of ices and highly decorated French cakes. The elegrant dresses of the ladies, blending with the gold braid of naval uniforms, added color to the scene as guests struggled to pronounce foreign names. Dancing, which began at 9:30 in the evening, continued until the morning sun gilded San Francisco's sand hills.

The editor's column in the November 22 Golden Era announced that "Florence Fane's Feuilleton, as charming as ever and containing a delightful account of the Russian Ball, is in print, but inevitably deferred until next week"—clear evidence that Florence in a dress of her own making and Henry in full-dress uniform had indeed attended the ball.[17] Her account opened with allusions to Russian folklore and history, ranging from sleds pursued by wolves to the Snow Palace in St. Petersburg and the emancipation of the serfs, before confiding: "It is very fortunate that some of the managers had been introduced to me else I should not have been able to be there to see the things I shall tell you."

As the wife of a ranking naval officer, Frances may have enjoyed some social recognition. But Florence Fane's claim that she opened the ball with Admiral Popoff because her dress was considered "more in harmony with Russian taste than those of other ladies present" smacks of a Mark Twain hoax. In fact, her description of her ornate dress suggests that she intended to parody the ball. However, she may very well have danced with the admiral; she was an excellent dancer and, at age 37, with auburn hair, large hazel eyes, and a lively interest in everyone and everything around her would have been an attractive companion at any special occasion. According to the customs of the day, the evening would have been spent dancing with her husband and his brother officers. In Frances Fuller Victor's account, "Florence Fane" had been escorted by "Will, in a handsome new suit," who told her that though she was slightly "passe," she looked "beautifully." Next to her, Admiral Popoff had been most attentive "to the bell of the evening [Admiral Bell] who . . . became very mellow toward morning." During the evening, Florence Fane also saw the Princess looking "superb," and Belle Jones flirting with Artemus Ward who had dropped in after "seeing his Babes safely out of the woods at the Metropolitan." She also observed the Poet, "contemplating an epic on the occasion." Friend Brown had been present, but Florence had refused to dance with him because he wore lavender gloves, which she abhorred. In closing, Florence noted "that a great mixing up of hats and overcoats had ensued to the loss of some and the gain of others — but these mishaps would only make the Russian Ball "long remembered by the citizens of San Francisco."

In any event, the Russian Ball was the highlight of Frances Fuller Victor's social life and the climax in her first series of Florence Fane columns, the last of which was dated December 6, 1863. In it, she admitted that should she ever conduct a paper of her own, she would likely include too many "moral-less tales," and thus lose the high moral tone to which she had always aspired. This admission was followed by this cryptic note:

> Leave of Absence
>
> Will and I have made up our minds to go on a hunting excursion to the head of the bay. I carry the ammunition, and count the game. I have Will's promise not to make a goose of me; but should he do so, mistaking me for the goose he often calls me, you will, of course, write a neat farewell address for me to the readers of ERA, and sign yourself, regretfully,
>
> Florence Fane.

In fact, the hunting excursion was a house-hunting expedition. After Henry submitted his resignation, he had agreed to settle somewhere on the San Francisco peninsula within commuting distance of the city and without its climatic defects. The Victors sought a place where Frances could write and he could recover his health while prospecting for opportunities to invest the prize money he had been assured he would receive at war's end.

On December 12, the overhauled U.S.S. *Narragansett* was secretly dispatched to Victoria, Vancouver Island, to search for Confederate privateers, reported to be outfitting there. Now a civilian, Henry was free to head south to explore the newly platted town of Half Moon Bay on the only protected bay between San Francisco and Santa Cruz on Monterey Bay.[18]

In her 1964 New Year column, Florence Fane did not reveal the name of "the small Arcadian village," where the Russian Ball and Washoe widows were unknown. But she did say that it lay by the sea and was "backed by noble mountains." Free from wind and fog, it had "all types of beauty and just enough wildness to make cultivation a delightful work of art."

In 1863, the village had some 300 inhabitants, served by a post office, a doctor, and a general merchandise store. The charming, low-roofed adobe houses of well-established Mexican families were interspersed with American-style frame houses. The Chapel of Nuestra Senora del Pillar, built a decade earlier, and the Pilarcitos Cemetary with Spanish grave stones dating back to 1820, stirred Frances Fuller Victor's sense of history.

The Victors returned to San Francisco to spend Christmas. Here Frances schemed to establish their residence at Half Moon Bay. In a letter to Mr. Era, Florence Fane observed that while she would be "a seldom correspondent," she regretted being denied "the pleasure of writing two volumes of nonsense weekly and being forgotten within a fortnight." She took formal leave of the Princess, the Poet, and Brown, but not of her colleagues, Inigo and Bret. The latter's last contribution to the *Era*, "Mysterious Dram, Story for the Holidays," appeared in the same number. Still employed by the Mint, Bret Harte quit the *Era* and wrote a few poems for the *Bulletin*. Webb continued to write for the *Era* for another month or two.

At Half Moon Bay, Henry did not share Frances' passion for home-making and landscaping. After a decade of shipboard living, adapting to civilian ways and to his role as the husband of a near celebrity left him frustrated. He apparently took refuge in drink and may have been under medication. Frances later credited him with playing a good game of chess; but his evasion of family responsibilities must have reminded her of Jackson Barritt's behavior in Omaha, Nebraska in 1856–57.

If she tried to write a history of Half Moon Bay she found that she needed a library and newspaper files, neither of which was available. Even more to be missed were the lectures, theaters, and social and political activities of San Francisco—and, of course, services at Starr King's recently dedicated Church of the Pilgrims. After six weeks of self-imposed silence, she advised her former colleagues of how she was feeling. Florence Fane's seventeenth column was datelined "Half Moon Bay, Midnight, February 12, 1864," and addressed to Mr. Era.

Sitting at her "half-moon bay window on this blessed saint's day," contemplating the same half-moon she had seen in other climes and times, she felt impelled "to write—write! But what and to whom?" In answer, she copied her poem, "Waiting," which she had penned in Omaha. Now she dismissed it as "melancholy stuff" and not "anyone's Valentine." This was followed by a tribute to "The Exception," addressed to Bret Harte, no longer a staff member.

"You are not one of the masses," she wrote. "You are society's saving clause, an Exception." Then she added, "You and your wife and your little ones are always welcome at Half Moon Bay. Will says that I need not put in the 'little ones' . . . But never mind Will. He can stand a little nervousness once in a while. Don't fail to come. Prove yourself an acception if not an Exception." Before closing with a valentine to *Era* and its readers, Florence Fane noted that it was a terrible tribulation to have a husband with a contrary opinion or an opinion with a contrary husband. It was even terrible having a brother who hated opinions. "Floy," Will says every now and then, "you may write what you please provided that you do not venture an opinion—I hate opinionated women!"

In his column "Things," dated February 28, 1864, Inigo noted that Florence Fane would not have refused him "her practiced pen were she not at present writing the history of Half Moon Bay." He further twitted her with the following "Pro-Fane" verses"

> I loved thee long and dearly, Florence Fane
> But you went away quite queerly, Florence Fane;
> I sometimes see a vision
> Of Half-Moon Bay,
> And I ask with some derision,
> "What's to say?"
> But fairest, coldest wonder
> Of Half Moon Bay
> Shell fish the sea-sands under—
> Oysters are they,
> And it boots not now to query
> When they reign
> Thou'll resume in the ERA,
>
> Florence Fane.

Webb's verses clearly parody these lines from Philip P. Cooke's "Florence Vane":

> I loved thee long and dearly,
> Florence Vane;
> My life's bright dream and early
> Hath come again;
> I renew in my fond vision,
> My heart's dear pain—
> My hopes and thy derision,
>
> Florence Vane.

At Half Moon Bay, Frances must have winced, and *Era* readers doubtless expected a spirited response. But this rivalry suddenly ceased on March 4, 1864 when San Francisco and the rest of the state were plunged into mourning by the untimely death of Starr King from diphtheria. According to the *Bulletin*, no other man on the Pacific Coast would be missed more. San Francisco had lost her chief attraction, the state its noblest orator, and the country one of its ablest defenders. The U.S.

Mint and other federal and state offices, and most places of business closed their doors. Flags on ships in the Bay, including those of foreign registry, hung at half-mast. Grief-stricken Bret Harte, King's protégé, composed an elegy, "Relieving Guard, March 4, 1864." It was published in the *Bulletin* two days after King's funeral on March 6 in the Church of the Pilgrims. A lofty, Gothic-style structure of stained glass windows and a splendid pipe organ, it was filled to overflowing for the impressive services, which included a military salute from guns in nearby Union Square and cannon on Alcatraz Island.

Webb paid tribute to King in his column, "Things," on the Sunday after the funeral. Frances wrote nothing on King's passing; but she certainly attended his funeral. One result of this visit to San Francisco and meetings with her colleagues there was a series of articles in the *Bulletin* about the exciting new Silver Mountain mining region written by Henry C. Victor.[19] He had written a travel letter for the *New York Times* during his round trip to Japan and China as an officer on the U.S.S. *Jacinto* in the mid-1850s. Now Henry accepted this new assignment to Frances' delight, as it meant that they could travel and work together; she would write a popular account of the tour.

By late April, the snow on the Sierra foothills was melting. Having rented or leased their house on Half Moon Bay for the season, the Victors set out on a month-long excursion, during which Henry, as an Occasional Correspondent for the *Bulletin*, wrote two reports. Frances, as a Lady Correspondent for the Sacramento *Daily Union*, wrote three chatty travel letters.[20]

Somewhere along the line, the Victors learned that the Scandinavian settlement of Konigsberg in the high Sierras had been renamed Silver Mountain after significant amounts of the previous metal had been found in the region.[21] Since then, miners from the southern end of the Mother Lode had been pouring in over the Ebbett Pass Emigrant Road, traveling by stage to Silver Valley, then by saddle train to Silver Mountain. In August, 1863, the California Geological Survey, traveling the route from the Big Trees (redwood) resort in Calaveras County, found a mining camp of some 40 houses and climbed to the summit of 11,000-foot Silver Mountain at the south end of the camp. In March, 1864, the growing population of Silver Mountain and nearby mining camps prompted the state legislature to create the county of Alpine and name Silver Mountain its county seat.[22]

Aware of these developments, the Victors decided to compare the old Placerville and the new Big Trees route to the region. This entailed traveling both routes. On their outbound journey, they took a steamboat from San Francisco to Sacramento, where they boarded a Sacramento-Valley Railroad train to Folsom. Here they transferred to a coach of the Pioneer Line, which ran daily stages between Folsom and Virginia City, Nevada, carrying the U.S. Mail and Wells Fargo Express as well as "inside" and "outside" passengers. These Concord coaches could carry nine passengers inside on padded seats and an additional six passengers outside, beside the driver, or "Jehu," and an armed "shotgun" on the top.[23]

On the five-hour ride from Folsom to Placerville in the foothills of the Sierra Nevada, the Victors suffered "discomfort" in a crowded coach. This prompted Henry, whom Frances called "Squires" and described as an "irrepressible male relative," to observe that there was no Sunday night steamer from San Francisco to Sacramento. Reasoning that, as a consequence, there would be little stage traffic on Monday, they stopped at a Placerville hotel to await the Monday coach. During their layover, they discovered that the old placer diggings were being replaced with quartz mining and that "there was yet plenty of gold in Placerville."

On Monday, they had an entire interior stage seat to themselves. This had put "Squires in a happier mood," though the manner in which the driver brought "the coach and six around the short turns the road makes above the heads of the ravines a thousand feet deep is as skillful as it is startling," according to Frances. After supper at "a romantic station in the woods," they reseated themselves. Before dark, they reached Sugar Loaf Mountain, where they saw snow as they rolled on to Strawberry station. Here they changed coaches. During the moonlit night they passed glimmering Lake Tahoe. At 3:30 A.M., they reached Van Sickle's. Since they were not going on to Carson City, they stopped for a nap and breakfast before boarding the 10:30 A.M. stage to Markleesville, where they arrived at 5 P.M., exhausted.

Finding comfortable quarters in a private home, the Victors spent several days here to accustom themselves to the rarified atmosphere. Founded two years earlier, the town had a population of 2,500, over 100 houses, and a quartz mill. Henry was intrigued with the silver-bearing ledges while Frances sampled the warm soda springs of the region.

In the first week of May, they boarded a stagecoach to travel the single track road to the town of Silver Mountain at an elevation of 7,000 feet. Frances described it as a "romantic eagle's nest of a town . . . . Fancy a valley two miles long and a quarter mile wide shut in by mountain walls from one thousand to fifteen hundred feet high, a blue sky overhead, bits of snow lying on the summits of silver-shining whiteness . . . and in the midst of all a brand-new, neatly built town of over one hundred houses."

With the prospect of returning by way of the new Big Trees road, the Victors settled in at one of the two well-stocked hotels for a fortnight. In Henry's "The Silver Mountain Mining Region," dated May 7, Silver Mountain, Alpine County, California, and published in the May 13 issue of the San Francisco *Evening Bulletin*, he reported that, unlike the Comstock Lode in Nevada, the Silver Mountain region had been overlooked because of its inaccessibility and lack of capital, though labor and cheap water power were available. However, its isolation would be ended when the road from Silver Mountain to Stockton, via the new Big Trees route, was completed this summer. He added that he did not have "quartz on the brain." He was simply visiting the region for "health, pleasure, and information." But should he succumb to "the insane desire to own stock," he would know where to invest.

The first of Frances Fuller Victor's three-part "Prospecting Tour," signed FFV, appeared in the May 18, 1864 issue of the Sacramento *Daily Union*. A first-person description, it contrasted sharply with Henry's matter-of-fact account. As they examined the mines and silver-bearing outcroppings, Henry questioned the costs involved. Frances wondered about the volcanic forces that had created the region. She saw mountain sides covered with finely broken stone, "which could dress a highway between here and Sacramento" as well as "impetuous mountain torrents forming cataracts and cascades of great beauty" before subsiding into "business-like streams" that lost their romance "in grinding quartz or sawing logs."

She regretted that the snow on Silver Mountain was too deep for a climb to the summit for a view of Mount Davidson, Carson Valley, and "the rest of the world." During the last week of their stay, wind, rain, and snow kept them inside, "making notes for future reference."

When bright weather returned, they visited a road camp at a completed section of the Big Trees road. Here they decided to head for Stockton over that route on May 22. By now, Frances had been identified as Florence Fane of the *Golden Era*; and their departure from Silver Mountain turned into a social event. A number of the ladies and gentlemen of the town accompanied them on the three-mile, uphill trek to the construction camp. The stage company provided horses for the ladies to ride, but most like Frances preferred to walk. Henry had arranged to have their luggage packed out earlier and was pleased to find it stowed in a company wagon, drawn by four horses that would carry them as far as the Big Trees. Their departure was delayed by a hearty lunch laid out by the superintendent of the camp, who was toasted in tea along with the new road and the construction company.

Henry's report on "The Big Trees Road Across the Sierra Nevada" appeared in the June 3, 1864 issue of the *Bulletin* a few days after the Victors returned to San Francisco. By the use of statistics and derogatory remarks about the Pioneer Line, he demonstrated that the Big Trees route was shorter and more comfortable than the Placerville route. The last installment' of Frances' "A Prospecting Tour," datelined San Francisco, May 28 and published in the June 1issue of the Sacramento *Daily Union*, gave readers a good idea of what traveling the Big Trees route entailed.

She had been impressed with the Big Trees resort, which they reached on the second day, but distressed at the sight of "a naked giant," the bark of which had been shipped to a fair in New York City. By stagecoach they arrived at Stockton in time to catch a steamer for "a good voyage down the crookedest of rivers, the San Joaquin, having had a highly interesting and very comfortable journey from Silver Mountain via the Big Trees, in easy stages, in three days."

Pleased with the results of their joint venture, the Victors decided to spend some time in the city before returning to Half Moon Bay. The

U.S.S. *Narragansett* had returned from Victoria without having located any Confederate privateers, but Henry would have been interested in any rumors of gold up north. Frances' chief concern was certainly the May 28 publication date of the first number of *The Californian* with its provocative motto: "There is a vein of silver, and a place for gold where they find it."[24] Charles Webb was the proud proprietor and editor. Bret Harte, chief contributor, would serve as editor during Webb's absence. The journal's handsome format of 16 three-column pages printed on firm, white paper surpassed that of the *Era*. The initial number featured sketches by Inigo and Bret and poems by Ina Coolbrith and Charles Warren Stoddard, which established its literary reputation from the outset.

Frances Fuller Victor had not been invited to contribute either as Florence Fane or as F.F.V. Determined to promote the latter, she turned to her old standby—the *Bulletin*. Presumably on her doctor's orders, though probably at the suggestion of her friend James Nesbit, she decided to travel for her health. While so doing, she wrote another travel series, titled "Summer Wanderings," signed F.F. Victor. Her four letters were published in the Bulletin on June 27, July 7, 13, and 16, 1864. Her poem, "By the Sea," was published in the "Poet's Corner" on July 12.

To this end, she and an unnamed companion visited the seaside resort of Santa Cruz on the north side of Monterey Bay with many fine beaches and surrounded with a scattering of lesser redwoods. Later they visited the historical port of Monterey on the south side of the Bay. It had been the capital of Alta California from 1775 to 1846, when it had been captured by American naval force. Now it was a quiet fishing and whaling village with a charming Mexican heritage.

"My friend and I took leave of our lords at the railroad station," Frances wrote in her first letter from Santa Cruz. They proceeded south by rail to the village of Santa Clara. Here they boarded a stagecoach for a ride through spectacular mountain scenery to the seaside village of Santa Cruz. At 5:00 P.M.. the stage drew up before the best hotel. Not finding "a room disengaged," the travelers took rooms in a private home. It was within easy walking distance of a secluded beach with a seal rock comparable to the offshore rock near Cliff House in San Francisco.

During the fortnight they spent at Santa Cruz, they skirted accessible beaches, on one occasion joining a party to round a dangerous point and explore a cave at the foot of a bluff. At low water, it was a living museum of fantastic sea wonders. They also joined picnic excursions to various points of interest—the ruins of a mission established in 1796, a modest stand of redwoods that did not compare with the Big Trees.

Of special interest to Frances was "a house of three, not seven, gables." According to her informant, it had been built and occupied for a time by Eliza Farnham. Prison reformer, feminist lecturer, and author, she was the widow of Thomas Jefferson Farnham, who had toured the Oregon Country in 1839 as captain of the Peoria Party.[25] After a colorful career in the Sandwich Islands and Monterey, he had died in San Francisco in 1848. After his death, his widow had tried to organize a company of young women to charter a ship to sail to California, where she was confident that they could find work. This enterprise failed despite the help of Horace Greeley and others. However, in 1849, Eliza Farnham had come west with her family and a few friends. She had built the three-gable house on land which her husband had acquired as "a thank-you offering" for having secured the release of an American party from Mexican captivity. At the time of Frances Fuller Victor's visit, the property was in ruins and had passed out of the hands of Eliza Farnham, then living in New York. There her last two-volume book had been published in January, 1864.

In another letter, Frances described five distinct changes in California scenery from the coastline to the Sierra Nevadas. She predicted that Santa Cruz, which combined the very best points of the whole" was destined to become "the Newport of California." She also reported that she had celebrated the Fourth of July by attending "a pic-nic-on-a-stick . . . . second to nothing less than a barbecue in flavor."

A few days later, she and her friend joined a party on an excursion to Monterey. They chose the slower, but safer, overland route—a stagecoach ride across the Salinas plains. Accommodations at the flea-ridden hotel were primitive. However, Frances focused on the discovery of Monterey, and on the missionary labors of Father Junipero Serra (1713–84) from

San Diego to Monterey. On another trip, Frances reported that her party, in a visit to a whale oil factory, saw every kind of fish they had ever heard of except "mermaids." On the fifth day, indebted to American families for "much politeness," the party left Monterey, rejoicing that there was such a place as Santa Cruz on the other side of the Bay.

By mid-July, Frances was back in San Francisco, expecting to resume life with Henry in Half Moon Bay. Rather, she was crushed to learn that he had scheduled a voyage of his own. As an "Occasional Contributor" to the *Bulletin*, he would sail to Victoria on Vancouver Island to investigate rumors of a gold strike. That his plan did not include her cut her to the quick and certainly reminded her of how Jackson Barritt had gone his own way in Omaha in 1857.

Both Henry and Frances were known to have quick tempers. A quarrel erupted. Just when and on what terms they parted is not known. That Henry sailed for Victoria in late July or early August is confirmed by a letter published in the August 10 issue of the *Bulletin*. Datelined Victoria, August 8, 1884 and signed Victor, it reported that the British colony was in a state of excitement over reported gold diggings along the Sooke River. A returning miner had pronounced the mines "No humbug," but Victor warned San Franciscans against "a general rush" until more particulars could be ascertained.

Frances, meanwhile, went to Half Moon Bay to collect her wits and her things. Faced with living alone, she returned to San Francisco, where she was confident she could earn her living with her pen. During these dark days, she expressed her emotions in poetry, as she did in times of distress. In a four-stanza poem entitled, "Peccavi," she confessed she was too stunned to feel the pity she entreated from the

> Shepherd, who gathereth up
> The weary ones from all the world's highways.

It appeared in the *Bulletin's* "Poet's Corner" on August 16. Four days later the *Bulletin* also published "The Overland Journey to Half Moon Bay," attributed to "Lud Fitz Hughlow and Friend." A parody of the travels of Fitz Hugh Ludlow and his painter friend, Albert Bierstadt, it described a fanciful journey from San Francisco to Half Moon Bay, during which Hughlow and Lagerstadt lost their handcart with all their belongings and each other in the coastal fog. Apparently written at Half Moon Bay in a merrier mood, its true authorship was obvious to insiders. In any event, the poem and the parody brought Frances needed income.

During the rest of the year, Frances published articles in the *Bulletin* on subjects such as the Christian Commission, the Mechanics fair, the need for an art museum, better education for women, and affordable housing for working widows. She also published revisions of previously published poetry. For instance, on September 7, a revision of her poem, "Memories," addressed to Metta, appeared under the title, "Verses." Three days later, a revision of her poem, "Palace of the Imagination," was published.

Meanwhile, on August 28, Florence Fane had picked up where she had left off at the *Era*. "When I left the Arcadian shades of Happy Valley to return to this earthquake-threatened and stock-ruined city," she explained, ". . . . I was only a little weary of uninterrupted simplicity and restless pining for the taste of a . . . Metropolitan society."

The second series of Florence Fane columns began with facetious comments on fairs, balls, theatrical performances, and current novels. Frances' love of the ridiculous and word play persisted, but she missed the stimulus of her former colleagues, Inigo and Bret. Henry remained the critical older brother; but Belle Jones was reformed. Her "stock-ruined" husband, Tom, and others probably represented new acquaintances.

Sometime during the autumn, Frances Fuller Victor accepted the editorship of *The New Age*, a weekly literary journal to be launched by the Independent Order of Odd Fellowship of San Francisco in January, 1865.[26] Whether or not she sought the position, her tenure as assistant editor of the *Monthly Hesperian*, sponsored by the Odd Fellowship Lodge of Detroit, Michigan, doubtless prompted her appointment. In preparation, she began researching the history of Odd Fellowship in the United States. It was published in 37 installments in *The New Age*, always on page 1, between January 4 and December 30, 1865—product of many hours Frances spent researching in the library of the San Francisco Lodge.[27]

That Odd Fellowship and Henry were both on her mind is confirmed by two items in the Florence Fane column of October 2, 1864. In
commenting on the Odd Fellows motto, "Friendship, Love, and Truth,"
she wrote: "The excellence and beauty of these principles are testified to
by many a widow left shelterless and now made comfortable, and many a
fatherless child, now fed, clothed, and educated." This salute to the local
Odd Fellows Lodge was followed by a more cryptic reference to Emma
Hardinge, a prominent spiritualist whom Florence Fane had heard and
who claimed that she had been directed to stump the state on behalf of
the re-election of President Lincoln, "the coming man," Though not a
spiritualist, Florence Fane was a loyal supporter of Lincoln and would
have offered to serve as Hardinge's "aide-de-camp," but because of "an
unfortunate disagreement with someone who shall hereafter be nameless," she could not clearly see her "coming man."

In the October 9 Florence Fane column, Frances was forthright. In
reviewing her literary career from the age of fourteen to the present, she
observed: "If I ever wrote anything right, it was out of my own brain—
not because some editor or publisher was just in either blaming or praising . . . I shall confess that I lost much valuable time from want of a
critic." In the next week's column, Florence Fane lashed out at the Cop-
perhead element (Northerners who sympathized with the South) and
vowed to illuminate her windows that night in support of President Lincoln.

Three days later, the *Bulletin* published Henry's final report on the
Sooke River mines. According to Victor, now billed as a Special Correspondent, British colonists on Vancouver Island, with the exception of
the Hudson's Bay Company, lacked the enterprise of Americans. Though
rumors had been "got up to start a mining experiment," he did not advise
San Franciscans to visit the colony for its gold mines.

The October 23 number of the *Era* carried Florence Fane's poem,
"Legend of Abrahm Lincoln," which closed with a tribute to

> *The man the nations saw from far*
> *Down Time's dim vista shining—*
> *The Coming Man, the Morning Star—*
> *Our liberties enshrining.*

Frances Fuller Victor, 1864.

In the same number, Florence Fane reported that Will had accused her of "expressing opinions." This she did not deny, including the opinion that it was "very trying to have a big, criticizing brother." She also expressed her unfavorable opinion of the performance of the Keans, a British husband-and-wife team, in an inferior play, "A Wife's Secret," at Maguire's Theatre. The next week, she revised her opinion of the Keans after she saw their performance in "Hamlet." She also reviewed two romantic novels, noting that when she wrote her novel, the heroine would "suffer to the end of her days," growing "nobler and holier" until she found the "blessedness of repose—the heaven of her own subdued spirit."

By early November, Henry advised Frances of his intention to settle in Portland, Oregon, and invited her to join him.[28] On November 5, to announce that she was about to be "banished" from San Francisco, she reprinted her poem, "Passing by Helicon," not in the *Bulletin* or the *Era*, but in the *Californian*—her only contribution to the journal. Whether Bret Harte, who had assumed temporary editorship during Webb's absence, solicited the contribution or whether she submitted it on her own initiative is not clear. In any event, by reprinting "Passing by Helicon," she alerted her family and friends to a drastic change in her literary venue.

It was about six weeks before Frances Fuller Victor headed for Oregon. Meanwhile, Florence Fane concocted a tale in which "Floy" invites her friend, "Mrs. Jonquil, a neglected wife, to a resort similar to Santa Cruz to meet her professor friend with a view to bringing Dr. Jonquil to his senses. Two episodes, dated December 9 and 10, were published in the December 12 number of *Era*. At the end of the last installment of the tale, which ends happily, Florence Fane boasted that she had "almost written a novel." Then she added: "Will says that he can wait no longer to commence the voyage around the world. So don't let anyone call me back again."

However, with the editor's connivance, the final Florence Fane column was published on Christmas Day, 1864. It featured a fanciful masked ball—perhaps inspired by the costume ball held on December 23, three days after Frances' departure from San Francisco at the Metropolitan Hotel. In this account, Santa Claus spirited Florence Fane away from her lonely room and packed traveling cases to the nearby masked ball. Here they had danced until he left her in the company of someone who had recognized her despite her masque. "Florence," a familiar voice had intoned, "Christmas times are times of peace. Shall there not be peace between us?" Florence Fane had forgotten her response, but she assured Mr. Era that "if Bal Masqué ever terminated in a pretty romance, this one is likely to."

Thus Florence Fane made her exit from the San Francisco literary scene during the waning years of Washoe widows and Nevada silver. France Fuller Victor never revived the alliterative pseudonym, but a decade later she would write a column for another San Francisco periodical in which she addressed current social issues. Fortunately, during her first foray in San Francisco, Frances had been more than a successful columnist. Her work as a lady correspondent for the *Evening Bulletin* and the Sacramento *Daily Union*, her history of Odd Fellowship, and her travels around California by steamboat, stagecoach, and railroad had prepared her for what lay ahead in Oregon.

CHAPTER 3

PROSPECTS &
PIONEERS IN OREGON
(1865)

W HEN FRANCES FULLER VICTOR decided to join her husband in Portland, she booked passage on the *Brother Jonathan* of the California
Steam Navigation Company.[1] This company provided tri-monthly service between San Francisco and the Pacific Northwest, with alternate first
landings at Victoria on Vancouver Island and Portland on the Willamette
River. In consideration of the travel letters she had contracted to write
for the San Francisco Bulletin and her own sense of adventure, she chose
the longer route, though it meant that she would be spending Christmas
Day at sea.

She boarded the *Brother Jonathan* on December 20, one of 30 first-class
cabin passengers along with 118 others,[2] the most conspicuous among
them a party emigrating from England to the Crown Colony. One of
these was a most irritating young man who persisted in sitting at table
beside the popular and handsome captain, though that position had been
reserved for a lady—none other than Frances herself. The captain seated
the offender two seats below her and himself, but this victory for Frances
was short-lived. The next morning, the steamer was rolling in rough seas;
Frances spent the next 36 hours in her berth, "shifting from head to foot
like a shuttle." By dawn of the fourth day, the steamship had passed the
turbulent mouth of the Columbia River and entered smoother waters in
the Strait of Juan de Fuca, named for an early explorer.

Restored to her feet, Frances enjoyed a fire in the grate of the upper
salon, and, warm and well fed, viewed the "unexpected beauty "of Vancouver Island. Three miles southwest of the city of Victoria, the

steamship dropped anchor in Esquimalt Harbor. Surrounded by forested hills, it was set in a basin of picturesque rocks covered in lichen of various shades of yellow, green, and brown. An amateur botanist and landscape painter, Frances wondered why celebrated California painters like F.A. Butman had failed to paint "the upper country."

Since the *Brother Jonathan* would not depart for Portland until the next morning, she joined a party of sight-seers. They set out in a carriage over a "fine graded road" through "agreeable scenery" to Victoria Harbor, which large, ocean-going steamers could not enter because of the rocks. However, local steamboats departed the harbor for points on the American mainland. There was no time to explore Victoria proper, but Frances predicted that it would become a popular resort to which she would return.

During the early morning hours of December 26, the *Brother Jonathan* took on freight and passengers for Portland and San Francisco. Among the latter was the theatrical troupe of Charles and Ellen Tree Kean, whom Frances had seen in their performance of *Hamlet* in San Francisco. While in Victoria, they had performed nightly since December 12 to overflow crowds at the Victoria Theatre.[3] Five hours after leaving Esquimalt Harbor, the Portland-bound steamship entered the stormy Pacific Ocean. By then, Frances had had an early breakfast and settled herself comfortably in the upper salon, her crocheting in hand. Later she reported that she had knotted away with "great industry," trying to distinguish between "seeing a ship" and "shipping a sea." If she had to die, she told a gentleman who remarked at her great calm, she wanted to have calm thoughts as she hated to be frightened.

After facing a gale all the way to the mouth of the Columbia River, the steamship crossed the bar on the afternoon of Christmas Day through a "seething sea of breakers." The captain and men on duty were lashed fast lest they be swept away by the wind. Oil was poured from cans to subdue the waves surging around the vessel. The crossing reportedly was accomplished in only 15 minutes, but according to the captain it was always a hazardous maneuver.[4] Once inside the fabled River of the West, dinner was served,[5] and Frances, seated next to the captain, satisfied both her appetite and her curiosity about Oregon history and geography. She learned that Astoria, perched on a high bluff on the Oregon side of the river, had been founded by John Jacob Astor in 1811. Now it intended to become the future seaport of Oregon, but only "with the permission of Portland," which she assumed was nearby. When the captain explained that Portland was over one hundred miles up the Columbia River and another 15 miles up the Willamette River, she confessed that she had never heard of the Willamette and always thought that Portland was on the Columbia. "It was put down when I studied geography," she told the captain, "and all eastern people thought as I did."[6]

Availing herself of "a traveler's and scribbler's privilege," Frances introduced herself to the Keans, then in their fifties. They had performed "The Merchant of Venice" in Portland on their way to Victoria, and were now returning to Portland to perform "Hamlet" and "Macbeth" before sailing back to San Francisco.[7] In her travel letter, Frances reported that she was indebted to them for a pleasant Christmas evening.

When the *Brother Jonathan* docked in predawn darkness at a dimly lit wharf on the Portland waterfront, it was pouring rain "in a fashion strictly Oregonian" as her husband rushed forward to greet her. The ship's lanterns revealed to his practiced mariner's eye that the pilothouse had been seriously damaged, and he feared that "the old tub" had narrowly escaped disaster. After a joyous reunion, he hurried her to a waiting hack for a short drive through the crowded riverside business district to a higher residential area on the west bank of the Willamette. The hack drew up in front of a two-story house on Third Avenue between Main and Madison Streets across from the two-block fenced public square. Henry evidently had rented rooms here as they had done in San Francisco, but with a Portland view of Mt. Hood from an upper east window on the first clear day.[8]

Always fascinated by place names, Frances soon learned the story of the naming of Portland and why it was located on the Willamette River, a major tributary of the Columbia., which had been controlled by the British Hudson's Bay Company from 1824 to 1846.[9] As early as 1832, American merchant adventurers, Methodist and Presbyterian missionaries, and later fur trappers and emigrants had settled on the admittedly American side of the Columbia. They had done so with the cooperation

The city of Portland. A G.T. Brown drawing from the east bank of the Willamette River and lithographed in San Francisco. The striking view features a number of business and dwellings well known to the Victors.

ORHI 49400

of Dr. John McLoughlin, chief factor of the Columbia Department of the Hudson's Bay Company, headquartered at Fort Vancouver on the north bank of the Columbia, a few miles above the mouth of the Willamette.[10]

In May, 1843, this growing American community, together with a few French Canadians, who had retired from the Hudson's Bay Company, had formed a provisional government. It was headquartered at Willamette Falls, which McLoughlin had staked out a two-mile-square land claim for himself.[11] In the winter of 1843–44, Asa L. Lovejoy, an

overland immigrant from Massachusetts, and William Overton took up a
640-acre land claim some 12 miles below the falls at the head of ocean-
going navigation as determined by Captain John H. Couch, master of
the trading brig, *Chenamus.*[12] Lovejoy was proprietor. Overton, a hired
hand who did not have money for a filing fee, traded his services for a
share of the claim. This he sold for $50 to Francis W. Pettygrove, who had
arrived on the Willamette with a cargo of merchandise from Maine.[13]
After laying out a townsite on the west bank, Lovejoy and Pettygrove
tossed a coin to determine its name. Winning the toss, Pettygrove named
it after the port city of his home state, Maine. When the Victors arrived
in Portland some 20 years later, the town had a population had a population of about 6,000. As a "half-rival of San Francisco" in the Pacific

Northwest, it was the largest municipality in the region. Its founders were still pursuing business interests in the Northwest, and many of Portland's capitalists—Henry C. Corbett, William S. Ladd, and Simeon G. Reed—were no older than they were.[14]

Christmas season when the Victors arrived in Portland was marked by the production of *Hamlet* and *Macbeth* at the Willamette Theatre at First Avenue and Stark Street by the Kean troupe that Frances had met aboard the *Brother Jonathan*. Christmas Eve was celebrated by the inauguration of service at a new, covered, two-level wharf at the Oregon Steam Navigating Company's riverside property between Ash and Pine Streets.[15] This innovative facility permitted vessels docking there to discharge and take on freight and passengers at all stages of the river's water. It was reportedly superior to most Pacific Coast wharves and, by initiating this service, the company, organized by Portland businessmen in 1860, hoped to compete more favorably with San Francisco-based lines.

January 1, 1865, fell on a Sunday when it would have been proper to call on Henry's employer, 39-year-old Governor Addison Gibbs and his wife, who maintained a home at Taylor Street and Park Avenue. Frances later recalled that the first person of importance in Oregon to whom Henry had introduced her had been the Governor.[16] When she alluded to her ignorance about Oregon, he replied that it was understandable and that something should be published that would correct the false impressions that many easterners had about the state. "If that is what is wanted," she had responded, "it's in my line." adding that she would enjoy studying the country and writing about its history and resources. Gibbs implied that the state legislature might appropriate funds for publishing such a book and suggested that she call on his friend, Judge Mathew P. Deady, "a man of literary interests," who, like herself, was a correspondent for the San Francisco *Evening Bulletin*. In his library she would find all the books she needed for historical research on Oregon.

Before calling on the judge, Frances finished her first travel letter on the Pacific Northwest, in which she noted that "the business of Portland is thriving, and the pioneer state of the Pacific promises to achieve a future for herself by rapid strides henceforth." The weather would keep her "a prisoner" for a while, but as soon as it permitted she would go

In the nature of things, Simeon Reed would have generated ambivalent emotions
in Victor. Her husband Henry felt duped by Reed, who was simply
practicing good business sense, as understood in the 1860s.
ORHI 9151

"sight-seeing on the Willamette and Columbia Rivers and north to
Puget Sound."

From the outset, Frances was an avid reader of the daily Portland
Oregonian.[17] An item in the January 6 issue reported that the editor of the
San Francisco-based *Pacific Monthly*, Leslie Lester, was in the region, gath-
ering engraved views of Oregon with which to illustrate a forthcoming

A view of Oregon City, the then influential settlement upriver from Portland,
where Frances Fuller Victor gave dramatic readings in 1865.

ORHI 21591

number. She was canvassing for subscriptions to her magazine by giving
dramatic readings at Oregon City, Portland, and old Fort Vancouver.
Frances did not seek out Miss Lester. Rather, she braved the rain and
called on Judge Deady.

At 41, the tall, bearded, and blue-eyed Deady was a commanding figure.[18] He had come to Oregon in 1849 with an Ohio law degree. After
teaching school and practicing law in the town of Lafayette, seat of
Yamhill County, he had served as an associate justice of the territorial
government and presided over the Oregon state constitutional convention in 1857. Two years later, when he was appointed U.S. district judge

for Oregon, he moved his family and office to Portland. Public-spirited, he became a pillar of the Episcopal Church, known for his public speaking, his contributions to the *Oregonian*, and his monthly column on "Oregon Affairs" in the San Francisco *Evening Bulletin*.

At 38, attractive and self-assured, Frances Fuller Victor evidently gave him pause. In an autobiographical sketch, she later recalled that when she announced that she was going to write a handbook on Oregon, he had run his hands through his reddish beard and stormed, "Oregon has suffered enough from itinerant scribblers!" Then he lashed out at a woman claiming to be a writer who had collected subscriptions for a magazine that proved to be a fraud. Frances later discovered that this "fling" was not only at the unknown woman but also at an article in *The Atlantic Monthly*. Written by Fitz Hugh Ludlow, whom Frances had met in San

Francisco, Oregonians considered it "an impertinence." But Frances refused to be dismissed. As a correspondent for the San Francisco *Bulletin*, she had called on him for reliable information. At her mention of the *Bulletin*, Deady relaxed and invited her to use his private library as if it were her own. "From that day until his death," she later declared," Judge Deady was the staunchest and the most helpful of my Oregon friends."

Frances learned that Judge Deady and other leading Portlanders in March, 1864, had organized the Library Association of Portland.[19] It admitted women to membership and maintained a library and reading room on the second floor of the Benjamin Stark Building on First Avenue. Here Frances found some 1,600 volumes on Oregon history and other subjects as well as files of magazines and newspapers of Pacific Coast and Atlantic states along with a few European periodicals. The Association's first president, William S. Ladd, was a banker and business promoter with the Oregon Telegraph Company as one of his interests. Harvey W. Scott, at age 27 was one of the first librarians while he was trying to learn to write and studying law in the office of Judge Erasmus D. Shattuck, a founder of the Library Association.[20]

Another literary oasis for Frances Fuller Victor was S.J. McCormick's bookstore at 105 Front Avenue,[21] established in 1851, and providing access to more eastern publications. In conversations with McCormick, she learned that he had published the first number of the *Oregon Monthly*, containing five poems and a story, all from his own pen. He had also published other short-lived magazines and books by other Oregon writers. One was the first book by Abigail Scott Duniway, eldest sister of Harvey W. Scott. Entitled *Captain's Gray's Company: or, Crossing the Plains and Living in Oregon*, McCormick published it in 1859. Frances found its subject matter interesting but its style pedestrian and did not seek out its author, who would become a militant woman suffragist and a publisher in her own right in the decade ahead.

Within a few steps of the bookstore was the store of Douglas Wright Williams, a cousin of Frances' mother. Still ruggedly handsome at 57, he was a successful commission merchant, dealing in feed, flour, and groceries. In 1859, Williams and his wife had migrated from New

York State to Portland via the Isthmus of Panama, much as the Victors had done in 1863. In 1865, the Williamses were living in downtown Portland and active in the First Baptist Church at the corner of Fourth Avenue and Alder Street.[22] Here Williams served as clerk of the church and superintendent of its Sunday School. Though an avowed Unitarian since her days in New York City and San Francisco, Frances knew her mother was a lifelong Baptist. Frances treasured family relationships, and she would find the Williams' substantial home a comfortable and congenial haven during trying days ahead.

Within easy walking distance of the business district, part of which was paved, Frances noted the darker side of the would-be city.[23] Some 20 retail liquor establishments were seeded among the new brick hotels. A great number of street-level general stores and specialty shops displayed a variety of products and equipment shipped from New York City via San Francisco. But she deplored the grog houses that tempted her husband and his companions to drink Still, the lively advertisements of doctors, lawyers, and skilled artisans of all sorts, including a photographer, on the outer walls of buildings promised a brighter tomorrow.

As soon as the weather permitted, Frances explored Portland proper much as she had the sand hills of San Francisco in 1863. The business and residential districts were confined within a narrow grid of avenues and streets on the west bank of the Willamette River. Front Avenue bordered on the waterfront lined with wharves. Double-wide Park Avenue bounded the grid of streets just below the west hills that overlooked the town and the river. Twice as many named streets crossed numbered avenues and footed on Front Avenue. Downriver lay North Portland, better known as Couch Addition for Captain John Couch, who had settled there. In this addition, streets were lettered, later to be named for prominent pioneers beginning with Captain Alexander P. Ankeny.[24]

On the east side of the Willamette lay the newly platted village of East Portland, surrounded by farms and orchards on clearings in the forested foothills of the Cascade Range to the east. It was reached from Portland by a steam ferry, boarded at the foot of Stark Street. On clear days, snow-capped, 11,237-foot Mt. Hood dominated Portland's eastern skyline, and to the north stood more modest Mt. St. Helens across the Columbia River.

In preparation for her proposed voyages up the Willamette and Columbia rivers, Frances explored the sometimes unsavory waterfront.[25] Three blocks downriver from the O.S.N. Company's two-level wharf stood Couch and Flander's recently improved wharf between C and D Streets. Nearby an incipient Chinatown had taken root. Here sailors were reportedly shanghaied for service on ocean-going vessels bound for distant ports. Upriver at the foot of Washington and Salmon Streets were privately-owned anchorages, where locally-owned steamboats shipped freight and passengers up and down the Columbia and Willamette Rivers. Here, too, San Francisco-based steamships arrived more or less on schedule, and an occasional sailing ship dropped anchor to discharge exotic cargo from the Orient and take on Oregon produce.

One popular excursion was a carriage drive south over riverside Macadam Road to view the upriver scenery. Another was over the Great Plank Road.[26] Opened in 1849, it had been planked in 1851 and 1856 and provided a wagon road from downtown through Portland's forested west hills to the fertile upriver Tualatin Plains. Built and maintained by subscription funds, it extended Portland's natural advantage as head of navigation.

The Victors had arrived too late to stake out a 640-acre land claim as those arriving prior to December, 1853 had been permitted to do. But it was not too late for Henry to invest his Navy back pay and expected prize money in Oregon enterprises and land, as other former military men were doing. Though money was tight during the Civil War in Oregon, as elsewhere, Portland merchants were profiting from trade with the mining regions in Eastern Oregon and the territories of Washington, Idaho, and Montana.[27] They were investing these profits in businesses and better transportation systems. This enterprise, in turn generated pride in civic buildings. In the spring of 1865, the Victors watched the construction of the Multnomah County Courthouse, also to serve as City Hall, on the blocks bounded by Fourth and Fifth Avenues and Salmon and Main Streets. When the massive three-story structure was completed in 1866, the promenade around the base of the wooden dome offered an unobstructed view of Portland's strategic location between the Coast Range and Cascade Mountains and the complex system of waterways that connected the towns and farms of the region.

While pursuing Oregon history, Frances Fuller Victor discovered that after 16 years of provisional and territorial governments, Oregon had been admitted to the Union on Valentine's Day, 1859. She expected that Oregonians, like Californians, would celebrate Admission Day. When it passed without notice, she was puzzled until she read Judge Deady's explanation in his February 25 column in the San Francisco *Bulletin*. Dated Portland, February 14, it read, in part: "On this day six years ago, we took our place in the sisterhood of states, and the star of Oregon was emblazoned on the family colors . . . . The day is going by, in fact nearly gone, without public notice . . . . The event," he concluded, "is yet rather recent and raw for glorification, especially for a people who are not glorious, *per se*."

When Frances called at the office of the *Oregonian* at 5 Washington Street, she was greeted warmly by 37-year-old Samuel A. Clarke, current editor.[28] He was also a regular correspondent for the *Sacramento Daily Union*, to which Frances had contributed a series of travel letters in 1864. Like her, he wrote poetry for diversion. He had been serving as a legislative clerk in his home town of Salem, Oregon, when the *Oregonian* publisher, Henry A. Pittock, had engaged him in 1864–65 to edit the most widely-read newspaper in the state. Frances acquainted him with her literary background before she announced that she proposed to write a book for "the glorification" of Oregon. The February 27 issue of the *Oregonian* carried an item headlined "A New Work on Oregon;" in it, editor Clarke noted that, from what he had learned of the author's ability, he judged the book would do much "to give Oregon the high reputation it deserves among the States . . . . Mrs. Victor will visit different parts of the state to procure the necessary information to make a correct and valuable report, and, as she is a very excellent lady and in former years has been known as a very popular and excellent writer, we feel assured her presence will be welcome in any community of our State."

This excerpt from Clarke's March 27 column in the *Sacramento Daily Union* further indicates that he was impressed with her abilities:

> Oregon is having its history compiled for publication, by a lady writer of considerable note; and whose well-known talents, it is hoped, will secure to a reading world, a graphic picture of our past and future. Mrs. Frances Fuller Victor is one of two talented sisters, known, each of them, for a graceful tendency to verse, each a contributor to the literature of America, and they have few superiors among the lady writers of our nation. What wind blew Mrs. Victor hither I cannot say, but not an ill one I trust for either her or us. I quite admire the enterprise that induces her to visit these distant shores and undertake the work of searching out our legendary lore, and penetrating facts of aboriginal and pioneer history. The field is ample, and the varied incidents of Oregon life, since the time when trappers first gazed upon our streams and cataracts down to the bustling present, when the steam whistle wakes the wilderness of nature and no longer astonishes the remnants of savage life, will suffice in the hands of a poetess, to cast a tinge of romance over the whole, to make a book most readable. Then, she ventures on the path where Irving trod, but his was a history of long ago, and the world will readily receive from some graceful pen the continuation of the story he so well commenced.

Clarke's prophetic remarks reflected Frances' own ambition. Her New York mentor, Nathaniel Willis, had entertained Washington Irving on his Idlewild estate on the Hudson River prior to Irving's death in 1859; and she later reported that while living in New York City she had read Irving's *Astoria*, published in 1837.[29] Like Charles Gibbs, Clarke evidently encouraged Frances to visit the places that Irving had only imagined and interview living pioneers who had experienced the Oregon story.

March, 1865 came in like the proverbial lion in Portland, Oregon. President Lincoln's second inauguration was marked only by the firing of

Though briefly employed, Henry Victor might have been in this group beneath the Oregon Iron Works blast furnace. Remains of "old growth" trees clutter the foreground of this 1867 Watkins photograph of this ill-starred installation.
ORHI 21596

a cannon salute at dawn, noon, and sunset, and a luncheon and supper sponsored by the Ladies of the Sanitary Aid Society. Attendance was small at both events, according to Judge Deady's column in the San Francisco Evening Bulletin. An exception to this lack of "a manifestation of patriotism and nationality" was in the small town of Oakland in southern Oregon. Here a pioneer of 1853, Jesse Applegate of nearby Yoncalla, delivered a stirring address to Union supporters. The Oregonian published passages of the address, which Deady noted in his April 13 column in the Bulletin as "a specimen of the philosophy of a distinguished Oregon farmer . . . . one of our earliest pioneers," whom he designated as "the Sage of Yoncalla." In planning her itinerary up the Willamette Valley and beyond, evidently with Deady's help, Frances wrote Applegate, asking for an interview.

Meanwhile, Henry Victor had quit the Oregon Iron Works (owned by Governor Gibbs) and advertised himself as a consulting engineer. The

John Hipple Mitchell was a state legislator when Victor arrived in Portland.
She and Matthew Deady would have discussed some aspects of the full-bodied life
of the later U.S. senator. He outlived them by years—always under indictment.
ORHI 26849

great number of steamships and steamboats on the rivers and plying the
Pacific Coast gave him his reason to believe that his naval engineering
skills would find a ready market. His first advertisement in the *Oregonian*,
dated April 1, stated that his office was in the Vaughn Building on Morrison Street and that he was prepared "to furnish designs and drawings to
order, supervise the construction and repair of machinery, and make surveys of engines, boilers, and hulls of vessels." A second advertisement a
day or two later added that "his acquaintance with the routine of official
business at the Department at Washington City will enable Mr. Victor to
manage cases of patent soliciting ably and efficiently."

During the rest of April, the Victors, like the rest of the nation, were
whipped by powerful emotions. Telegrams from San Francisco by way of
Yreka, California, announced the fall of Richmond, the Confederate
capital, on April 3, and the surrender of General Robert E. Lee's Army of

FRANCIS FULLER VICTOR

Northern Virginia on April 9. On the afternoon and evening of April 12, Portlanders gathered to rejoice at the end of the fratricidal struggle. According to Deady's column, businesses and residences staged "illuminations" of bonfires, candles, and transparencies for a mile along Front Avenue and several parallel avenues. For a couple of hours after nightfall, crowds assembled to admire the lights and greet family members and friends. About 9 P.M., a procession, headed by a military band, marched and counter marched for a couple of hours before proceeding to the public square near the Victors' lodgings. Here dedicated Unionists listened until 1 A.M. to speeches by Governor Gibbs, Senator John Mitchell, Judge Erasmus Shattuck, Col. C.H. Larrabee, and the Rev. Henry K. Hines of the Taylor Street Methodist Church.

At noon April 15, Portlanders were struck "dumb with horror and shock" at a telegraphic report that President Lincoln had died from a gunshot wound inflicted at Ford's Theater in Washington City on the evening of Good Friday. Stores and residences draped their doors in mourning. Portlanders again assembled, in small groups, to share their shock and sense of loss. Frances Victor would have been able to share her memory of having seen Lincoln and his family being driven down Broadway to the Astor House in New York City on his journey to Washington City for his first inauguration, as well as her poem, "Legend of Abraham Lincoln," published under her pen name, Florence Fane, in an October 1864 number of the San Francisco *Golden Era*. In his April 26 column in the San Francisco *Bulletin*, Deady spoke for many Oregonians when he predicted that "the removal of Mr. Lincoln by the hand of violence at this particular juncture, will tend to embalm him in all hearts, and his name will be even more potent dead than living."

The dispatch announcing that the funeral of the President would be held in the East Room of the White House at noon, April 19, did not reach Portland until the previous evening. The *Oregonian* recommended that businesses close and that churches hold appropriate services at that hour. Governor Gibbs proclaimed statewide services to be held on April 17. In his May 11 column in the *Bulletin*, Deady described "The Obsequies of Abraham Lincoln" in Portland.

The day was fair, but flags hung at half mast, and the city was dressed in mourning. At a midtown location, a procession of four divisions, each with its own marshal, was formed under the command of General John McCracken, who had served during the Indian Wars of 1855–56. The lead division displayed a catafalque, "a superb piece of mechanism," which contained a coffin. Drawn by four black horses, it was escorted by a military guard and pallbearers, of whom Judge Deady was one. In following divisions marched members of civic societies of Portland as well as clergymen; city, state, and federal officials, and citizens at large. Church bells tolled and minute guns were fired as the procession wound its way down Front Avenue. At 1 P.M., it entered the upper level of the O.S.N. Company's new wharf. Here some 3,000 persons, among whom were the Victors, crammed themselves into a space filled with chairs for the occasion. Appropriate band music, a hymn sung by a choir, a prayer, and a reading from Scripture preceded the funeral oration delivered by Governor Gibbs. Then the audience rose to its feet as one to sing the national anthem and receive the benediction rendered by the Rev. Thomas Hyland of Trinity Episcopal Church.

May transformed Portland gardens into bowers of flowering fruit trees—cherry, peach, and prune—with birds nesting everywhere. By mid-month, Frances Fuller Victor left her husband to pursue his new vocation and apply for Navy prize money now that the Civil War was over. Traveling as a lady correspondent for the San Francisco *Bulletin*, she intended to gather information and documents for her proposed Oregon handbook. According to her second travel letter, entitled, "Wayside Pictures from Oregon: Up the Willamette Valley," she rose before dawn and rode across town to the Couch-Flanders wharf to board the steamboat *Rival*.[30]

Departing at 6 A.M, the *Rival* made its first stop at Milwaukie in Clackamas County six miles up the Willamette.[31] Founded in 1848 as a rival to Oregon City, a flourishing fruit nursery and a boat-building industry had insured its existence. Here Henderson Luelling and his son-in-law, William Meek, had established the first nursery in the Pacific Northwest with fruit roots that they had brought across the plains from Iowa. Lot Whitcomb, who had migrated with Luelling, had founded

Milwaukie and had launched the first steamboat on the Willamette there, but had soon been outmaneuvered by a shrewder lot of Portlanders.[32] As the *Rival* steamed up the Willamette River to Oregon City at the Falls there, Frances was approaching one of the most historic sites in the state, Oregon City.[33] Here she hoped to learn more about its founder, Dr. John McLoughlin, Chief Factor of the Hudson's Bay Company. She knew that after his retirement from the Company in 1846, he had settled his family on his land claim there and had died an American citizen in 1857. In 1850, British-born Daniel Harvey had married McLoughlin's widowed daughter, Elois McLoughlin Rae, and had handled his father-in-law's affairs before and after McLoughlin's death.

Upon reaching the landing and wood yard below the Oregon City Falls, Frances observed that they did not compare with Niagara Falls; but they did obstruct and increase the cost of navigation. All freight and passengers had to be portaged around them. Talk of building a canal around them struck her as foolhardy. The capital needed for such a venture would be better invested in a railroad up the Willamette Valley.

When she met Daniel Harvey, her artful questions won his confidence. During this visit or later, he entrusted her with several valuable documents. Foremost was "A Statement to the Parties in London," in which McLaughlin defended his benevolence to Americans living south of the Columbia River and his decision to allow Company retirees to join the efforts to organize the Oregon provisional government. Other materials related to efforts of Methodist missionaries and others to deprive him of his land claim at the Falls, where as early as 1829 he had erected a sawmill and laid out a town site. A paragraph in her travel letter to the *Bulletin* indicates what Harvey told her about McLoughlin's declining years:[34]

"The jealousy of American citizens gave him little enjoyment of his well-chosen property, and finally the town was taken away from him by Act of Congress . . . . The confusion of titles and the continued occupation of the doctor's heirs, whom no one could be found unscrupulous enough to eject, put a stop to its growth and prosperity for a time, and in the winter of 1862 the floods added their cruelty by sweeping away many of the buildings, mills, and shops." The town was recovering, she added, and the recently built Oregon City Woolen Mills, of which Harvey was a director, would soon be running looms for the manufacture of heavy woolen goods.

A mule-drawn car on the portage railroad on the east bank, built by the People's Transportation Company after the recent flood,[35] brought passengers to Canemah, a depot and boat-building site at the head of the Falls. Here Frances scrambled down a bank to board the Company's upriver sternwheeler, *Reliance*, bound for Salem.

She found the state's capital situated on the extensive plain on the east bank of the Willamette River and framed by rolling hills on the opposite shore that made "a pretty landscape." In contrast to Portland's crowded waterfront, Salem displayed "a thoroughly comfortable and tidy look." Its regularly laid out streets were wide and clean and a square and small parks reserved by "sagacious owners for the enjoyment of the public" added to its charm. Capital buildings were still "wanting." The legislative hall and state offices were located in a rented, fireproof building on the principal street. However, Willamette University, under the patronage of the Methodist Church, was "in a very flourishing condition." The old Oregon Institute, a plain wooden building, was still in use; but a fine brick building "with quite the air of "academic halls'" was under construction. A woolen mill and several flour mills made up the principal businesses, as they did in most towns in the valley.[36]

During her week-long visit in Salem, Frances stayed with Samuel and Harriet Clarke. Earlier that month, they had returned to Salem. Pittock had engaged Harvey W. Scott to edit The Oregonian. The Clarkes introduced Frances to their Salem friends, among whom was Belle Walker Cooke.[37] Though eight years Mrs. Cooke's senior, Frances considered her a pioneer. In 1851, at age 17, Belle had crossed the plains with a folding melodeon, her widowed mother, and her Baptist uncle, the Rev. George C. Chandler. She had taught at the Oregon Institute before she married Joseph Cooke. After proving up on a land claim, they had returned to Salem. Here Belle had been in charge of the Primary Department of Willamette University and was one of the first music teachers in the region. In the company of such congenial companions, Frances took a 70-mile trip to the Santiam gold and copper mines east of Salem—which would be of great interest to her husband, now a would-be capitalist.

At sunset of a lovely May day, Frances again boarded the *Reliance*, this time for Albany, only 20 miles south by land but farther away by way of the winding Willamette River. At the landing, she was met by a Mrs. Shepard, at whose home she stayed during most of her visit. In her travel letter, Frances observed that the homes, churches, and the new county courthouse were among the finest in the state, but the schools were "wanting" as were schools throughout Oregon. This she attributed to the fact that "many communities divided by the Slavery question in 1862 still remained divided, sending their children to separate and generally very poor schools."[38]

Through Mrs. Shepard, Frances met several prominent pioneers. Most notable was self-promoting Judge J. Quinn Thornton, who was practicing law, and his wife Nancy. The Thorntons had come to Oregon in 1846, and had suffered severe hardships while pioneering the newly blazed South Route from Fort Hall on the Oregon Trail to the Willamette Valley. These they had blamed on Jesse Applegate, who had helped survey the route. Frances would have known that in 1847 George Abernethy, first and only governor of the provisional government, had appointed Thornton judge of the provisional Supreme Court, a position he had resigned in order to go to Washington City, where he claimed that he had helped secure territorial status for Oregon. In any event, Frances readily accepted the Judge's invitation to visit him and his wife at Fairmount, their land claim in nearby Benton County and to inspect his historical collection.

In her autobiographical sketch, Frances later recalled that the judge had researched Oregon history from the point of view of the Hudson's Bay Company. Therefore, she questioned him about Dr. John McLoughlin, whose lawyer Thornton claimed to have been and whose autographed photograph he showed her. He also let her read items presented to him by Catherine Sager Pringle. One was her poignant manuscript about her life with Marcus and Narcissa Whitman at their Presbyterian mission on the Walla Walla River and their massacre there, which she and her sisters had escaped. Another was a 30-page pamphlet of "facts" about the massacre, compiled by the Rev. H.H. Spalding, an associate of Whitman at the time of the massacre. Spalding presently was serving as Indian agent at the Lapwai Indian Reservation in Idaho Territory, where he and his first wife, Eliza, had established a mission after having crossed the plains with the Whitmans in 1836. Their massacre was a sad and tangled tale that Frances would unravel in the decades ahead. But in 1865 her interest in McLoughlin and Whitman and her keen intellect impressed Thornton, for later that year he sent her the photograph of McLoughlin and let her copy in her own hand the Pringle items.

Mrs. Shepard also introduced Frances to other prominent pioneers such as Walter and Thomas Montieth.[39] When they arrived in Oregon by ox team in 1847, they had bypassed Oregon City and Salem and purchased 320 acres from an earlier settler. This land lay on the east bank of the Willamette near the mouth of the Calapooya River, which heads in the Cascades. When they surveyed their parcel, they set aside 60 acres for a townsite, which they named Albany after the capital of their home state, New York. In 1849, the Montieth brothers, along with hundreds of other migrants, headed for the California gold fields. In 1850, they returned with enough gold to build the first house and open the first store in Albany

When Frances met them, they were family men and enterprising mill owners. Their families took her on excursions to see the surrounding countryside, and she reported that the farms were well cultivated and the scenery delightful, especially from the top of Knox Butte, which was terraced nearly to the top with fine farms. On another occasion, she accompanied a party to the top of Washington Butte, some 11miles from Albany. Though clouds obscured the promised view of snow peaks in the Cascade Range to the east, the profusion of wild flowers and wild strawberries on the trail made the climb worthwhile.

Departing Albany, again by sternwheeler, for Corvallis in Benton County, some 15 miles distant, Frances found it strategically located on the west bank of the Willamette and the north bank of Mary's River, which heads to the north of Mary's Peak, one of the highest in the Coast Range to the west.[40]

To Victor's romantic eye, this farm town of some 800 inhabitants enjoyed several advantages over other upriver towns. It lay in the heart of the state's agricultural region at the confluence of two rivers, and a projected military wagon road from Corvallis to Yaquina Bay on the Pacific Coast would provide an outlet to the sea. However, Frances pointed out that a wagon road was no substitute for a railroad, without which the state would never gain commercial prosperity.

During the few days she spent in Corvallis, Frances talked with its most prominent woman, Martha Marsh Avery, whose hospitality was legendary. She had much to tell about crossing the plains with an immigrant party in 1867 and early days in Corvallis, founded by her husband, Joseph C. Avery.[41] In 1845, Avery had traveled with a party of men from Illinois to make a home for his family in Oregon. He had purchased 640 acres from the Calapooya Indians, where he built a log house and a granary and operated a ferry across Mary's River. In 1847, his friend, Mark Sawyer, returned to Illinois to bring out his own family, that of Avery, and anyone else who wanted to come. Martha Avery and her three small children joined Sawyer's company with two milk cows and a single wagon drawn by oxen. Her husband had met the party in eastern Oregon and piloted them to the Willamette River by way of the Barlow Toll Road, then under construction around Mt. Hood.

In 1848 and 1849, Avery had gone to California where he accumulated a small fortune in the mines. This he invested in merchandise, which he shipped to Portland and then upriver to the town he called Marysville. In 1852, now its postmaster and leading merchant, he built a frame house for his family. In 1854, the territorial government, of which Avery was a member, authorized changing the name of Marysville to Corvallis, a Latin compound meaning "heart of the valley." In 1855, by then a vital link on the road to California, the town was designated the capital of the territorial government for ten days.

Intrigued by stories of Albany and Corvallis from the lips of pioneers who had founded them, Frances boarded a stagecoach for the next leg of her journey to Eugene City in Lane County at the head of the Willamette Valley.[42] Some 35 miles south of Corvallis and 125 miles south of Portland, Eugene City seldom enjoyed more than a few months of access by steam navigation. Since 1859, it had been served by the California Stage Company, headquartered in Sacramento, California. With 60 way stations, 30 "mud wagons," and 28 stages powered by 500 head of horses, the 700-mile route between Sacramento and Portland delivered passengers, United States mail, and Wells Fargo express in seven days on its summer schedule and as many as twelve in the winter. In 1863, when Henry W. Corbett, Portland merchant and banker, purchased the line and the mail contract, it was the second longest stage route in the nation.

A stagecoach veteran accustomed to the jolts and lurches of the sturdy vehicles, Frances enjoyed the ride and arrived to find Eugene City located on the main fork of the Willamette, joined by the McKenzie River, both of which head in the Cascade Range, and by the smaller Coast Fork, which heads in the Coast Range, as the name implies.

In 1846, Eugene Skinner, a disgruntled Californian, had come north over the California Trail and settled on the bank of the Middle Fork of the Willamette at the foot of a 681-foot butte that soon would bear his surname. Here he had operated a ferry and in 1852 had platted a townsite, called "Skinner's Mudhole," until it was designated the Lane County seat. Then the territorial government upgraded the name to Eugene City—a fitting memorial to Skinner, who had died there in December, 1864. Arriving six months later, Frances Fuller Victor could not interview Skinner, but she sought out Harrison Kincaid, owner and editor of the *Oregon State Journal*.[43]

Kincaid, at age 17, had crossed the plains with his parents, who had settled in newly formed Lane County. After splitting rails and building fences, like a young Lincoln, he had struck out for San Francisco by way of Crescent City, California, only to return and move with his family to Eugene City. Here he helped build the family home while attending Columbia College. It had opened in 1856 under the sponsorship of the Presbyterian Church. During the last years of its existence, 1859–60, Kincaid had been a classmate of the more talented C.H. Miller, later known as Joaquin Miller, whom Frances had met in San Francisco in 1863.

Miller would find literary fame elsewhere; but Kincaid would be identified with Oregon newspapers and politics for the rest of his life.

In her travel letter, Frances mentioned "a lonely ruined college" standing on an eminence south of town. She called it "another token of the educational barrenness of Oregon." Not that people did not care for education, she explained, but "the sparseness of the population and the necessarily scattered support schools receive baffle all attempts at systematic education." She noted that a woolen mill was contemplated and that all Lane County would have a market for its produce in eastern Oregon and Idaho Territory upon the completion of the Oregon Central Military Road from Eugene City to the eastern boundary of the state. One of such military roads projected or under construction, it was unique in that it was being surveyed by B.J. Pengra, state surveyor, headquartered in Eugene City and president of a stock-issuing company of the same name.[44]

When she boarded the southbound "mud wagon" the next morning, she was only 35 miles from her final destination—the home of Jesse Applegate, "Sage of Yoncalla." Vistas of golden wheatfields interspersed with groves of ash and fir repaid her for the bruising passage over the mountains. She noted that alder and vine maple, with which she was familiar, lit up the dark green forest as did flowering shrubs and wild flowers that were new to her. Equally diverting were "the astonishing gymnastic feats" of the deer as the mud wagon thundered by.

Down in the Umpqua Valley, the driver pulled up at the foot of Yoncalla Mountain in front of a handsome two-story building with elegant pillars and a climbing rose spreading a riot of color over the east porch. It was the home of her host, but Frances was surprised to learn that the homespun figure standing at the gate to greet her was the "Sage of Yoncalla." He gave her a reception she never forgot. Many years later, she recalled "his philosophical head close shaven with its large ears set almost at right angles with his face, his large mouth stretched wide in a cordial yet half-quizzical smile, together with his gaunt figure and farmer's garb made an altogether unexpected picture—for I had heard a good deal about this Oregon statesman, and looked for something different."

Inside the spacious, well-furnished home, described as the finest in southern Oregon, Frances was greeted by Cynthia Anne Applegate. Her domain was the kitchen, the gardens, and the small dairy on this wayside retreat of 54-year-old Jesse Applegate, surveyor-statesman turned gentleman farmer. During her two-week stay, Frances, who had spent many of her 39 years living in inns and boarding-houses, appreciated the thought that had gone into the design of the house that Jesse had built in 1858, after his retirement from public life.[45]

The first floor was a generous version of a familiar lay-out: parlor and living room, dining room, kitchen and pantry, a hall, and three downstairs bedrooms for the older Applegates and their guests. An ornate stairway led to the second floor, the west side of which was divided by a hall, with the girls' rooms on one side and boys' rooms on the other. During Frances' visit, these rooms were overflowing with young people and their belongings. Some of the girls played the melodeon in the music room, which like the parlor below, was furnished with chairs and sofas constructed of walnut and upholstered with hair cloth. These pieces, together with Brussels carpets and additional furnishings, had been shipped from San Francisco to Scottsburg on the Umpqua River and hauled to Yoncalla over the Scottsburg Military Road that Jesse helped to survey in 1853–54.

Indeed, she was an ideal guest. By day, she visited other family members and neighbors or went sight-seeing. Shortly after her arrival, Jesse took her to the top of the mountain that the local Indians called Yoncalla, or "Home of the Eagles," for a view of the Umpqua Valley. In her account of this excursion, Frances wrote: "Up that mountain at whose foot he lives, he and I toiled together, and I found him the younger of the two." At the summit, he pointed out the natural landmarks: Diamond Peak, 8,750 feet in height, and the Three Sisters in the Cascade Range to the east, and to the north, 2,000-foot Spencer Butte, south of Eugene City from which she had just come.

From this vantage point, she could see that the Umpqua Valley was "a collection of isolated mountains with narrow strips of bottom land winding about their bases." Timber was dense on the steep mountain sides; but the slopes of the loosely timbered hills were covered with grass, "excellent pasturage for sheep." However, there was not a carding machine in the country; so farmers had to haul their wool to Scottsburg, or north to Salem or Portland. The shearing being over, many Umpqua farmers were setting out in covered wagons with beds and camping equipment. They visited family members and friends on their way to the nearest market town. Though enthralled with the romance of the covered wagons, Frances reminded her readers: "There again the railroad want comes in; nothing but to supply that want will ever bring out this portion of Oregon."

During the winter of 1829–30, while boarding at the Green Tree Tavern in St, Louis, Jesse had received a more encouraging picture of the American fur trade from partners of the Rocky Mountain Fur Company, who customarily met at the tavern to settle their accounts and recruit new trappers. After listening to their tales of adventure and easy money, Jesse might have turned mountain man had not Colonel McKee promoted him to the post of deputy surveyor. His marriage to Cynthia, the birth of their first child, Roselle, and the counsel of his older married brother further discouraged him from becoming a Rocky Mountain fur trapper. In 1833, the three brothers settled their growing families on a large tract of land in central Missouri. As a surveyor and cattleman, Jesse earned a good living until 1840. Then hard times wiped out the cattle business; and Jesse, who abhorred slavery, had to borrow slaves from his neighbors because he could not find free men to work his farm.

A letter from Oregon written by bachelor Robert Shortess, who had lived in their homes while teaching school in Missouri, had rekindled the Applegates' interest in this distant country.[46] In 1839, after hearing the Methodist missionary, Jason Lee, lecture on Oregon, Shortess had joined the Oregon-bound Peoria Party which broke up en route. Traveling in the company of Rocky Mountain fur trappers or mountain men like Joe Meek and Robert Newell, Shortess reached the Willamette Valley in April, 1840. His schoolmasterly descriptions of the lush valley and the availability of free land prompted the Applegate brothers and others to think about following his tracks with their wagons, families, and livestock.

Victor's feelings for the estimable O.C. Applegate (left) could have been robust.
They found much to admire in each other. Joaquin Miller (right)
was a San Francisco acquaintance who flowered later, notably in Europe
upon the publication of his notable *Land of the Modocs*.
ORHI 56449

By early 1843, parties of immigrants from all over Missouri and bordering states were assembling in western Missouri with plans to cross the plains and the Rocky Mountains by wagon train. Jesse loaded four wagons of provisions from his farm as well as household goods, clothing, tools, especially his surveying instruments, and a great number of books, some on Oregon, but more were textbooks for his children. He and his sons rounded up some 200 head of cattle. Late in April, the Applegates and some of their friends headed west for Independence to join hundreds of others, equally eager to make a transcontinental trek to an unknown land.

When the train departed Independence on May 22, it numbered almost 900 men, women, and children in some 120 wagons, drawn by oxen or mules and followed by several thousand head of livestock. At the outset, they traveled in a single train, under the command of Peter H. Burnett, who had helped organize the migration. But those without livestock soon claimed that they were being slowed down by those driving herds that raised pillars of dust. In response, those driving stock, about half the train, formed a rear division, known as the "Cow Column," with Jesse Applegate in charge. So at age 33, he entered the annals of Oregon history.

As Jesse recounted the story of the Cow Column, which he later published, Frances learned that in July, 1843, Dr. Marcus Whitman and his nephew, Perrin Whitman, had overtaken the disjointed wagon train in time to guide the lead division across the Platte River and deliver the first baby to be born on the trail. In his account to Frances, Jesse Applegate simply noted that Whitman had been helpful. He did not explain that in the winter of 1842–43 Whitman had traveled east from his Presbyterian mission on the Walla Walla River in eastern Washington to attend to urgent missionary business in Boston and to visit his own and his wife's families. Rather, Applegate noted that by early August the lead division of the migration reached Fort Hall, built in 1834 by Nathaniel Wyeth, a New England merchant-adventurer, who had sold it to the Hudson's Bay Company in 1836 when he returned to the East. Here, according to Jesse, a dispute had arisen over the wisdom of taking wagons and families over a trail untried for such travel except by mountain men like Joe Meek and their Indian families. When Whitman agreed to escort the wagons as far as his mission on the Walla Walla, most followed him. Arriving in early October, they procured provisions there before pushing on to the Columbia River and down its south bank to a dangerous set of rapids known as The Dalles.

At this gap in the towering Cascade Range, the Applegates had been met by Robert Shortess, who had come upriver from the Willamette Valley with a canoe filled with supplies. Like other immigrants, the Applegates had to decide whether to engage Hudson's Bay

Handsome mountain man and storied trapper "Colonel" Joe Meek was
seeking a biographer when Judge Deady introduced Victor to him.
ORHI 47320

Company bateaux or build rafts of their own on which to transport
their families and wagons downriver to Fort Vancouver on the north
bank of the Columbia and then up the Willamette to the falls. Live-

stock that was not sold or traded was driven down the south bank of the Columbia and over a trail through the forested Mt. Hood foothills and into the Willamette Valley.[47]

While trying to pass the rapids, the Applegates had suffered a heart-wrenching tragedy. A canoe carrying three men and at least two of the Applegate boys capsized. Seventy-year-old Alexander McClellan was drowned while trying to save Lindsay and Elizabeth Applegate's son, Warren, who was drowned, as was his cousin, Edward Bates, oldest son of Jesse and Cynthia Applegate.

In subsequent conversations, Frances learned that the Applegates had spent the winter of 1843–44 in the abandoned buildings of the first Methodist mission on the Willamette River, 40 miles down stream below Salem. Dr. McLoughlin was laying out a town he called Oregon City. So Jesse was well situated to make surveys for McLoughlin and the Oregon provisional government, headquartered there. At the same time, his older brother Lindsay, built a ferry boat for James O'Neill, who had settled across the river from the original mission site in 1835. According to Lindsay's son, Jesse, his father caulked the boat with a bushel of religious tracts the Methodists had left behind. These he had forced between the planks with a hammer and chisel and sealed with hot pitch.

Frances later recalled that she had found Jesse Applegate's far-ranging knowledge "phenomenal" and that he was the most independent thinker she had ever met. Further, she agreed with him on every subject they discussed except "woman's rights." He clung to the old-fashioned idea that a woman needed only enough education to be a good wife, but Frances was confident he respected her physical stamina, her intellect, and her literary abilities; for as he handed her into the coach bound for Eugene City, he remarked, "I would be proud if I could call you my daughter."

Frances appreciated the epic nature of his pioneer experiences and did not turn them into grist for her own literary mill, knowing that he was best able to do justice by them. Some two decades later, when she wrote Chapter 20, "The Immigration of 1843," for Bancroft's *Oregon*, she wove together several accounts of the migration, of which Applegate's manuscript, dated 1878, was only one. Another was Peter Burnett's *Recollections of a Pioneer*, published in New York City in 1880.

During her visit, Jesse Applegate, in his candid, but prickly, fashion, had rehearsed his autobiography for her. What the effort had cost him he revealed in his reply two years later to Elwood Evans, a lawyer and historian of the Pacific Northwest, living in Olympia, capital of the Washington Territory.[48] After explaining that he could fight off male authors seeking information, he admitted that he was "no match for ladies of the pen." On one occasion, he had been "the helpless victim" of such a lady. He had written her that if she wanted information from him she would have to come to him for it. She had taken him at his word. In about two weeks, she had pumped him "so dry of historical matters that the memory and imagination were utterly exhausted." There had been nothing that he could conceal from her scrutiny. Then he added: "Yet she is so little grateful for the information thus wrung from me as you are for my strictures on Chapter 17 (of Evans' projected history), if you really seek the truth, go to her for it. Perhaps she will give you the benefit of her investigations. What she derived from me is now hers. I cannot object if she gives you my autobiography. The lady is Mrs. Frances Fuller Victor of St. Helens."

In late June with Jesse Applegate's "autobiography" and much more in her notebook, Frances returned to Portland to write her "Wayside Pictures from Oregon: Up the Willamette Valley." When she apprised her husband of investment possibilities in the Santiam mines near Salem, and the Oregon Central Military Road, headquartered in Eugene City, he countered with news of his own. During her absence, Simeon G. Reed, 35-year-old president of the O.S.N. Company, had engaged him to draw up specifications for a steamship, suitable for the competitive run between Portland and San Francisco. This assignment would command a substantial fee which, like the prize money he expected to receive from the federal government, would be paid in gold, not in discounted greenbacks.[61]

Frances Fuller Victor's report to Judge Deady on her trip to interview Jesse Applegate was followed by her decision to seek out "Colonel" Joseph Meek, who had lived on a land claim on the Tualatin Plains with his Indian family since 1840. Judge Deady told her that Meek predated both the Applegates and Thornton in Oregon.[48] In 1843, this self-educated, former Rocky Mountain fur trapper and cousin of President Polk's wife had helped organize the Oregon provisional government. In the winter of 1847–48, after the massacre of Marcus and Nercissa Whitman and the outbreak of the Cayuse Indian War, he had been delegated to proceed overland to Washington City to help secure territorial status for the beleaguered Oregon "Republic." Moreover, this jovial political leader, now no longer in the midst of current events, was seeking someone to help him write his autobiography.

Intrigued with Meek's story, Frances agreed to interview him, but first she must complete her promised 400-mile "Columbiad" from historic Astoria at the mouth of the Columbia River to Lewiston on the Snake River in Idaho Territory, a major tributary to the Columbia. She decided to break her voyage into two round trips—the first from Portland to Astoria and return in time to greet a New York City acquaintance, Albert D. Richardson, a correspondent for Horace Greeley's New York *Tribune*. He was a member of the celebrated Schuyler Colfax party, touring the country west of the Missouri mainly by stagecoach.[49] Colfax was speaker of the U.S. House of Representatives. William Bross, editor of the Chicago *Tribune* and Lt. Governor of Illinois, and Samuel Bowles, publisher of the Springfield *Republican*, were also members of the party. The group was scheduled to arrive in Portland on July 19, with Judge Deady to be a member of the welcoming committee. Frances also decided to write to William L. Adams, a former Willamette Valley newspaper man.[50] In 1861, President Lincoln had appointed him collector of customs, headquartered in Astoria, reportedly because Lincoln had been amused by Adams' political satire, *Breakspear; or, Treason, Stratagems, and Spoils*, A five-act play, which the *Oregonian* had serialized in 1852, it was written in the "Oregon Style" of invective that Adams and his political opponents were practicing at the time. Another potential contact was Dr. William H. Gray (1810–89), an associate of Dr. Marcus Whitman. It was rumored that Gray was writing a history of Oregon, based on his personal experiences, to be published serially in the Astoria Marine Gazette.

Between June 24, the Portland dateline for her "Wayside Pictures from Oregon," published in the San Francisco *Bulletin*, and July 10 when she boarded the O.S.N. Company's sidewheeler, *John R. Couch*, for its regular Monday morning departure for Astoria, Frances secured a copy of Washington Irving's *Astoria* together with relevant passages from the Lewis and Clark journals and *Narrative of the U.S. Exploring Expedition* by Lt. Charles Wilkes. All were in Judge Deady's personal library or in that of the Library Association. As she noted at the outset of her third travel letter, "A Voyage Up the Columbia," she was determined to "get a good ready" by commencing at the beginning.

She left with the knowledge that Simeon Reed had advised Henry that the board of the O.S.N. Company had authorized "building in the Atlantic states . . . an Ocean Steamer." She would have been less sanguine had she known that three days later, in writing fellow board members in New York City, Reed remarked:[51] "Mr. Victor, a practical engineer and draftsman here in town, is getting up for us the dimensions of a ship with such machinery which in his judgment would meet our requirements. This will doubtless be sent to you, but you can take it for what it is worth, as merely to corroborate what ideas you can obtain from other parties. I believe we all concur in this, that Capt. Wm. S. Dull's judgment as to a ship that would be adapted to our wants, and his ideas of the general planning and arrangements is superior to any person we know of, and should be secured by all means possible to do so."

Henry Victor's career as a commercial engineer was doomed from the outset. However, like many of his peers, he would speculate with his own (anticipated) prize money and other people's money. In contrast, his wife had already discovered a career for which she was uniquely qualified—producing the written record of her own adventures and those of others. These differing approaches to the prospects and pioneers in Oregon would strain their already fragile marriage.

CHAPTER 4

A TIME OF
GOOD FORTUNE
(1865-68)

FRANCES VULLER VICTOR carried a copy of Washington Irving's *Astoria* in her pocket when she left her husband absorbed in his drafting and boarded the steamboat *John H. Couch*, bound for Astoria on July 10, 1865. In her mind were extracts from the Lewis and Clark journals. When the steamer docked at Astoria that evening, she was much more favorably impressed with the village of some 400 inhabitants than when she had observed it from the deck of the *Brother Jonathan* six months earlier on a stormy Christmas afternoon.[1] The oldest part of the town, where the fort and trading house of John Jacob Astor and subsequent British companies had been located, was also the handsomest, she noted. But enterprising citizens were improving, by grading and otherwise, the cliffs along the Columbia River.

The next morning, invigorated by a fresh sea breeze, Frances set forth "with the inquisitiveness usual" to her to respond to an invitation from the collector of customs, William L. Adams, and his wife, Frances Goodell Adams, to visit them at their home. There, to her surprise, Adams presented Frances with a file of the first newspaper published on the Pacific Coast, the Oregon City *Oregon Spectator*, published in 1846. At its demise in 1855, Adams had purchased its printing press on which he had published the *Oregon Argus*, a Whig newspaper, until President Lincoln had appointed him collector of customs.

Later that day, Frances had a less fortunate experience with William H. Gray, a lay Presbyterian missionary, who had accompanied Dr. Whitman and Henry H. Spalding to Oregon in 1836.[2] Frances called on Gray's wife, who received her graciously and also let her borrow one of her husband's two copies of *A Voyage Around the World: With a History of the Oregon Missions* by Gustavus Hines. A few hours later, Frances was surprised and shocked when a messenger appeared at her lodgings to reclaim the volume. Gray apparently resented a newcomer, especially a woman, borrowing his source materials, for he was writing a history of Oregon, which the Astoria *Marine Gazette* would begin publishing serially the next month.[3]

Despite Gray's rebuff, Frances enjoyed a idyllic week in and around Astoria. With the Adamses, she visited the site of old Fort Astoria, where nothing remained to mark the historic events enacted there except "the fine grass of cultivation which time does not eradicate." Sitting on the grassy slope in the sun, they conjured up that tranquil scene which Captain Robert Gray and the crew of the good ship *Columbia* beheld for the first time on the morning of May 11, 1792—among the first of the white race to do so. They fancied Astor's ship, *Tonquin*, some 19 years later, sounding out the channel in small boats and losing eight of her crew in the undertaking. They imagined the small ship crossing the bar and anchoring alongside the bluff on which they were sitting, sending on shore the stores of the Pacific Fur Company with business haste, eager to be off to those northern waters where the *Tonquin* met her fate. On another day, Frances and the Adamses took advantage of an ebb tide to proceed south along the shore of Young's Bay to visit an Indian lodge and obtain a view of Saddle Mountain, Lewis and Clark River, the Clatsop Plains, and environs. By day's end, she was certain that at this point there would be "a great and important city."

Before Frances departed Astoria on July 18, the Adamses decided to accompany her aboard the sternwheeler, *John R. Couch*, to Portland to meet the Colfax party as well as on her scenic excursion up the Columbia and Snake rivers. Frances found little of interest below St. Helens, a village on the Oregon side of the Columbia, but she waxed enthusiastic about the townsite of St. Helens where she enjoyed a view of Mt. St. Helens on the Washington side of the river. In 1839, the mountain had erupted, throwing ashes all over the ground to a depth of one to two inches, she was told. As the sternwheeler entered the mouth of the

Willamette River, she felt that on this fine July evening, the scenic beauty of "the mingling rivers, the numerous low islands covered with groves of cottonwood and oak, and three lofty snow peaks could scarcely be equaled anywhere for singular loveliness."

When the steamer docked at Vaughn's wharf at the foot of Morrison Street, Henry doubtless greeted Frances and her traveling companions, who planned to continue their voyage up the Columbia River of the O. S. N Company's new sternwheeler *Cascades*, scheduled to make her run in regular service to the Cascades Rapids.[4]

In Portland, excitement was building over the impending visit of the Colfax Party. Since May, city residents had been following the party's progress, mostly by stagecoach across the continent from Atchison, Kansas, the most western point of the eastern railroad system. Traveling day and night, they had endured the hazardous journey in the Concord coaches of the Overland Stage Line by way of Fort Kearny in Nebraska, Denver in Colorado, and Salt Lake in Utah to Placerville in California. Here the party had entrained for Sacramento, thence by steamboat to San Francisco. After a brief interlude in the Bay City, the party had headed north, again by stagecoach, through northern California and southern Oregon. While traveling through Douglas County, the party had stopped at Jesse Applegate's farm, as self-invited breakfast guests. His fame as an old pioneer, honest and incorruptible in thought and act, and a maker of good cider, had increased as they approached his home. While enjoying the ample meal furnished by their hospitable host, they discovered him to be "a man of genius, too proud to practice the politician's arts, and therefore in private life."[5]

During a brief stopover at Salem, the party was honored at a state reception. Meanwhile, in Portland, "The Colfax Ovation," as Judge Deady termed the event, was already underway. In the early morning hours of July 19, a committee of prominent citizens, headed by Mayor Henry Failing, boarded the steamboat *Senator* bound for Oregon City to meet the party. About sundown that evening, Frances and Henry Victor joined the crowd along the waterfront. Cheers rose as the *Senator*, carrying the party and welcoming committee hove into sight with colors flying, drums beating, and cannon firing. From the wharf, the committee escorted the party directly to Lincoln House, built earlier that year at the corner of Front and Washington streets. Here the Colfax Party was headquartered during its stay in the city.

The first night, a banquet at the Lincoln House was hastily dispatched because of the lateness of the hour and the clamor raised by the noisy crowd outside, demanding that the guests speak. Frances and Henry were among them. Lt. Gov. Bross led off and was followed by Speaker Colfax. Though he spoke for an hour and a half, the audience listened with great interest. Next they called for Mr. Albert Richardson. Just as he got "cleverly under way," Judge Deady retired. He evidently anticipated that the levee in honor of the party to be held at the governor's residence in Portland the following evening would be even more demanding.

The gala affair was attended by some 150 ladies and gentlemen among whom were the Victors. Frances, attractive, vivacious, and aware of her growing recognition as an Oregon author, thoroughly enjoyed herself. In talking with Mr. Richardson, whom she had met in New York City before the Civil War, Frances told him that she was writing a book about Oregon for which she had yet to find a publisher. To her pleasure, he gallantly offered to carry her manuscript to New York City, where he was confident he could locate a publisher for her, but not before December because he intended to make a tour of the Pacific states after the other members of the party returned to the East. Encouraged by his interest, Frances left the governor's levee determined to complete her manuscript by December.

Early the following Monday, Henry escorted Frances to the O. S. N. Company's wharf where, with the Adamses, she boarded the *Cascades*. After the trim sternwheeler pulled away and breakfast was served in the dining salon on the hurricane deck, Frances caught her first glimpse of Vancouver, former site of the Hudson's Bay Company headquarters. Now, she noted in her travel letter, it was a quiet place, important only as the Pacific Northwest headquarters of the United States Army.

As the steamer moved upriver smartly at the rate of 15 miles an hour, Frances realized that not until they approached the Cascade Mountains was the majesty of the Columbia River fully apparent. Though Mount

Hood seemingly diminished in size as they proceeded upriver, the scenery became more spectacular as the Cascade Mountains lifted their towering peaks on either side. She also observed fantastic forms of rocks in the river and alongside with equally fantastic names. Still others were pointed out by the captain, who tendered them the use of the pilot house for observation. About 11 A.M., the steamer approached the Cascades Rapids. Here, in the heart of the Cascades Range, Frances observed "a pretty piece of bottom land on the north side of the Columbia." Here was a little town called Lower Cascades, fronted on the south by a 3,000 foot mountain. Between it and the town flowed the rapid and mighty river, just escaped from the rocks and falls that for six miles tortured it into a sheet of foam. At this point, Frances and her friends transferred from the sternwheeler to a small coach of a portage railway train waiting near the landing. After an hour's wait while freight was trundled on hand carts from the wharf into the train's boxcars, the short string of cars, drawn by a small engine with a big smokestack, rolled rapidly along the river in sight of the foaming rapids. This ride of six miles, Frances later recalled was "a delightful one, affording such opportunities of wonderful sightseeing as occur but seldom in a lifetime." These rapids did not have the force that one sees "when the Niagara rushes to its fall, but the variety of the play of the water is infinitely greater."

At the Upper Cascades landing, while waiting to board the steamer, *Oneonta*, for The Dalles, Frances picked up a few pieces of petrified wood as souvenirs and explored the little town of Cascades, "once taken by Indians and several citizens massacred." This mountain hamlet, she felt, ought never be anything more, else "the soul of nature is profaned." The *Oneonta* had superior accommodations: from its open deck, Frances could enjoy the scenery without moving from her chair. As it churned upriver, she marveled at a high and bald, perpendicular cliff of red rock, pointed like a pyramid at the top, which looked as if freshly split off or parted from some other mass of rock nowhere visible. This, she thought, is surely the site of the "Bridge of the Gods."[6]

Frances admitted that she could not describe the height and grandeur of the river and mountains above the Cascades. She could only compare and isualize past adventures here. The Hudson River, which had

The Upper Cascades on the north bank of the Columia, 1867.
Victor passed through here two years earlier on her Columbia River trip.
ORHI 21109 NO. 1100-A

been the pride of Americans, now seemed to her to be but "the younger brother" of the majestic Columbia. "Triple the height of the Palisades," she wrote, "and you can form an idea of these precipitous cliffs. Elevate

the dwarfed evergreens of the Hudson Highland into firs and pines like these and then you can compare."

Here Frances paused to visualize the historical and romantic events that had taken place on these wild, western waters in years past. Some fifty years ago the annual brigades of the Hudson's Bay Company

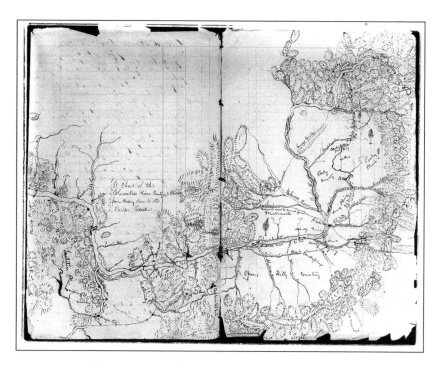

There is some evidence that Mrs. Victor used this map
in preparing for her Columbia River voyage.
ORHI 9834-A

brought the year's accumulation of peltries and the express from the Red
River settlement in Canada. Ten years earlier, Lewis and Clark had
descended this great river in the service of the federal government, and a
few years later a part of Astor's overland expedition had suffered all but
death passing down this river in the winter. Only twenty years ago, the
1843 immigration to Oregon, arriving late at The Dalles, were dependent
on Hudson's Bay boats to bring them down to the settlements. It had
been a difficult passage; immigrants and boatmen alike had been lost in
the fearful rapids.

After this historical aside, Frances recounted her own adventures.
Some 13 miles above the Cascades, the paused at a wood yard to take on
fuel. Not far above the point where Hood River flows into the Colum-
bia, Mount Hood glistened in a mantle of snow and the crest of Mount
Adams was sighted between the cleft heights on the north bank of the
Columbia. As they neared The Dalles, Frances found herself in "a very

desert of rocks — rocks, nothing but rocks on every side but the heaven-ward one."[7]

Frances and the Adamses found rooms at the Umatilla House, where the parlor was warm and filled with lively children who occupied the few sofas. Relief came that evening when they sat on the hotel's wide, cool balcony. The next morning before dawn they boarded the portage rail-road that passed dpwn the main street of The Dalles, then whirled east between the bluff and the Columbia. At Celilo, passengers emerged from the railroad cars into the O. S. N. Company's 900-foot warehouse and directly into the Company's waiting steamer, the *Nez Perce Chief*. From Celilo to the mouth of the John Day River, the Columbia was a tumult of rapids, but they posed no obstruction to the sharp-nosed steamer, which slipped through them like a salmon. Above the John Day, only a wood yard and a sail added interest. About unset, the *Nez Perce Chief* reached the village of Umatilla, where it paused only briefly, to the disap-pointment of Frances and the Adamses. They had to settle for a view from the steamer's deck of a village of perhaps 100 inhabitants and to look forward to their destination in Lewiston on the Snake River in Idaho Territory. However, when they retired that night, the captain refused to assure them that he could navigate the Snake.

The next morning when Frances came on deck she learned from the captain that they were already fifteen miles up the Snake River. Then, at what seemed but a slight shock to her, he rushed away, and Frances heard the pumps working. Three or four hours passed before the repairs were completed. Until 4 P.M., the captain cautiously piloted the steamer up the narrow, rapid stream, a smaller version of the Columbia River above Celilo. Suddenly all progress ceased. The captain sent out a small boat to search for a deeper channel. When the search proved fruitless, he announced that he must unload his freight and retire to Celilo for a smaller steamer.

The next morning, the steamer, relieved of its freight, commenced its return to Celilo. Then all at once, Frances heard "bump, thump, jump, crash!" The captain beached the water-logged craft and after eight hours of hard work at the pumps, its crew succeeded in refloating it. Then they ran it down to Wallula, one side of its lower deck underwater and its

The Columbia River town of Wallula, Washington Territory,
the site of the Hudson's Bay Co.'s Fort Walla Walla.
ORHI 80952

pumps working to keep it from sinking. While waiting for the regular steamboat to return them to The Dalles, Frances and the Adamses went ashore. They walked along the main street past the former fort, now a hotel, and down along the beach to the mouth of the Walla Walla River. Here they hired a boat to take them to the opposite shore of the Columbia River so that Frances and Adams could settle a wager they had made on the length of time it would take them to climb the bluff on that side. To her chagrin, Frances gave out halfway up the bluff. As Adams waved his handkerchief from the highest point, she envied him his view. As she descended the bluff, with loose stones rolling under her feet, a rattlesnake, coiled and ready to strike, blocked her path. Instinctively, she retreated. The snake uncoiled and glided away. But she did not feel comfortable until Adams reached her side and they returned to the waiting boat. That evening, he taunted her by describing his bird's eye view of the Walla Walla Valley.

FRANCIS FULLER VICTOR

Early the following day, they boarded the steamer headed for The Dalles, arriving in time to see some of the town's historic sites and Mount Hood bathed in sunset glow. Then at dawn the next day, they boarded the *Oneonta* to enjoy, in reverse, the beauty of the Columbia on their homeward voyage. They reached Portland just as the overland telegraph from Jacksonville, Oregon brought news of a maritime disaster. On the afternoon of July 30, the *Brother Jonathan*, after striking a reef, had foundered off Crescent City, California. All but sixteen of its 183 passengers and crew had been lost.

Remembering the stormy passage she had endured just six months earlier on that ship, Frances shuddered. How close had she been to disaster? As she scanned the newspaper list of lost passengers, she suffered a sharp sense of personal loss. The name of James Nesbit, her friend and benefactor as editor of the San Francisco *Evening Bulletin* was there. She had been looking forward to talking with him during his visit to the Pacific Northwest. But she did not indulge her sorrow. Rather, she wrote an account of her voyage up the Columbia and Snake Rivers for the *Bulletin* and finished her book on Oregon.

On October 11, the Portland *Morning Oregonian* published a news item featuring "The Coming Work on Oregon." It read, in part:

"We learn that Mrs. F. F. Victor is now engaged upon the final preparation of her work on Oregon. The lady has been very energetic in prosecuting her researches for information on the subject since her arrival in Oregon, and we may expect many things that have come under her observation, which were speedily becoming extinct, that now will be made matters of history. Mrs. V. is ably qualified to consummate this purpose in which she is engaged, and we look with interest for the publication of her work, believing it will be a faithful view of Oregon. Last week Mrs. Victor returned from a trip up the Columbia River. Recently a tour of the Willamette Valley was made by her, and sketches from her ready pen where there is so much of interest to take note of, must become very popular."

During the late summer, Frances Fuller Victor continued to correspond with other pioneers and interview some in person.[8] In September, she received from J. Quinn Thornton three almost illegible letters and

Every detail but a leaping salmon is included in this breathtaking historical stufy of
sternwheeler loading from a wheat chute on a favorite Victor river, the Snake
ORHI 1727

the autographed likeness of Dr. John McLoughlin. He wrote that he had
known McLoughlin well, as he had been his professional adviser during
McLoughlin's last days in Oregon City. Thornton praised McLoughlin

for his humane treatment of the early American settlers and decried their later treatment of him. Thornton also dwelt at length on his own trip in 1848 to Washington, D.C., where, he claimed, he had influenced Congress to create the Oregon Territory, and he had introduced a donation land bill. Though it had not come to vote before the session ended, Thornton assured Frances that it had later become the Donation Land Law with but four changes.[9]

In the midst of her correspondence, Frances paused to do some volcano-watching.[10] On the morning of September 23, she noticed a "singular looking cloud" hanging off the top of Mount Hood. First there was black smoke, then alternate puffs of smoke and steam, and then steam alone. Two weeks later at about 8 A.M., she observed a great volume of steam rising from Hood's summit. Settling herself in her observation post, she resolved to see "what the grand old titan was doing that he needed to be puffing away at that rate." There she remained until 4 P.M., observing no diminution in action. With Mount Hood smoking and steaming, she joined in the widespread speculation about the relationship between volcanoes and earthquakes. Could there be a connection, she wondered, between the first eruption she had seen on Mount Hood and the earthquake off the California coast eight days later? "I recommend," she declared, "that when the operator at Portland telegraphs an eruption of one of our volcanoes, San Francisco citizens should make fast all their loose property and sit with open doors ready for an exit . . . ." It may be," she concluded, "we shall witness something grander in the way of an eruption."

Frances' interest in and fear of volcanoes may have set her apart from most women of her day. In fact, she was more upset at being quoted out of context at home. On the morning of October 11, the Portland *Morning Oregonian* carried a front-page two-column article, captioned "Railroads and Railroad Routes in Oregon." It was prefaced by this brief editorial statement: "We are kindly permitted to make the following extracts from the coming history of Oregon in preparation for the press by Mrs. F. F. Victor." Frances likely fumed as she read it. The statement was misleading. The excerpts were from the descriptive, not the historical, part of her manuscript, which was not in press.

However, excerpts demonstrated that Frances, a railroad enthusiast since her youth in the Midwest and East, understood the need for a railroad between San Francisco and the Columbia River and from here to Puget Sound—the best natural naval depot in the world. She pointed out that increased prosperity would accrue to Oregon with development of her resources and expansion of her trade. To help finance the venture, she suggested that Willamette Valley farmers donate from their land claims the right-of-way needed for the railroad. She added that in 1850 the citizens of Illinois had paid for its first railroad by so doing and had laid the foundation of its future prosperity. Frances further argued that the railroad "is a great educator" and that there "can be no Rip Van Winkle within the sound of the railroad whistle." In her article, Frances was clearly trying to goad the people of Oregon into action.

Misleading statements about her book continued to plague Frances. In Judge Deady's October column in the San Francisco *Evening Bulletin*, she came upon his two-paragraph comment on "Mrs. Victor's forthcoming *History of Oregon*—a Word About Slowness." In the first paragraph, he announced that "this morning's *Oregonian*" contained two columns from *The History of Oregon* by Mrs. Frances Fuller Victor, "now in press." The extract in question, he explained, "is kindred to railroad and transportation, or rather the lack of them. The historian (I believe the word is common gender) raps us over the knuckles in a kindly way about our special peculiarty—slowness." The rest of the paragraph took issue with Frances' contention that Oregon should build a railroad through the Willamette Valley and on to the California border. It was equally certain, he editorialized, it was to Oregon's advantage, now and in the future, that she had been blessed with sufficient slowness, not to attempt it before she was ready and able. However, in his second paragraph, Deady's evaluation of Frances' work doubtless mollified her: "Mrs. Victor is a good writer, neither flashy nor foggy; has a clear and correct eye for the natural resources, scenery and material of a country. She had examined the State and its surroundings in greater extent than anyone else I know of, who has attempted a book or pamphlet about it. The work will be published in two volumes. The first will be devoted to business—a description of the country and its resources, including the neighboring mines. The second will be more devoted to history proper and will deal with the men and events that illumine or darken the period of our colonial existence. I bespeak for the work a good word and a wide circulation."

Deady had repeated the *Oregonian* editor's error in terming Frances Fuller Victor's book a history of Oregon. In fact, his description sounds more like a recommendation. The book was primarily a descriptive handbook which included historical information about the state along with a map. However, Deady had Frances' interest in view. About his time, he introduced her to Joseph L .Meek, who was in search of a collaborator. She was charmed by the tall, handsome mountain man and Oregon pioneer. Fascinated, she listened to his deep, resonant voice recount his Rocky Mountain and early Oregon adventures, engagingly embellished with humor and mimicry. She sensed that the experiences of this original and gifted frontiersman could add much to the history of Oregon she hoped to write, now that her descriptive work on the state was ready for publication. Flattered by her attention, Meek began sending her, every now and then, batches of notes in pencil, likely edited by his daughter, Olive.[11]

During October and November, Frances also received three voluminous letters in the legible hand writing of Jesse Applegate, to which she replied in the order of their receipt. In his letters there was no self-serving. Rather, he asked her to show his letters to Judge Deady for verification of the facts. In his first letter, he characterized Dr. McLoughlin, chief factor of the Hudson's Bay Company, and his contribution to Oregon, especially his aid to American settlers and his influence on the settlement of the Oregon boundary in 1846. The last two letters narrated events that influenced the fortunes of McLoughlin and the hostility of the Methodist missionaries and their eventual success in depriving him of his land claim at Oregon City. Though Frances prized Applegate's account of one of her own heroes, she took offense at a postscript to his second letter, in which he remarked: "Your Railroad Chapter is very prettily arranged collection of words and sentences, but there is no sense in it. The relation of Chicago and New York City was somewhat different than that between Portland and San Francisco." In her reply, she voiced her indignation, but only after requesting additional information.

Quick to speak her own mind, she was equally careful to respect the knowledge and views of others. In turn, Applegate tried to appease her in his third letter. "When your work is printed, please send me a copy," he began. "I wish it as a memento of the author." After defending his belief that building a railroad to the California boundary was premature, he added: "but I know that you are a woman with a will and what you have said you will adhere to."

The next day, he wrote his friend, Judge Deady, that he had written "Madam Victor" three letters about Dr. McLoughlin and had requested her to show them to him (Deady) and adopt any corrections he might suggest. It went "much against the grain," he confided, "to write anything for her history." But he could not "forbear when called upon to do a good man justice. I think I have offended the Madam with a rather harsh judgment upon her railroad chapter."[12] By this time, whether she realized it or not, Frances was both admired and criticized by two of Oregon's foremost intellectuals.

For her part, Frances was finishing her handbook on Oregon, which entailed corresponding with a growing number of interested parties. Among them was George T. Allan, William H. Gray of Astoria, and Elwood Evans, a pioneer of Washington Territory who lived in Olympia. In a letter dated November 6, Allan noted that, agreeable to his promise from Astoria, he was enclosing some memoranda of Fort Vancouver, extracted from a letter he had written while serving the Hudson's Bay Company, as well as anecdotes concerning Dr. McLoughlin. Overlooking Gray's unfriendly behavior in Astoria, Frances wrote him of her wish to borrow a pamphlet on Oregon, written by Charles Saxton in 1846. In talking with the former Governor George Abernethy, the first and only provisional governor (1845–49), she had learned that it had been lent to Elwood Evans and afterward to Gray. As bait, she offered to lend Gray a leaf that the Rev. Griffin had given her. Before sending her greetings to Mrs. Gray, Frances closed with a pointed remark. She would be glad to buy one of Gray's two copies of Mr. Hines' book. She had written Elwood Evans, who had "very politely" furnished her with a copy of his article on the Hudson's Bay Company. She regretted that she did not have "a perfect file of the *Gazette* since the beginning of your history, as

The Portland photographer, Twaites, captured the steady gaze and solid qualities of
Victor's constant friend and ally, Elwood Evans, of Washington Territory,
whose papers now reside at the Yale University Library.
They exchanged views on H.H. Bancroft.

ORHI 104249

no doubt it would be an important guide for me informing opinions on
°difficult subjects."

In this letter, Frances indicated that she had corresponded with
Evans in the past and may have initiated the correspondence by asking

for a copy of his article that she needed for the history of Oregon that she intended to write. In any event, in mid-November, Frances thanked Evans for his "full and courteous reply."[13] It placed her under an obligation to say how much their views and plan of work seemed identical. She was convinced that they had nearly the same understanding of "the interest, the moral, and the *romance* of that history which attaches to the Northwest Coast." His synopsis of subjects sounded almost as if she were giving an outline of her own sections of history. It was true, as he had said, that the *theory* underlying their respective works may differ widely and from the fact of this difference, future historians looking back may be able to make philosophical deductions in support of the truth.

As "distance lends enchantment" so also it often lends clearness of view. "We, in our own humble way may be serving posterity by presenting the several sides of an argument to the dispassionate criticism of another generation." She added it was still too early to write the history of Oregon, but not too early to collect the material for the writing of that history. In that connection, she warned Evans that he was not to judge her proposed history from reading her "newspaper scribblings, the chit-chat of the pen written without effort or revision." After explaining that the *Oregonian* had wrongly stated that her railroad article was from her history, she noted that she hoped to publish a summary of the geography and resources of Oregon to enlighten the Eastern public. She regretted that she had yet to visit Washington Territory, but she assured Evans that she had said all she could in its favor without having seen it. Putting his generosity to the test, she asked him to aid her by furnishing, or tell where she could find, records of the Indian Wars of 1855–56 since it was necessary for her to "advert to them." Then she asked whether he was convinced by any known evidence of "the complicity of the Hudson's Bay Company and the Catholic fathers in the massacre at Waiilatpu." Though she had been assured of such complicity by one of the missionaries, she did not believe it. She trusted that Evans would not think that she was "prying" into his beliefs "in an unwarrantable manner." At one point in her letter, Frances indicated that Evans had invited her to Olympia. "It would give me great pleasure, and profit also, I do not doubt, to converse with you on these topics," she wrote, "but an Oregon winter is so full of horrors for me that I could not undertake to visit Olympia except after it is over."

While Frances was preoccupied with historical correspondence and completing her manuscript, Henry was considering how to invest the prize money he expected to receive from the federal government. In late July, when Frances was steamboating up the Columbia River, he had moved his office from Vaughn's building to the Chapman Building. Here he had finalized his plans for the O. S. N. Company's steamship. His business advertisement in the *Morning Oregonian* ran through August, then ceased. Apparently there was not sufficient demand for his services to justify the expense of maintaining an office. After the Civil War ended in April, Oregon's economy, along with the rest of the nation, had weakened. The price of gold had fallen. Nevertheless, Oregon businessmen continued the West Coast practice of receiving payment in gold coins. Greenbacks were regarded as merchandise in San Francisco and Portland, where brokers bought and sold them for almost 75 cents in coin on the dollar. But no man who prized his credit or financial standing dared pay his debts in greenback currency.[14]

Henry knew that the decline in the price of gold would lessen the purchasing power of the money he would receive for his services in the Union Navy. Investing these declining funds in order to earn the greatest capital gain in the shortest time, even though risky, seemed to be his wisest course of action. Unlike Frances, Henry was a speculator. At 37, he wanted to establish himself in Portland. Both he and Frances wished to live in the city. In order to achieve his ambition, Henry arranged to act as an agent for San Francisco capitalists, who wished to import Oregon products or invest in Oregon real estate. It was a role for which Henry was fitted; but because of his tendency to drink and to prevaricate, it would finally lead to his downfall. At some point, he approached Franklin A. Davis, whom he had met in San Francisco the previous year. Through Davis, a partner in the firm of Sedgly & Davis, wool dealers, Henry secured a commission to act as the company's wool purchasing and shipping agent in Oregon.[15]

During September, 1865, Henry toured the Willamette Valley, purchasing wool and exploring two investment opportunities, which he and Frances thought were promising—the Santiam mines east of Salem in the Cascade Mountains and the recently organized Oregon Central Military Road Company, headquartered in Eugene City. At the Santiam mines, he used his knowledge of geology to determine the prospects for making successful investments there. Back in Salem, Henry took the stage south to purchase wool and learn more about the Oregon Central Military Road Company.[16] Here Henry met J. Benson Underwood, a Eugene wool dealer and secretary of the Company, who advised him that James B. Chapman, a Portland physician, was a stockholder in the Company and a member of its board of directors. He had stock to sell. Henry may already have known Chapman. If not, upon his return to Portland, he made his acquaintance and found him congenial, with similar ambitions.

In mid-October, Henry received some back pay for his Union naval service as well as minor awards for aiding in the capture of Confederate battleships.[17] On the 23rd, Chapman wrote Underwood that he had sold Victor ten shares of Oregon Central Military Road stock, valued at $2,500 and would collect the $625 assessment due on them. Early in November, Chapman notified Underwood that he had sold Victor the balance of the stock he had to sell—20 shares worth $5,000. He added that Victor had not yet paid his assessment because he had to send to San Francisco for the money. However, he noted that H. C. Victor was "an engineer & a very good geologist & a first rate gentleman & perhaps may go with party next summer on the trip through the Owyhee."[18] By the end of the month, Franklin A. Davis had agreed to be Henry's partner in some of his Oregon investment ventures—including mining claims in the Santiam mines and stock in the Oregon Central Military Road Company. At last, Henry had realized his dream to be known as a capitalist. On October 30, the Salem *Weekly Oregon Statesman* published a news item, captioned, "A Capitalist Visits the Santiam." Victor was identified as a gentleman who represents a large amount of San Francisco capital . . . . We understand that he is prepared to purchase mines now, or make contracts for the disposal of mining interests in San Francisco."

Between November, 1865 and February, 1866, most of the prize money for the capture of the *Princess Royal*, in which Henry had been involved, was distributed, so he must have received a fairly large sum or word of the amount he could expect. In any case, he decided to buy property in the town of St. Helens with Frances' approval. She had already written favorably of its location and the resources in the immediate area. Only men and money, she had noted, were lacking to develop the town and the deposits of coal, iron, and timber. Further, the Pacific Steamship Company of San Francisco had bought waterfront property and intended to compete with the O. S. N. Company, headquartered in Portland, for the Columbia River trade. In any event, Frances approved of Henry's decision on November 20 to purchase from Elizabeth J. Knighton, administrator of the estate of her husband, Henry M. Knighton, for $1,000 in gold, the portion of the town site still in her possession.[19]

By this time, Frances was looking forward to sailing to San Francisco in order to escape the Oregon winter. On December 1, Colfax party member Albert D. Richardson stopped in Portland for a few days. Before he departed by ship to San Francisco, Frances gave him her finished manuscript. On December 6, Richardson advised Judge Deady that he was sending him, via Wells Fargo, two copies of his book, *The Secret Service, the Field, The Dungeon, and the Escape*—one for him and one for Mrs. Victor.[20] Whether she received it before she sailed on December 11 on the steamer *Sierra Nevada* is uncertain. But she did demonstrate that she approved of Henry's business ventures by giving him power of attorney. He could not accompany her because he was involved in yet another St. Helens land deal.

On Christmas Day, the Salem *Oregon Statesman* published a private letter confirming the rumored sale of the St. Helens town site. It was noted that Mr. Victor, who has been up at the Santiam mines a few weeks ago, was the agent making the purchase and that he represented a company, having a capital of three million dollars. Capt. W. L Dall and S. J. Henaly of San Francisco were reported to be the principal shareholders of the company. A fine new line of steamships to the Columbia, stopping at St. Helens, was named as part of their plan to make the town a rival of Portland.

Meanwhile, Frances had arrived in San Francisco on December 14. At the dock, she boarded the coach for her favorite hotel—the Russ House. The next morning she set out to enjoy the city at its holiday best. But first she paid her respects to her friend, James Nesbit, at the office of the San Francisco *Evening Bulletin*. Here she was pleased to learn that her poem, "Sunset at the Mouth of the Columbia River," had been published in the newspaper's "Poets' Corner" the week before and that her contributions were still welcome. Recalling her *alter ego*, Florence Fane, she paid a sentimental visit to the rooms of *The Golden Era* to greet editor Joseph Lawrence. He told her that he too was leaving the *Era* in the spring to return to his boyhood home on Long Island. Later that week, Frances discovered this personal item in the *Era*: "Frances Fuller Victor (Florence Fane), the coming historian of Oregon, who has traveled all over the State and closely studied its mineral resources, says that Oregon will equal, if not surpass, any of the Pacific States or Territories in the future development of mineral wealth."

Determined to see her *Era* fellow columnists again, Frances made her way to the office of *The Californian*. Inigo, her rival on the *Era* staff in satirical writing, was on vacation. Bret Harte was there. However, her pleasure at seeing him was somewhat diminished by her irritation about a book he was known to have edited, *Outcroppings, Being a Selection of California Verse*, published by Anton Roman for the Christmas trade. Only 19 of California's poets were represented in the selection of 42 poems. Frances, who has been publishing poetry in California publications since 1861, joined the ranks of the other aggrieved poets. Nevertheless, she did revel in being in San Francisco again during the Christmas season to enjoy the shopping and the music. She also made Christmas calls, one at the home of Franklin A. Davis and his wife, Sarah.[21]

Shortly after, Frances sent Henry $200 of her own with which to buy property joining St. Helens in her name alone. Henry complied with her request. On January 15, 1866, Francis Lamont and his wife, Jane, for $200 conveyed to Frances Fuller Victor five acres adjacent to the St. Helens township.[22] On January 21, Henry departed for San Francisco to join Frances, but he had waited too long. The steamship *Sierra Nevada* on which he booked passage went aground just above the mouth of the Willamette Slough and, though it was freed in time to sail on schedule, it was delayed for a week in Baker's Bay at the mouth of the Columbia River.

While waiting for Henry, Frances caught up with her correspondence. Among unanswered letters she brought with her was one from Elwood Evans, dated December 6. In her reply she recalled that in her last letter to him she had stated that all old Oregonians had one time or another cherished the idea of writing a book about Oregon. She still thought it was true, though it often made it difficult for her to obtain "their hoarded historical treasures." This only proved to her that all of them possessed "a strong sense of the peculiar points of their history." And that only inspired her, she wrote, to acquire what these pioneers considered valuable. She added that he, for one, shared his knowledge. She still wanted to see whatever material he had collected about the West Coast and talk with him should he visit Portland after her return there in April.[23]

When the *Sierra Nevada* docked in San Francisco on February 1, 1866, Frances greeted Henry warmly. He had much to tell her about his real estate ventures and other matters. A week later, he, and eventually Governor Gibbs of Oregon, became involved in helping Frances' friend, William L. Adams, collector of customs at Astoria, when he was was robbed of $20,000 in gold coin, Custom House money he was bringing to deposit with the assistant treasurer of the United States. In the days that followed, Adams was mercilessly attacked by the press and not until early March, when detectives assigned to investigate the theft of federal money discovered leads to the identity of the robbers in California, did Adams return to Astoria.[24]

Despite their concern for Adams, Henry and Frances consolidated their partnership with Davis and his wife and reviewed Henry's financial ventures. Frances also was considering the purchase of a painting of Mt. Hood by a California artist by the name of Butman. In December, he had been painting in Oregon. Henry reported having seen a canvas of Mount Hood which Butman had presented to Simeon G. Reed in Portland. After his return to San Francisco, Butman's entire collection was placed at auction. Frances was among those who attended. When it was over, she owned two Butman paintings: a 28 x 52-inch canvas of Mt. Hood and another oil painting titled "Sunset Scene."[25]

On February 19, Henry drew up his will, evidently at Frances' urging with an eye to protecting her ownership of the property she had purchased as well as her interest in Henry's investments. It is written in her reliable hand and signed in the presence of two San Francisco witnesses. Briefly, Henry's will acknowledged his indebtedness to others such as F. A. Davis, and appointed Frances as the sole administrator of his estate. Further, she was to have one-half of all his possessions free from any interference or control. The other was to go to his only child, Mary Edwards Victor, then living in Cincinnati, Ohio, to be held and controlled by Frances until her step-daughter reached her majority.[26]

Just prior to the Victors' departure for Portland, Frances wrote Judge Deady.[27] The previous day she had received a note from A.D. Richardson of New York City. After reading her manuscript, Harper's had written him that they would undertake to publish the book, provided that the Oregon state legislature would purchase 2.000 copies. To Deady, Frances admitted that she doubted that the state cared that much about its interests. However, knowing his opinion of her book, she asked him to write Richardson if he felt that there was any hope that the state might subsidize publication. She added that she would be quite "content if it pays the publishers." But she did feel that the book would have considerable influence in encouraging settlement and development of Oregon if the state could buy and distribute 2,000 copies in the East.

At midday, on April 17, H. C. Victor and his wife boarded the steamship *Montana*, owned by the Anchor Line.[28] This was the first time they had sailed together since their voyage three years ago from New York City to Acapulco, Mexico. As the San Francisco skyline receded, Frances felt no regrets. She was going home to Oregon to play out their good fortune. She could hardly have envisioned what lay ahead.

CHAPTER 5

"FORTUNE IS A FICKLE GYPSY"

(1866-68)

A S THE STEAMSHIP *Montana* passed through the Golden Gate and headed north, Henry and Frances Fuller Victor eagerly anticipated their return to Portland. Beyond a doubt, Oregon was the place where the success they desired seemed assured. Meanwhile, however, strong northerly winds caused the ship to roll with an awkward motion and Frances, always susceptible to seasickness, was soon reduced to a helpless condition in their stateroom while Henry enjoyed himself on deck and in the saloon.

During the early evening of their third day out, Henry appeared at the door of their stateroom to tell Frances that Mr. Ela, a fellow passenger, wished to talk with her in the hope of helping her forget her wretchedness. With her consent, two chairs were pulled up just inside the doorway, and the visitor began to talk.[1] Frances formed a favorable impression of him, and soon the Victors were listening to the incredible tale of his pioneering experiences in Oregon. It developed that at age 19 in the early 1850s, Mr. Ela had moved from his land claim in the Willamette Valley had because of a crop failure. He drove what remained of his 250 head of livestock south to the Rogue River mountains where he became a hermit, living behind an 18-foot-high stockade he had built to protect himself from the local Indians. The next year he began to sell beef to mining camps in the Rogue River Valley. Frances lay spellbound as Mr. Ela's story, replete with peril, mystery, and romance, centered in his secluded home, unfolded. Just as it reached its dramatic conclusion, the lights in the saloon began to go out. Hastily departing, Mr. Ela exclaimed, "There is always in this world, someone going around putting out the lights. Good night!"

Early the next morning, Frances ventured out on deck. The *Montana* had reached the Columbia River bar, crossed the dreaded line of breakers, and docked six miles up the river at Astoria to clear customs and unload freight. The Victors went ashore to call upon William L. Adams at the Custom House to celebrate with him the restoration of his good name. On the eve of their departure from San Francisco they had read in the *Evening Bulletin* a detailed account of the arrest of his robbers in New York City by detectives assigned to the case and the recovery of part of the stolen money. [2]

As the steamship resumed its voyage to Portland, Frances reveled in the beauty of the heavily timbered shores of the lower Columbia and noted the historic places along its banks now that she and Henry owned property there. As they steamed toward the town of St. Helens, where they intended to move later that year, she thought of Nathaniel J. Wyeth, who, in an attempt to establish American commerce on the lower Columbia River had built a fort and trading post, Fort William, on the west side of Sauvie Island in 1834–35. There he had hoped to establish a town. But his trading enterprise had failed and he had returned to the East in 1836. Eleven years later Captain Henry M. Knighton had purchased the land claim on which he founded the village of St. Helens, named after his birthplace in England and located in view of Mt. St. Helens on the Washington shore of the Columbia. Frances could envision Knighton, town plat in hand, beginning to promote the town of St. Helens just as she and Henry hoped to do now, 15 years later.

Finally, that evening, the *Montana* docked at Portland and the Victors hurried to their Third Avenue home to assess their financial situation. [3] In accordance with the agreement he had just re-affirmed with Franklin A. Davis, Henry increased his wool buying in Oregon after he conferred with Dr. Chapman about divesting the interests the Victors had acquired in "coal lands" adjacent to St. Helens. Henry had begun to realize that he had overextended himself in his investments. As yet he had not received the long-awaited Civil War prize money, and the assessments on his Central Oregon Military Road stock were larger than he had antici-pated. But most alarming to him was the failure so far of Captains W.L.Dall and S.J. Henaly of San Francisco and Commodore William H. Webb of New York City to place on the Columbia River their proposed new line of steamships which would stop at St. Helens.[4]

On April 25, with Henry signing for Frances, Victor and Chapman deeded to Davis the 13/16th interest they had acquired for $1,800 in Janu-ary for 680 acres of coal land they had purchased for $1,000 the previous November.[5] That deal completed, Henry then traveled through the Willamette Valley to investigate progress at the Santiam mines and to arrange for the purchase of wool for shipment to the San Francisco firm of Sedgley & Davis.

In Portland, Frances noted the progress during her five-month absence. The new courthouse across the public square from her rented home was in its final stages. Most impressive was the three-story struc-ture under construction at the corner of Front and Alder streets.[6] At the *Oregonian* office, she met Dewitt Clinton Ireland, the new city editor, who had recently joined the staff. She then called on Judge Deady to learn his reaction to Albert Richardson's report that Harper's would not publish her handbook on Oregon unless the state legislature purchased 2,000 copies for distribution within the state. Though Deady agreed with her that "the state of Oregon does not care $2,000 about her own interests," Deady had written Richardson to suggest that he try another publisher.

Impatient to resume collecting material for her proposed history of the state, Frances planned another trip up the Willamette River later that spring to acquire additional source materials. First she wanted Joe Meek to resume his story-telling visits and notes about his past adventures. She also wanted a Joseph Buchtel photograph of Meek to use as a fron-tispiece in his published biography. By chance she met Meek the day he posed for the photograph and noted later that

> He was looking . . . limp and white from drinking. When
> he recognized me, the gentleman in him asserted itself and
> he said with a deeply apologetic air, "Punish me any way
> you please, Mrs. Victor. I know that I am unworthy to

speak to you, and I promise on my sacred honor not to be seen by you in this condition again!" Nor did I ever see him really intoxicated afterwards—perhaps because when he came to town he usually reported to me, and I took measures to prevent him from meeting too many of his acquaintances on the street. For this, and because he was made hero of *The River of the West*, he entertained for me a profound affection, as refined and loyal as one could wish from the most cultured of men.[7]

On May 16, while reading the *Oregonian*, Frances received a pleasant surprise. The lead item in the "City News" column, titled "The Final Word", began: "Mr. A.D. Richardson, of the Colfax Party, copies the following poem—entitled "Sunset at the Mouth of the Columbia"— written by Mrs. Frances Fuller Victor of this city, as his closing words to the New York *Tribune*, on a subject on which he has written so much, entitled 'From the Missouri to the Pacific.' Mr. Richardson says: 'I copy it from the San Francisco *Bulletin* in slight atonement to the reader for leading him so long over the desert that by no means blossoms like the rose and among quartz mines whose owners would have their richness told in Gath and published in the streets of Askelon.'" Then followed the complete text of the poem, the final stanza of which reads: [8]

> *A noble scene! All breadth, deep tone, and power,*
>   *Suggesting glorious themes;*
> *Shaming the idler who would fill the hour*
>   *With unsubstantial dreams.*
> *Be mine the dreams prophetic, shadowing forth*
>   *The things that yet shall be,*
> *When through this gate the treasures of the North*
>   *Flow outward to the sea.*

Five days later an item appeared in the *Oregonian* about F.A. Butman's painting of Mt. Hood, which Frances had purchased in San Francisco. It announced that "this celebrated painting, said by competent judges who have seen both, to be equal to Bierstadt's, is now on exhibition at the art gallery of Messrs. Shanahan and Dufrene, corner of Morrison and First Streets."[9]

The following day, May 22, Henry's younger brother, Jacob N. Victor, arrived from San Francisco.[10] Henry, who had not seen Jacob since the outbreak of the Civil War, had been urging his brother to join him and Frances in Portland. Unable to serve at the front because of a physical disability, Jacob had been in charge of the Union military railroad and Henry was confident that this experience would assure his brother employment whenever construction began on the railroad through the Willamette, Umpqua, and Rogue river valleys to the border where it would connect with the California railroad.[11] He introduced Jacob to his business acquaintances and took him to see the Santiam mines near Salem and to Eugene to inspect the completed portion of the Oregon Central Military Road, being built up the Middle Fork of the Willamette River—all in the hope that Jacob might be interested in becoming Henry's partner, and perhaps help pay off the assessments on his military road stock. Frances, meanwhile, visited friends in the Salem area and, always working on her Oregon handbook project, continued to interview other pioneers in the area.

When the two brothers returned to Portland there was unwelcome news from George A. Ladd of St. Helens, who had been acting as Henry's wool-purchasing agent. J.B. Underwood, Eugene wool dealer, was demanding payment for the wool he had shipped to Portland. Ladd, in turn, informed Henry that he had written Underwood that the money to pay for the wool had not yet arrived from the San Francisco firm of Sedgley & Davis. Ladd assured Underwood that Victor would not let him lose a cent. "Mr. Victor," he added, "is very anxious to close up this business. They have treated him so badly he wants it off his hands."[12] The nightmarish business dealings that preoccupied Henry Victor would only get more convoluted.

It was imperative that Henry expedite a plan to stimulate the growth of St. Helens, even though making it the steamship terminus on the Columbia River appeared to have been abandoned. Further, he and Frances had to decide where they would live in St. Helens when they moved there later that year, as planned. So Henry and Jacob traveled by steamboat to St. Helens to see the property Victor and Davis owned there and to tour the Lower Columbia region. When they returned to

Portland, Frances handed Henry his mail. Their worst fears were realized: J.B. Underwood, in his role as secretary of the Oregon Central Military Road Company, was demanding payment of the $1,000 in assessments Henry owed on his stock. Henry was now the company's largest stockholder, having increased his holdings to forty shares, worth $20,000, earlier that year.

During Henry's absence from Portland, his friend, Dr. Chapman, realizing that Henry was in a shaky financial situation, had made an attempt to rescue him. He had written Underwood to tell him that he was thinking of making a trade for Victor's stock and asked how many shares he had as well as the total of assessments on them.[13] The answer Chapman received evidently discouraged the trade. In the meantime, Henry angrily advised Underwood that he had been out of town and informed him that the stock standing in his name was actually owned in San Francisco, brusquely adding: "I await the disposition of the owners to adjust matters to suit themselves. Will in due time inform you of it."[14]

During the last week of July, the Victors moved to St. Helens to promote the sale of their town lots. On August 4, Henry sold to Benjamin F. Giltner and Sebastian C. Adams a desirable lot near the old steamship dock.[15] Young Giltner told the Victors that he planned to establish a store on the property with Adams, brother of William L. Adams of Astoria, as his non-resident partner.[16] Five days later, Henry sold two more lots. Then, just as everything seemed to be progressing well, he received a notice from the O.C.M.R. Company that he would be sued if he did not immediately pay the $1,000 in assessments he owed on his stock. Henry was cornered. Davis had not sent the promised money from San Francisco nor had Henry received the expected Civil War prize money from the federal government.[17]

Alarmed by their precarious financial situation, the Victors turned to their major resource. On September 19, they quitclaimed to F.A. Davis all of their "one undivided half-interest in the St. Helens townsite." Before Frances signed the quitclaim, she was examined privately and testified that she had executed the deed freely and without fear or compulsion from anyone.[18] But she did establish her individual ownership of the St.

Helens property that she had purchased with her own money or had received from Henry.[19] On October 20, 1866, she filed in the Columbia County Courthouse a declaration of her intention to hold separate property, described as the property she had purchased from Francis A. Lemont and his wife, Jane. She also included all the lots in Block 14, four lots in Block 17, and eight lots in Block 25. All of this property had been deeded to her by Henry "on his own part and as attorney for F.A. Davis and his wife, Sarah." Henry continued to sell lots with and without buildings. In some cases, standing buildings were required to be repaired or converted to new purposes. In other cases, new buildings were constructed on empty lots. Certainly, St. Helens was growing, thanks to Henry's activity. But all too soon the blow the Victors feared fell. The O.C.M.R. Company filed suit against Henry. In order to establish that Frances had received the lots he had deeded to her from someone other than himself, on November 12 Henry and Frances deeded them to Charles H. Williams and his wife, Almira.[20] Three days later, the Williams deeded them to Frances. Meanwhile, the suit of the O.C.M.R. Company vs. H.C. Victor appeared on the calendar of the Circuit Court of the State of Oregon, published in the *Oregonian*.[21] On November 17, Frances filed a new declaration. In addition to the land deeded her by the Lemonts and the lots acquired from Williams and his wife, she included "a large painting of Mount Hood painted by F.A. Butman with a carved walnut frame."

On November 23, the *Oregonian* carried at the head of the "City News" column a short article on St. Helens, with Frances' positive touch. It summarized the town's past misfortunes before describing its present prosperity and bright future. "This advancement of St. Helens is permanent," she wrote, "and it is destined at some future day to become one of the most beautiful places in the State." She had come to love the marine landscape visible from St. Helens. As December approached, she decided to spend the winter here despite her abhorrence of Oregon rain at this season. Certainly she needed to work with Joe Meek on his biography, and staying in Oregon also would enable her to keep her eye on Henry's financial transactions and legal entanglements. In any event, late in

December, after granting power of attorney to his brother, Jacob, for himself and Davis, it was Henry who sailed alone for San Francisco, confident that he would succeed in securing the money he needed to pay his delinquent assessments before the suit against him came to trial.[22] Upon his return, he assured Frances that his mission had been successful.

But Henry's temper flared when he read a letter from Underwood that had arrived during his absence. Underwood informed him that he must either assign to him the stock held in his name or "sign it in blank to be held by the Company until such time as they may choose to dispose of it, provided a purchaser can be found."[23] Replying immediately, Henry advised Underwood that he expected to receive funds with which to pay the assessments and enclosed a promissory note for the $1,500 he owed the Company. There matters stood when, in February, 1867, the Victors decided to build a home of their own in St. Helens. Henry gave William Pickering a bond for $500 to be paid within eight months, provided that he erected on Lot 18, Block 20 a house fit for occupying.[24] The carefully chosen site commanded an unobstructed view of Mount St. Helens across the Columbia River and an equally charming view of the southwestern end of Sauvie Island, entrance to the Multnomah Channel of the Willamette River, and of the ocean-going steamships and river steamboats passing by. Now convinced that Henry would soon be able to pay his debt, Frances was delighted that at last she would possess a home of her own. But her happiness proved to be short-lived.

A fortnight later, while reading the *Oregonian*, Frances discovered a notice dated "St. Helens, Feb. 16, 1867" and signed by Henry. Incredibly, it read: [25]

> B.F. Giltner, of this place, has this day paid a judgment of $35 and costs in favor of the Willamette Salt Works, in *green backs*. This being the second time said Giltner has recently been publicly noticed for his dishonorable transactions, attention is called to the following advertisement published in the Oregonian of January —, 1865. The status of the man may really be seen.
>
> H.C. Victor

"NOTICE – All persons are hereby notified not to purchase two certain promissory notes given myself to B.F.
Giltner of Yamhill County, dated Nov/5, 1864, or about
that date—one for four hundred dollars gold coin, payable
nearly three years after date, the other for three hundred
and twenty-five, payable nearly three years from date – as
both of said notes were obtained by misrepresentation and
fraud, and without any consideration, and the same will not
be paid.

William Carson
"Yamhill County"

Frances was shocked. She liked Giltner, his young wife Susan, and
her parents, Dr. James and Mahala McBride.[26] To her it seemed incredible
that Henry had publicly insulted Dr. McBride's son-in-law Giltner, who
had invested so much in St. Helens. Surely he must have mailed these
notices to the *Oregonian* in a fit of anger after drinking too much
whiskey—a weakness he had acquired in the Navy. She had become
increasingly aware of his fondness for liquor and his temper after drinking too much. She also knew that, as co-owner with his brother, Jacob, of
the Willamette Salt Works, Henry did have a reason for exposing Giltner's payment of his debt in green backs. But why had Henry dug up a
past transaction? Frances had been proud of Henry's salt-making enterprise. Earlier that year he had leased the salt spring on Enoch Meeker's
farm near the Multnomah County line. Presently the Victor brothers
were producing about two tons of salt a day, which they sold for $35 a
ton. Evidently, Giltner had purchased a ton, needed for salting butter and
curing meats, for his grocery business.[27]

Soon Henry received notice that Giltner had filed a complaint of
criminal libel against him in Multnomah County. On the appointed day,
Henry proceeded to Portland to appear in Circuit Court. Here he was
bound over to the Grand Jury, but was released on bail of $800 posted by
Dr. Chapman and his partner, Dr. W.A. Watkins. The trial for the case of
State of Oregon v. *H.C. Victor* was set for the June, 1867 term.[28] Before long
Henry was also notified that Enoch G. Adams of St. Helens had filed in

Multnomah Circuit Court an action against him for $250 in damages to a house owned by Adams, an active member of the Independent Order of Good Templars, an organization that was taking measures to discourage patronage of the several drinking establishments in St. Helens.[29]

Meanwhile, Underwood had accepted Henry's $1,500 promissory note and had requested that the Company's case against him be dismissed. In late April, Henry, now confident that Davis would provide funds with which to pay his promissory note, sent Underwood this letter from St. Helens:[30]

> I shall without doubt be up to Eugene at the coming meet-
> ing of the O.C.M.R. Co. . . . . I prefer to transact all business
> such as paying assessments, direct with you. You will
> remember that there is ten more shares to be issued to me,
> upon which I am to pay $500 more. This we can arrange
> when I come."
>
> Please tell Mr. Pengra that I duly received his letter and
> accompanying map, for both of which I thank him. Tell
> him also that I highly approve of his views on the matter of
> the proposed railroad. I will heartily co-operate in any rea-
> sonable move in that direction. We had the Chief Engineer
> of the about-to-be-constructed valley railroad here yester-
> day . . . . Action of vital interest to us as a Company will
> soon be taken and which if we act right, we can control for
> our benefit. I am not at liberty to state what has been con-
> fided to me, but there will be some unexpected development
> in railroad matters soon.

The following day the Victors deeded to F.A. Davis an undivided half of the 80 acres of land, together with all the buildings on them, that B.F. Giltner had deeded to Henry the previous October.[31] They were either encouraging Davis to forward the needed money or seeking to protect themselves in the event that Giltner won his libel suit. About this time, it was discovered that Henry had been signing deeds improperly; and on May 6, the Victors signed an "instrument to correct the infor-mality of the signature of certain deeds given by H.C. Victor to others."[32]

The June 7 *Oregonian's* list of cases to be tried in the Multnomah County Circuit Court's June term included the suits of Giltner and Adams against Henry Victor as well as one in which Henry and his brother, Jacob, were suing a Portland businessman. The next day, Frances, humiliated by Henry's actions, revoked the power of attorney that she had granted him in December, 1865. Though she still felt affection for Henry, he had undermined her confidence in him and destroyed any hope of a happy life in St. Helens. Actually Henry deceived Frances more than she knew. On May 16 he had signed an article of agreement with Franklin A. Davis, which he did not file in the Columbia County Courthouse at the time. As part of this agreement, Henry had contracted to sell one-half interest in all property he then held in Oregon and in Washington Territory and supply a deed within two years, provided Davis pay him $6,000 within that time. Davis granted Henry power of attorney for two more years, but required that Henry agree not to sell any of the property without his consent. Moreover, all proceeds received by Davis in management, sale, or development were to be applied toward the $6,000.[33]

In a June 12 letter to Underwood, Dr. Chapman asked whether Victor had paid his assessments or his promissory note. In a footnote, Chapman warned that if Victor had not paid his note Underwood had "better go for it without fail, for I think he intends making a change in his affairs."[34] Henry had apparently confided in Chapman, who now, as an O.C.M.R. Co. stockholder, was turning against him. Underwood, nearing the end of his patience, was glad to follow Chapman's advice. Within a few days, he came to Portland and, finding that Henry was in St. Helens, wrote him a letter demanding payment of the note and assessments. Henry's immediate reply, dated July 18, could only increase Underwood's frustration and contempt:[35]

> I have your note & in reply have to state that the San Francisco party jointly interested with me in it having failed to 'come to time,' I make you the following proposal. I have contributed to the coffers of the Co. $3,000 in assessments. I will give you up the stock now standing in my name, you

giving me a release from all dues on its account. I think this is as well as you can do. If you should insist on pressing matters I will contest the thing to the end in the courts & as I think with some view of success as I was induced to purchase said stock by misinformation and a portion of it was bought for me without my knowledge or consent.

Underwood quickly filed a suit in Multnomah County Circuit Court for judgment for the principal and interest on the promissory note given by Victor in February. And he also filed again the suit for $1,556.45 in stock assessments that Henry owed. Both were scheduled for the Court's July term. Meanwhile, the Court's June term had just been opened by Judge E.D. Shattuck, who adjourned all civil business of the Court until July 8.[36] Before that date, however, Henry received good news about the verdict reached on one of the suits pending against him. The Grand Jury, which had remained in session, discharged him on June 26, after returning a not true bill on the charge of criminal libel brought on the complaint of B.F. Giltner against him.[37]

It so happened that a decision by Judge Deady concerning the separate property of a married woman recently had been published in the *Oregonian*.[38] Within a few days, Frances wrote Deady commenting on the decision and asking whether it would be out of place for her to consult with him on the subject. Then she continued:[39]

What I wish to ascertain is whether my husband can *deed* to me a certain piece of property (a house and lot) in St. Helens, and whether I can register the same as my separate property. If this should not be the proper course to pursue in order to secure to myself some separate property, then what would it be?

Can you spare a day or two from legal or judicial duties to fetch Mrs. Deady down to visit me and our pretty town? I should enjoy such a visit very much—whether you and Mrs. D. did so, would depend on whether 'rural felicity' had any charm for you.

Regards to Mrs. Deady and sisters—

With the date of the trial of the case of the *O.C.M.R. Co. v. H.C. Victor* approaching, Jacob, still living in Portland, agreed to a scheme to help Henry as well as F.A. Davis and his wife, Sarah, to protect their interest in St. Helens. On July 1, Davis and his wife deeded to Jacob all of their right and interest in the town of St.Helens, which had been deeded to them by Henry Victor, as their attorney in fact, on December 26, 1865. [40] The transfer was made none too soon. Gibbs and Parrish, Portland attorneys for the O.C.M.R. Co., on July 18, sent Secretary Underwood a terse notification of the Circuit Court's verdict in the case of the *Company versus Victor.* [41]

"We have this day obtained judgment against H.C. Victor in the action on note for $1,500 with interest thereon, amounting to $1,518.75. Also judgment in action on three assessments with interest thereon, amounting in all to $1,556.75." Henry had entered no defense. Now he must pay $3,025 plus costs.

Henry soon suffered two more blows. On August 1, the Circuit Court tried two other cases in which he was involved. In the suit of Enoch Adams against Victor, Adams was awarded a judgment of $175 for damages done to his house plus costs. Henry's only defense had been a demurrer in hope of obtaining a dismissal of the case. [42] The verdict in the case of *H.C. Victor and J.N. Victor v. J.H. Davenport* was in favor of the defendant; and the Victors had to pay the costs.

Four days later, Jacob returned to Davis and his wife their share of the St. Helens property. In consideration of $1,000 paid by Davis, Jacob released to them all their interest in the town. Significantly, the instrument of release was signed, sealed, and delivered in the presence of A.C. Gibbs and C.W. Parrish, attorneys for the O.C.M.R. Co. They had pressured Jacob to restore the property to the Davis family. The St. Helens property would be Henry's chief asset on which the O.C.M.R. Co. could place a lien if he failed to pay the judgment against him. However, Gibbs and Parrish—especially Henry's one-time employer, former Governor Gibbs—showed some concern for Henry in trying to allow him more time in which to raise the money he needed to pay his debt.

On August 5, Henry sailed for San Francisco. About two weeks later he returned to Portland, a dispirited man. When he reached St. Helens, Frances made a last attempt to save their marriage. She suggested that they sail together to San Francisco. Hopefully, she could help him persuade Davis to lend him the money he needed. She would take along her cherished painting of Mount Hood by Butman and attempt to sell it. With the proceeds, she would buy furnishings for their almost completed house in St, Helens. Regardless of the outcome of Henry's business affairs, she was determined to live there.

Henry and Frances Fuller Victor sailed for San Francisco the evening of September 16. That morning Gibbs & Parrish had received a letter from Underwood, to which they replied:[43]

> Victor now refuses to sell his stock unless he can get all he has paid for it including the judgment and costs. Neither Ladd or Corbett will give that. He has gone to San Francisco to raise money to pay the judgment. I think he will get it. The Salt Works stands two thirds in his name and one third in the name of his brother. St. Helens is in the name of F.A. Davis but he is to have at least a half interest. I suppose we can make the money on the judgments out of his property, but I think we had better wait two weeks for his return. We will act under your instructions however.

Underwood fired back a telegram directing them to obtain the judgments. Five days later Parrish reported that he had gone down to St. Helens immediately after securing the judgments and had them "docketed there thus securing a lien on Victor's property in Columbia County."[44] Five days later Henry sent an optimistic note from San Francisco to Gibbs, which read in part: "I think all my creditors will now feel secure as I have considerable to show for security. I have little doubt of getting all the means I want &of getting my business in first shape."[45]

On October 14, Gibbs received a surprise note from Jacob Victor, then living in St, Helens. He inquired if any arrangement could be made about the judgment in case he and Henry succeeded in raising only a limited amount of money. Then he added: "It may be advisable to use the money we raise in our business, & in that case it might be best to even

Addison "Guts" Gibbs served as Oregon's governor in Civil War times (1862–66).
Victor met the Republican leader in the first twenty-four hours
of her arrival in Portland from San Francisco.

ORHI 71432

lose the amount that has already been paid & return the Stock, if thereby
they will cancel the judgment and release H.C. from any further payment."[46] Within the next ten days, Jacob reported to Gibbs that Henry
would be up on the next steamer with his affairs in good shape.[47] But he
did not appear.

While Henry struggled with his financial affairs, Frances pursued her own interests in San Francisco. Within a few weeks, she succeeded in selling her valuable Butman painting of Mount Hood. [48] Elated by her good fortune, she was determined not to lose her hard-earned money accumulated from her writing efforts as she had to her first husband in Nebraska. For days she happily shopped in the city's finest stores for furniture to be shipped to her new St. Helens home. Then she called on her literary friends in the city by the Golden Gate. During the past months, while writing her history of Oregon with Joe Meek as its central character, she had maintained literary connections in San Francisco, first as a correspondent to the *Evening Bulletin* and then by her visit to the city. Earlier in the year, three of her poems had been included in an anthology of verse of the Pacific states. The poems—"Palma," "El Palo Santo," and "Sunset at the Mouth of the Columbia"—all first published in the San Francisco *Bulletin*, were among the best in the volume. [49]

Frances first stopped at the Bulletin office, where she talked with the editor who had succeeded her friend, James Nisbet. Then she paid a sentimental visit to the *Golden Era* office. Her friendly mentor and competitor Inigo (Charles Henry Webb) and other colleagues such as Mark Twain and the *Era* editor, Colonel Lawrence, had all departed to live in the East. Only Bret Harte remained in San Francisco. Copies of Harte's newly-published book, "Condensed Novels and other Papers," were in the city's bookstores; Frances naturally would convey to him her congratulations and solicit his advice on the book she had in progress.

Meanwhile, Henry was making little progress in raising money; and in Eugene, Underwood was becoming restive. With his wife and daughter, he sailed for San Francisco, where he hoped to track Henry down and learn the true state of his financial affairs. When they did meet, Henry proposed that Underwood take back the stock and release him from the judgments and costs—a proposal that Underwood apparently accepted at the time. Relieved of their anxiety, the Victors boarded a steamship bound for Portland and arrived there December 1. [50] Frances' first concern on returning to St. Helens was to file in the Columbia County Courthouse an affidavit claiming her separate right and title to the personal property she had purchased in San Francisco "by means independent of my husband and in no way liable for any debts which he may contract or may have contracted previous to the date of this instrument, the articles above enumerated having been procured by the sale of property before declared to be separate property."

The property listed reveals Frances' taste and varied interests. Floor coverings included 36 yards of carpeting called three-ply, 12 yards of carpeting for stairs with rods, one large rug, and two mats of velvet carpeting. Furniture included one spring bed and bedding, one painted chamber set, one Turkish easy chair, two parlor chairs, one spring back rocker, one work table, one Gondolier lounge, one centre table, one library table, one hat rock, one commode with what-not, and two brackets. For dining there was one set of china, one set of fine cutlery for the table, one set of silver-plated forks and spoons, table linens, napkins, etc. For her personal use there was one set of ivory chessmen and board, one fine work box, two hundred volumes of books, writing and drawing portfolios, drawing material, pictures, and vases.

About a week later, Frances read with relief in the *Oregonian* an important decision rendered by Judge Deady in the U.S. Circuit Court upon the rights of creditors and married women's property. In the case of *David Dick* v. *Christina Hamilton et al.* that certain lots purchased by Mrs. Hamilton from Daniel Lownsdale were not subject to the claims of her husband's creditors.[51] Now Frances was confident that her right to the lots in St. Helens and adjacent land she had acquired from persons other than her husband would be protected.

Other items in that issue of the *Oregonian* also pleased Frances. The St. Helens correspondent noted the rapidly increasing lumber production in the town, which was nicknamed "Little Stump Town" in a joking reference to Portland's "Stump Town" cognomen. She also noted approvingly the opening of a private academy to help fill the need for better schools. But to Frances the most pertinent comment was in the concluding sentence: "The Indepedent Order of Good Templars have broken up the traffic in spirituous liquors in this place, having captured a large proportion of the customers of the saloons. That way of breaking into the arrangements of those chaps who expect to draw their subsistence from destroying others is as good as any."[52] Privately Frances rejoiced at the work of the Good Templars. She knew all too well that too much liquor could destroy a man.

When the Victors returned to St. Helens, Jacob had informed them that the O.C.M.R. Co. had filed judgments against Henry in the Columbia County Courthouse and secured a lien on his property. But Henry had not been worried; he was waiting for official confirmation of the proposal he had made to Underwood in San Francisco. He knew that Byron J. Pengra, president of the company and superintendent of road construction, would have the final word.

Meanwhile, during December, 1867, Frances and Henry were moving into their new home. Jacob, disillusioned with his attempts to help Henry and to establish himself in Oregon, had decided to return to his railroading career in the Midwest.[53] He celebrated Christmas with the Victors in St. Helens, and two days later they regretfully watched him sail for San Francisco. He departed none too soon. The following day, snow began to fall, and arctic cold invaded Oregon. On January 1, 1868, Portlanders were skating on the lake near the iron works. A week later, no steamboats left port— the Columbia River was closed by ice. Communication was even severed between Portland and East Portland, as the ferry could not push through the ice on the Willamette.[54] For Frances, the long, cold days meant time to concentrate her energies on what had become an obsession: melding Joe Meek's fantastic anecdotes and the Oregon history she had gathered into a flowing biographical narrative.

Suddenly, in the first week of March, Henry received word that Pengra had refused to grant his request that the O.C.M.R. Co. repossess his stock and release him from judgments in both Columbia and Multnomah Counties.[55] On March 17, Henry managed to save a valuable portion of his St. Helens property from being auctioned off by the Columbia County sheriff. Acting for Davis and his wife as their attorney, he deeded to Frances three lots, together with all the buildings on them.[56] They adjoined the refurbished hotel in the first block above the old Pacific Mail Steamship dock.

In March 1864 the leading jurist and diarist Mathew (his spelling) Deady
and several friends founded the Portland Library Association—
both institutions attractive to Victor.

CN 0002391

At the end of April, 1868, Judge Shattuck, who had rendered the
decision in the case of *O.C.M.R. Co.* v. *Victor*, attempted to aid Henry and
at the same time procure a valuable investment for himself. He wrote
Underwood a letter, requesting that if he had not made a levy on Victor's

stock to hold off as long as possible. The judge thought he had "negotiated a bargain with the Willamette Salt Works whereby V. will get the money to take up those judgments this week." He also offered to buy Victor's stock if it had not been sold. In closing, Shattuck commented: "The stock certificates are in my hands."[57] Shattuck wrote to Underwood again on May 11, this time to rescind an offer he had bid in Victor's stock for $1,000. He stated that he did not intend to pay any more than the amount equal to the judgments. However, he assured Underwood that he withdrew his offer reluctantly, for he thought that the stock would be par in gold within five years. He concluded his letter with this plea on Henry's behalf: "He thinks it simply just that the Co. take the stock and the donations already made by way of assessments paid, & let him off, & really does it not look somewhat so 'to a man up a tree?'"

Henry made yet another trip to San Francisco late that spring. At Enoch Adams' request, Davis had bought from him for $100 the $175 judgment that the Court had awarded him for the damages Henry had inflicted on his (Adams') house.[58] After learning that the O.C.M.R. Co. had placed a lien on all of Henry's property, Davis decided it was time to sever his partnership with Henry, at least to the extent of nullifying the articles of agreement they had signed on May 16, 1867. Now well aware of Henry's lack of character and incompetence in business management, on June 16, 1868 in San Francisco, Davis paid Victor $1,000 in gold coin for release of the articles of agreement between them. Victor gave Davis a receipt for the money and that same morning sailed for Portland.[59]

Back in St. Helens, Henry Victor received a disappointing counter-proposal in mid-July from Bynon J. Pengra, O.C.M.R. Co. president. Henry expressed his frustration thus:[60]

> I have your late note from Eugene City. I regret you did not
> see Judge Lancaster who went to Portland last Friday to
> meet you. He and he alone is my authorized agent to act in
> the matter at hand. As for the proposition of Judge Shat-
> tuck . . . . I do not recollect its tenor but think it was
> offered to sell the stock for $2,500.00. My proposition to,
> and accepted by you in San Francisco . . . was that you were
> to take the stock back for a release of judgment and costs.

The 'costs' have mainly been made since Shattuck's proposition to Kelly and your legal agent has made me all possible cost & trouble, intendedly, and for a purpose without doubt. I am not responsible for your costs & you have no moral right to ask me to pay them. Having already paid $3000.00 into the coffers of your Co., it is as little as you can do to accept that without asking me to give you another $500.00 in accordance with the (aforesaid) Shattuck, Kelly negotiations. I repeat my (accepted) proposition made to you in California to give you up the stock & you release claims against me. This is fair, honorable & right & you ought to ask no more of me. I leave with Judge Lancaster the settlement of this matter. Whatever may be Gibbs' disposition, through you as his authorized agent of the Co., I shall expect a right & just settlement of the affair.

A week later, Pengra sent the following instructions to the Company's attorney, Gibbs:[61]

Enclosed I send you the last of two letters from Victor, as evidence that the man is either a fool or crazy—

I want you to see Judge Lancaster, and, for me, as a properly authorized agent of the Road Company have the stock that Victor holds assigned to me, on his paying the causts [sic] and the five hundred as he offered to do in a letter written for him by Judge Shattuck, or get any amount you can from him down to the payment of causts [sic] and release of the judgment. If you cant do that let me know without delay and I will sell his stock and leave the judgment hanging over him.

I would like to have the man understand that mine and his relations to the company are the same, only I pay the assessments due on my stock & he don't. The case admits of no more delay.

On July 31, F.A. Davis and his wife finally terminated their business relationship with Henry Victor. They revoked his power of attorney to act for them and granted it to Columbia Lancaster, Henry's attorney.[62]

While Henry was carrying on his controversy with Underwood and Pengra, Frances pressed ahead with writing her book on Joe Meek and making plans to travel East in search of a publisher. Metta and Orville Victor had sent her a warm invitation to spend the fall and winter with them in their home, The Terraces, on the Saddle River in New Jersey. Over five years had passed since she and Henry had parted from her sister and brother-in-law on the dock in New York City. She was eager to see them and their first five children and the two new arrivals.[63] She also felt a deep need to talk to Metta about the past two troubled years and her disillusionment with Henry.

But it was her formidable friend, Judge Deady, to whom she wrote for literary advice:[64]

> Will you do me the favor to furnish me any anecdotes, papers, or facts, concerning Meek's career in Oregon that you may chance to have? I am pretty well on in my book now, and want to get everything in that I can. He tells me that in a number of *Harper* September or October of '59, he thinks, there are some anecdotes of him. Have you got and will you lend them?
>
> I would like to give a correct view of Meek's official acts—perhaps a few words from you would help me in that.
>
> It is my intention to go to New York in a few weeks. My time is limited, and whatever you can do for me will be gratefully remembered—for really it is as much a matter of bread and butter with me now, as of literary reputation. I must publish my book this winter, and I must get off to New York as early as possible.
>
> Regards to Mrs. Deady.

Judge Deady answered promptly. He granted her request for additional information on Joe Meek. And he told her about the publication of the first number of the new San Francisco magazine, *The Overland Monthly*, with Bret Harte as editor. Included in this first number was Deady's historical article, entitled "Portland—on Wallamet," which he thought she might find useful.[65] Pleased with his helpful response,

Frances ventured in her reply to request two additional favors she was certain that he would grant her:[66]

Hon. M.P. Deady—Dear Sir:"Am in receipt of your obliging note, and shall try to come up to Portland soon in order to have that 'hour's conversation' in which I expect to learn much of our friend Meek. Please bear in mind, while cogitating on the subject for my benefit, that although anecdote constitutes the principal capital in writing Meek's life—I wish to impart what dignity can properly be imputed to him in a more serious light, and so try to remember what is good and useful about him, as well as amusing.

Since you offer your services without specification, there is a matter about which I will ask you to inquire. I have a lot of books, new, which I do not care to leave to the mercy of vermin during my contemplated absence in the East; and I would if I could, sell them to the Portland Library Association or any other party, who would take them at what they cost me. I suppose there is something over $300.00 worth which are to be disposed of in some way. I send you the bill (original) and have marked out such books and articles as are not for sale. If the Library will take the remainder of the list I will bring up the boxes when I come to Portland.

In addition to all this, I shall ask you for an open letter to whom it may concern, or better, perhaps, a letter addressed to myself in which it is shown that by writing Meek's life I am supplying a 'literary want' of this country, and any other fol-de-rol which in your judgment will influence the skeptical Eastern press, and assist me in the matter of getting my book published.

For all of this I shall remain,
Yours truly—

F.F. Victor

Please retain bill until I see you.

As soon as she could after receiving Deady's encouraging reply, Frances boarded the steamboat for Portland with her boxes of books. She anticipated talking with the judge, obtaining more information on Joe Meek, and the letter of introduction she needed. On August 19, the morning *Oregonian* published a brief paragraph about Frances' forthcoming book:[67]

> History of Oregon—Mrs. H.C. Victor is writing a history
> of Oregon for the past forty years. Col. Joe Meek, who
> came here when 'Mt. Hood was a hole in the ground,' has
> kindly furnished this authoress with many facts connected
> with the early settlement of this part of the Pacific. We
> suppose that Joe Meek knows more of the past in regard to
> our young State than any other man in the world, and he
> can tell it, too.

The following day, Frances sailed for San Francisco aboard the steamship *Continental*. Among the 55 cabin passengers were two of her pioneer informants, J. Quinn Thornton and the Rev. Myron Eells.[68] Finally, on August 23, the fog lifted enough for the *Continental* to pass safely through the Golden Gate. However, the next Pacific Mail steamship was not scheduled to depart San Francisco for Panama City for another six days. During her stop-over, Frances had planned to call on Bret Harte. She was excited about the first two numbers of *The Overland Monthly*, which had begun publication in July. At last the West Coast possessed a magazine of the caliber of Eastern periodicals. It even resembled *The Atlantic Monthly* in appearance.[69] Now Western writers like herself could offer their articles, short stories, and poems to a first-class literary publication. Moreover, it was edited by one of their fellow authors, Bret Harte.

Frances found the debonair editor in his luxuriously furnished office on Clay Street.[70] He received her warmly as she complimented him on his successful editing of *The Overland Monthly* and the favorable reviews in the first two numbers. When she commented on the articles in them by Mark Twain, signed Samuel L. Clemens, Harte passed on to her the good news about his friend. He had secured an unusually liberal contract for the publication of his second book, tentatively titled *The Quaker City*, through Elisha Bliss, Jr. of the American Publishing Company, a sub-scription-book publishing house in Hartford, Connecticut.[71] In May, Mark Twain had arrived in San Francisco to persuade the *Alta* and the *Tribune* to release their copyrights on his Quaker City letters, that they had published, so he could reprint them, with revisions, as chapters for a book. After spending two hectic months in San Francisco doing just that, Twain had given three of them to Harte to use in the first numbers of *The Overland Monthly*. Then, on July 2, Twain had delivered a farewell address to a full house at the Mercantile Library before returning East.[72]

Frances confided to Harte that she was on her way East to locate a publisher for her nearly completed book manuscript—a lively narrative based on the humorous anecdotes of the famous mountain man, Joe Meek, about his Rocky Mountain fur trade adventures and his role in Oregon history since 1840. Harte expressed interest in the book and encouraged her to approach Twain's publisher in Connecticut. He also suggested that she submit to him historical articles for publication in *The Overland Monthly*. On Saturday, August 29, she sailed for Panama City aboard the Pacific Mail Steamship *Colorado*.[73] She anticipated retracing in reverse her memorable voyage from New York City to Acapulco, Mexico, with Henry in 1863, even though she was saddened by the circumstances that had led to her return east without him.

While the ship steamed south in the calm waters of the Pacific, Frances relaxed on deck and enjoyed the view of the shores of California and Mexico as the vessel's course neared the land. When it swung farther out to sea, she retreated to her cabin, where she continued the writing of her book. On the voyage to Panama, the *Colorado* stopped only at Acapul-co to coal and replenish supplies.[74] As the ship entered the beautiful Aca-pulco Bay and the town came into view, Frances indulged in sentimental memories of the fortnight that she and Henry had spent there five years before, when they explored the town and the fort and skimmed over the waters of the bay in the captain's gig to board Henry's ship, the U.S.S. *Narragansett*. Then, she mused. Henry, a successful naval engineer, had been master of himself and his work. After the lovely bay faded from view, Frances retired to her cabin, overwhelmed with regret and grief for Henry in his present state. She expressed her emotions in a three-stanza poem, titled "A Reprimand,"[75] that ended with:

> Scorn you I do, while pitying even more
>> The ignoble weakness of a strength debased.
> 'Tis vain to invite you—yet come up, come up,
>> Conquer your way toward the mountain-top!

CHAPTER 6

THE RIVER
OF THE WEST
(1868-70)

Frances fuller victor, from a vantage point on the deck of the steamship *Arizona*, thrilled to the sight of the spires of Lower Manhattan and the flags of the world's nations flying from the masts of hundreds of ships anchored in the harbor. Her former enthusiasm for New York City returned as the vessel moved past the Battery and up the Hudson River to the Pacific Mail Steamship Company's pier—one of nearly two hundred girding both sides of the island from the Battery to the Harlem River.[1]

It was early afternoon of September 20, 1868 and Frances was seven and a half days out of Aspinwall on the Caribbean shore of the Isthmus of Panama when the *Arizona* steamed through the Narrows of Upper New York Bay.[2] Scanning the crowd waiting at the pier as the ship docked, she suddenly spotted her beloved sister, Metta, as beautiful as ever, on the arm of her attentive husband, Orville. They were soon reunited and Frances was warmly greeted as "Frank." After a journey by ferry, railroad, and carriage, they turned into the driveway of The Terraces, the 30-acre, riverside estate that, for Frances, brought back painful memories of her estranged husband Henry, who had left The Terraces a Civil War hero. But these thoughts were soon dispelled as seven lively children with their governess emerged from the mansion and greeted their aunt. Five were now grown almost beyond recognition since she had left in March, 1863.[3]

Metta conducted a tour of the new two-story north wing that greatly increased the living space for the growing Victor family. In the mansion's old wing, Metta had prepared a comfortably furnished second-story bed- and sitting room with a view of the Saddle River for "Frank." She was delighted to have this secure, trouble-free haven where she would soon complete the first draft of her tale of the adventures of Joe Meek, the mountain man and political leader in Oregon. Since her account was historical, Orville held out the hope that Albert D. Richardson, who had failed to find a publisher for her Oregon handbook, probably could find one for the Meek book. Orville was still general editor for all Beadle and Company publications, and was planning to assume the editorship of a new periodical, *The Illustrated Western World*, early in the coming year.[4] While Orville worked at the company's editorial office on Lower Manhattan, Metta worked at her desk at home. The Beadle Company continued to publish her novels under various pseudonyms, and she also contributed to weekly New York journals, which vied to publish her popular stories serially, and paid her well for the privilege.[5]

The chief topic of conversation at the Victors' menage at the time of "Frank's" arrival was the upcoming November election for a president to succeed the ill-starred Andrew Johnson. The Republicans had nominated General Ulysses S. Grant and selected Schuyler Colfax, Speaker of the House, as their vice presidential candidate. Frances had met Colfax in Portland in 1865. In Orville's view, the reconstruction of the South now hung in the balance. With the fourth and final volume of his *History of the Southern Rebellion* yet to be published, he was deeply concerned, and he and Frances followed the election developments with great interest.

Frances admired Metta's financial success but regretted that her sister had compromised her youthful desire to write enduring literature. As for herself, she held fast to their shared youthful aspiration. Now without financial support from Henry, she would need to exist on what she could earn by her pen. So finishing her account of Joe Meek's saga and finding a publisher by fall became her goal. That autumn she spent many hours driving the soft gold point of her favorite pen swiftly over sheets of paper. She must complete her manuscript by mid-November if she was to secure a publishing contract, make revisions, read proof, and return to Oregon with "a book in press."

Word from Henry in mid-October revived her hope that he was a changed man.[6] Early on a lovely autumn morning, she accompanied Orville to Ho-Ho-kus, to entrain for the ferry to Lower Manhattan. She had an appointment with Albert Richardson on the staff of Horace Greeley's *Daily Tribune*, one of the four newspapers that fronted on Printing House Square.[7] She wanted to consult with him about offering her manuscript to the American Publishing Company in Hartford, Connecticut, which had published two of his books, copies of which he had given her. Richardson greeted her warmly, and reminisced about his visit to Portland as a member of the Colfax Party in 1865. When he expressed his regret for having failed to find a published for her Oregon handbook, she handed him the manuscript of her new book. As he scanned the lively first chapter of her account of Joe Meek's boisterous life, she noticed that his handsome countenance, adorned with a neatly-trimmed black mustache and beard, registered an expression of rising enthusiasm.[8] Encouraged, she summarized the main events of Meek's career and shared some of the humorous anecdotes she had included in her book. In turn, Richardson predicted that Elisha Bliss, manager of the American Publishing Company, would publish her manuscript. Her readable style and coverage of two subjects of interest to subscription-book readers— the Rocky Mountains and the settlement of the Oregon Country— would guarantee good sales.

Then Richardson noted that Mark Twain had called on him last January before signing a contract for the publication of his *The Innocents Abroad*, about which Bret Harte had already told her. Twain had wanted to know more about subscription-book publishing and what advantages, if any, it had over traditional book publishing. He also wanted to know how much Richardson had received from the sales of Twain's books. He had assured Twain that he had realized from his four percent royalties contract far more than he had anticipated. In fact the sales of each book had grossed well over $100,000.

Excited by the possibility of a similar contract, Frances asked Richardson about Elisha Bliss as well as his publishing, distribution, and sales policies. He recalled that in 1867 Bliss had joined the American

Publishing Company as secretary and manager just two years after the company was formed by the merger of several small subscription-book companies in Hartford, the center of the industry. In 1865, the new firm had published only one book—Richardson's *The Secret Service, The Field, The Dungeon, and The Escape*. The following year two books had emerged from the company's press: Joe I. Headley's *The Great Rebellion* and a deluxe family Bible. The sales of each of these three titles had exceeded 100,000, for interest in the Civil War remained at fever pitch, and Biblical publications had perpetual appeal.[9]

Bliss had initiated aggressive publishing, distribution, and sales techniques. He produced more books annually; and in his search for manuscripts by popular authors, he had offered Mark Twain a contract for the publication of his *Quaker City* expedition letters, which he had read in the San Francisco *Alta Californian*. They suited his preference for first-person narratives possessing a popular or sensational allure.

Richardson added that Bliss had also established subsidiary companies headed by his relatives. Under their imprints they published works of lesser known authors and also served as distributors of books to agents, who canvassed from door to door in assigned territories. These agents received at least 20 percent of the book's retail price, which ranged from $3.50 to $5.50, depending on the type of binding.

These 600-page volumes included a large number of illustrations, usually woodcuts, some of which were page-size. Because pre-publication sales accounted for a large percentage of the number of copies eventually sold, agents entered the field armed with an attractive dummy or prospectus. It contained sample pages of the book, including full-page illustrations, a table of contents, and some fifty pages of text—all bound together in a cloth cover. At the back of the dummy were strips of alternate bindings, half or all leather, and a blank page for the subscriber to sign. As a rule, subscription books were not sold in bookstores or advertised in magazines and newspapers, though review copies were sometimes distributed after publication. Frances, who later used subscription-book techniques in distribution and sales of her self-published books, improved on some of those techniques.

The arresting personality of Bret Harte caught Victor's eye and they wrote
and dreamed for years among Bay Area journalists. He, too, would die in 1902,
but his stories of the mines had reached readers around the world.

ORHI 63383

Richardson told Frances that Bliss had not released his *Beyond the Mississippi* to agents in the field until pre-publication orders had reached 41,000 copies. So far this year, Bliss had produced only two books. Richardson's *Personal History of Ulysses S. Grant* had been issued after a long delay caused by Bliss' insistence that Richardson pad it to meet the Company's new 600-page requirement by adding a biographical sketch of Grant's vice president, Schuyler Colfax. The second book was a reprint of Kane's *The U.S. Grinnell Expedition in Search of Sir John Franklin in 1853-1855*. Bliss' publishing schedule for 1868 had included *The New Pilgrim's Progress*. But the conservative directors of the company had strongly objected to his irreverent treatment of the pilgrimage to the Holy Land. However, Bliss appreciated humor in literature and felt that because of Twain's popular appeal as a journalist and lecturer, his book would outsell any previous publication. So its typesetting had proceeded.

Frances was relieved to learn that Bliss appreciated humor. Hope for her own success was heightened when, on parting, Richardson offered to recommend to Bliss that he publish her book on Joe Meek. Elated, she departed Printing House Square to return to The Terraces and plan a trip to Hartford to present her manuscript to Bliss in person.

She traveled on the New Haven, Hartford and Springfield Railroad with its station located three blocks from Bliss' office in the center of the city. When she met Elisha Bliss in his office, she was grateful to Richardson for having prepared her for the interview. A middle-aged man, he was bald except for longish hair on the back of his head. His handle bar mustache blended into long sideburns, and a goatee on his determined chin did little to soften the expression in his eyes. However, he greeted her warmly and assured her that he was interested in reading her manuscript so highly recommended by his best-selling author. If she would leave it with him overnight he would read as many pages as possible and give her his decision in the morning.[10]

Frances spent the afternoon visiting some of the historic buildings of Hartford, joint capital with New Haven of the native state of both her Williams and Fuller grandparents. The next morning she returned to Bliss' office, confident that he had made a favorable decision, as he had—provided that she met the 600-page requirement. Until she did so, he could only offer her a tentative contract. Then he explained the details of the production and sales of the book for which she would share responsibility—obtaining illustrations, proofreading the text as it was set in type, and promoting the sales of the book by giving talks on its contents prior to it publication.

Though pleased with the result of her trip to Hartford, it meant a winter filled with work. As the railroad car rumbled south, she determined that a quick solution to the problem of adding more pages would be to append an account of contemporary conditions and future prospects of the Pacific Northwest. Her unpublished handbook on the Oregon Country would provide such material!

She returned to The Terraces to find Metta absorbed in writing two novels—one a mystery story, the other a tale of disappointed love.[11] So it was that, while one sister dealt with her imaginary world, the other toiled to meet Bliss' demand for a 600-page book of historical events. Frances set about adding five chapters to her original manuscript, stating in the opening sentence:

> It was no part of the original intention of the author of the
> foregoing narrative to extend the work beyond the personal
> adventures of one man and such portions of collateral his-
> tory as were necesary to a perfect understanding of the
> times and events spoken of. But since the great interest
> which the public have taken in the opening of the first
> Pacific Railroad has become apparent, it has been deemed
> expedient to subjoin some facts concerning the Western
> Division of the Northern Pacific now in contemplation,
> and to become a reality, probably within an early day.

She concluded this transition from Meek's story as a fur trader and pioneer politician to the descriptive chapters with the following paragraph:

> The Northern Pacific Railroad will have its eastern end
> somewhere on Lake Superior and its western terminus at a
> point on Puget Sound, not yet determined. As that por-
> tion of the road lying west of Fort Union on the Mis-
> souri River traverses much of the country spoken of in

the adventures of the fur-traders as well as all the northern part of what was once the Oregon Territory, whose early history we have already given, it will not be found altogether irrelevant to enter into a brief description of the country so soon to be opened to the traveling public. Hitherto we have roamed it in imagination as the fur traders did, bent only on beaver skins and adventure. Now we will briefly consider it as a country fit for the permanent settlement of industrious people seeking homes for themselves and the coming generation.

These additional chapters added another dimension to her book, which she documented by quoting at length from several local sources, thereby honoring them. For instance, in a section on sheep-raising and the manufacture of woolen goods, she included a two-page excerpt from an essay by her friend, John Minto of Salem, Oregon, an authority on the subject. In a ten-page section on Eastern Oregon, she included a three-page extract from the report of Col. C. S. Drew of the First Oregon Cavalry on his reconnaisance through Southern Oregon to Fort Boise, Idaho in the summer of 1864. She also alloted a nine-page chapter to Washington Territory, in which she quoted excerpts from the Pacific Railroad Report of the late Governor S. I. Stevens on the Strait of Juan de Fuca and the waterways of Puget Sound. It was followed by a 17-page chapter on the Columbia River, which she knew so well. In her six-page summary on Montana Territory—its scenery, climate, resources, and development—she leaned heavily on Governor Stevens' report for physical features of the area.

Her final 13-page chapter contained general remarks on the Pacific Northwest. Among her sources was Capt. John Mullan's *Miners' and Travelers' Guide: A Report on the Wealth and Resources of Oregon*, and a newspaper clipping about a visit to Crater Lake in the Cascade Mountains, which Frances had yet to visit. In the last page of this chapter, she neatly reintroduced the subject of railroads by discussing "possible railroad routes in the Pacific Northwest."

By mid-February. 1870, President Ulysses S. Grant and Vice President Schuyler Colfax had received formal notification of their election, and Frances Fuller Victor had completed the work on her five additional chapters. When the winter weather moderated, she returned to Hartford, confident that Elisha Bliss would approve of the additional ballast, as it were, but wondering about the terms of her contract—especially the amount of royalties and the title of the book. Bliss had not approved of her simple, straight-forward title, *The Life and Times of Joseph L. Meek.*

She found Bliss in a good mood. He was confident that the humor in her book would make it a good seller. A few days were required for considering the terms and signing the contract, agreeing on a title, and arranging for illustrations and proofreading as the printing of the book proceeded. Bliss also wanted his new, attractive, widely-traveled, and witty female author to meet as many people as possible during her Hartford stay.

While reading the additional chapters, Bliss found a title for the book. Noting that two names had been applied to the Columbia River during the exploration of the Pacific Northwest—the "Oregon" and the "River of the West"—he thought that the latter was a romantic and appropriate title that would help sell the volume. Because of her love of the river and her knowledge of its romantic history, Frances acquiesced, but insisted that Meek's name appear in the subtitle. Again she had to yield. The subtitle read, *Life and Adventure in the Rocky Mountains and Oregon: Embracing the Events in the Life-Time of a Mountain-man and Pioneer with the Early History of the Northwest Slope* . . . . Finally, she won an important point: Bliss accepted her suggestion that the photograph of Joe Meek taken by Joseph Buchtel in Portland in 1865 be used as a frontispiece, facing the title page. The prefix "Mrs." which preceded her well-established signature, "Frances Fuller Victor," conferred a status of respectability which was cherished in 1869.

Whether Bliss granted her the four percent royalty is not known, but she was not pleased when he told her that her book would be published by the subsidiary publisher, R.W.Bliss of Hartford and Newark, N.J., which would obtain the copyright. Agents for her book in the west would be W.E.Bliss in Toledo, Ohio and R.J.Trumbull in San Francisco. With respect to illustrations, she agreed to furnish Bliss with ideas which he could send to the engraving firm with which the American Publishing

Company dealt. As for her reading page proofs, those ready before mid-March, 1869 were to be sent to her at The Terraces. After that until the end of May they should be sent to her mother's home in Marysville, Ohio where she would be visiting for a few weeks. Sheets run off after that should be mailed to her agent in San Francisco until mid-July, at which time they should be mailed to her in Portland, Oregon.

She departed Hartford, elated with her success and confident that she would be receiving a substantial sum in royalties, especially if she and her collaborator, Joe Meek, canvassed for sales in the Pacific Northwest.

Before beginning her return journey to the Northwest, Frances and her sister Metta called on Albert D. Richardson in his *Tribune* office in New York City and on their old friends and mentors, the Cary sisters, Alice and Phoebe, in Gramercy Park,[12] to inform them of the forthcoming book. Metta had heard that Alice Cary was seriously ill; they found that, though not yet fifty, her beautiful black hair was already turning white, and her glowing skin had become colorless. However, she questioned Frances about her book on the faraway Oregon Country; and the author was happy to report that publication was underway. She assured them that the Cary sisters would have one of the first copies off the press.

During that spring Frances also wrote a historical essay, entitled "Manifest Destiny in the West," which she mailed to Bret Harte, hoping that he would publish it in *The Overland Monthly* by the time she returned to San Francisco by way of the new transcontinental railroad from Omaha, Nebraska to Sacramento.

A one-sentence opening paragraph stated the theme of the essay: "That remarkable succession of circumstances quoted oftentimes as 'Manifest Destiny' is nowhere in history more wonderfully illustrated than in the rapid spread of Americanism from the eastern to the western shores of North America." Then she asked: "Does this opening sentence seem to smack of national self-praise and confidence in our sacred mission as exemplars of all the highest virtues of republicanism and free institutions? Belief in a manifest destiny ought indisputably to inspire us with enthusiasm to fulfill it to the utmost. But it was not of this belief or that sentiment we were thinking when we took up pen to write our dogmatical first sentence. It was the result of mental review of the written and unwritten history of the last eighty years as it applies to the march of empire in the western hemisphere."

After reviewing historical highlights beginning with the Spanish retirement from the Northwest and the arrival of the British and Americans, she revealed the extent of her own belief in the manifest destiny of the United States:

> "The dream of Thomas Jefferson, and the desire of Thomas H. Benton's heart, have been wonderfully fulfilled, so far as the Pacific Railroad and the trade with the old world of the East is concerned. But even they did not prophesy that Chinese should build the Pacificward end of the road. It was the Columbia River, and Puget Sound as a harbor, that the first projectors of the Pacific Railroad dreamed.
>
> Nor is the scheme of Jefferson, of Astor, of Benton, and other far-seeing men of a past generation, an unlikely one at this day. Another decade may see the ships of China and Japan unloading at the wharves of the Northern Railroad in Puget Sound, than which there is no more safe and commodious harbor in the world. . . .
>
> The only lion in the way of making the Sound a great naval depot is the British Lion, who has his lair upon Vancouver's Island, at the entrance to the Sound. It was an oversight on the part of the United States, the giving up of an island of Quadra and Vancouver on the settlement of the boundary question. Yet, 'what is to be, will be,' as some realist has it; and we look for the restoration of that picturesque and rocky atom of our former territory as inevitable.[13]

Early in April, 1869 Frances bade farewell to Metta and Orville and their children. After a five-year stay in the West, she was eager to visit other family members and share with them the news of her good fortune. As she retraced journeys of past years to Ohio and Iowa, she fulfilled Bliss' request that she promote her forthcoming book, and found that she "was called upon to do volumes of talk about the Pacific Coast, especially Oregon and Washington . . . ."[14]

As she traveled by train and stagecoach and family carriages, Frances caught up on events in the lives of her mother, sisters, and cousins. At the same time, she was obligated to read proof on the pages forwarded by the publisher to her planned destinations. She also wrote a second essay, entitled "The Search for Fretum Anian," which she intended to submit to Bret Harte when she reached San Francisco.

To reach the fabled City by the Golden Gate, Frances boarded the Union Pacific train at Omaha, departing daily on the thousand mile journey to Promontory Point, Utah. She paid $8.00 for her Pullman sleeping car space and $7.00 for her meals along the way. Her through ticket from New York City to San Francisco cost $112.50 in gold or its equivalent in devalued currency.[15] When the engineer sounded a warning whistle and the train pulled out of the station, a new adventure was underway for the passengers, including Frances. Some were fearful that Sioux Indians would derail the train, as they had on one occasion, but, because the crews of all trains were armed, they had been able to defend themselves until federal cavalry arrived. Besides the Indian peril, there was danger of being derailed by a herd of buffalo or cattle crossing the track. Fortunately, the usual speed of the train was about 30 miles per hour.

When Frances had traveled with her first husband, Jackson Barritt, along the Oregon Trail route in 1855, Indians had lived in the vicinity. Now, more than 20 years later, she saw no Indians except for some friendly Pawnee, who provided a sensation for some of her fellow passengers, After a breakfast stop (with antelope steaks for some!) at Cheyenne, Wyoming, Frances was thrilled by her first sight of the Rocky Mountains. In writing of *The River the West* she had visualized them from descriptions furnished by Joe Meek. Now she was experiencing their grandeur for herself. Beyond Cheyenne, the train labored up a steep grade and paused at Sherman station—the highest point on the Union Pacific Railroad line. The landscape was wild and bleak. Long's Peak to the southwest and Pike's Peak, due south, were plainly visible. The next stops for meals were on the backbone of the continent. The watershed—191 miles west of Sherman Station and 1,034 miles east of Sacramento—divided the waters flowing east from those flowing west.

Early the next morning, passengers were routed out to take breakfast in Mormon country. The train had just entered the Territory of Utah. Before the next stop at Unitah lay the most scenic views on the line—Echo and Weber canyons, Devil's Slide, and Devil's Gate. Though passengers were permitted to cross the platforms in walking the swaying length of the train, they were cautioned against standing there for sight-seeing. Some of the most curious and daring did so anyway, naturally. Corinne was the last stop before the train reached its western terminus at Promontory Point, where, on May 10, 1879, rails from the east and west had met, prompting Frances to write her essay, "The Search for Fretum Anian."

At Promontory Point, transcontinental passengers on the final 780-mile run to Sacramento transferred from Union Pacific Pullman cars to the Central Pacific Railroad's "Silver Palace" cars, considered somewhat inferior. Frances, nevertheless enjoyed the views as the train ran along the shore of the Great Salt Lake. She remembered that her Uncle Almond some 20 years earlier had accompanied Brigham Young in his search for a place to build a Mormon city in the wilderness

Veering west, the train entered the Great American Desert, covered with the alkali dust that permeated the cars until they reached Elko on the Humboldt River in northern Nevada, some 200 miles to the west. During the stop here, Frances was among passengers who explored the small town, finding that many inhabitants were Chinese who had helped to build the railroad. After Reno the train crossed the California line, some 127 miles from Sacramento, and Frances rejoiced with all the Californians on board. Soon the two engines now drawing the train were laboring up the eastern slope of the Sierras. She could see Donner Lake, nestled among the trees. From Summit station, 7,000 feet above sea level, the descent into Sacramento was rapid, and Frances soon arrived in San Francisco after an absence of almost ten months.[16]

It was now mid-July, 1869, and, after settling herself in for a brief stay, Frances Fuller Victor claimed the page-proof for *The River of the West* awaiting her at R. J. Trumbull & Company. Then she hastened to the office of *The Overland Monthly* to tell Bret Harte that a subsidiary of the American Publishing Company would publish her book later that autumn. After complimenting her on her success, Harte told her that her essay, "Manifest Destiny in the West," would appear in the August number of the *Monthly*. And he handed her $44 in payment.[17] She, in turn, handed him her second essay, "The Search for Fretum Anian," which he agreed to publish later that year, as well as her poem, "Nevada," which she had written *en route*. He also invited her to submit contributions on Oregon after her book on Joe Meek was in print.

In the second essay Frances mused on the search for a mythical northwest passage across North America, summarizing voyages of discovery from those of Columbus, Magellan, Cortez, and de Soto, to Coronado's and Drake's, among others. In so doing, she revealed her considerable knowledge of the world's geography. She concluded her exercise with this reference to a contemporary accomplishment:

> It is about eighty years since Europe abandoned the long
> pursuit for a shorter route to India around Cape Horn. In
> this year of our Lord 1869 we of the degenerate Yankee
> nation have discovered one passing right through the heart
> of the continent. It is divided, as the ocean once was,
> between two powerful companies, and seeks as they did to
> monopolize the trade of the Chinese and Japanese Seas.
> The *Fretum Anian* of the nineteenth century is a few feet
> wide of solid earth mounted by a parallel line of iron rails.
> Its ships are of wood, mounted on iron wheels, and they
> outsail all the white-winged navies of the world.

Frances returned to Portland July 31 aboard the steamship *Pacific*, four days out of San Francisco. The front page of the *Oregonian* of August 2, 1869, devoted two columns to the first half of her essay, "Manifest Destiny in the West," without crediting her as the author. She was, however, acknowledged in a brief item heading the local news column on August 2:

> Mrs. H.C. Victor, already well-known as a talented writer,
> has just returned from the East, where she has been engaged

for some time upon a 'Life' of the old pioneer Joe Meek.
We have no doubt that the book will possess much historical value and shall await its appearance with interest. It will
be out, we learn, sometime this fall.

To that end, Frances was occupied reading the last of the page
proofs for *The River of the West* and collecting illustrations to submit to
Elisha Bliss. She worked on her projects while she was a guest at the
Portland home of her cousin, Douglas W. Williams, and his wife, Harri-
ett. She found that her cousin's grocery and produce business was flourishing, especially after a Portlander, George T. Myers, had become his
partner.[18] Frances also visited St. Helens, where her furnished home was
leased or rented; Henry's whereabouts were unknown. She retrieved her
drawing portfolio and began to paint again, while staying with friends,
B.F. Giltner and his wife, Susan, a member of the McBride family.[19] In
late September, she departed St. Helens to spend the fall and winter in
Salem. She had received an invitation from another friend, Louisa
McBride Woods, and her husband, Governor George Woods, to visit
them.

However, Frances first spent a few days with yet another friend, Belle
Cooke; both had been anticipating the opening of the Oregon State Fair
in Salem. Belle entered several floral arrangements from her own garden,
and Frances entered several of her water color paintings of autumn
leaves, field flowers from the St. Helens area, and California fruit.[20]
According to the newspaper account, Frances Victor of St. Helens was
awarded a blue ribbon for the autumn leaves painting—dogwood, vine
maple, oak, ash, alder, willow, cottonwood, laurel, as well as wax and rose
berries, and Belle Cooke won a premium prize for her floral arrangements.

After the fair, in mid-October, Frances moved into the home of Governor Woods and his family, located at the corner of Capitol and Marion
streets. There she received the November *Overland Monthly*, featuring her
"*Fretum Anian*" essay, for which she received $49—funds she needed for
personal expenses while waiting for publication of *The River of the West.*

Feeling much at home, Frances felt free to question the young governor about his experiences in crossing the plains and his early life in Ore-

gon.[21] She learned that he had migrated at age 15 from Missouri in 1847 with his parents, Caleb and Margaret McBride Woods. Traveling with them had been his mother's brother, Dr. James McBride, his wife, Mahala, and their ten children. Both families had settled on land claims in Yamhill County, where George had attended the county school and then McMinnville College—at that time a day school with only a few students.[22] It had been opened in 1856 by Sebastian C. Adams, a Christian Church minister and the sole instructor.

In 1857, before embarking on the private practice of law, Woods had decided that he wanted some adventure. So in July he joined a party of six who had set out from Oregon City on an extended mountaineering expedition with two objectives: to acquaint themselves with eastern Oregon and discover the famous but elusive Blue Bucket Mine. On their return to the Willamette Valley, they decided to scale the highest peak of the Three Sisters. Rather than relating his adventures to Frances, the governor produced a worn copy of the Oregon City *Argus,* dated October 17, 1857. The front page carried a six-column account, entitled "Notes of a Trip to the Mountains," which Woods had written upon his return. Delighted with the narrative, Frances asked permission to use it as a basis of a mountaineering tale for The *Overland Monthly.* In her essay, "Trail-Making in the Oregon Mountains," she assumed the role of narrator.[23]

Late in November in the *Oregonian,* Frances read in horror and grief that Albert D. Richardson, her valued friend and publishing counselor, had been shot while sitting at his desk in the office of the New York *Tribune.* Mortally wounded, he had been carried to the nearby Astor House. His assailant had been Daniel McFarland, a confirmed drunkard and divorced husband of the woman Richardson was planning to marry. A widower and father of five, the 36-year-old Richardson had become engaged to Abby Sage McFarland soon after her divorce in 1869. On December 3, Frances read in the *Oregonian* a description of Richardson's deathbed wedding to Mrs. McFarland at the Astor House with Henry Ward Beecher and Octavius Brooks Frothingham officiating.[24]

Shortly after observing the year-end holidays with her Salem friends, Frances received her first copy of *The River of the West*—an auspicious beginning for the new year. The excellent printing job and the numerous illustrations, especially that of Joe Meek in his trapper's outfit, delighted her. How pleased and proud Meek would have been had not his eldest son, Courtney, been in hiding after having been attacked by a local bully whom he had killed in a scuffle in a local saloon.[25] On January 4, 1870, the Salem *Daily Oregon Unionist*, published by her friend, Samuel A. Clarke, announced that her book on Oregon and the life and adventures of Joe Meek would soon be issued. On the 27th Harvey Scott commented in the *Oregonian* on a specimen volume of *The River of the West*, which he had received from Joseph Wolf, the agent who would canvas for subscriptions in the Pacific Northwest. Scott's editorial states, in part:

> This is a book written by Mrs. Frances Fuller Victor of St. Helens, Oregon, a lady well known to all literary circles on the Pacific Coast, from matter furnished by Col. Jo. Meek, one of the most noted of the pioneers of Oregon—a mountain man who was in many respects the most remarkable of his class . . . . Of the contents of the book, we may say that, containing as it does the life and adventures of the best living specimen of a mountain man of the period when the great mountain and desert regions of the West were the scenes of the wildest romance and adventure, they could not fail to be the most deeply interesting even if written by the clumsiest of pens; but when told in the easy graceful narrative style which Mrs. Victor understands so well, the story is frequently thrilling and always captivating. Aside from the principal plot of the book, we find that it contains, incidentally, a good deal of the veritable unwritten history of the Northwest, of the old fur traders, Indian tribes and early missions; descriptions of the country, with its rivers, mountains, deserts, and natural resources . . . . As a literary effort, we think we can trust this Oregon book to the critics with confidence and pride, assured that its authoress has thereby extended and enlarged a fame in which Oregon had before a right to feel a just pride.

When *The Overland Monthly* for March, 1870 was received in Salem, the governor read with pleasure Frances Fuller Victor's version of his mountaineering expedition featured in the lead essay in this prestigious magazine. Soon she received $47 from the Overland office. Only Bret Harte among the contributors to that number received more. Altogether she had received from the magazine $140 for her three essays plus $15 for her poem, "Nevada," published in the December, 1869 number. However, she was worried about her finances. While in Portland to meet Joseph Wolf, the subscription agent for Oregon, she had learned that Henry was being sued by his physician, Dr. Julius Mack of Portland.[26] Fearing that she would have to pay Henry's debt if he defaulted, she inquired of Mack the amount still owed and was appalled to learn that it totalled $677.77 in gold coin plus court costs.

In late February, her peace of mind had been somewhat restored when she read in the *Oregonian* that a copy of her book had been presented to the editor and that it would be delivered to subscribers about March 10. That meant pre-publication sales had reached the number that Elisha Bliss required before releasing the book for distribution; in the case of Richardson's *Beyond the Mississippi* pre-publication subscriptions had totaled 40,000 copies. About that time, she discovered the first critical review of her book heading the column of reviews of new publications on the front page of the San Francisco *Bulletin*.

After introducing her as a former correspondent and a contributor to *The Overland Monthly*, the reviewer continued:[27]

> She is well-qualified for the task she has undertaken, possessing, in rare degree, the investigating, analytical and judicial faculty. She has, moreover, the patience of the student, to whom labor in the cause of truth is sweet, and the zeal of the true worker in the field of historical research. A resident, for many years, of Oregon, she has made herself thoroughly acquainted with the people whose annals she proposed to write. Much—indeed, we might say most—of her information is derived from the lips of those who were the actors in the scenes she describes. By far the most interesting portions of the work are those in which are detailed the narratives of the pioneers. In many instances the exact words of the narrators are given. Mrs. Victor had made

good use of her feminine art of 'drawing out' the hardy founders of our sister State. Of these her special pet and hero is Joseph Meek, whose adventurous career is graphically sketched. She presents him to our wondering gaze as the Bayard of the forest, a man without fear if not without reproach. As drawn by her partial pen, he is the embodiment of all that is heroic, the most excellent, the most doughty, the most daredevil, the most seductive in the frontiersman. His career is indeed a remarkable one. . . . In short, Mr. Meek is the real hero of the story. . . .If we were to criticize Mrs. Victor's performance, it would be to say that her history of Oregon is just a little too much a history of the life and adventures of Joseph L. Meek. Oregonians would possibly like it better if there was less of personal narrative and more of general historical data. But as the author wrote not for Oregon, but for the American people at large, and as the great mass of readers are more interested in the movements of individuals than the movements of events, she probably—looking to the question of financial success—adopted the wiser course. Authors are but human, and we must not be severe with Mrs. Victor for having written rather a popular book than a model history. That it will prove popular there can be little doubt. It is attractive in style, attractive in method, attractive in make up, attractive in printing, binding and illustration. It is true that the pictures have a cheap look, but the subjects are generally the kind that take the fancy of millions.

Then the reviewer cited criticism that Frances was soon to suffer:
Of course the book will be criticized by our neighbors up north—criticized not only for its sins of omission, but its sins of commission. The author is a woman of positive character and pronounced opinions. She 'speaks her mind' with a frankness that is commendable, but we fear not always palatable. She does not have a very good opinion of some of the early missionaries, and says so in the plainest

kind of English. She represents them as clannish, exclusive, uncharitable, intolerant, grasping—caring more for their temporal welfare than for the souls of the heathen, and being more concerned with accumulating fortunes than in spreading the gospel. She does not say this in so many words, but this is the impression her picture of some, if not all, of the missionaries, leaves on the mind of the reader . . . .

The paragraph concluded with a one-sentence summary of the descriptive chapters added to the book. Then the reviewer offered eight extracts "from Mrs. Victor's readable volume." Among them was a three-paragraph quotation in which she expressed her opinion of the missionaries and mountain men. It was followed by the incident in which Meek prayed for a cow. The longest extract was her four and one-half page description of the Whitman massacre at Waiilatpu Mission in 1847.

On the morning of March 8, Frances found on the editorial page of the *Oregonian*, a lengthy review of her book similar to that of the San Francisco *Bulletin*[28] In an introductory paragraph, the reviewer noted that books of adventure biography like *The River of the West* fill

an important place and are invaluable to him who studies the habits, manners, modes of thought and other character-istics of the community. These things cannot be traced without going back to the beginning. To know what our own State is we must know what manner of men they were who first settled it, and the circumstances which surround-ed them.

Then the reviewer presented the following critical evaluation:

Mrs. Victor's book supplies a tolerably full and well con-nected narrative of early events in Oregon. It is certainly the best that has yet appeared. Her work takes the form of a biography of one of the most widely known of our early pioneers, Joseph L. Meek; and into her narrative she has wrought many interesting details relative to the settlement of Oregon, the trials of the pioneers, their hopes and objects and the early policy of the National Government toward this most important part of our domain. On the whole the book is a fair and generous estimate of Oregon and the country drained by the *River of the West*. Much is said of its resources, and the author evidently writes with a faith that a great future awaits it.

Of Joe Meek everybody in Oregon knows much, and the book will help everybody to know much more. The story makes him quite a hero. It is told very attractively, and can hardly fail to prove popular. But the book is by no means so exclusively devoted to the one hero as to exclude mention of other persons who are entitled to a place in the early history of Oregon. Every person prominent in our early annals obtains notice, and the part they bore is generally outlined with satisfactory fullness. Doubtless there will be some who think that certain parts of the narrative are not fair, for Mrs. Victor has positive opinions and does not hesitate to state them, and in her study of the characters and events of early times in Oregon, she has found matters for censure as well as for praise.

"The story," the reviewer noted," is introduced with speeches, etc. after the manner of all good writers of tales of adventure from Homer to the present." That statement was followed by an extract describing Meek's induction into the fur trade by William Sublette in 1828. A second extract involved Meek's separation from his company on the Yellowstone River. After quoting Frances on the Methodist missionaries, the reviewer wrote, "We give the above as a specimen of the writer's independent style of criticism and leave her to those who may be disposed to take a different view of these things." After quoting her account of the Whitman massacre, the reviewer promised to present at another time something from the book "relative to the organization of a government in Oregon . . . . We will only add at present that every one who takes a pride in the history and growth of Oregon should encourage the authoress whose performance, on the whole, is one that will be of real service to Oregon."

By this time, Frances was experiencing repercussions from her comments on Oregon missions, ignited by the featured quotations from those comments in the reviews in the Portland *Oregonian* and the San Francisco *Bulletin*. Many persons associated or sympathetic with the missions formed the opinion that she was critical of all missions and was herself irreligious.

One of her defenders in Salem was Samuel A.Clarke. In his review of *The River of the West* in the March 17 issue of the *Sacramento Union*, he noted:[29]

> . . . the tale is well told, and in the main does justice to all parties concerned. It touches rather heavily upon some acts of the missionaries, while it does not appear to be intended for malicious comment and accords Dr. McLoughlin of the Hudson's Bay Company a mead of deserved praise as having been a generous friend to the early emigrants
> . . . . The book is written fairly and closes with a somewhat full allusion to different portions of our State and a recital of its resources. The reader will recognize that the authoress is not lacking in strength of mind and may somewhat wonder that she found it possible to use the free and sometimes profane vocabulary of the mountains as readily as she has done . . . .

Toward the end of the month, Frances received a complimentary letter from Jesse Applegate, who seldom gave compliments:

"I have received a copy of your book on Oregon, and have read it with much pleasure. It is certainly the best book yet published on the early history of our State, and I hope the sale will fully reward you for the labor you have bestowed upon it. Tho' some of the incidents narrated are not just as I have understood them to have transpired yet the book bears upon its face the evidence of the impartiality of the narrator. Nearly all of the mountain men you mention I have known either in Oregon or St. Louis. Many of the adventures you narrate I have heard before."[30]

Not having received his opinion of *The River of the West*, Frances wrote Judge Deady a brief letter on March 25:[31]

> I rather thought that when you read my book you would have something to say about it—critically, at least. Quite to

my surprise, I find myself much talked about; having forgotten that writers of contemporary history were liable to
notoriety—sometimes unenviable. Up here in Salem there
is a good deal of feeling among the class connected either
in former times and now with the Methodist Mission or
Church; however, as they avoid **me**and only quarrel with my
friends, there seems to be no present opportunity of 'reasoning together'—to the end that a compromise of opinion
may be made.

Well—no doubt Col. Meek is pretty well pleased with
himself as seen in print—and I am glad of that. I have been
waiting to hear from him as regards his impressions, but he
has not yet written.

About the fourth or fifth of April I expect to go to
Portland, when I hope to meet Mrs. Deady and yourself.
When I come down I will deliver the *French Dictionary*, which
so far I have had no suitable opportunity of sending.

Four days later, in his reply Deady included this paragraph concerning her book:[32]

The book [*The River of the West*] reads well and is interesting.
So far as I know or believe, in the main it is true both in
fact and opinion. Indeed, I am surprised that such a
stranger as yourself could have gotten as correct a view of
the field and the heterogeneous and scattered action thereon
as soon as you have.

Frances replied promptly on April 5:[33]

It was my intention to have sent you one of my books. I am
sorry that those I have are in cloth binding but such as they
are, if you will accept one for *your* library, I shall be very
happy to leave one with you when I come again to Portland.

I recognize the apparent justice of the only criticism
you make in your note—and still there is an error in it. I
did not *name* any denomination in likening the processes,
which in pagan rites made a medicine man and in Christian
rites a saint. As there are several sects who use a good deal

of muscular power to excite their spiritual fervor, it is not necessary to apply the remark to the Methodists particularly—certainly not to the Oregon Methodist . . . . Still, I admit the thought may be suggested to others as it was to you by the general tenor of the history of those things. And—I am such a scorner of humbug, that really I cannot find it in my nature to be very sorry that I said it!

Would it be convenient for you to hand to Gov. Woods for me the amount due for the books I sold to the Library Association: $30.

Agreeably to Mrs. Woods' request I shall remain in Salem until the Governor's return from the convention, and I shall have need of some money at the time of my departure. Like a prudent woman, I am going to earn my living this year by pen work which I am preparing to do, in order that what accrues from the sale of my book may be kept together for a yet greater need than the present, or as you pleasantly put it—that I may be able to find leisure 'to disport myself beyond the seas' at no distant day.

Kind regards to Mrs. Deady.

Yours truly,

F.F.Victor

CHAPTER 7

ALL OVER OREGON & WASHINGTON

(1870-72)

C URIOSITY AND COURAGE were, of necessity, Frances Fuller Victor's constant companions when she traveled alone through Oregon and the territories of Washington and Idaho from mid-May through July, 1870. From Portland by way of river steamers, stagecoaches, and an ocean-going steamship, she went as far east as Lewiston on the Snake River and as far north as Puget Sound and Vancouver Island. By then she was a controversial celebrity in the Pacific Northwest, and her primary purpose was to help her agent, Joseph Wolf, canvass for subscriptions to her book, *The River of the West.* She also wanted to gather material for a second book about the Pacific Northwest (which she eventually published at her own expense), and to meet her cousin, Jane Williams Wilson, and her family in Walla Walla.

Before Frances left on her voyage of discovery, however, she wrote a humorous jingle about the Willamette Slough.[1] And she decided she needed a place to call home. A personal item in the *Oregonian's* new city column announced that "Mrs. F. F. Victor, author of *The River of the West,* has again taken up her residence in Portland and continues to give her attention to matters of public interest." The city editor, DeWitt Clinton Ireland, would have known; Frances had made arrangements to stay with him and his family in Portland.[2]

Prior to her departure, Frances also took time to compose an indignant yet conciliatory response to a critical letter of protest from the Rev. Henry Harmon Spalding, a former colleague of the martyred Dr. Marcus Whitman. She wrote:[3]

The reading of your note of the 2nd was quite a surprise to me. Why you should accuse me of saying in my book anything that needed to be denied and defended, concerning the missions east of the mountains, I do not understand. I have said that the Methodist mission in the Wallamet Valley did not sustain its missionary character and that its members were selfish and grasping; and I shall be able always to maintain that assertion by the testimony of the whole State, with here and there an exception. I never did say that the Presbyterian Mission was either grasping or dishonest. In fact, I took great pains to do them justice by describing their years of honest and earnest labor among the Indians.

That the mission was a failure I did not charge to them, but to the circumstances which surrounded them. I fairly considered all the causes which led to the massacre, and formed my judgment thereon, as I certainly had a right to do. My account of the ladies of the Presbyterian Mission was altogether kind and flattering.

Truly I am tired, not to say disgusted, with the carping spirit of so many of the people of Oregon. My book is doing much good in the East by bringing into notice this state, its history and resources; and I believe I deserve the kindly assistance of the people instead of their jealous criticism.

Hoping that when you have read my book you will form a more liberal opinion

I remain . . .

Yours respectfully,

F. F. Victor

Should you come to Portland you can hear of me from Mr. Ireland at the *Oregonian* office.

The Reverend Mr. Spalding, then living in Brownsville, Oregon, prior to going East to seek redress from the federal government,[4] would not have been pleased with the *Oregonian*'s review of Mrs. Victor's book any more than was W.H. Gray of Astoria, a long-time adversary of the author. Gray's resentment deepened after both the *Oregonian* and the San Francisco *Bulletin* published favorable reviews of *The River of the West*, and especially after the *Bulletin* carried a hostile review of his volume:[5]

> A short time since we noticed Mrs. Victor's work, *The River of the West*; we now have a *History of Oregon,* by W. H. Gray of Astoria. Both authors substantially go over the same ground, but from how different standpoints do they write! One would hardly suspect, from reading the two books, that they treated the same events, or even referred to the same country. Mrs. Victor, for instance, represents the Methodist missionaries as intriguers and mischief-makers; Mr. Gray holds them up to public admiration as models of all the private and public virtues. The former gives a rose-colored picture of the Hudson-Bay [*sic*] Company; the latter denounces them as little better than moral monsters. The one surrounds the "Mountain Men" with a halo of romance; the latter stigmatizes them as a lot of "squaw men," scapegraces, and Commandment breakers. The feminine chronicler makes Mr. Joseph L. Meek the central figure in her historical tableau. If historians thus widely differ with regard to events that occurred "within the memory of men still living," what shall be said of events that occurred thousands of years ago!"

After terming Gray the "Pioneer of Pioneers," the *Bulletin* reviewer continued:

> . . . He therefore knows whereof he speaks, and his words have something of the weight of historical authority. We need hardly add that he carries into his events much of the prejudices of the partisan and the intolerance of the zealot. Belonging to the missionary party, it is natural that he should have seen with their eyes, heard with their ears, and understood with their understanding. He hates the English; hates the Hudson's Bay Company; hates the Jesuits; in

short, hates everybody who were not on good terms with
the missionaries . . . .

One week later Gray's wrath had increased. The *Oregonian*, he discovered, had devoted only a single lengthy paragraph to a review of his book, relegated to the city news column on page three.[66] After noting the size of the book and the names of the local agents, the reviewer stated:

> The author in his introductory remarks that he had endeavored to narrate events in plain language, and in order of occurrence as near as possible, without laying claim to literary merit or attractive style . . . . He claims that this is a standard history of the country from the time included within the period of its discovery by Capt. Robert Gray, to the year 1849, as the contents are based on the author's personal knowledge and observation and participation in what is stated for one-half of a century; and that the written and quoted statements of others have been so compared that conclusions are intended to be without a possibility of truthful contradiction. We leave the readers of the work to judge for themselves as to the merits or demerits of its contents.

Frances Fuller Victor, before undertaking her long northwest excursion, called on Jesse Q. Thornton to get his response to *The River of the West*, in which she incorporated historical information he had given her. She found him critical of her use of Joe Meek's testimony, and she left his office aware that, in addition to Spalding and Gray, she had a third critic in the offing. Thornton's own review of her book was scheduled for publication in the Portland-based weekly *Pacific Christian Advocate* later in May.

As a traveling correspondent for the *Oregonian*,[7] Mrs. Victor set the tone for her subsequent reports in her first article, datelined Dalles, Oregon, May 20, 1870:

> It is five years less a few weeks, since I first made a voyage
> up the Columbia —I should say, perhaps, the Middle
> Columbia—for the navigation of the river is so divided that
> the hundred miles from the mouth of the Wallamet to the

sea have obtained the distinctive appellation of *Lower* Columbia; while that stretch beyond The Dalles following up to the sources of the north fork of the great river is known as the Upper Columbia. That intervening section, then, from the mouth of the Wallamet to The Dalles, one hundred miles in length and most interesting of any in scenery, I shall, on my own responsibility, and in ink the color of the haze which mantles its mountain borders, hereupon christen the *Middle* Columbia. It has been so often described by tourists in the past four years that to capitulate would be superfluous.

After summarizing the Indian legends of the creation of the obstructions and rapids at the Cascades and The Dalles, Frances commented on the bill before Congress that year to remove these obstructions to navigation. In a good example of her ability to combine historical romance with the contemporary and practical, she further noted the perils of passage when winds were blowing fiercely through the Gorge of the Columbia. In fact, the steamboat that met hers at the Cascades was two hours behind schedule, owing to one of her bulkheads having been crushed.

Frances found The Dalles looking "fresh and pretty against its background of spring green." Her friends there entertained her handsomely by driving her on excursions outside the city, proudly pointing out flourishing orchards on fertile creek bottoms and on arable hillsides as well as superlative views of Mt. Hood.

Among the people she met she discovered "considerable cultivation and taste for intellectual pursuits." She was delighted that "from a lecture delivered here last winter by Dr. McKay—a descendant of that McKay who had perished in the *Tonquin,* as related in [Washington] Irving's *Astoria,* and who is more conversant with Indian languages and ideas than any man in Oregon—I was able to obtain the Indian names of many places about The Dalles, together with their significance."

She did, however, experience one disappointment—failure to see Thomas Condon and his collection of fossils again. In expressing her regret that Condon had not been at home, she wrote:[8]

I had before had the opportunity of looking through his 'Second Book of Genesis,' as he calls his collection of fossils, but it is so extensive a volume that it bears a great many readings, and besides, it is a real pleasure to meet with a man whose soul is so evidently in his work. Mr. Condon is a pastor of the Congregational Church in Dalles, and labors zealously for the good of his people; nevertheless he finds time to devote to the collection and study of geographical, mineralogical and paleontological specimens. From the contents of his cabinet, it is evident that the northwest coast is rich in the remains of extinct species of animals, together with numerous indications of the ocean life which once existed where now are elevated mountain peaks. Mr. C's lectures, aided by a valuable set of charts, with which he illustrates them, have dine much toward developing a scientific taste in the young people of Dalles, as well as much toward instructing and entertaining 'children of the larger growth.'

Before departing Dalles, Frances notified the editor of the Walla Walla *Weekly Statesman* that she intended to arrive soon. On May 21, he published the following notice concerning her:

'*The River of the West*'—Mrs. Victor, the charming writer, in a private note informs us that she will be at Walla Walla in a few days with a view to seeing the country and learning of its resources. The information thus obtained will be embodied in a book which Mrs. V. is now preparing. Whilst here she will also receive subscriptions for her book, entitled "The River of the West," a work mainly devoted to the illustration of scenes in the early settlement of the Northwest coast. We trust that our readers will be prepared to receive Mrs. V. kindly and liberally."

Mrs. Victor, the only lady passenger and a stranger to all the others, boarded the train of The Dalles-Celilo portage railroad for the 15-mile journey to Celilo on May 24. After it pulled up at the O.S.N. Company's dock there, passengers were transferred to the *Yakima*, "a fine, commodious steamer, which was lying alongside the great warehouse of the O.S.N. Company with steam up, ready for departure." [9]

Once board, Frances indulged in a substantial breakfast; and, as no more ladies appeared, she had "the after-cabin" to herself. Seated in a little sewing chair which the attentive steward found for her, she divided her time between reading Isacc Taylor's *Natural History of Enthusiasm* and taking notes on the passing scenery.

The *Yakima* arrived about 6 P.M. at Umatilla, a "bit of a town" on the sands of the Umatilla River about 97 miles above The Dalles. After a brief stop, it steamed the 25 miles to Wallula "in the rosy sunset and purple twilight." [10] As the steward guided her and a few male passengers to a boarding house, she recalled that, though historically interesting as old Fort Walla Walla of the Hudson's Bay Company, the town lacked any local charms. Soon she discovered the sand had panatrated her room and her bed. Even the food served at breakfast the next morning was gritty.

The 35-mile stagecoach ride to Walla Walla only added to her misery, [11] as well as to the journey's accumulation of evidence of her physical stamina and writing ability:

> On taking my seat in the coach after breakfast, for Walla
> Walla, I found that the female element was in the minority
> again. Eight specimens of the male sex, and one insignifi-
> cant woman! Of course I subsided into my corner over the
> right wheel, and submitted to having sand thrown in my
> face without venturing to utter a word of remonstrance.
> The simple audacity of being a woman up here in this mas-
> culine territory was so powerfully impressed upon my mind,
> that I felt compelled to sit in speechless immobility during
> the whole drive of thirty-five miles.

She privately rejoiced when a slight shower fell, tempering the heat and laying the dust, and silently admired the flowers along the way. As a seeker of knowledge, she became interested in the comments of her fellow passengers. But she did "confess to a slight feeling of distrust when one of them declared that the soil of the Powder River valley was so rich that if a man chanced to leave his crowbar sticking in the ground at night, in the morning he would be sure to find it had sprouted eight-penny nails!"

When the stage pulled up at the noon station on the Touchet River, Frances. Discovering that there was no place to sit inside the house except in the public room, seated herself on the door step with the land-lord's ague-stricken children. They entertained her while "the eight mas-culines went to dinner within," and she went without—nobody thinking her of "sufficient importance to be asked to dine." When the stage resumed its journey to Walla Walla, she gathered from comments made on the dinner that she had been the winner.

Later that afternoon, the stage entered Walla Walla and stopped in front of the hotel. In this paragraph, dated June 5, she summarized her first impression of the town:

> Perhaps it is by contrast that the town of Walla Walla
> impresses itself so pleasantly upon the vision on first enter-
> ing it from the direction of Wallula. It does, at all events,
> surprise the traveler with the aspect of cheerfulness and
> thrift—with its neat residences and embowering trees, and
> the general air of comfort and stability which it posseses. A
> commodious hotel, quite as good as the best in Portland,
> receives the dust-stained inmates of the coach, and the gen-
> tlemanly proprietor does his best to furnish them with
> everything needed for their refreshment. I had some letters
> to prominent citizens of Walla Walla which were duly hon-
> ored; and I found the people generally hospitable and social
> in their habits. A week looking about furnished me with
> many interesting facts concerning that considerable tract of
> country known as the Walla Walla Valley.

While Frances was exploring the town and the surrounding country, her cousin, Jane Williams Wilson, and Jane's husband, Oscar, arrived from their home, located just south of Pendleton, Oregon. Twelve years had passed since she had been with them while visiting her uncle, Jane's father, on his Iowa farm. While in Walla Walla, where he moved later that year, Oscar provided Frances with the highlight of her visit—an excursion to the site of the Whitman massacre. On May 31, 1870, the Rev. Cushing Eells recorded in his diary that "Mrs. Victor, Mrs. Rees, Mr. Wilson and wife have been here."[12] At the time, Eells owned the land once occupied by the Mission, which lay on bottom land near the junction of the Walla Walla and Mill Creeks.

A few days later, Frances Fuller Victor wrote this moving description of the state of the site as she saw it:[13]

> While in Walla Walla I took a ride out to the scene of the Whitman Mission and massacre. Mr. Eells, one of the members of the early mission in this country, is now residing on the identical spot where the buildings of Dr. Whitman's establishment formerly stood. Having been built of adobe, after the burning of the buildings, the walls dissolved into mounds of clay indistinguishable from the earth around; unless, in thrusting a stick into one of the heaps you came to bits of burned glass, iron, charcoal, or broken earthenware. Another mound of dry alkali earth, enclosed in a rough board fence, marks the spot where Dr. and Mrs. Whitman and their fellow victims lie buried in one common grave in rude uncoffined sepulchre. It is a sorry spectacle, and appeals to the sympathy and proper sense of every beholder for a more suitable column than this unsightly mound unadorned with grass or shrub. The most affecting reminders of wasted effort which remain are the two of three fruit trees which escaped the general destruction, and the scarlet poppies which are scattered broadcast in the creek bottom near the houses. Sad it is that the flower whose evanescent bloom is the symbol of unending joys should be the only tangible witness left of the womanly tastes and labors of the victims of savage vengeance and superstition.

It was a picture Frances never forgot, and would form the basis for one of her favorite poems, "The Poppies of Wa-ii-lat-pu," first published many years later.

At the time, Frances Fuller Victor noted that Dr. Whitman's labor and suffering had been commemorated by the founding of the Whitman Seminary in Walla Walla. It has been chartered in the winter of 1859–60 after the Reverend Mr. Eells had donated one-half of his land claim toward raising funds for its construction. In 1867 the Seminary had been built by subscriptions from the people of Walla Walla with the help of additional financial aid from Eels. For lack of a principal and teachers of sufficient quality, no classes were being held at the Seminary when Frances was in Walla Walla. She did find, however, that the town had two nigh schools, one Protestant and one Catholic; and just that year a Teacher's Institute had been organized. In the entire Walla Walla Valley she observed "a more than ordinary spirit of enterprise in educational matters."[14]

She was surprised by the progress that the people of this isolated area had made since its opening for settlement only eleven years before. She was delighted that during her visit Walla Walla celebrated the completion of the telegraph line. Now only a branch of the Northern Pacific Railroad was needed to assure a prosperous future for the region; and Frances was confident that the Walla Wallans would obtain it. She concluded her observations on the region with this admonition to the people of Western Oregon:

> It is our fashion to grumble because Californians do not
> understand or appreciate us. With equable propriety the
> people east of the mountains may complain of our igno-
> rance concerning them, their institutions and resources.
> One thing is very certain: the Northern Railroad Company,
> with their policy of settling their employees along the line
> of their road, is going to bring a great influx of settlers into
> this fertile and delightful valley; and with the start it has
> already established, we shall have to look to our laurels if
> we do not have to yield the palm or the bay to our eastern
> neighbors in point of mental and physical advancement, in
> material prosperity and intellectual development.

About June 5, Frances departed Walla Walla in the two-horse hack that also carried the mail to Lewiston, Idaho. To her delight, she was the

FRANCES FULLER VICTOR

only passenger and because of the heavy load of mail that day the driver took a longer but more pleasant route. In her travel letter, she waxed poetical over views from high points in the road. "Perhaps it was by contrast with the uniform rolling expanse of grass land on either side that the little valley looked so lovely; but I thought it the perfection of home-like peaceful beauty, and felt my bucolic tastes strongly appealed to," she wrote.

By ten o'clock that morning, they came to "the six-year-old town of Waitsburg—as pretty a spot, and as thriving a new town as there is on the Pacific Slope."[15] Here, Frances learned, Mr. Wait had settled in the winter of 1864 and built a flour mill from which he had made $5,000 in two months. Tradesmen settled near the mill; and soon stores and a hotel were constructed. In reporting on the four or five days she spent in Waitsburg, Frances noted that "all the farmers seemed to have money, and trade was all the time brisk. There was also considerable packing from here to the mines." With regard to the town's educational and social development, Frances noted that it did not yet have a church, but it possessed the largest schoolhouse she had seen in the Pacific Northwest except in Portland. Fifty pupils attended the school; and on the Sabbath, a Sunday School and Bible class met there. She also observed a Good Templar's Lodge, numbering 80 members, and only one "very sickly saloon in the place."

On two occasions, Frances saw most of the twonspeople assemble to hear political speeches—one by Washington Territory's Governor Salomen, the other by a "Democratic gentleman" from Walla Walla. She was most impressed by the German-born governor's discourse, which he delivered "in English so pure and scholarly" that she could not help regretting "that all our public men are not compelled to learn their mother tongue in foreign schools."

The Waits took Florence on a drive to show her how water for irrigation was brought to the land from wells and springs in the ravines. But it was only when she headed for Lewiston, again in the mail hack, that she fully appreciated the basis for the town's prosperity: "a constant succession of thrifty-looking farms, with a neat, commodious white-painted schoolhouse every few miles." [16]

When the hack climbed out of the valley some 20 miles northeast of Waitsburg, the scenic change was dramatic:[17]

> From the greatest elevation there are splendid views—wonderful for extent, and rather awful, inasmuch as one is able to realize that we are traveling like the fly on the rind of an orange, and can look down its slopes to dizzy descents of curvature. Just before coming to the descent to the Tucanon River, there is a fine view of the Bitter Root mountains, and of several buttes, among them Steptoe's Butte, where the colonel of that name had a disastrous fight with the Indians, in the breaking out of the Indian war of 1855. Going over the ground now, it strikes one with a strong sense of the difficulties and dangers of such a march through such a country, and of amazement that a small company of whites ever were able to retreat out of it alive.

Then Frances described the perils and discomforts of stage travel in this rugged terrain:

> The hill of the Tucanon is frightful. Seeing the preparation made for its descent prepares the traveler for something of a hill; but when once the narrow winding grade with a coach seeming minded to tumble over the backs of the horses it is the most natural things in the world to wish you had not taken the ride down. Walking, you reflect, if not an easy mode of locomotion, had the advantage of being eminently safe, compared to this. A mile and a quarter of such useless reflections prepared one to be thoroughly glad when the lowest level is reached, and crossing the Tucanon you come to the house of Mr. King, a very comfortable stopping place for the night; a house set in the midst of a cottonwood grove, with a little village of barns and outhouses in front of it. Plenty to eat and a good bed had seemed almost more than could be expected in so isolated a situation; but Mr. King has a farm here, and there are other farms in the neighborhood.

To Frances, the drive to Lewiston the next day was more tiresome than any other part of her journey from Wallula. However, after an excellent dinner at the noon station, she walked up a long hill, which was "nothing to the heat and fatigue of walking <u>down</u> the long and ugly looking hill into the valley of the Alpowah." When the coach pulled onto the ferry at the Snake River crossing to Lewiston, she was among the passengers who eagerly accepted a glass of ice water provided by the ferryman. After spending a few uncomfortable hours in a Lewiston hotel, she was unexpectedly rescued by friends, Judge Kelly and his family, who took her home with them "to the comforts of private life and social intercourse."[18]

Though Frances appreciated the hospitality of her hosts, her description of Lewiston, Idaho was less complimentary than those of Walla Walla and Waitsburg. She found the town located on a sandspit between the Snake and Clearwater Rivers. From a business point of view, she wrote, "the roads, navigation, etc. shall demand a commercial centre."[19]

The only place of historical interest in the region was the Indian Agency located on the site of the Lapwai Mission, established in 1836 by the Rev. Henry Harmon Spalding and his wife, Eliza Hart. Since a visit there and a voyage on the Snake River to its junction with the Columbia above Wallula were the two chief objectives of her trip to Lewiston, Frances was delighted when Levi Ankeny offered to drive her to the Indian Agency. In recalling the early morning ride across the high prairie covered with a profusion of wild flowers, she wrote:[20]

> The little valley of the Lapwai is exceedingly pretty, The
> effect is picture-like, seen from the hills bordering it—
> with the military post and the Agency, nestled each in its
> own little nook not far from each other. This, everybody
> will remember, is the scene of early missionary labor,
> under Mr. Spalding. Here, Mrs. Spalding, if not the most
> devoted, yet the most successful missionary of the
> A.B.F.M. in Oregon, taught Indian women religion and
> civilization together for eleven years of patient conformity

to savage wants. Small reward had she in time. Let us hope 'her works do follow her.'

At the Agency, Frances met the interpreter, Perrin Whitman, nephew of Marcus Whitman. He lived there with his family in a pleasant home; and the Indians regarded him as the only person who could properly represent them. "Mr. Whitman," Frances noted, "was kind enough to show me about the grounds, pointing out each piece of special interest—among them the old mission building, now fallen into decay, and the new mission church, 'Lyon's Folly,' as it is called—which will soon be nothing better than a ruin, as its massive stone walls have no covering. Uncle Sam must be a very good natured relative to allow so many of his nephews to set up expensive monuments to themselves out of his material, and to pay them handsomely at the same time for doing it."[21]

She was equally critical of the policies of the Bureau of Indian Affairs in Washington, D.C.:

> There never was a more stupendous piece of nonsense in the world than erecting handsome buildings or providing enlightened institutions for the use of the average aborigine. The Nez Perce have always been the exemplary 'good Indians' of the Northwest; but to regard them as civilized, or to expect them to become such, is in error . . . .It is true that they cultivate a little ground under superintendency which looks well, but it is only a little . . . . Some of them are fine enough looking fellows and many of the young women are pretty. The latter can learn to sew quite nicely, but are too indolent to keep themselves decently clad without constant urging. They prefer lounging like the men, and amuse themselves in the Indian room at Mr. Whitman's by chanting together in their low, lazy, not unmusical though decidedly barbarous and unpronounceable, sing-song.

The high point of France Fuller Victor's visit to the Agency was talking with Chief Lawyer:[22]

"Asking to be introduced to Lawyer, Mr. Whitman took me to see this renowned chief. He is a rather short, stout-built man, with a good face of the Indian type, very dark—almost African in complexion—and dressed in a rusty suit of white men's clothes, with the inevitable high silk hat. His manner on being introduced is a very good copy of the civilized man's; but his English is quite too imperfect for much conversation. I told him I had come a long way to see the man who talked with Lewis and Clarke; at which he smiled in a gratified manner. When I asked him how old he was when Lewis and Clarke were in the country, he indicated with his hands the stature of a five-year-old child; but he must have been older than that to have remembered all he claims about the great explorers. It was his father who kept their horses through the winter while they explored the Columbia to its mouth."

At the Agency, Frances learned of the then existing conflicting claims to the land on which the old mission was located. In her travel letter to the *Oregonian*, published July 7, 1870, she wrote, in part:

When Congress passed an act denoting a mile square to each of the mission establishments in Oregon, requiring settlement to be made previous to 1850, it practically cut off the missions in the upper country from the benefits of the act; for from the breaking out of the Cayuse war up to 1859, that country was closed against settlement by military order. Thus it happened that while the Methodist missions west of the mountains were enjoying the bounty of the government, the A.B.F.M. on the east were dispossessed. However, when Washington Territory, being set off from Oregon, began to act independently, she also passed an act confirming the previous act of Congress giving a mile square of land to the missions within her boundaries. Subsequently, the U.S. government took possession of the Lapwai claim for a post, and the erection of garrison buildings. In opposition to this, Mr. Spalding, as agent for the A.B.F.M., sold the claim to a private party; and here comes the conflict. The law on the subject seems very much mixed—I think if I were an advocate I should like such a case. Whether it is U.S. *versus* U.S. or *versus* Washington Territory or *versus* private individual seems difficult to determine. Meanwhile, Mr. Spalding thinks he ought to have a claim as a settler, and is about going to Washington to insist upon it. If he gets his claim in the Lapwai valley his worldly affairs will need little further attention, for the land is held at a high evaluation. . . The spot must be much prettier now than formerly, owing to the present good state of cultivation; and certainly made a much pleasanter impression on my mind than Waiilatpu.

During her three days at Lewiston, Frances also enjoyed "an elegant little dinner with Mrs. A. and a few friends; after which there were seats on the piazza in the moonlight for the party, with cigars for the gentlemen and flowers of poetry, and wit, and merriment for whoever liked to participate."[23]

She departed Lewiston on a Monday morning aboard the weekly steamer from The Dalles. A terrifying thunderstorm the night before had brought refreshing rain and insured a cool voyage down the Snake River to the Columbia and then on to The Dalles by way of the railroad portage at Celilo. Upon departing The Dalles by steamer the next morning, Frances enjoyed a parting glimpse of Mt. Hood. She noted that "his majesty was draped from summit to base in a golden-tinted tissue of mist." The steamer docked at Portland that evening, June 15.[24] The next morning the *Oregonian* reported that she had returned from her tour of the Columbia and Snake Rivers. She was glad to be back after four weeks of travel and intended to remain only long enough to write the last of her articles describing the journey east of the Cascades.

Frances was also pleased to read her reply to the first installment of J. Quinn Thornton's review of her *The River of the West*, published in the May 21 issue of the *Pacific Christian Advocate*. She had earlier been advised of Thornton's attack and at some point *en route* had sent a reply to the magazine, which published it on June 11—just a few days before her return. Though appalled at Thornton's assertions, Frances could see them as an adverse advertisement for her book and an opportunity to establish her historical veracity. In the opening sentence of her reply, she stated "it is not my intention to enter into a wordy defense of myself or my book." Then she continued:

Some little notice I do feel compelled to take, however, of Mr. Thornton's characteristic 'Review.' In the first place, it is only fair that what I am about to state concerning Mr. Thornton's previous communications to me should be made known to the same set of readers who have been reached by the article in question. About a month ago I called on Mr. Thornton, after having sent him a copy of my book, and asked him his opinion upon the correctness of the historical mater it contained. On that occasion, Mr. T. proceeded at once to the Mission question, and took exceptions to some of my views. I allowed him to go over the ground, explaining what he conceived to be my mistake, for an hour, perhaps. After all that had been said in an hour, I still found no reason the reverse my judgment in the main, and told him so. He then remarked that it was not singular that I had gotten such an impression from the stories or representatives of Col. Meek. In answer that that remark, I assured him at once, and plainly, that I had not taken Mr. Meek's views on the Mission subject at any time; that the only time when Mr. Meek had mentioned the Mission to me was when he related the incident of praying for a cow. 'And,' I said, 'I cannot swear to the truth of the story; I tell it as it was told to me; and that is all any biographer can attempt to.'

During this conversation with Thornton, Frances also summarized her methods of historical research:

I further said to Mr. Thornton that my course had been from the first in gathering material for my book, one of impartial hearing of all sides; that I had sought information far and wide, of all classes and denominations alike; that if there was aparty who had not had a fair hearing, it was their own fault. And I reminded Mr. Thornton that in former conversations with himself, in 1865, he had related to me what had contributed not a little to form some of the opinions he now took exception to. . . . What his object is (for I do not doubt he has an object more than appears in the criticism) I cannot pretend to know. It is enough for me to say that while I gave Mr. Meek's mountain stories as he furnished them to me, as the exponent of a class of man and style of living now passing away, and while I do not doubt the truth of them myself, leave them to the judgment of the public as the tales of a well-known mountain man—I claim something more than that for the historical sketches interwoven with the adventures. Having access to old files of papers—all the books previously written about the country and its history—private papers and public documents, it would be strange if, with a disposition to write the truth without fear or favor, I had not arrived at something approximating to it"

In conclusion I wish to state that in regard to the disposition finally of the estate of Ewing Young, I received both from Mr. Thornton and Judge Deady a correction which I immediately sent to my publishers, and which will appear in the next edition. Could any similar error be pointed out I am in honor bound to correct it. But while I feel this to be my duty, I do not feel that I ought to be expected to make a reply to any future attacks from such a pen as that wielded by Mr. Thornton.

By the time Frances Fuller Victor returned to Portland, Thornton had responded to her reply to the first installment of his review of *The River of the West*, published in the June 11number of the *Pacific Christian Advocate*. A third article, titled "Mrs. Victor Again and *The River of the West*," in the June 18 issue of the *Advocate* heaped additional censure on her and her books, as the following excerpts indicate:

Mrs. Victor had no right to indulge in a tone of complaint, and assuming the air of one injured, to inform her readers that while she does not know what object I had in view in criticizing her book, she does not doubt that I was seeking by indirection to arrive at one which is not visible to the

casual observer . . . . But it is not surprising that I should
thus be accused by one I have taken some pains to follow in
her tortuous policy along the by paths and crooked ways by
which she would possess herself of every ill natured rumor
which dressed in a pleasing style of agreeable speech would
enable her to malign Methodist preachers and especially the
Methodist Missionaries of Oregon.

But if she really desired to find some legitimate motive
for my criticism, she might well have imagined that I
regarded her book as a nuisance to public morals, as incul-
cating irreligious sentiments and opinions by sneering at
preachers; and especially at Methodist preachers . . . .

Then he consigned *The River of the West* to the oblivion he thought it
deserved:

. . . It is the office of the critic to expose such a vicious
taste in literature, to censure it as hostile to morality, to
correct whatever misrepresentation it may contain, and to
refute its sophisticated reasoning. This I did and nothing
more. I believe Mrs. Victor now understands what were my
motives.

The critic does a great service to the public who writes
down any vapid or useless publication such as ought never
to have appeared; he . . . . prevents people wasting both
their time and money upon floating trash that ought to be
permitted to hasten on to the sea of oblivion and the dead
past.

Though Frances was not surprised at Thornton's continuing attack,
she realized that it would take her several weeks to prepare for publication the documentary proof from the material she had gathered for the
writing of her book. But that would have to wait until she returned from
a projected trip to Salem as a traveling correspondent for the *Oregonian*.
That meant boarding a steamboat bound for Oregon City. On that June
day, she later reported, even the Willamette River lacked its usual charm
and she had wondered why so little poetry had been written in Oregon—surprisingly little when the character of the scenery is considered.

Then she explained the reason for Oregon's poetical deficiency:

> It is a country for an artist, not a poet, contrawise to California, which is a country for poets more than painters. In Oregon one sees—in California one *feels*, the beauty lavished abroad. True, there occasionally gets into the local paper a bit of rhyme, which, if not showing the hand of culture and genius, gives evidence of the stirrings of the subtle element called the poetical gift. And true, there has lately glinted on our appreciative vision rays from that diamond in the rough, the gifted, if not polished, Miller.[25]

On her way south, Frances had the opportunity again to visit Salem where previously she had stayed with Governor Woods and his wife, Louisa. The governor, who had been defeated in his bid for a second term, would in mid-September relinquish the office to a Democrat, Lafayette Grover, but planned to practice in the capital city.[26] In her "Summer Wanderings" column in the July 12 issue of the *Oregonian*, Frances described the city which, with its business, educational, and social advantages, would become "the great central city of the State fifty years from now." But if it did not, it would be because it was just next door to it.

A highlight of that June visit to Salem was accompanying an unnamed party to one of the several camp meetings then in progress in Marion and Polk counties. Her description of the Disciples of Christ meeting being "held by the Christian denomination (usually nicknamed Campbellites)" provided interesting reading material as well as an insight as to her own religious views.

The campground, located in a fine grove of firs, had been donated to the church for that purpose by the late Col. Ford. In the midst of the trees, Frances saw a structure for which she did not know the name—"all of the style called in architecture, rustic. . . .A tent it is not; nor a tabernacle, nor a church, and I do not like to call it a <u>shed</u>. I think I will manufacture a name and call it a *penumbraum.* Well, beneath this penumbraum is a pulpit and many benches—the latter usually well filled, as to numbers, and the former well filled as to zeal and talent."

That morning the pulpit was occupied by Sebastian C. Adams, minister of the Christian Church in Salem, "a ready and pleasing speaker and an amiable Christian gentleman," according to Frances, who found the meeting inspirational:[27]

> That 'the groves were God's first temples,' strikes one
> forcibly who has ever attended worship under circumstances
> like these. The devotional spirit comes much more easily
> and quickly, and with more power, in immediate contact
> with nature, than when coaxed and stimulated into exercise
> by the appliances of art. In the days when architecture was
> really and truly an art, this truth was realized; and those
> grand cathedrals which still remain the glory of Europe, in
> their pointed roofs and fretted arches, and long colon-
> nades—their deep shadows and chequered windows of col-
> ored glass, were made to express much of the solemn beauty
> of the forest, and in the presence of great Nature lift the
> heart above and away from mean or trivial considerations.

Soon after the close of the Christian camp meeting, heavy rain interfered with later camp meetings and disrupted Frances' plans to visit several places of interest in Marion, Linn, and Benton counties, and Siletz Bay and the Indian Agency on the coast. Instead, she returned to Portland where, to her distress, the temperature ranged from 98 to 102 degrees during the first week of July. To escape the heat, she and her friends traveled to St. Helens for a Fourth of July picnic, according to her "Summer Wanderings."[28]

During this time, she had been working on her reply to Thornton, which she titled "*The River of the West* Vindicated," and which the *Oregonian* published on the July 14 and 15 front pages. Before introducing her documentary evidence, she stated her reasons for publishing it:

> For the enlightenment of that portion of the public who
> may have read Mr. Thornton's attack upon me, as author of
> *The River of the West*, wherein he charges me with gross false-
> hoods, and also with subsequent falsehoods uttered to my
> reply to his *Review*, I have thought it best to publish one of

Mr. Thornton's letters to me, and to follow that by some documents furnished me in 1865 by Mr. Harvey, the late son-in-law of Dr. John McLoughlin. As a bit of history, these papers are interesting; and certainly they confirm any statement I have made or opinion I have uttered in my book on this subject. I had, and hope I still have, when they can be found, other letters of Mr. Thornton's concerning *Mission* matters, which will go to show whether or not he contributed anything to my opinions in the matter he is so vituperative over.

Then Frances cited Thornton's letter to her, dated September 8, 1865, in which he had praised Dr. McLoughlin and put in a word for himself. She noted that this was Thornton's testimony to McLoughlin's "integrity and benevolence" before she cited a document prepared by McLoughlin in which he recounted encroachments by members of the Methodist Mission on his land claim at Oregon City. As she penned this concluding paragraph she hoped they would be the last words on her controversy with J. Quinn Thornton concerning her historical veracity:[29]

If Mr. Thornton believes what he has himself emphatically stated concerning the unimpeachable integrity of Dr. McLoughlin, he could not attempt to deny the truthfulness of the above statements by Dr. McLoughlin's own, or his attorney's hand. These, statements, if true, show that in *The River of the West* there have been no exaggerations of facts—certainly no falsifying them, in my account of the Mission affairs at Oregon City. There is no partisan spirit in my book, and, whatever its other faults may be, it is fearless and independent. It is with reluctance that I have taken up the instrument 'mightier than the sword,' in my own defense, but since I am fairly compelled to it by an infamous charge against my veracity, I shall not lay it down again until the right is vindicated. Truly, I do not wish to irritate the feelings of any class of men, but if I am forced to produce other documents to substantiate my former statements, I fear there are those now rejoicing in having got a first-class anathematizer upon the track of *The River of the West*, who will be brought to exclaim, 'Save me from my friends, and I will take care of my enemies!'

F. F. Victor.

Now that her rebuttal to Thornton's attack on *The River of the West* was in print, Frances Fuller Victor prepared for a long delayed journey—an excursion to Olympia to examine Elwood Evans' Pacific Northwest historical collection and to observe western Washington Territory first-hand. It had once been part of the Oregon Country and would always remain a part of Oregon's early history. On July 18, a local news item in the *Oregonian* announced that "Mrs. F. F. Victor will start this morning on a tour to Puget Sound and British Columbia. Readers of the *Oregonian* may expect to see some useful and entertaining letters from her pen, the fruits of her usually close observation and discriminating judgment."

After a six hour voyage by steamer from Portland to Monticello on the Washington side of the Columbia River, Olympia-bound passengers found several stages waiting for them at the landing to carry them and the mail to the territorial capital. Intense competition among the drivers enabled travelers to be transported to Olympia for $4.00 each. In her front page "Summer Wanderings" column, dated July 17, 1870, Frances recounted her experiences and offered advice to ladies planning to make a similar journey.

As a member of a party of five, including the driver, she had set off at 2:00 A.M. in an uncovered wagon with three wide seats, pulled by two stout horses. The seats had been "pretty well loaded with mail matter and freight before taking on passengers." Since neither she nor the lady who occupied the second seat had sun umbrellas, they hoisted "a large cotton affair," which soon wearied them. Fortunately, "a gentleman in the back seat volunteered to carry it, and thus all three had the benefit of a partial shelter." She warned ladies without sun umbrellas that there was no certainty of their "meeting with so polite and patient a gentleman. A warm dress with a linen duster over it, a heavy shawl for morning and evenings, and a sun hat and sun umbrella are required for comfort."

Frances reported that the road followed the Cowlitz River bank for several miles before beginning the ascent of the Cowlitz Mountains. During the 17 miles over the mountain road, she was struck by the abominable condition of the road and the magnificence of the timber. In fact, she "would not have missed crossing the mountain for a pretty sum."

Then she added:

> Such a forest as this is something to remember having seen, and fills our conceptions of solemn and stupendous grandeur. Fir and cedar are the principal trees. They stand thickly upon the ground, are as straight as Ionian columns, so high it is an effort to look to the top of them, and so large that their diameter corresponds admirably with their height. If there is anything in nature for which I have an affection resembling love to human creatures, it is for a fine tree. The god Pan and the old Druidical religion are intelligible to me as an expression of the human soul struggling 'through nature up to nature's God;'—and as a religion free from arrogance and the temptation to built upon worldly ambition, it will bear recommendation even in the nineteenth century. Being a lover of the woods, I could not but enjoy this splendid forest, both in the aesthetical and religious point of view.

However, the stage broke down about seven miles from the lodging for the night. Passengers had to walk over bad sections of the road and amuse themselves watching the driver repair the stage and lock its wheels with rope. It was 8:00 P.M. before the stage pulled up at Pumphrey's Landing at the head of navigation for canoes on the Cowlitz River. After a satisfying supper, with a cup of coffee, they rode in the chill darkness over a rough road through an awesome forest to McDonald's on the edge of the first prairie. Here the benumbed passengers relished a good breakfast before a fire blazing in an open fireplace.

Nine miles beyond McDonald's, the stage crossed the Chehalis River, and Frances saw a signboard advertising the nearby Claquato Academy. After the second crossing of the Chehalis River, the stage entered the Grand Mound Prairie, from which she enjoyed views of Mt. Rainier—"the grandest snow peak of the Cascade Range." Though it hurt her "patriotic Oregon pride" to admit it, she realized that Rainier is the chief of the snow peaks, and the one altogether lovely."

At the head of the Sound where the Des Chutes falls into its waters, Frances could see the small lumbering town of Tumwater, which was really a suburb of Olympia. Passing through the town, the stage soon drew up in the classically named territorial capital, described in her July 17 letter to the *Oregonian*:

> Olympia depends upon its location for its claim to beauty. Like all towns cut out of the forest it is rough in its primitive aspect, and has to contend with stumps, fallen timber and burnt trees unfallen. Still, it is a cheerful looking place, with pleasant houses, good sidewalks, and the longest and most delightful bridges! In time it must become a second Venice. The habits of the people are eminently social, and the tone of its society good. Its business is not of the noisy and bustling kind of the lumbering towns. There are large and commodious wharves, but as yet little commerce . . . .
>
> What interests me most in Olympia is the historical library of Hon. Elwood Evans, to whom the future state of Washington is going to be immeasurably indebted for a collection of books already very rare. Mr. Evans has taken pains to collect every volume by every author relating to the Pacific Coast. Those which could not be obtained in the United States have been procured by orders sent to London. All the matter printed in newspapers referring to the early history of Oregon and Washington has been carefully preserved and as carefully arranged for reference. I do not know of anyone in Oregon who has anything so extensive a collection of such matter; and I would suggest that the Portland Library Association is the proper party to commence and prosecute the work of collecting similar material for Oregon. By advertising, no doubt a great many valuable books and papers might be obtained for preservation which are now lying in dusty corners of old pioneer houses, and which will be destroyed as waste paper by the rising generation, if not secured in the lifetime of the present one.

During her few days in Olympia, Frances Fuller Victor haunted the Evans' library and Mrs. Evans took her on a popular drive to Chambers's Prairie. Divided into farms where newly cut hay had been gathered into windrows, it had been named for "its first settler, a 'colored individual' from Missouri, who had for his wife a white woman." He had also planted the oldest orchard in the region.

Cool and showery weather denied Frances the best views of the mountains and the pleasure of clam-bakes as well as boating and riding parties. She commented on "the railroad fever" raging in Olympia and warned its residents that with "a railroad train arriving two or three times a day they will find their pleasant socialities departing." She met acquaintances from Portland, Walla Walla, and Astoria, and when she attended the Presbyterian Church that Sunday, she had never seen a more stylish looking congregation north of San Francisco.

Happily anticipating her first voyage on Puget Sound, Frances, armed with letters of introduction by Evans, boarded the elegant, 180-foot sidewheel steamer *Olympia*, bound for its weekly run from Olympia to Victoria, British Columbia. The *Olympia* first docked at Seattle, the largest town on the Sound. It was, Frances, pronounced, "a city set on a hill that cannot be hid." She reported several ships loading and unloading and "a great buzz and whirr of mills in operation." From the landing she could see on the very brow of the hill a large courthouse and an enormous hotel signboard, proclaiming Seattle the "Western Terminus." However, in spite of its busy appearance, Seattle did not impress Frances as pleasantly as Olympia. She also thought Port Madison, the next stop, a prettier town, located as it was in a grove of maple trees on a less abrupt hillside. After stops at other mill towns like Port Gamble and Port Ludlow, the steamer paused at Port Townsend, seat of the U.S. Custom Service, and then entered the Strait of Juan de Fuca where Frances could see the New Dungeness lighthouse to the south and the archipelago of San Juan to the north. She was reminded of the continuing dispute between the United States and Great Britain concerning the possession of the largest island, San Juan, still jointly occupied by military encampments of the two countries. Settlement of the conflicting boundary claims awaited a decision on the best passage for ships among the island into the Gulf of Georgia. The United States contended that the channel to the west of San Juan Island was more desirable. After studying the dispute, Frances advised her Oregon readers that from "the appearance of the channels as represented on the best maps we have it would seem that the British claims are unfounded."[30]

While the *Olympia* headed for Victoria Harbor, Frances reveled in views of the snow-covered peaks of Mount Rainier and Mount Baker to the east, the rugged Olympian Range to the south, and the rocky shore of Vancouver Island to the north. In Victoria, she registered at the St. George Inn, which she designated "the best ordered hotel north of the southern boundary of Oregon." Its attentive host, clean room, comfortable bed, immaculate table linen, and delectable meals brightened her visit to the capital of the Crown Colony of British Columbia. Here she met other travelers like herself and was well positioned to observe the present condition of the city.

Following the collapse of the Fraser River mines, the fortunes of Victoria has stagnated and had continued to do so when Vancouver Island and the mainland were united in 1866 to form the new Crown Colony. In 1870 at the time of Frances' visit, Sir James Douglas, the first governor of the colony, was living in retirement in Victoria. Now a tall, impressive 67-year-old man with an aristocratic bearing, the former chief factor of the Hudson's Bay Company, was a familiar figure on the quiet streets of the small city. While there, Frances had the pleasure of "hearing his reminiscences of early times."[31] He recounted his overland journey from Fort Vancouver on the Columbia River to Vancouver Island when the Hudson's Bay Company had transferred its business in 1849. In speaking of his friend and former colleague, Dr. McLoughlin, Sir James declared that "he had never known his equal in genuine goodness of heart and forbearance under circumstances of great trial."

From "table talk" and the morning papers, Frances soon learned that Victorians were agitating for a railroad with as much fervor as the Americans in the Pacific Northwest. In spite of the poor financial state of the Crown Colony, there was widespread demand for building a Canadian Pacific Railway from the St. Lawrence River in the East to the Gulf of Georgia in the West. In hope of hastening its construction, many people in Victoria advocated either confederation with Canada or annexation by the United States. By tactfully questioning those whom she met, Frances discovered that three out of four preferred confederation. Property owners, suffering as they were from continuing depreciation of their property, favored annexation. Government officials were among the majority who opposed it.

In her strolls around the city, Frances, always an enthusiastic walker, discovered a photographic gallery. Here the owner gave her permission to inspect his albums of scenes around Victoria and the Fraser River country. Thus, she was able "without fatigue to see some of the wildest and most beautiful scenery on the continent." She concluded that "the scenery of the Fraser is a combination of the Columbia and the Colorado." Frances also stopped at a bookstore displaying many works about the Northwest, especially British possessions. In exploring dry goods stores, she found them "handsomely fitted out with show goods fit for a large city." Patrons were chiefly the aristocratic class connected with the government and American visitors taking advantage of the chance to purchase coveted articles for less than they could at home. Frances searched for "a good specimen of the slate carvings done by the Queen Charlotte Island natives." But finding only "some very clumsy and badly executed pipes," she ended her quest for native art.

On the day of her departure, Frances enjoyed an eight-mile excursion around the head of Esquimalt Bay before boarding the steamship *California* for Portland, where she arrived the evening of July 30.[32] During the last two weeks she had added immeasurably to her knowledge of the geography and history of the Pacific Northwest. Now she had only to pen the last of her travel letters for the *Oregonian*, on which she intended to base her next book, in part.

Frances Fuller Victor spent August, September, and the first week of October in Portland, preparing for this new publishing venture. In order to improve her knowledge of railroading and stage coaching, she decided to make an overland journey all the way to San Francisco. There she hoped to find a publisher and renew her acquaintance with Bret Harte, editor of *The Overland Monthly*, to whom she intended to submit her first western short story, "Mr. Ela's Story." Along the way, she intended to bring her Oregon friends up-to-date on her adventures. That meant leaving Joe Meek to canvass for subscriptions to *The River of the West*, still selling well, perhaps because of her controversy with J. Quinn Thornton.

Confident that she had a second successful book in the making, Frances boarded a car of the Oregon Central Railroad in Portland. Her first stop was Salem where, for a few weeks, the capital city had been the end of the railroad line while track-laying progressed slowly south to Albany and Eugene City. After a two-day visit, she continued south in a coach of the California and Oregon Stage Company.[33] She found it crowded inside with four gentlemen and two ladies with children; several men were perched on top with the driver. As the stage rolled toward Albany, the scene was enlivened by the sight and sound of Chinese track-layers at work.

Following the supper stop at Albany, Frances was the only inside passenger for the night ride to Eugene City under a brilliant moon. Shortly, a gentleman whom she had once met descended from the top of the coach and asked permission to share the inside back seat. Pleased to have company, she welcomed him, only to be subjected to a lecture on the mysteries of creation. When the stage reached the Eugene Hotel at 4:00 A.M., the gentleman disappeared,[34] and Frances welcomed a day of rest before boarding the stagecoach for Yoncalla. She was the only passenger on a cold, bright morning and was glad to huddle under a blanket until the sun warmed the atmosphere and she was able to join the loquacious driver on the box for a better view of the colorful autumn landscape. She had hoped to talk to Jesse Applegate about her forthcoming book, but, unhappily, he was not at home. After spending the night with his family, she resumed her trip and was glad that two fellow inside passengers could help to balance the coach as it swayed and pitched over the rough mountain road.

At Oakland, Frances began another night ride. By the light of a full moon, she observed with great interest an area of Oregon she knew only from oral or written sources. At Roseburg, the stag stopped briefly, then proceeded on to the breakfast stop at Canyonville at the entrance of the Umpqua Canyon. Here she recalled the perilous passage of one party of early emigrants, who had been nearly swept away as they struggled through the torrents of waist-high water, rushing over the road every mile of the way.

Beyond the Umpqua Canyon, in Cow Creek and Grave Creek valleys, she observed abandoned cabins and discarded rockers and sluice boxes scattered about the terrain—mute evidence of the turbulent gold-rush years in Southern Oregon. After traveling in view of the Rogue River for over an hour, the stage entered the village of Rocky Point about 8:00 P.M. Here on the bank of the Rogue River, the traveler dined at a place so inviting that Frances regretted that she could not stop over for a day. Oregonians like Mr. Ela had told her that the Rogue River Valley was paradise. Now she believed him.

From Rocky Point the road to Jacksonville was level, though dusty. About 8:00 P.M. the stage pulled into the historic mining town; then, after an hour's delay, resumed the journey with a full load of passengers. Ahead lay the dreaded night ride to California over the Siskiyou Mountains—a fearful grade of six miles up and six miles down. But Frances enjoyed "the sublimity of the rugged heights, the gloomy shadows of the depths, the intense brilliancy of the heavens" in the moonlight as well as the autumn colors on the mountain sides after sunrise.

At the foot of the Siskiyous, the travelers were revived by an ample breakfast at Cole's Station and the knowledge that travel would be easier after crossing the Klamath River on the way to Yreka, California. Here Frances looked to the mountain range to the east for a view of famed Mt. Shasta, but saw only its triple summit above the morning mist.[35] Yreka, where she had hoped to lay over for a rest, was swarming with visitors enjoying the county fair; and at the suggestion of the stage driver she continued on to a place called Forest Home. Here, amid "plenty and pleasantness," she relished a quiet twenty-four hours which prepared her for another three successive day and night rides through the rugged terrain of northern California. At daylight of the fourth day, she arrived at Chico, then the end of the railroad line being rapidly extended north to the Oregon border. Frances boarded the waiting train with relief. Though fatigued, her strenuous and scenic journey had provided her with the makings of a first-person, western article.

FRANCES FULLER VICTOR

Suskiyou Tollhouse on the rod wouh from Ashland to Yreka, California.
ORHI 61491

By the end of October, Frances Fuller Victor was back in San Francisco, comfortably settled in the home of long-time friends. Here, in undisturbed privacy, she hoped to finish her new book, which she had already titled *All Over Oregon and Washington*. She also hoped to write for *The Overland Monthly*. But when she called on Bret Harte at the magazine's office, she was both delighted and disappointed. He advised her that her first fictional contribution, "Mr. Ela's Story," would appear in the December, 1870 number, and she would receive $30.00.[36] Then he revealed that he had just resigned as editor of the magazine and would soon depart for the East. He admitted that he could not resist the lucrative offers he had received from eastern literary journals since the publication of his *Plain Language from Truthful James*, popularly known as *The Heathen Chinee*.Frances was not surprised. She had seen broadsides of his poem being hawked on the streets of San Francisco.[37]

But news that her mentor was leaving San Francisco dismayed her. It had been his novelette, *M'Liss*, featured in the *Golden Era* in 1863 that had made her realize how passé her sentimental stories were. At the time, she had resolved to publish no more fiction until she could write from her own observations and experiences, using western characters and settings. Now he was urging her to submit more stories to the magazine, even though he was leaving. However, Frances knew that *The Overland Monthly* had been sold to the publisher of the San Francisco *Commercial Herald*, John H. Carmany, and hoped that after Harte's departure, he would maintain the same policies and literary standards. On November 19, the San Francisco *Bulletin's* front-page review of the December, 1870 *Overland Monthly*, merely stated: "The stories, of which there are three, are unusually good." Though the names of the authors and titled of the stories were omitted, Frances resolved to contribute both short stories and essays to the *Overland* in order to support herself while she was writing and publishing *All Over Oregon and Washington*, and to keep her name before the public.

CHAPTER 8

A VENTURE IN
PUBLISHING

(1871-72)

O N NEW YEAR'S DAY, 1871, Frances Fuller Victor read a favorable
newspaper account of a public lecture on woman suffrage delivered by Abigail Jane Duniway of Albany, Oregon. Frances would later
learn that Mrs. Duniway had come to San Francisco to transact
millinery business and attend the January convention of the California
Woman Suffrage Society as a delegate of the Equal Suffrage Association of Salem, the first such association in Oregon.[1] Frances had heard
of its founding from her friend, Belle Cooke. One of its most active
members, Mrs. Cooke had praised her friend, Abigail, for her devotion
to the movement for the past two years. Though generally sympathetic
to the woman rights movement, France Fuller Victor had been preoccupied with personal and publishing matters. Now she looked forward to
following the sessions of the forthcoming second convention in the San
Francisco *Evening Bulletin*.[2] There is no evidence that Frances attended
any of the sessions, but she doubtless noted that the delegates had tendered a vote of thanks to Oregon for having sent a delegate and that
Emily Pitts-Stevens was the owner and publisher of *The Pioneer*, the first
newspaper in San Francisco dedicated to woman rights.[3] Abigail Scott
Duniway soon would emulate Emily Pitts-Stevens with a newspaper of
her own in Portland.

On a foggy morning on January 25 the delegates gathered in a room
in Dashaway Hall with Elizabeth T. Schenck, vice-president of the
National Woman Suffrage Society in New York City, presiding. Chief
architect of the California Woman Suffrage Society, she had been presi-

dent during its first year. In the afternoon session, after disposing of the details of organizing the convention, the delegates elected Emily Pitts-Stevens to succeed Mrs. Schenck as president.

On the second day the delegates, some of whom were men, voted on several resolutions. They commended the Board of Regents of the University of California for offering the educational facilities of the institution to both sexes. They passed three resolutions critical of masculine control of government. Another two resolutions concerned the two existing national societies—the American Woman Suffrage Association, headquartered in Boston, and the National Woman Suffrage Society in New York City, organized by Elizabth Cady Stanton, Susan B. Anthony, Lucretia Mott, and others.[4] The delegates were critical of the American Woman Suffrage Association for spurning the offer of consolidation, tendered by the National Woman Suffrage Society, and resolved to remain independent of all national associations until they were unified. On the third and last day, the delegates censured local newspapers for their coverage of the convention. Only the *Bulletin* was credited with having reported the business of the meetings daily. In closing the convention, President Pitts-Stevens advised the delegates that a truthful report of the convention proceedings would be published in the next number of *The Pioneer.* Just before adjournment, the delegates tendered a vote of thanks to Oregon for sending a delegate. But Abigail Duniway was not there to enjoy the recognition. She had been summoned home by her husband before the convention had opened, but not before she had decided to emulate Emily Pitts-Stevens in Portland.[5]

Thus was Frances Fuller Victor introduced to the younger and more militant Mrs. Duniway. These two strong-minded women would soon meet. From the outset, Mrs. Duniway was critical of Mrs. Victor's failure to embrace the woman rights movement enthusiastically; but they respected each other's talent and ultimately helped each other on occasion.

In the meantime, Frances had written and submitted to Bret Harte her last contribution before his departure on February 2 aboard the overland train to Chicago.[6] Supporters of the city's literary journal, *The Lakeside Monthly*, had urged Harte to become its editor. Two weeks after his departure, while reading the *Bulletin's* review of the March, 1871 number of *The Overland Monthly*, Frances was heartened by a statement about the magazine's future: "Mr. Harte is gone, but the *Overland* remains. If it has lost its gifted editor its goodly corps of contributors to whom its success in the past has been so largely due, continue in its service." As an example, the reviewer characterized Frances' "A Short Stay in Acapulco" as "a fine piece of descriptive writing."

Published in the same number was a piece by Frances Fuller Victor's new friend, Josephine Clifford, who was Bret Harte's secretary and a writer in her own right. Harte had employed the gifted and attractive young widow as his assistant the previous year after he published her first *Overland* article, "Down Among the Dead Letters." In the December, 1869 number. Reading it in Oregon, Frances had been captivated with Mrs. Clifford's account of her experiences as a clerk in the dead letter office in Washington, D.C. Earlier that year, Mrs. Clifford had been impressed with Mrs. Victor's first two contributions to the *Overland*: "Manifest Destiny in the West" and "The Search for Fretum Anian." When Frances arrived in San Francisco in the fall of 1870, the women became friends, though their origins scarcely could have been more diverse.

Josephine was born at the Castle of Petershaven on the bank of the Wesier River in Prussia. Her mother, the Baroness Charlotte Von Ende, was a member of a noble German family. Her father was part German and part English. He had been born in Hanover, then a possession of England, and had served under the Duke of Wellington at the Battle of Waterloo in 1815. After the birth of their daughter, Josephine, they had migrated to the United States. Here she had been educated and married Clifford, a U. S. Army officer.[7] After the Civil War, she had accompanied him while he served in forts on the frontier in Arizona and New Mexico. Following a successful Indian uprising, Josephine had been held captive until she managed to escape, only to find that Clifford and disappeared. Presuming him dead, she had joined her mother, brother, and sister in San Francisco to begin a new life, part of which was her responsible position at *The Overland Monthly*.

Frances Fuller Victor's good fortune continued. In February she received word from Elisha Bliss that the Columbia Book Company would soon issue an 1871 printing of her *The River of the West*.[8] Sales of the book had surpassed expectations, exhausting the 1870 printings. She was jubilant! Not only would she continue to receive royalty payments, but Joe Meek could continue to earn good money by canvassing for sales of his biography in the Pacific Northwest—and for her new book when she got it into print.

Encouraged by the success of *The River of the West*, Frances decided to return to Oregon to update her information on various areas of the state and to secure sufficient financial commitment from Oregonians concerned with the economic development of the state to enable her to interest an Eastern publisher in her proposed book. Before her departure, Carmany paid her $36.00 for her second *Overland* short story, "On the Mexican Border," scheduled for inclusion in the May, 1871 number. She also received from Bliss the first issue of *The American Publisher*, the monthly trade magazine of the American Publishing Company. It promoted books published by the company and its subsidiaries and contained ideas on subscription-book publishing.[9] In this April, 1871 number, Frances discovered a review of her *The River of the West* and a reprinting of her poem, "Sunset at the Mouth of the Columbia." In response, she sent Bliss an article entitled, "A Stage Ride in Oregon and Washington," the first half of which appeared in the August, 1871 number of the magazine.

Frances arrived in Portland on April 17 aboard the steamship *Oriflamme* which, by coincidence, carried in its cargo the printing press for Abigail Duniway's new newspaper, *The New Northwest*. After plans to bring *The Pioneer* to Portland were abandoned, Mrs. Duniway decided to launch her own woman rights paper in the city.[10]

When the first issue of *The New Northwest* emerged from the press on May 5, Frances was in St. Helens. Here Joe Meek called on her to celebrate the new printing of *The River of the West* and to arrange for his subscription-sales canvassing in other parts of the Pacific Northwest.[11] Later that month Frances returned to Portland and, to keep her name and her ideas before the public, began to write for a new newspaper there. This was the *Democratic Era*, founded by Urban E. Hicks, a long-time Oregon newspaperman. Her initial contribution was an essay, entitled "The Romance and Poetry of Oregon," in which she recycled images she had introduced in a "Summer Wanderings" article in the *Oregonian*—presenting California as "a girlish Cleopatra" and Oregon as "a young Anthony."[12] Then she lamented that since [William Cullen] Bryant, "the greatest American poet," had written of the Columbia as "the Oregon," very little poetry about the state had appeared. As a result, one of her own poems, "Sunset at the Mouth of the Columbia" had been repeatedly copied. After a brief overview of the romantic episodes in Oregon's past, she asked: "Has Oregon no native poet or painter, no genius fired by the splendor of his surroundings to represent worthily the spirit of this country?" She would answer this question at the end of the book on which she was now working. In her essay, she simply noted that "Oregon ought to have a literature of its own of a very high order."

This remark caught the attention of the fledgling editor, Abigail Duniway, who reprinted it in the *New Northwest*. In her editorial comment, Mrs. Duniway lauded Frances Fuller Victor before waxing critical:[13]

> Our present issue contains a graphic picture from the pen
> of Mrs. Victor, copied from the *Democratic Era*. We have
> looked in vain over all our exchanges for anything that will
> compare with the literary excellence, beauty of fancy, or
> originality of conception. We are proud of Mrs. Victor,
> but we are sorry she uses her magic power to lend grace
> and interest to the columns of a journal which disclaims
> the claim of woman to the free exercise of her inherent
> immunities, and thus debars discussion from his journal
> because he has more important topics to talk about than
> the best interests of the human family.

Frances responded with an article entitled, "The Woman Question," which Hicks published in the May 25 issue of the *Democratic Era*. The following opening paragraphs of her first known public statement on woman suffrage reveal her disapproval of the aggressive militancy of some promoters of the cause:

> Once the most momentous question a woman had to answer was—'Will you marry me?' But when, now-a-days, that other question—'Are you a Woman Rights woman?' is plumped at one at unexpected times and in inappropriate places our answer is not always ready.
>
> The aggressive manner, the 'Stand and deliver your opinion' air with which one is assaulted, makes the greater portion of the difficulty. And yet the question itself is one not at all easy to answer in a definite manner . . . .
>
> Perhaps it is right that people should demand from us . . . .a perfect opinion of a vastly important moral and social question. But the subject is so large, so long, and so broad, in its many points of view, that it would be a liberal education to have canvassed it thoroughly, involving as it does all the interests of humanity— religious, moral, social, and political. We do not yet feel prepared to say whether we shall insist upon our 'rights' or not.
>
> It does, we confess, seem absurd to attach gender to the question of human rights. Absolutely and without prejudice, one human being, can have no rights which do not belong equally to all other human beings, circumstances being equal. Circumstances! Aye, there's the rub. Expediency or inexpediency, after all, must ever govern the question of rights . . . . The Suffrage is the one great right for which women are now contending, and whether they are justified in demanding it or not depends upon its expediency, and that alone . . . .

At this point, Frances came close to committing herself fully:

> The present desire of women for political rights is founded in their conviction that without the franchise they have

no individual existence; and that without an individual existence it is vain to attempt the accomplishment of any worthy object . . . .If, then, women, having found out that there is work for them, good paying work in which both inclination and profit are united, wish to be made politically alive . . . we do not know of any good and sufficient reason why they should not begin to exist in this new sense.

We say we do not know of any sufficient reason. Now that commits us to the affirmative side of the Woman's Rights question, doe it not? . . . .If enfranchisement will secure to them any important good, such as higher education, better social positions, larger pay for competent work, more full and perfect home influence, and greater happiness, then there is ground enough for their demand . . . .

Frances then developed the reasons for the objections of men to the enfranchisement of women. But to the end, she maintained ambivalence concerning her final decision:

Have we committed ourself on the question? If we have, we do not know it, but like that ostrich with its head in a bush, imagine ourself hidden. If too doubting or too uninformed to have an opinion, we know that we would not lay a straw in the way of any woman striving to reach higher toward an earthly or heavenly good.

In the June 2 issue of the *New Northwest*, Mrs. Duniway responded sarcastically to parts of Frances Fuller Victor's essay:

The *Democratic Era* is the most readable paper we get. Its articles upon the woman question are more voluminous and very nearly as good as our own. We sometimes think that it is hardly necessary to run two equal rights organs in the community and have almost made up our mind to propose consolidation.

If offended by Frances' modest stand on the question, that did not deter Mrs. Duniway from reassembling and reprinting selected passages from Mrs. Victor's essays that conformed to the former's opinions. This collection, titled "Mrs. Victor's Views," she published in the same issue of the *Era*.

Needing the good will and support of all regional publishers, Frances did not respond. Rather she turned her attention to updating her information about Oregon and Washington and seeking financial assistance for the publication of her projected book. In July she sojourned at Clatsop Beach.[14] "No one is presumed to be in fashion, who has not been to Clatsop Beach," she wrote, "therefore to Clatsop we are going – have gone." On July 17, the *Oregonian*, under the heading of "Seaside Items," noted that "yesterday the steamer *U.S. Grant* took a party of pleasure seekers to Young's River falls," and that "today the steamer *Varuna* took a party to Cape Disappointment at the entrance of the Columbia on the Washington side of the river, among whom was 'Mrs. Victor, who is collecting material for her new book'."

Frances Fuller Victor's adventures there were detailed in her article, "About the Mouth of the Columbia," published in the January, 1872 number of the *Overland Monthly*. Her party had visited Fort Canby at the harbor of Baker's Bay and the fortifications near the summit of the cape. Here all has been "militarily neat;" but Frances had been more impressed with views of the ocean and the surf dashing over the bar. Even more exciting had been climbing the steep steps to the lighthouse on Cape Disappointment. From its iron balcony, where the keeper polished the glass of the powerful light, he pointed out Shoalwater in Washington Territory to the north. At Frances' request he pointed out the location of Peacock Spit, scene of the wreck of the U. S. S. *Peacock* in 1841, and South Spit, some two miles outside the Cape, where the U.S.S. *Shark* had been lost in 1846. The party also visited Fort. Stevens on the Oregon side at the mouth of the Columbia, "one of the strongest and best armed on the Pacific Coast," and saw the mouth of the river on which Lewis and Clark and their party had wintered in a log hut late in 1805 and early 1806.

After a brief stop in Astoria, Frances departed for Portland on the *Dixie Thompson*, one of two elegant sternwheelers built that year to serve the increasing number of visitors to resorts in the area. En route she gathered current information with which to update her coverage of the settlement and commercial development of both sides of the lower Columbia. Her observations, beginning at Cathlamet, a salmon fishery on the Washington side, and Westport, a fishery and cannery on the Oregon side, are recorded in her article, "From Astoria to the Cascades," published in the February, 1872 number of *The Overland Monthly*. In this article, she speculated on lumbering and railroading on both sides of the Columbia, as well as the location of the future city that would distribute the commerce of the country. At St. Helens, which Frances thought would profit from the building of the railroad, she was overcome by memories of the grief and frustration she had suffered because of Henry's actions and the collapse of their plans for St. Helens' development. "'Hope deferred maketh the heart sick' has been its fortune from first to last," she wrote.

By August, refreshed from her voyage, Frances was back in Portland to finish her book. But first she tried to interest Portland businessmen in subsidizing a portion of the cost of its publication in the East. On the 19th she wrote Judge Deady to this effect:[15]

> I have been wishing to speak to you on a matter of business, and would have done so when you called, but for the interruptions. I went so far as to mention my intention of publishing a book—*All Over Oregon and Washington*—but did not get into detail.
>
> The book will be about 400 pages, and with a dozen or so illustrations. It is general in its nature, descriptive, gossipy, historical, and with enough of statistics to impress the reader with the possibilities and actualities of the country; and with enough about what is to be *seen* to attract tourists. Such, at all events, has been my aim.
>
> It has cost me considerable effort, time and money so far, and now in order to get the work where it will do good—that is, into print—will require more of all these, and certainly more money. I have seen several gentlemen of

the Board of mmigration and the Chamber of Commerce, but all say there are no funds which can be used for such a work as this of mine. Very well, then men who have money and interests in the State, should put their hands in their pockets and produce a fund for this special pocket. Nordhoff's *California* settled half that state, and set tourists on going there. I want $500 just not to go at once to eastern publishers with the book and see it rhough the press. It ought to be twice that amount, but perhaps I can manage with that, *and argument*. I do not know how to approach businessmen, or who to select to approach. Could you aid me in this matter? Would not some of your friends among rich business men see the point? I put this request in writing because I am not sure of an opportunity to talk it over even should I call in person. Mrs. Gaston is very anxious I should go East with her the first of the coming week, and I am equally anxious to get about publishing. Please let me know your mind about speaking to other gentlemen . . . .

While awaiting a reply from Deady, Frances sent *The New Northwest* a clever essay, titled "All About Looking Glasses." An amusing description of household mirrors, true and crooked, it concluded with a consideration of the need for a true mirror in the head and for moral mirrors of true friends who encourage but do not over-praise. Abigail Duniway used Frances' contribution to fill most of the first two columns on the first page of the August 25th issue.

Though mainly engaged in writing and promoting *All Over Oregon and Washington* during the summer and fall of 1871, Frances noted the vigorous Woman Suffrage campaign conducted in Portland and other Pacific Northwest towns. Near the end of August, Susan B. Anthony arrived from San Francisco in Portland, where she was scheduled to give a series of lectures on Woman Suffrage during the first two weeks of September. In welcoming Miss Anthony to Oregon, Abigail Scott Duniway presented her with a plan of lecture tours in Oregon, Washington Territory, and Victoria, British Columbia. In appreciation, Miss Anthony agreed that Mrs. Duniway should manage the tours and receive one half of the gross receipts of the sales of lecture tickets.[16] The Portland audience received Miss Anthony's first lecture, "Power of the Ballot," enthusiastically; and newspaper notices were mostly favorable. Among Miss Anthony's critics, J.Quinn Thornton, writing in the *Pacific Christian Advocate*, was the most vehement. The most encouraging and constructive comments appeared in the *Oregonian*, edited by Harvey Scott, Mrs. Duniway's brother.[17]

Frances Fuller Victor may have attending one or more of Miss Anthony's lectures in Portland, but in September she was deeply engaged in her own literary work. That month she completed a substantial portion of *All Over Oregon and Washington* and sent an article on Oregon Indians to *The Overland Monthly*. The October 3 *Oregonian* published this notice praising her work:

> In the October *Overland* appears the first of a series of articles by Mrs. Victor on the Oregon Indians. Much research is evinced in its preparation. Mrs. Victor's doing much to fix and give permanency to the recollection of events of long ago in Oregon history. Her efforts are timely, for many of these events are fast becoming traditions merely, and are seen and heard but dimly 'through the dark backward and abysm of time.'

Four days later, Frances, apparently remembering a conversation she had with a fellow passenger aboard the *Dixie* about a new townsite, Columbia City, decided to invest in it, as some of her St. Helens friends had already done. In the Multnomah County courthouse, she signed a document in which Mary C. Holman and her husband, Dillard, bonded themselves for $660.00 to carry out an agreement to sell her 12 lots on their as yet unsurveyed land. The property consisted of 20 acres of the original donation land claim of Jacob Caples, once an agent for Henry C. Victor. Notably, it was bounded on the north by B.F. Giltner's land; on the south by Sebastian C. Adams' land, and on the west by land owned by James McBride and B.F. Giltner. If Frances did not intend to live here she hoped to profit from the sale of the land. Her action further suggests that she was not without funds, as is so often stated.

About the time she concluded her land deal, she received the October, 1871 number of *The American Publisher*, Bliss' trade magazine. It included the Joe Meek story she had written to help Bliss promote *The River of the West*, then in its third 1871 printing.[18] She had narrated the tale as it supposedly unfolded in the home of Mrs. W. [Williams], where she and the hero of her book, *The River of the West*, had "chanced" to be visiting. When "the lady of the house" urged them to accompany her to a festival of the church of which she was a member, "the old mountain man" excused himself, "saying that festivals of this sort were not much in his line." When Mrs. W. persisted that he come along and tell a Rocky Mountain tale, Colonel Meek responded that he would be as badly frightened of "all those ladies" as he had been when President Polk introduced him to Mrs. Polk.

Just then, according to Frances, "someone inquired if the letters for the house had been brought in." This reminded the Colonel of an "incident that happened in the mountains," which he proceeded to relate. One day one of his young mountain companions, named Harvey, received a sealed package from home, which had been delivered by "some person passing through the mountains." His companions had insisted that he share its contents with them, which he did, seated in a circle in a quiet place of their own. Breaking the seals and taking off the wrappers, he came to a little box. Inside was "a beautiful velvet-bound copy of the New Testament , inside the cover of which was his name in his mother's handwriting." According to Meek, the first man to speak said, "Read!" Opening the book, Harvey read the story of Jesus from his birth to his crucifixion. When he came to the passage where Jesus "gives his mother into the care of the beloved disciple," Harvey's voice broke, and his companions cried with him. "I tell you," Meek remembered, "our hearts were mighty 'little,' as the Indians say when they are afraid. It wasn't the last time that little velvet-bound book had listeners, either!" the Colonel concluded.

Mrs. W. urged him to retell the story at the church; but he could not be coaxed to do so; and Mrs. W. and Mrs. Victor were forced to tell the story "only one third as well as he could have done." This sentimental account, which Bliss had published to promote *The River of the West* was evidence of Frances' respect for her aging collaborator.

By this time, Frances despaired of receiving any financial aid for publication of her new book in Oregon. The only solution, she decided, was to finance a limited edition herself to sell on the Pacific Coast. She would also have copies to take East, where she hoped to persuade a publisher to undertake an additional printing. She was confident that her book about the Pacific Northwest would sell well in the East. While promoting *The River of the West* in the East in 1869, she had answered innumerable questions about the region.[19]

Frances Fuller Victor, filled with great expectations, boarded the steamship *Oriflamme* for San Francisco on October 21.[20] With her she carried the first draft of her manuscript of *All Over Oregon and Washington* and a Western short story, "El Tesoro," to offer John Carmany for *The Overland Monthly*. She had decided to ask him to print and bind her new book at her expense. To her delight, he not only agreed to undertake and printing and binding jobs but also accepted for his magazine three articles, that she had extracted from the book's early chapters embodying her 1871 travel observations.[21]

In early December, Frances delivered the final draft of her manuscript, copyrighted in her own name, to Carmany. Anxious about paying the printing bills as they became due, she took a page from Bliss' book: she decided to canvass for sales by mail. She appealed to Elwood Evans for help in marketing her book in Washington Territory.[22] After apologizing for making so many demands on his time, she explained that because "there are so few people who are sufficiently literary, or public spirited, or progressive to apply to for aid or appreciation, that the few must bear the burden of all such demands." She added that she had written the postmaster of the Territory to take names of subscribers to her new book called *"All Over Oregon and Washington"*—"and to collect the money in advance." She was forced to pursue this course in order not to overwhelm herself "in debt." She did not think that businessmen in Oregon and Washington would "refuse to give their aid in the manner proposed. Some of them ought to take several copies for distribution by mail." As for the book itself, it described every part of the country from her own and other persons' observations with "flattering notices of its scenery, resources and general desirability." She had arranged it to read "as interestingly as any book of the kind can be expected to." She was making arrangements for its sale in the East, and contemplated "reproducing it abroad." Her final paragraph was straightforward and practical:

> I write to ask you to speak a good word for it among your
> citizens, and get them to send me one, two, or three hun-
> dred dollars right off. I must have fifteen hundred at least
> for the first edition; and after that more to defray the
> expenses of getting it into the market in good shape.

In Oregon, the December 29, 1871 issue of the *New Northwest* announced that her new book would soon be released. The editor added: "A rare treat to lovers of literature will doubtless be found in its pages, judging from the well-deserved fame of the author." This announcement proved to be premature. Though the three articles Frances had published in the January, February, and March, 1872 numbers of the *Overland Monthly* may have stimulated sales of her book, the stereotyping and printing proceeded slowly.

Its brief preface, penned by Frances in Portland, March, 1872 read, in part:

> . . . It is difficult to write with absolute correctness of
> those countries whose rapid development outruns the
> printer and publisher. Since this volume was put in the
> hands of the compositor, numerous corrections have been
> made; and, between that time and this, new town-sites have
> been laid out, and other improvements commenced, which
> do not appear in these pages. But the slight omissions do
> not affect the general faithfulness of their contents; the
> whole constituting an amount of information which could
> only by obtained, otherwise, by a considerable expenditure
> of time and money.
>
> The beautiful and favored region of the North-west
> Coast is about to assume a commercial importance which

is sure to stimulate inquiry concerning the matters herein treated of. I trust enough is contained between the covers of this book to induce the very curious to come and see for themselves.

The 34-chapter book itself, with an elaborate front cover designed by Frances, was an example of fine printing and binding in the style of the time. Embossed in gold on the purple cloth was the title, the author's name, Mrs. F. F. Victor, and a two-inch circle depiction of Mt. Hood looming above a Pacific Northwest forest—all within the border of a curved sheaf of wheat.

To Mrs. F. F. Victor's delight, on April 6 she read the following brief review by the *Bulletin*'s literary editor:

> Mrs. Frances Fuller Victor is pretty sure of a respectful hearing whenever or wherever she speaks. Few women in this country—certainly no woman on the Pacific Coast—has higher claim to popular regard. Whatever she writes, whether it is poetry or prose, has the 'ring of true metal.' Her mind is eminently germinative. She never puts pen to paper unless she has something to say. She is a quick and close observer, and possesses in large degree the power of re-producing impressions made upon her plastic mind. Her style is terse, vigorous and free from affectations. Some of the best articles that have graced the pages of the *Overland* were from her pen while her work entitled 'The Rivers [*sic*] of the West' was most favorably received not only here but in the Atlantic States. A new volume from her fertile pen, entitled 'Oregon and Washington—Observations on the Country,' is published by John H.Carmany & Co., San Francisco. It describes the scenery, soil, climate, resources and improvement of Oregon and Washington Territory. It also considers their early history, geology, botany, and mineralogy, and gives useful hints to emigrants and travelers concerning routes, cost of travel, the price of land, etc. It is a book of substantial value, and deserves a wide circulation. It is neatly printed and tastefully bound.

Six days later Frances arrived in Portland, bringing with her a plentiful supply of her new book.[23] Gratifying response appeared promptly. The April 17 *Oregonian*, in an editorial review, said: "In her new book, *All Over Oregon and Washington*, Mrs. Victor has done herself as much credit as she has done this section of the country service." The *New Northwest*, two days later, declared: "*All Over Oregon and Washington* is a work of decided merit . . . . "It is one of the most valuable publications to circulate with a view of securing immigration to this far western country that we have seen." After summarizing the contents, the reviewer added that readers of Mrs. Victor's *River of the West* "need not be told that Mrs. Victor's latest work should have a place in their libraries. To all we say, buy a copy and thereby benefit not only yourself, but also encourage the meritorious author in her chosen field of literature." Another item in the paper announced that J. F. Curtis was canvassing the city for sales of the book. By April 27, Col. Joe Meek, who had been lecturing on and selling copies of *The River of the West*, was canvassing for and selling copies of *All Over Oregon and Washington* in Linn County.[24]

Meanwhile, on Sunday, April 17, Judge Deady called on Frances at the home of her cousin, Douglas W. Williams, where she was staying. Later Deady noted in his diary that she had been to Salem and that he had promised to write a notice for the *Oregonian* on her visit to the state capital, which he did.[25] Frances had tried to interest the legislature in funding the publication costs of her new book, as it advertised the state and would attract settlers. In a later autobiographical sketch, she noted that the state, faced with paying soldiers' bounties, could spare no money on advertising.[26] She also noted that Abigail Scott Duniway, who was in Salem at the time, had opposed her request as punishment for "saying something not radical enough on the suffrage question."

Both of these strong-minded women sailed for San Francisco on board the steamship *Oriflamme* on April 27. Mrs. Duniway was bound for New York City, where she would attend the annual convention of the National Women Suffrage Association.[27] After a lay-over in San Francisco, Mrs. Victor planned to promote her new book in the East. To her dismay, she found her book business in disarray and herself facing a financial crisis, as she explained in this letter to Joe Meek, dated May 3, 1872:[28]

> I went to see Mr. Trumbull about the *River of the West* and found he had only a few copies over 100, and most of these in cloth. With what you have however there will be about 150. These with the other books will keep you busy until I can get to Hartford and arrange to send you the *Life and Times of Joseph L. Meek* to go to Idaho with. And the sales you can make up the valley will pay that debt to Hill & Williams, $500, which must be attended to in time—that is, before the 27th of June.
>
> Now about more money.—I am sorry I did not let you get me that $500 you offered to, because I don't see how I am to get along without it. My agent here [it is Capt. Noble- formerly of Oregon] neglected his business for whiskey, and so I found very little on hand when I got down here. I have not money enough to pay Carmany & Co. and go east with. So I am forced to make some arrangement with Carmany to wait a little longer for a portion of it—say $200. Now what I shall ask you to do is this: if you can get $400 of Thompson, as you thought you might, please do so, on your own account, immediately, and send a draft for two hundred to *John H. Carmany, 409 Washington Street, San Francisco, Cal.* The other two hundred send by draft in a letter to me at Hohokus, Bergen Co., New Jersey. If you cannot get 400 and can get 200 only, send it to Carmany. I will repay you as soon as I can get things started.

This part of her letter, contrary to the opinion of some critics, shows that Frances was not exploiting Meek. Rather, she was providing him with an opportunity to earn much needed money and enjoy himself in the process. As the book's author, Frances received a royalty of four percent or less. It was to her advantage to act as her own agent and pay

Meek a percentage of the discount allowed her. That Frances trusted Meek implicitly is confirmed by these concluding paragraphs:

> I know that I can rely on you—and I cannot on anybody else, to do anything right in my absence. I wish you to keep my address—Hohokus, Bergen Co., New Jersey—in your notebook, so you can write me if necessary from any point you happen to be. Keep me informed just how affairs are going; what you have done, and what you intend to do.
>
> The bill for the box of *River of the West* which I send up, will accompany it but I think I shall be able to arrange for its payment down here—so that all the money you may get may be applied to other uses. If I can have four or five hundred sent to me by the 20th of June it will make everything easy for me.
>
> One thing more—will you please inquire whether my school land was taxed last year, and if so attend to the payment. I quite forgot in my hurry to ask about it.
>
> I hope you are well, and in good spirits. I will write to you a brief note before starting, and as soon as I arrive in New York. Please remember me kindly to the family, and when you write send my love to Olive.
>
> I think I will send some books by express so that you will not have to wait long to start up the Columbia. In the meantime you can do what you can with the other new book.
>
> I shall be thinking over that lecture and should not wonder if you went east next fall to deliver it, and make your fortune and mine!
>
> Yours very sincerely,
>
> F. F. Victor

When Frances conferred with Carmany concerning what she still owed for the production of *All Over Oregon and Washington*, she learned that it had been reviewed in the May, 1872 number of *The Overland Monthly*. She was pleased to note that the only adverse comment closed with a word of praise: "The descriptive parts are easily, almost carelessly written, yet contain some striking word pictures of the remarkable scenery of Oregon and Washington." Further, in the concluding sentence, the reviewer declared: Mrs. Victor has done the eastern public, as well as our own, a service in the publication of this book."

Before heading East, Frances, who was staying with a long-time friend in Alameda, a suburb of San Francisco, decided to clear up a misunderstanding which had occurred when Judge Deady had called on her in Portland. In a note, she wrote, in part:[29]

> In the haste of my last interview with you it did not occur
> to me to note a query you inserted into my running talk
> about the book. You said I had done Portland better jus-
> tice than in my former accounts of it, and I replied that I
> had drawn largely from your *Portland on Wallamet* article.
> Then you queried about giving credit. If I then had time I
> should have said that I learned to avoid giving credits
> wherever such avoidance was possible. To you, of course, I
> wished to acknowledge it; but my experience in these mat-
> ters is that it provokes disputation . . . . a certain clique
> would say—'she adopts Judge Deady's spelling of Wal-
> lamet, and Judge Deady's statements concerning other mat-
> ters'—and in short make that an excuse for getting up a
> party spirit about it disagreeable both to you and me . . . .
>
> The weather down here just now is nearly 'paradisacal'
> as it ever is anywhere on earth. Alameda is as green and
> flowery as Eden. I almost regret leaving for the East while
> this lasts, but I go on the 9th. Please give my love to Mrs.
> Deady.

On May 9, Frances Fuller Victor boarded the overland train for her second scenic journey across the continent, savoring the prospect of once again visiting her sister Metta and the family, which now included a widowed sister, Martha Rayle, who now served as the children's governess.[30] As always, "Frank" received a warm welcome at The Terraces, but after a few days at this pleasant country estate, she entrained for

Hartford to talk with Elisha Bliss about a special printing of the *River of the West* which Joe Meek could sell in Idaho. Because he was so well known there and it was the birthplace of his Nez Perce Indian wife, Virginia, Frances wanted the title of the book changed to *The Life and Times of Joseph L. Meek*, her original title. But she had to settle for Bliss' title, *Life of Joseph L. Meek: Record of Early Times in the Rocky Mountains and Oregon*[31]

If Frances asked Bliss to reprint *All Over Oregon and Washington*, he did not grant her request. However, she may have approached other publishers in Hartford. A copy of the book, sold in Olympia, Washington Territory in June, 1872, and inscribed to Hazard Stevens, son of the former governor, has pasted inside the front cover a small printed notice identifying the printer as Case, Lockwood & Brainard, Hartford, Conn. The title page remained unchanged.[32]

Frances enjoyed the rest of the spring at The Terraces with her two next sisters. Before bidding them a reluctant farewell about June 20, she extracted a promise from Martha that she would join Frances on the West Coast if Frances could find her a position whereby she could support herself. In the meantime, Frances' own publishing venture had been a modified success, though how to keep All Over Oregon and Washington up to date and in print would prove a continuing challenge in the years ahead. Once again, Frances decided to spend the winter in Marysville, Ohio with her mother and two younger sisters, who boarded with their mother. canvass the East and Midwest for sales of *All Over Oregon and Washington* and *The River of the West*. On October 27, 1872, she wrote to Judge Deady about the state of her affairs:[33]

> Your note in reply to mine from San Francisco reached me
> in New York, since which time I have been on the move
> most of the time. I have not found that Oregon is much
> appreciated in the east—nor is it likely that I shall make a
> fortune out of my interest in it, literary or otherwise. The
> weather this summer is past description trying and dis-
> agreeable—so, had it seemed best I should have gladly
> returned to the Pacific Coast this autumn. Now, however, I
> shall not try to return before March.

I write to propose a question, in my own interest as usual. It is this: would it be possible to secure the post of librarian in the Portland Library for myself, or a sister of mine whom I am trying to induce to share my fortunes in the west. If the place could be filled by, or obtained for a lady, no more suitable person need be desired than Mrs. Rayle—who is next younger than myself in the family—a teacher by profession, with executive ability and fine manners.

I could think of nothing else to attempt for her if we lived in Portland, as I would like to. I have no *home*—never shall have as long as I am alone in the west—and it is a very ardent wish of mine to set up my lares and penates somewhere soon, as I observe the gray beginning to show among my auburn locks; and I prefer being carried from my own house to 'that bourne' etc.

I am writing—trying to retrieve some of my quixotic errors by hard work. Have hope that if I live long enough I may die comfortable!

How is Mrs. Deady and the handsome boy? I desire [to send] my very warm regards to them.

By the way, I do not know anything about your Librarian's salary.

A letter full of such literary gossip as Oregon affords would delight me; have you time to write it; and something about Jesse Applegate. My address for the winter will be Marysville, my mother's address.

Driven by her need to recoup her publishing and promotional costs for *All Over Oregon and Washington*, Frances had been writing western short stories. Carmany had encouraged her by publishing three of them in the *Overland Monthly*: "Sam Rice's Romance," in April; "What They Told Me at Wilson's Bar," in May, and "A Romance of Gopherton," in October. All of them were laid in the California mining country. At Marysville, she wrote her first short story based on her Oregon observations and experiences—"On the Sands." In November, she submitted it to the Lakeside Monthly in Chacago and, to her great satisfaction, it was accepted by Bret Harte, the editor, for immediate publication.[34] Then she began to write a two-part story titled "The Old Fool," in which all the action takes place on the Lower Columbia River. Carmany would publish it in the June and July, 1873 numbers of *The Overland Monthly*.

Late in November, Frances received Judge Deady's answer to her October letter. He advised her that the Portland Library had a new librarian, named Henry Oxer. In her reply, dated December 1, 1872, she commented on Deady's Oregon news, literary and otherwise. After reporting that it was snowing hard and that the mercury was six degrees below freezing, she thanked him "for the letter and information. In the good time coming we will put the Oxen to some serious occupation, and give women the inside places." She was surprised to hear that Jesse Applegate had retired to Goose Lake in Eastern Oregon and was glad he had done so, for she wanted to visit "that romantic region" and now had "a fair excuse" for her "folly."

With regard to the recently published volume of poetry by her Salem friend, Samuel Clarke, she noted that he "sometimes gets off a verse or two without serious blemish; but he cannot hold out, and runs into twaddle in his longer efforts." As for the copy of *Deady's Reports*, published by the Bancroft Company in San Francisco, which he proposed sending her, she was "very much honored" but asked that he keep it until she returned lest it be lost in the winter mail. She added that she always read his "Reports" published in the *Oregonian* with interest. Her curiosity about "legal matters" was considerable and she regretted "not having time to read law." Then she thanked him "for the offer." Was she thanking him for an opportunity to read law in his Portland office? She added that she had heard that Portland was "about to have horse cars." A line past the new Post Office building would quite suit her, for her "ideas of locality in Portland" clung to that part of town between 7th and 9th and Washington and Main Streets. She was glad that Mr. Hill was still editor of the *Oregonian* and hoped his health would permit him to perform "the duties of his position." [Harvey W.] Scott is "a fair

AGENTS WANTED.

NOTICE. - The Subscription Department of H. H. BANCROFT & Co. has removed, with the general business, to 721 MARKET STREET. MR. A. L. BANCROFT assuming the active management of the business, the firm-name is changed to A. L. BANCROFT & Co.

GOOD LIVE MEN

Can make money by Canvassing for Books which are sold exclusively by Subscription.

Address, either personally or by letter, **A. L. BANCROFT & CO.,**

721 Market St., San Francisco, Cal.

Advertisement in the *Overland Monthly* for subscription agents to sell the publications produced by H.H. Bancroft.

ORHI 104261

writer," she noted, " but the *Oregonian* had a surly way not quite the thing for a leading journal." She hoped "the day of better things" was at hand.

This letter suggests that Frances was looking forward to returning to Oregon in the spring as a successful self-publisher and short story writer. However, what actually awaited her was beyond her wildest imagination, and on January 21, 1873 in the Columbia County Courthouse in St. Helens, her long-time friends, James and Mahala McBride, recorded a deed that transferred the ownership of one of their lots in Columbia City to Frances Fuller Victor

CHAPTER 9

AFTERMATH OF THE MODOC INDIAN WAR
(1873)

FOR FRANCES FULLER VICTOR 1873 was a pivotal and romantic year, both as a writer and as a woman, then in her late 40s. When she stepped down from the overland train in the San Francisco station of the Central Pacific Railroad on Sunday, April 13, she planned to spend a few weeks with her friend, Mrs. Bissett, in Alameda, and to attend to her own publishing affairs before proceeding on to Oregon.[1]

But, when she arrived at her hotel, she was shocked by an article in the San Francisco *Evening Bulletin*, filed by its correspondent in Yreka, California, near the southern Oregon border.[2] Just two days earlier, on April 11, a few renegade Modoc Indians, under a leader dubbed Captain Jack, had fatally shot two unarmed members of a federally appointed Peace Commission. Shortly after the Commission arrived at the appointed place, General E.R.S. Canby, U.S.Army, and Dr. Eleazar Thomas of Yreka had been fatally shot. Alfred B. Meacham, superintendent of Indian Affairs for Oregon, also had been shot and knifed, and was thought to be mortally wounded. Only Leroy S. Dyar, newly appointed Indian agent for the Klamath Indian Reservation, as well as an Indian Scout, Frank Riddle, and his Modoc Indian wife, Toby, managed to escape. In Portland, flags had been lowered to half-mast, and the newly-organized City Rifles had offered their services to the governor.[3]

Though concerned about the situation in Oregon, especially the welfare of Jesse Applegate and his relatives, who she knew had cattle ranches in the Klamath Country, Frances needed to tend to her business affairs first. She offered John Carmany of the *Overland Monthly* her two-part story, "An Old Fool."[4] Then, after checking at the house of Trumbull & Co. on the number of copies of *The River of the West* available, she boarded the ferry for Alameda to contemplate her future. Within three weeks, a solution to her dilemma arrived in the form of an unexpected letter from 27-year-old Oliver C. Applegate, who had been an assistant to his father, Lindsay Applegate—Jesse's next oldest brother—when Jesse had served as Indian agent at Fort Klamath in Eastern Oregon. In her letter to the Applegates accepting their invitation to visit the Klamath Country and "write up" the Modoc Indian war as they had experienced it, Frances sent the following message:[5]

> "Only last evening your note of March 5th came to my hands from Oregon, having been advertised, and rescued from oblivion in the P.O. Department by some of my friends there.
>
> I regret extremely that so flattering and kind a proposition should have lain so long unanswered. Of course, so far as I am concerned, the work of writing such a history would be very agreeable to me, and I should hope to make it acceptable to those who have known the facts and also suffered the ills connected with the war of races on the frontier.
>
> A letter from Hon. Jesse Applegate of date 9th March, reached me at the same time with yours. It contains a similar proposition, and invites me to come to the country made memorable by these events.
>
> I am to leave San Francisco for Portland about a week hence, and shall be occupied in the latter city for ten days, probably. After that I propose to spend the summer in Southern Oregon in pursuit of every species of information which may enable me to represent it truthfully either historically or by descriptive articles for the magazines. The assistance which you, and others of your family, can render is not underestimated by me, and I thank you for the preference of the offer.

Would it be possible for you to secure copies of the photographs taken by official means [as these would help to assure the] success of the book, and certainly add greatly to its interest to the reader. I shall wish to secure as many views as possible of interesting and historical points. It will be well to commence back to the earliest known Indian history, and to secure views of all famous places if possible.

Thanking you once more for your note and the compliment it implies to my former efforts in Oregon—

I am very Sincerely

Your friend

F. F. Victor

Frances Fuller Victor arrived in Portland aboard the steamship *Oriflamme* on May 1. Two days later the *Oregonian* published a brief personal item welcoming her back:[6]

Mrs. F. F. Victor, the authoress of "River of the West," "All Over Oregon and Washington," besides various other productions of acknowledged literary merit throughout the land, returned on the last steamer after a protracted visit to the East. The many friends of this estimable lady and talented writer will be pleased to learn of her safe return to the State of her adoption, which is proud to claim her as one of her most gifted daughters, after so long an absence.

While she stayed for several days at the Portland home of her Williams cousins, Frances counseled with Joe Meek and Judge Deady. The latter had served as a pallbearer at the funeral of General Canby on April 18. In his diary entry of April 25, the judge observed "that if it had not been for gross errors and want of common sense on the part of the whites, there would not have been any Indian war."

Frances was entering a region unfamiliar to her when she finally set forth on her journey to the Klamath Country.[7] At the outset, she had felt some qualms; based on what she had heard about the Modocs, she did not "aspire to an encounter with them." Moreover, "there were rumors afloat of Indian agents scarcely less formidable than their barbaric wards;" and she had been told "that alkali and volcanic ash" constituted most of the Klamath Country. In fact, she doubted that her "wanderings in that direction would provide either pleasant or profitable." However, she enjoyed the ride on the Oregon and California railroad between Portland and the end of the line at Roseburg, Oregon. She had been allowed to ride on the locomotive through the most scenic part of the route, including the Yoncalla Valley, former home of Jesse Applegate. From Roseburg, Frances proceeded by stagecoach to Ashland, a charming foothill village where she was welcomed at the home of Lindsay and Elizabeth Applegate. Jesse Applegate and his family also had been staying there during the last stages of the Modoc War, and, now that Capt. Jack and his cohorts had been captured, were eager to return to their California ranch. Frances was delighted at the prospect of a three-day journey over the Cascade Mountains to the village of Linkville in Klamath County, Oregon.

Near the end of June, the travelers departed Ashland in a mule-drawn ambulance, a horse-drawn baggage wagon, and on horseback. For Frances, the 62-mile trip across the Cascade Mountains was a long-awaited but harrowing alpine adventure; she permitted herself "to become so effeminate and awkward as not to be able to ride a hard-trotting horse." But she had not given up walking. And walk she did, "conversing meanwhile with a companion of inexhaustible resources." (Jesse Applegate.)[8]

The first night out the party camped in the Jenny Creek Valley and feasted on trout taken from the creek. On retiring, Frances left her shoes outside the tent and found them wet with dew the next morning. Though fond of nature, she shrank from sleeping "without the interposition of a French bedstead and a good spring mattress." But to her surprise, she slept well. The second night, the travelers camped on the summit of the Cascades. The hunters, traveling in advance of the party, had killed a deer; and that evening everyone ate venison, which they roasted on sticks around a blazing fire. Later, they told stories and sang songs until it was time to retire. At three in the morning, Frances had been awakened by the "Sage of Yoncalla" for a view of the star, Venus; and she was grateful that he had done so. The next morning the party broke camp in a jubilant mood. It was July 3, and later that day they expected to arrive at Linkville, located on the main traveled road into the Klamath Country. As Frances and Jesse Applegate walked along, he related how he and his brother Lindsay had helped to open the road, and near the Klamath River he pointed out a tree on which some of John Fremont's exploring party had carved their names in 1843.

At the close of the day, the Applegate party arrived at the Link River. Crossing the narrow wooden bridge, they entered the village of Linkville to find great preparations underway for the Fourth of July. The celebration would be doubly joyous. The cruel Modoc Indian War was over. The war was over, but what the Modocs made of it was still not clear. Capt. Jack and his cohorts had been captured on June 1. Two weeks later, 150 Modoc Indians had been imprisoned in a stockade at Fort Klamath on the Klamath Indian Reservation.

On the morning of the Fourth, the young ladies of the Applegate party invited Frances of join them in the festivities of the day. First, they heard 33-year-old Ivan Applegate, a son of Lindsay and a captain during the Modoc Indian War, discourse on the nation's history "in a manner rather more original than anniversary orators are accustomed to." The day closed with a ball held in the largest building in Linkville—the two-story Nurse Hotel. In her letter, Frances declared that "if anyone is malicious enough to aver that the grave and revered author of this letter danced, I should state uncompromisingly that they told the truth."[9] Among those with whom she danced may well have been her correspondent, Oliver C. Applegate, a younger brother of Ivan and the sixth son of Lindsay and Elizabeth Applegate.[10]

On Saturday, July 5, the members of the close-knit Applegate family separated. Jesse and his immediate family headed south in the baggage wagon for their ranch on Clear Lake. Lindsay's party, which included Oliver and Mrs. Victor, set out in the mule-drawn ambulance to the Klamath Indian Agency on the Klamath Indian Reservation to the northwest. Here they would stop overnight before proceeding the next morning to Fort Klamath, where the trial for Capt. Jack and his cohorts was just beginning,

To reach the Agency on Agency Lake at the western edge of the Reservation, they entered a forest, and Frances was enchanted with the Agency's white buildings nestled among the tall pines. At the home of the Indian Agent, Leroy S. Dyar, she was warmly greeted by his wife, Sarah, eldest daughter of her Salem friends, Samuel and Harriet Clarke. Her sojourn in the Klamath Country would be even more pleasant than she had anticipated. The Agency, she learned, would serve as the base for her travels to gather information about the Modoc Indian War and other Indian tribes, as well as the geographic and scenic features of the country.[11] For her, Dyar, who had already testified at the on-going trial, was a reliable source of information.

Together with Dyar, the Applegate party drove the six miles to Fort Klamath on Sunday, July 6, to attend the third day of the trial, scheduled to begin the next morning. As they approached the Fort, Frances could see a white building on the open, pine-fringed prairie, encircled by low mountains. On the bank of a stream flowing along their base, stood the officers' quarters and a hospital. Several hundred feet from the Post, an 11-foot rectangular log stockade was visible. Within were confined 155 Modoc Indians—44 men, 49 women, and 62 children. Nearby stood a small jail, in which the six Modoc Indians standing trial were imprisoned. A short distance away, two companies of soldiers, who guarded the stockade and jail, were encamped.[12]

On Monday, Frances, in the company of the Applegates, entered the building provided for the trial. In the long room in which the proceedings were being held, they saw seated at the south end of a narrow table the five uniformed members of the military commission, appointed by General Jefferson C. Davis to act as the trial court. Lt. Col. Washington Elliott of the First Cavalry acted as the senior officer. At the north end of the table were seated the judge advocate for the California area, Major H. P. Curtis, and the official shorthand reporter. Sitting behind them were Frank Riddle, a government scout, and his Modoc Indian wife, Toby. They had been scheduled to serve as interpreters for the condemned imprisioned Modocs.[13]

Seated on the bench to the right of the trial court were four of the Modoc prisoners: Capt. Jack, Schonchin, Black Jim, and Boston Charley

— all of whom had participated in the murders of General Canby and the Rev. Eleazar Thomas. Lying on the floor in Indian fashion were two other prisoners, Barncho and Slolux. They had yelled and jumped from ambush with rifles for their fellow conspirators. At each end of the room stood a file of soldiers "with muskets ornamented with polished bayonets" to prevent the prisoners from attempting to injure anyone in the courtroom. Near the door stood four more Modocs: Hooker Jim, Shacknasty Jim, Bogus Charley, and Steamboat Frank. Though just as guilty as the charged prisoners, they had been granted their freedom as a reward for having surrendered their arms and serving as government scouts for the remainder of the war.

In the crowded spectator section, Frances Fuller Victor jotted down notes as the drama continued to enfold. In the two previous sessions, the prisoners had been arraigned and had refused counsel. Two charges had been lodged against them: the murders of Canby and Thomas in violation of the law of war, and assault to kill in the cases of A. B. Meacham and L .S. Dyar. Then the judge advocate had questioned three witnesses: Frank and Toby Riddle, the interpreters, and the Indian agent, L.S. Dyar. The testimony of the Riddles had confirmed the charges against the prisoners, and that of Dyar had identified the accused.

The judge advocate began the third day's session by questioning the first witnesses for the prosecution: the four Modocs who, though guilty, had been granted their freedom. First to testify was Shacknasty Jim. He readily admitted that he had attempted to shoot Frank Riddle at the Peace Conference, and he identified the prisoners as having been present at the murders of Canby and Thomas. Similar testimony was given by the other three witnesses. Then the prosecution called its star witness, Alfred B. Meacham, former superintendent of Indian affairs for Oregon. As he entered the courtroom, the prisoners stared at him in disbelief. They had been convinced that the wounds they had inflicted on him had been fatal. Meacham, who had been serving as chairman of the Peace Commission at the time of the attack, testified at length and would later lecture in the East and write a book about the Modoc Indian War.[14]

On July 8, the last two witnesses for the prosecution were called. H. H. Anderson, a lieutenant in the 4th Artillery, identified General Canby and stated why he had been at the Lava Beds. H. C. Elderly, assistant surgeon, U. S. Army, established that both Canby and Thomas had died from gunshot wounds. Then the court accepted testimony from the defense. Capt. Jack was permitted to choose witnesses to testify in his defense. The three he named—Scarfaced Charlie, Dave, and One-Eyed Mose—were duly sworn in. The chief burden of their testimony was that the Klamath Indians had encouraged the Modocs to resist the demands of the federal government. Now the trial reached its climax. Capt. Jack was granted permission to speak. through the interpreters, in his own behalf and that of the Modoc people. Rising slowly from the bench, he stood gazing at the chain on his leg for a time before launching into an impassioned speech. He admitted that he had killed General Canby but declared that his own men, including the four then at liberty in the courtroom, had forced him to do it. Finally, he placed the blame for the Modoc attack on the Peace Commission on white people. Over the years, he claimed, they had killed many of his men, including his own father, who had then been attending a peace parley at the time.

At this point, Frances leaned forward to study the shackled leader.[15] Many years later she wrote that there was nothing about him "to indicate the military genius that was there. He was rather small, weighing less than 145 pounds, with small hands and feet and thin arms. His face was round, and his forehead low and square. His expression was serious, almost morose, his eyes black, sharp, and watchful, indicating cunning, caution, and a determined will. His age was thirty-six, and he looked even younger. Clad in soiled cavalry pantaloons and a dark calico shirt, his bushy, unkempt hair was cut square across his forehead . . . . but for the darting of his watchful eyes, he looked like any other savage."

Capt. Jack contended that he had done nothing wrong until he killed General Canby. He had always followed the advice of the good men of Yreka. He had never opposed the settlement of his land by white men. Soldiers had come to his village on Lost River and started firing when he had expected Ivan Applegate to come alone and talk peace. He had run away to the Lava Beds without returning the soldiers' fire and had not known that white settlers had been killed until Hooker Jim had told him about it. He had not planned to kill the general—his men had called him an old squaw and forced him to do it. Pleading that he did not know how to speak in this place, he asked for permission to finish his defense the next morning.

The other prisoners defended themselves in differing ways. Slolux denied that he had taken part in the crimes with which he was charged. Black Jim, Capt. Jack's half brother, pleaded for his life so he could take care of Capt. Jack's band. Boston Charley created a sensation in the courtroom when he admitted that he had killed the Reverend Thomas with the help of Steamboat Frank and Bogus Charley. Sub-Chief Schonchin spoke last. He was an old man, and had taken no part in the war or the murders of the peace commissioners. He had turned his oldest son over to Old Chief Schonchin at Yainax.

The next day, Capt. Jack concluded his defense. His men had talked of killing General Canby because they did not want to live on a land they did not know. Indian messengers—not the Riddles—sent to him in the Lava Beds told him that the Peace Commission were armed and intended to kill him.

Neither Capt. Jack nor his cohorts were examined further. Rather, the judge advocate took pains to read aloud and enter into the record documents that showed that Capt. James Jackson of Fort Klamath had been authorized to move Jack's band to the Yainax Sub-Agency, by force if necessary, in compliance with the Modocs' treaty with the federal government. Then he directed the trial court to consider the evidence against each of the accused, reach a verdict, and impose an appropriate penalty. Not surprisingly, the court quickly found each defendant guilty as charged and imposed the penalty of death by hanging.

For Dyar and the Applegates justice had been rendered. Back at the Agency they would discuss the effect of the hangings on the Klamath Indians and the final disposition of Capt. Jack's band. The next morning, Lindsay left the ambulance in Oliver's charge and boarded a stagecoach for Ashland by way of Linkville. For Frances Fuller Victor, the trial had been her first brush with military jurisprudence and its tragic overtones. She was glad to settle down at the peaceful Agency for a week or two to prepare for a ten-day tour of the Klamath Country with special emphasis on the principal sites of the Modoc War. Prompted by her probing questions, Oliver, a one-time school teacher and occasional poet, instructed her in the history, customs, and legends of the Indians east of the Cascades—Klamath, Modoc, Snake, and Paiute. He may even have sketched a map of the Klamath Country for her, including the volcanic "gem of the Cascades"—Crater Lake.

During these sessions, Frances was increasingly impressed with Oliver, whom she later dubbed "a master of Indianology."[16] At this time, she expected to write a history of the Modoc War, which she later called "in some respects the most remarkable that ever occurred in the history of aboriginal extermination."[17]

Early on the morning of July 22, Oliver and Frances were rolling east in the ambulance toward the Yainax Sub-Agency. After they crossed the Williamson River, the Sprague River Valley narrowed and the road ascended a ridge, where it became a trail. Here Oliver pointed out high caves stained with the smoke of ancient Indian campfires as well as rock fortifications which the Klamath Indians had erected against hostile Snake Indians in the past. After entering the Yainax portion of the valley, the trail broadened into a road again. Frances was enchanted by the wild flowers, bleached elk horns, and an occasional butte that rose directly from the valley floor. One near the Sprague River crossing was called Yainax, or "The Mountain." Now it served as a convenient landmark for the Sub-Agency. But for centuries, according to Oliver, Indians east of the Cascades from the Columbia River to the headwaters of the Sacramento River had regarded it as sacred. In times of peace, they had gathered here. Bartering for slaves and gambling by day, at night they feasted, boasted of their prowess on the warpath, and danced in the light of fires set on the sacred butte.

With the sun low in the sky, Oliver did not stop at the Sub-Agency; but he told Frances that in 1869 Meacham, then superintendent for Indian affairs for Oregon, and their friend, Leroy Dyar, had established it and appointed his brother, Ivan, its first agent. At the outbreak of the Modoc War, he himself had been agent, in charge of some 500 Klamath, Modoc, and Paiute Indians, with no garrison on which to rely. He had been able to persuade Old Chief Schonchin and his band not to join Capt. Jack in the Lava Beds.

Four hours of driving southwest of the Sub-Agency lay Swan Lake Valley, their first night's destination for Oliver and Frances. On the way, Oliver explained that his brothers, Ivan and Lucien, now made their homes on a large cattle ranch they had purchased in 1869. About the same time, he had purchased a ranch of his own in the upper reaches of the same valley. When the weary travelers reached the home of Lucien and Lizzie Applegate, Frances was greeted like family. Then, when Oliver set out in the ambulance to visit his ranch, she insisted on accompanying him. They drove north through the meadow-like valley, where countless cattle grazed on waist-high wild rye grass. Manned by hired hands, Oliver's ranch was named "Lone Rock," after the saddle-shaped rock that encircled it. The Klamath Indians called the rock "Bliwas" (Eagle Mountain), and they called Oliver "Bliwas-Eagle of the Klamaths," a title he treasured.

Back at Lucien's ranch home, Frances was busy. She jotted down the lines of a poem entitled "He and She," which she had composed on the way to Yainax. She also enjoyed the company of Lizzie and her children "in their quiet home in a quiet place;" and she delighted in the pure mountain air as she trapped and bottled insects for later examination.[18]

After this idyllic interlude, Oliver and Frances headed towards California for Uncle Jesse's ranch home on the north shore of Clear Lake just south of the Oregon border. On the way, Oliver explained that his uncle, as an agent for Jesse Carr of California, had figured in the opening and closing episodes of the Modoc War. At the isolated ranch house, the younger Applegates, followed by their elders, Jesse and Cynthia, greeted the travelers warmly, and with many questions about the Modoc trial and its outcome. Upon learning that Capt. Jack had said he did not know the white men were "mad" at him, Jesse related his first experiences with the condemned chief. In 1870, after Jack's band had fled the Klamath Indian Reservation, he had demanded fees from settlers on the six-mile square tract lying athwart the Oregon-California border, which he claimed as his reservation. When Jesse and most of his neighbors had refused to pay the fees, Jack's band had raided their ranches and threatened to kill the settlers. While waiting for federal authorities to rule on Capt. Jack's claim, the settlers had invited him, with a small unarmed band, to meet with them at the Applegate ranch. However, he had arrived with 29 warriors, decked out in war paint and feathers, and demanded the disputed tract as their reservation. Frances Fuller Victor now knew that had not come to pass, and that an unsympathetic superintendent of Indian affairs had inadvertently triggered the Lost River battle, which had launched the Modoc War.

Jesse's recollections were very much on Frances' mind the next morning when she and Oliver rolled along the north shore of Clear Lake in the ambulance on the way to the initial battle site and the Lava Beds. On the eastern side of Tule Lake, Oliver pointed out the ranches of the murdered settlers; and at the place where Lost River entered Tule Lake, he showed her the ashes of the Modoc villages on either side of the river. Then he headed for the Lava Beds which had served as the Modocs' first line of defense. As the travelers explored this subterranean stronghold, Oliver related how Jack's warriors, secure in their impregnable fortifications, had repulsed all initial attempts made by the army to dislodge and defeat them.

Next they visited the nearby site of the April 11, 1873 massacre of the Peace Commission.[19] Had not Jesse Applegate resigned from the commission and had not Oliver, secretary of the commission, been otherwise engaged that day, they both could have lost their lives here. It was here that Frances recognized that the history of the Modoc War would be best written by its participants—Meacham, the Riddles, the Applegates, and the Warm Spring Indian scout, Donald McKay.[20]

As they backtracked for a farewell supper and a good night's sleep at Uncle Jesse's ranch, Frances was beginning to see the Modoc War as only the last in a series of Indian wars in the Oregon Country. Writing about them would be a painstaking task. In the meantime, she would have to earn her living by writing stories and travel essays for the *Overland Monthly*. To that end, she was looking forward to the promised trip to Crater Lake.

A few days later they returned to the Agency by way of Linkville, where they stopped to feed and water the mules. On the way, Oliver prepared Frances for one of the greatest adventures of her life. As clerk for his father at Fort Klamath, he had become acquainted with Crater Lake and its history.[21] At the Agency, they found the Dyars well prepared for the three-day trip to the lake, and the party departed on July 31 in the ambulance and on horseback by way of Fort Klamath. Many years later Frances recalled waking from a "mosquito-tormented sleep" to see bear tracks and those of a deer in the ashes of their evening fire where they had camped overnight.[22]

Oliver managed to get the ambulance up the grade to the lake, but he and the ladies had to walk all the way because of the skittish mules and patches of snow. At a low point on the rim, Frances caught her first glimpse of the lake. "A choking sensation arose in our throats," she recalled, "and tears flowed over our cheeks . . . . The water of Crater Lake is of the loveliest blue imaginable in the sunlight, and a deep indigo in the shadow of the cliffs . . . . It impresses one as having been made for the Creator's eye only, and we cannot associate it with our human affairs. It is a font of the gods, wherein our souls are baptized anew into their primal purity and peace."[23]

In this description Frances Fuller Victor noted that rocks and points had been named after persons and resemblances such as "Cathedral Rock, Phantom Ship, and—I mention it with due modesty—Victor Rock, in compliment to my early visits to this then almost unknown wonder, and a trifling feat of daring performed to get a view of a beautiful reflection under this overhanging stone parapet."

By August 3, the dusty and elated party was back at the Agency, and Frances spent the last of her six weeks in the Klamath Country here, assembling her notes and artifacts and writing an article on her travels, which she mailed to John Carmany with instructions to publish it in the September, 1873 number of the *Overland Monthly*, or not at all.

At week's end, Oliver left the ambulance at the Agency; and he and Frances boarded the stagecoach to Linkville where, by pre-arrangement, they met Uncle Jesse for a stagecoach ride to Ashland by way of the Southern Oregon Wagon Road that followed, in part, the Applegate Trail. After enjoying the hospitality of the Ashland Applegates and meeting some of their friends, Frances departed for Roseburg on August 20. As Oliver handed her up to the seat on top beside the driver, he asked her to write him in Swan Valley. On August 2, a great fire, reportedly arson-caused, had destroyed much of Portland's commercial district, and he wanted a first-hand report.

Her first letter, dated Portland, Oregon, August 27, 1873, brought him up to date on their common friends and her writing prospects:[24]

> . . . After you saw me perched up beside the driver, I continued to keep my lofty position all day, and enjoyed the ride very well but not well enough to keep me from feeling the bruises inflicted on unhappy shoulders . . . . However, I survived it . . . . The day following my departure from Ashland found me at Mrs. Clarke's in Salem. At the depot I met Clarke, who was just starting for San Francisco where he thinks of locating. Mr. Anderson, expressman on the train, told me that C. said he had 'exhausted the subject [the Klamath Country]—there was nothing left for Mrs. Victor.' Perhaps so. If he did not do it he certainly meant to; but what comes out of my brain, even on the same subject, is likely to differ from the product of his."

She added that she had found everyone "well and merry at Mrs. C's", and looking forward to his autumn visit. It reminded her of her own "girlish days when music and merriment sounded forever in a happy home which no later home has ever equaled." Coming down to Portland on the early Monday morning train from Salem, she was relieved to see that the fire had not filled up the boarding houses and private residences. She had come to her old place "in the house of D. W. Williams Esq. of the firm of Williams and Myers, Commission Merchants on Front Street." Mrs. W. having gone to Hood River for a visit, Frances was housekeeping "for the first time in five years."

Frances had expected to remain in Portland for only a short time before sailing to San Francisco to meet her sister, Martha Rayle, who had accepted a teaching position in Alameda. But upon her arrival in Portland, she learned that Martha's arrival date had been delayed until October. So Frances decided to stay in Portland, as she told Oliver, to put her affairs in somewhat more satisfactory order. Two days later, the *Oregonian* noted that Mrs. F. F. Victor had returned to the city from Southern Oregon, and on that same day *The New Northwest* announced: "Mrs. F. F. Vic-

In the 1870s, Victor became aquainted with the pleasant people and the parkways of Oregon's capital, Salem. This spacious late-winter afternoon in the play fields belies her observation that "Oregon winters are too long—at both ends."

ORHI 5463 NO.1080

tor has recently returned from the Lava Beds. Look out for an interesting article from her pen next week." On September 5, the promised article occupied almost three columns on the front page of Abigail Scott Duniway's newspaper. Later that month, in her answer to Oliver Applegate's first letter to her, Frances explained how she came to write the article:[25]

> The letter you saw in the 'New Northwest' was quite
> unpremeditated. Calling on Mrs. Duniway, she asked me
> for a letter for her next issue. I told her that I could not *give*
> the use of the material I had been collecting; but I would
> write a letter which should contain nothing in particular;
> and so went home and threw it off in an afternoon—rather
> glad to have a chance to say what I did about Indian affairs,
> without appearing to mean to do it.

Frances devoted over one half of her published letter to describing her trip to Ashland, her three-day journey with the Applegate families to Linkville, and the Fourth of July celebration there. Then she summarized the opening incidents in the Modoc War in a brief paragraph before waxing philosophical:

> The history of the events which led to the Modoc War will hardly be written in this generation; and the unwritten facts will be those possessing the most intense interest, even when something like a history will be produced. It is not the fault of the interviewers, be it understood, if no account of these things is furnished to the public in proper form. One of this uncanny tribe myself, I felt some compunctions of conscience when I beheld the rapacity of my kind. Be it known that Job's patience would scarcely have been sufficient to meet the exigencies of the quizzing which the officers of the Agency, particularly, had to undergo. The courtesy and kindness extended to us is, and always will remain, a wonder to my mind.

At this point, Frances launched a defense in their behalf:

> It is so much the fashion to berate Indian Agents that I shall likely astonish a majority by taking their side . . . . Everybody knows of what they are accused—stealing, peculation, unfairness to Indians, cruelty, lying, and the rest of the Decalogue of sins. It is curious to me how the agents of the Klamath Reservation contrived to make anything out of a position where the appropriations were so small and so slowly remitted . . . .And then the salaries behind, too. At this rate an Indian agent may be looked upon as an underpaid and suffering rather than a money-making individual. The duties required of one are anything but agreeable, the servant rather than the master of his wards—attending to every want from a gunstock to a baby's shroud . . . . I am satisfied that the affairs of the Klamath Agency will bear the strictest investigation, and that the tales afloat concerning the provocation given to Jack and his band are both false and foolish. Having an opportunity of observing the administration of the present Agent, and being competent to say that not only was there no ground for complaint

against them, but that they seem to have acted with singular manhood and good faith toward the Indians and the Department. Yet in California, and even in Oregon, the contrary opinion is recklessly stated by people totally uninformed of the facts of the case."

Having vented her anger at the charges brought against Indian agents, who had become her friends, Frances brought her *New Northwest* letter to a clever conclusion:

> I did not set out to defend anybody; that last paragraph slipped in unawares. What I meant to tell you of was the many pleasant excursions I enjoyed while stopping at the Klamath Agency from taking notes at Jack's trial, to visiting the wonderful Crater Lake. But I cannot tell you everything in one number of your paper—I don't know that I want anybody to know the half I enjoyed on this summer voyage. Suffice it for the present that to travel in Eastern Oregon requires you to wear stout shoes, a linen duster, a dust cap, an immense hat, to carry a field-glass and a carbine; to know how to make a hemlock bed, or to sleep in a haystack, and to talk jargon. With these accoutrements and accomplishments, if you are a good and indefatigable rider, you can get along

Frances added this note: "Eastern Oregon is settled by cattle raisers, and for that purpose the country is best and good for little else than good beef, butter, and cheese." In the "Moral" that followed, she advised anyone who was well off to stay where they were. She concluded with a postscript, "the most important part of a true woman's letter: I will just say here that the only reason that I do not put more information about the country into my letter is that I do not resemble Mark Twain, who cannot help being sensible and wise when he only means to be amusing. If I fail of being sensible or amusing, so much the worse for me."

About ten days after Frances sent off her first letter to Oliver, she received his reply, written at Swan Lake. She must have read his salutation and opening paragraph with great pleasure:[26]

Mrs. F.F. Victor,

Dear Friend,

Yours of Aug. 27 has just found its way into my sylvan retreat. The mountain Bliwas ruffles his plumes with delight and taking a pen in his claw undertakes briefly to reply.

'Thy symbol be the mountain bird
Whose glistening quills I hold;
Thy home the ample air of hope
And evening's sunset gold.'

Well, after I saw you safely located beside the stage driver, I spent another day about the pleasant little village, enjoying the society of relatives and friends and then mounting my charger plunged into the evergreen forests of the Cascades, about which our friend Miller has expressed himself so grandly . . . ."

After stating that there was no news about the Modoc prisoners about which she had not heard, Oliver turned to news of their friends, Leroy and Sarah Dyar: "Mr. Dyar is East on a visit to his aged parents and Mrs. D. and Mr. Sykes Worden are manipulating the I.D. machinery at Klamath with good success I believe. The Government has often commissioned less capable public servants than Mrs. D. would make and I expect to see the day when merit shall be regarded as the chief qualification for office, and sex shall not debar any capable individual from mounting to any round of the political ladder." Then he noted that he was sending her "the Modoc portraits and seed of the "sky-blue snapdragon" which she had admired so much on the road to Yainax. However, the elk horns remained "in the bosom of the interminable forest" from which he had yet to extract them. His brother, Ivan, and his wife, Maggie, sent their friendship. After a formal "Ever truly yours, O. C. Applegate," Oliver had added, "If I can favor you in any way please write— but write anyway, Bliwas."

Frances responded to Oliver's letter on September 17. After addressing him as "Dear Bliwas," she began laying the groundwork for a declaration she wanted to make about their unique friendship:

As the regard in which I hold my 'plumed' friend is quite different from the ordinary friendships of mortals *without* wings, I have, upon mature reflection adopted the above style of address which if not distasteful to him shall be adhered to in the future. It has a certain air of romance about it, and an aroma of sentiment which seems to suit with the scenes with which the personage addressed is associated, and may be tolerated I think upon the score of 'poetical privilege' at least. There are some minds, you know, which prefer to avoid the designation which by power of association brings before my mental vision many pleasant scenes and agreeable recollections.

In a second paragraph, Frances spelled out the nature of her affection:

Perhaps you do not guess that it pleases me to invest you with a title, which might be written thus wise: 'Oliver Applegate: Gentleman, by the Grace of God and the nobility of his own nature.' Here again the 'poetical privilege' comes in with which the poetical sad soul of a too worldly-wise woman comforts itself. To endow with rare virtues a 'Chance Acquaintance' of whom just so much may be known as not to destroy whatever pretty theories and fine imaginations said soul, being in want of cheer, warms itself with . . . . Bring a poet, and your Senior, I may without circumlocution say, that I take great pleasure in liking you and esteeming you a number of degrees more than other chance acquaintances every day met with; and I think it a privilege to cherish and enjoy the sentiment; holding it a gift of God when anything is sent to us to which our faith can pin itself. These gifts have their 'sweet uses' like adversity . . . . Very barren and unhappy is the soul in which none of the affections can grow to ripeness and exist independently of 'that on which it throve;' poor and uncultivated is the mind in which love exists only as a passion of the blood; and both unhappy, and barren and uncultivated, the life of that person who cannot or does not sometimes own a sentiment above and apart from those ordained by conventionalities.

In her final paragraph on this delicate subject, Frances wrote:

If I had not dubbed you "Gentleman by the grace of God" I might fear you would misconstrue what I have written to mean some silly and unbecoming sentimentality. But you will not; knowing that I am a perfectly self-poised woman, whose appreciative regard is as pure and simple as it is sincerely avowed. There may happen times or events in your life when to know of this regard may be of some now unguessed use to you; therefore it is here recorded. Have I 'risen and explained' sufficiently?"

Then Frances changed the subject abruptly. Mr. Carmany had failed to publish her article on Klamath Land in the *Overland Monthly*, though he had given her leave to choose her subjects. Today she was parceling out the seeds of the blue snap-dragon, which is *"not"* a snap-dragon, to send to friends and florists. She would look up the seeds "in the latest Botanical work." In the meantime, she had sent her bottle of beetles and bugs to a Mr. Fuller in New York. If he thought them of any value, she would report.

In a letter to Oliver, dated October 23, 1873, Frances noted that she would be "jolting off soon" to California, where she expected to spend the winter with her sister in Alameda. Otherwise she would remain in Oregon as she would be compelled to return for the spring term of court, some important property rights being about to be established. She concluded this letter with an unexpected piece of good news: "I have just come from an interview with [Brig.] Gen. [Jefferson C.] Davis, who sent me word that he was at my service if I wished assistance from his office in writing up the Modoc War. I explained to him that my intention was not to hurry a History of that matter before the public; but to include an account of it in a general history of the Indian Wars of Oregon—and accepted his offer very gratefully of course."

Since returning to Portland from the Klamath Country, Frances had begun to write fiction again. Her short story, "How Jack Hastings Sold His Mine," first published in the *Lakeside Monthly* in Chicago, was featured on page one of Abigail Scott Duniway's *New Northwest in Portland* on

November 7. A fast-moving tale of a California gold mining camp episode filled with suspense, it is reminiscent of Bret Harte's stories in the same settings. Two weeks later, Mrs. Duniway announced that a new story, written for the *New Northwest* by Mrs. Frances Fuller Victor and titled "Judith Miles; or, What Shall be Done With Her?" would begin in December to appear serially each week well into the next year. Mrs. Duniway further noted, "Mrs. Victor has long been a resident of Oregon, and is well known as the most popular and gifted contributor to the *Overland Monthly*. The proprietor of the *New Northwest* feels confident that the people of Oregon will aid her in her efforts to sustain our brilliant home author in her literary labors."

In mid-November, Frances reported to Oliver that she was taking notes from military documents at General Davis' headquarters. He had provided her with an office, access to all documents, his own assistance as well as that of Col. E. C. Mason and Major W. H. Boyle. But she soon discovered that "this is the *military* side of the subject alone" and "to become a faithful historian" she needed to get the other side as well. To that end, she listed several questions as they had occurred. Had the Klamath Indians been "over-bearing" toward the Modocs and Snakes? Why had the Modocs been settled at Yainax? Who had been inspector general in 1871 and had he reported fairly? And why had Meacham been removed? Finally, she asked for a history of Fort Klamath and the regular succession of commanders, as it was not to be obtained in this office. "Here is inquiry enough to give you employment for some time," she commented. "I beg pardon for being so troublesome; but 'facts are stubborn things' and not always easily obtained."

Turning to personal matters, Frances stated that it was "useless for the present to look for F.F.V. in the *Overland*." She had given orders to use the Klamath article in the September number or not at all. Certain things seemed to indicate that it would be best to remain in Oregon. If she did, she would give considerable time to the "Indian History," and he could expect to be called upon the help her out. She wished she could shorten the distance between Portland and Ashland. His father doubtless had many interesting documents, and certainly had much more information which he could communicate orally. "The labor of getting together all the material for a well-written history," she wrote, "is very considerable—the writing is nothing, in comparison."

In mid-December, Frances dispatched to Hon. Lindsay Applegate a brief letter requesting his aid in obtaining information on the Indian Wars of Southern Oregon:.[27]

> You are already aware perhaps, that I am working this winter upon a history of the Indian Wars of Oregon. I know of course that you could be of the greatest assistance to me if I were in Ashland. But it is impossible for me to do my writing there, so far from other authorities, the Military Records, libraries, etc. It would therefore be the greatest favor if you were able to collect in your neighborhood. Some little explanation might be needed in writing, and certainly would be very desirable, if you can take the time to give it. I will preserve carefully any and all papers entrusted to me, if desired . . . .
>
> I really need some one to give me a sketch of their origins, and of their principal events. Old newspapers are of course very useful, but not always exactly reliable.
>
> My compliments to Mrs. Applegate and to all your family.

Three days before Christmas, Frances wrote Oliver to thank him for his "copious notes" in reply to her queries:[28] "I feel at length that I am becoming sufficiently imbued with the facts and the *animus* of the intricate Indian question to dare to call myself a historian. But I shall take all the time necessary to make an unquestionable work, and therefore am 'making haste slowly' so far as the writing is concerned."

Then she listed additional questions about the Modocs, beginning with Joaquin Miller's dealing with them. Next she sympathized with Oliver, whose article on the Modoc War, written for the New York Times, had not appeared. "It is very provoking," she agreed. "I wish I had them, since they are rendered objectless by the publication of others less reliable." Then she shifted to her plans and prospects for her ongoing literary work:

The Modoc uprising on the California borderlands elicited a taut statement from
Victor: "I feel at length I am becoming sufficiently imbued with the facts
and the animus of the intricate Indian question today to call myself a historian."
This was humbly entered.

ORHI 5463 NO.1080

Do you observe that I have a story running in the *New
Northwest*? I thought it advisable to cultivate the acquaintance of the Oregon public even in this way, as it might
possibly bring me a larger number of readers when I have a
book to sell—I have not yet begun my book which is to be

written *to please myself*, the plan of which I got while summering in Klamath Land.

By the way that is the name of the article in the *Overland* by Clarke—a very pretty article, but *thin*. If Mr. Carmany had not behaved so unreasonably I should have written him a much better one on the same subject. He is now appealing to me for *short stories*. It is comforting to know, since I cannot afford to refuse an assignment, that he has at last taken as editor to conduct the magazine—a gentleman of ability too—Mr. Avery of the *Bulletin* staff."

Here she was not referring to her novel, "Judith Miles," published in the *New Northwest*, when she spoke about writing a book "to please herself." It was apparently a "fugitive" novel which she may have planned while in Klamath country during the summer of 1873.

As she concluded her letter, Frances Fuller Victor's thoughts turned to Christmas:

We have been having a little winter, sleighing and all. But today has been Springlike and beautiful. Everybody is running to find Christmas things—and Portland is quite gay. I hope the holidays will be enjoyed by the inmates of Swan Lake as merrily as by right of its venerable use it should be .
. . .

Write me of your goings-on—I should be greatly interested.

Most Sincerely Yours,
F. F. Victor

CHAPTER 10

HISTORIAN &
JOURNALIST

(1874-75)

THAT FRANCES FULLER VICTOR published a 60-page pamphlet entitled "The Women's War on Whisky; or, Crusade in Portland" was large-ly a matter of happenstance. She happened to be at the scene, and she was certainly interested in the subject. But it was not all that she was doing.

She had greeted the New Year with optimism. She was still corre-sponding with her friend, Oliver Applegate, about the Modoc War. Sure-ly Benjamin F. Avery, the new editor of the *Overland Monthly*, would accept the sketches and stories she was prepared to offer him. On January 3, 1874 she wrote him a letter that read, in part:[1]

> I send a sketch for the O.M. in the shape of a story . . . .
> Mr. Carmany has so bewildered me in the last year by
> ordering and then declining articles, that I have about given
> up any intention of writing any more. He seemed to wish
> for stories more than anything else—if that is the need of
> the magazine, please indicate the same to me, and I shall try
> to send an occasional one . . . . .
>
> I was glad to see that you have taken the editorial chair.
> My observation of the O.M. the last year or two, has shown
> me that very much depends upon the editor in regard to
> keeping the contributors up to their best work . . . . So far
> as I am concerned, I could furnish either of three classes of
> articles—historical, Northwest Coast, of course—descrip-
> tive, the same—or short stories. Better than all these, I

should like to furnish a sauntering novel something after
the style of "A Chance Acquaintance," but with the plot
laid among the new scenes of this coast. I have been saving
up material for it for a long time.

Less than three weeks later, Frances was shocked to receive a letter of
rejection from Avery on the grounds that her sketch of the old Indian
chief, named Nittinat, would not appeal to the average reader. Replying
immediately, she mildly disputed his decision.[2] She pointed out that to
someone like herself, who was sensitive "to the finest shades of savage
character," the acts of the old chief possessed "a quaint and peculiar
interest." Further, the fact that the events that he had detailed were "in
the main historical" enhanced the value of the sketch.[3] But she was not
discouraged. She offered to furnish the *Overland* with a first-class article
on the very peculiar early history of Oregon or some biographical
sketches of interest, especially one on Dr. John McLoughlin. In closing,
she assured Avery that she had always felt a special interest in the *Overland*
as "an exponent of western literature."

Meanwhile, she had been collecting information on the early Indian
wars of Oregon. From Capt. J. M. McCall of Ashland, she requested the
facts on the campaign of 1864 in the Snake country and asked him to
name all the military forts in Southern Oregon, together with their locations and how they had been officered during the Indian wars of the
1850s.[4] Especially she wished to determine the truth of the prevalent
opinion of many people that the Rogue River Indian War had originated
with the unprovoked massacre of Indian men, women, and children by
Major Lupton. "Who was he, she asked. "I wish to get at the facts," she
continued, "yet am wholly unable to decide as to the truth, from the
contradictory testimony of responsible persons on both sides."[5] She
ended her plea for assistance with these words:

The causes of, and first steps toward, a war are the most
difficult parts of history to get at. Any light you may throw
on the subject will be a 'lamp to my feet' in these intricate
mazes. Could you induce somebody who has saved a file of
newspapers of that time to loan them to me? Or were there
none published in Southern Oregon at that time? I can

gather the people's views better from local papers than any-where else. Please put yourself in my place and set every-body to producing material for history.

In mid-January, Frances expressed her gratitude to Oliver for his "long and instructive" answer to her queries.[6] After posing a few more questions regarding events before and after the Modoc Indian War, she expressed her frustration with his Uncle Jesse. She had written him for an explanation of some of the acts of the Peace Commission, of which he had been a member, but he had declined to answer her. "He is very pro-voking," she wrote, "and if I did not admire him so much for some qual-ities, I should certainly have to strongly condemn others. There are many things he could help me about going back twenty-five or more years; but at present, he is like a Sphinx—a grim and silent puzzle."[7] Near the end of her letter, Frances confessed that she had "a great ambition to have enough of those beautiful silver gray fox skins," such as the one she had seen at Clear Lake, "to make a set of furs, or a traveling jacket." If some of the boys in his employ could trap them they could consider her "as a purchaser of—say four skins or five." In closing, she expressed her regret that Oliver could not attend Professor Thomas Condon's geological lec-tures then underway in Portland. "They are really a very great treat," she noted, even to someone like herself who had been over the same ground in her reading. "Mr. Condon's warmth and earnestness win him applause, especially upon those points where science is supposed by many to conflict with religion. He saves his religion—but he vindicates the truth of science nobly."

During the latter days of January, Frances was caught up in the Port-land celebration of the centennial of the American Revolution, organ-ized by Abigail Duniway. Hoping to emulate the Centennial Tea Party held in Boston on December 16, where members of the New England Woman Suffrage Association had gathered at Faneuil Hall to protest "taxation without representation of one half of the citizens of the U.S.," Mrs. Duniway appealed to friends of the New Northwest to contribute supplies for a Portland Centennial Toast and Tea Party to be held at the Masonic Temple.[8] Among other arrangements, she prevailed upon Frances to write a pertinent paper, which she read during the program offered at the Portland celebration. In the February 6, 1874 issue of *The New Northwest*, Mrs. Duniway, the editor, noted that though the event had been socially successful, it had failed financially.

On the front page of the same issue, Frances found her contribution to the celebration, entitled, "An Open Letter to the Boston Commonwealth," which Mrs. Duniway had read during the program. In her essay, addressed to "Dear Athenians," Frances had deftly presented the historical links between Boston and Portland and the pioneer history of Massachusetts and Oregon. In closing, she looked to the future:

> Having shown you, dear Athenians, the bond of kinship, which exists between Portland and Boston, we herewith tender our congratulations upon a marked event in your history. And close with an expression of hope that a hundred years from now, you may join us in a National Jubilee upon the Pacific shore at which the finest Pekoe teas shall be furnished *ad infinitum* by us to every delegate from your glorious commonwealth; and the *toasts* by the finest classicists of old Harvard of the 'Hub,' whose health we are about to drink in aromatic Oolong.

The following week, Frances submitted to Avery a two-part article, entitled "The Pioneers of Oregon." With her offering, she sent this explanatory note:[9]

> I send you a double-article on the Pioneers of Oregon, which I judge will prove interesting reading to the largest class of your subscribers. I know that you prefer a less lengthy contribution; but as it now stands it is complete, and fit for reference, and will explain any historical incident that from time to time may be contributed about Oregon by myself or anyone else.
>
> I submitted it to Gov. Curry who is well versed in Territorial matters, and he approves of it. Do not fear I mean to crowd articles upon your attention the year round as I have done the last two months. I have much serious work on hand which will take up most of my time for the present year, in which fact lies your security.

Victor was much taken with the enormous drive and intellectual vigor of
Thomas Condon; part geologist, part minister, part prickly paleontologist,
She may have seen her own personality reflected in the forever questing Irishman.

ORHI 6808

On that same day, February 12, Frances departed for Salem by train to take part in the sessions of the Oregon State Woman Suffrage Association, scheduled to meet February 12 and 13 in Reed's Opera House. First, however, she attended to a personal matter. Most of the 1,500 copies of *All Over Oregon and Washington*, which she had paid Carmany to print, had been sold. Now she wanted to issue a new edition. Although she had failed in 1872 to obtain from the Oregon state legislature a $1,500 appropriation with which to publish the volume then, she now planned to approach the 1874 legislature, now in session, with the same request. She was confident that her book, describing Oregon's historical background, natural resources, and scenic wonders, as well as its economic and cultural progress, would benefit the state by attracting new settlers who would contribute to its future growth. In her quest for support, she consulted Representative Cyrus A. Reed of Salem, of one of the owners of the Willamtte Woolen Mills and builder of the Reed Opera House. To her delight, he agreed to introduce a bill in the House, authorizing an appropriation of $1,500, which would enable her to reprint *All Over Oregon and Washington* in the East.[10]

With this mission accomplished, Frances hurried to the home of her friend Belle Cooke. Both were scheduled to present papers at the State Woman Suffrage Association meeting. Frances, who still shrank from speaking in public, prevailed upon Belle to read her paper as well as her own on the final evening of the two-day convention. After the applause for her reading of her own paper subsided, Belle announced the title of Frances' paper: "Some Thoughts About Ourselves." These opening paragraphs set the tone:[11]

> Women, trained for so many centuries to entire dependence, are not good at a long, steady defiance to association and habit. That they are capable of it, the world knows, but if it is forced on them, the sustained effort which it costs them, makes them course, fierce, and unwomanly. This continued effort at defiance will soon make, from habit, a woman's voice hoarse and manlike. So says a very observing writer, and there is a great deal of bitter truth in the statement . . . .

If it is true, and no doubt often may be, that women who go out of the narrow circle, usually denominated their 'sphere,' become less charming and refined in appearance, is not here the reason? Mind is the same, whether it resides in a man's form or a woman's. All the laws of the mind, the soul, the affections, are the same in men and women, so far as observation or science can determine. What affects one affects the other in exactly the same way. What makes the woman who has to do battle with the world—as earning one's own money in one's own way is called—more awkward, or cold, or less lovely than her sister? . . . And whether she had undertaken to do battle solely for the sake of truth; or whether 'unmerciful disaster' has forced her into the world's broad arena to struggle for the poor privilege of a joyless existence—she suffers the same . . . .

But a more curious question even than this and one of greater import to women, is, why women so rarely stand by women in any undertaking. Whatever the reason may be, it is a fact, and one not at all creditable to the womanly head and heart, that they do not *sustain each other*. The phrase 'a lone woman'—the saddest in the world, I think—is fairly a decisive one. It means one who has no legal right to the support and protection of any man—and lacking *that*, she has nothing!—for women who belong to men will not care for her, aid, or uphold her . . . . "But why enumerate the disabilities of the 'lone woman'? Whatever she might have been with liberty to use her natural, God-given abilities, she is nothing now. And why? Primarily, because men claim for themselves all the privileges of life; and secondly, because more fortunate women agree to sustain men in this assumption and become the most merciless critics of their helpless sisters . . . . A man of brains is a prince among his peers. A woman of brains is, among women, a crow to be picked at. If she gets recognition at all, it must first come from men. Women have no coherency about them . . . .

Abigail Scott Duniway lost her mother to the Oregon Trail as the family wagon
lurched toward Oregon and the settlement of Lafayette.
Staunch in the battle for women's rights, she was sometimes an ally,
other times a competitor, to Victor.
ORHI 78930

The reason for this is not far to seek. The civilization
of a dependent class must be inferior to that of an independent one. Proper pride, self-esteem, honor, and loyalty
are qualities belonging to the highest culture, and we do not
look for them along serfs. Women should study history and
learn from whence comes their enslavement. There they will

discover that it did not come from the hand of God—he made all things free. It began with barbarism, when rude physical struggle governed . . . .

Let women investigate for themselves the means by which men, in Church and State, have for ages hindered their advancement in mental and moral culture. The world is ruled by precedent. A precedent established centuries ago keeps women in chains, even in this age of refinement and culure. Let there be once established the precedence of an intelligent, independent womanhood, and the ages to come will abide by that, until the words 'slavery' and 'equality' will have become obsolete in their relation to women's legal or intellectual estate.

On February 27 in *The New Northwest*, Abigail Duniway summarized the two-day meeting in Salem. After noting that "Essays by Mrs. Belle W. Cooke and Mrs. F. F. Victor were read by the former lady, and were well-written, well read, and well received," she added, "Mrs. Duniway followed for an hour giving cogent reasons why women should be allowed the ballot." Frances was pleased to note that the remainder of the front page of the paper for that day was devoted to the publication of her entire essay.

On her return to Portland, Frances found a 21-page letter from Oliver Applegate awaiting her.[12] In her reply for February 19, 1874, she thanked him for his "full and complete explanations" to her questions before commenting on the failure of Eastern Oregon ranchers to obtain federal reparations for their losses during the Modoc Indian War. "So the settlers must pocket their griefs and their losses together," she wrote, "It is the history of the frontier from first to last." After sympathizing with him for losses of cattle during the severe winter weather, she cited her own ill luck: "There has been such a constant pouring upon me, for at least six years, that I sometimes am inclined to believe that there will never be a rift in the clouds. Getting used to it, is half the battle anyway, and am well used to adverse luck by this time, and do not wish to be understood as complaining whatever happens. But I would like to see my friends succeed." As for her history of the early Indian wars of Oregon, she continued to "make haste slowly," for it is very difficult to get people to take trouble about anything in which they are not financially interested."

A month later Frances sent Oliver a promised "gossipy" letter about herself and Portland. But first she lectured "O.C.A., otherwise Bliwas, otherwise the Klamath Eagle" on isolating himself on his ranch as "poor Uncle Jesse—our common relative" was doing. He was not to think that she was "venturing advice." She would "wait to have it asked for . . . . But 'what will it profit a man if he gain the whole world [of cattle] and lose 'the best enjoyments of life?'" She then shifted to the conflict between her desire to write creative works and her need to publish articles to sustain herself. "How much I wish myself pecuniarily independent!" she exclaimed.

> So much time and thought is *wasted* on contriving ways and
> means, and in writing fugitive articles for present pay, that I
> cannot get ahead as rapidly as I ought with any of my work.
> Besides, this horrible bread and butter business does so clog
> the fancy and bind the wings of imagination, that I am
> often willing to cry quits with Fate, and give up the battle
> of life, disgusted with my ill success in being and doing
> anything I most desire. But I shall never do it, I presume.
> The inexorable policeman Pride, backed by Necessity, will
> keep urging me to 'move on' to the end. Therefore if I live
> long enough I shall write my Klamath Romance, and in it
> you will find a great deal of myself that you do not yet
> know of (its poorest recommendation, certainly) and many
> hints, perhaps of others, not so completely disguised but
> that you may guess one or two of them out. I wish I could
> write it next summer up among the Cascades, or among the
> pine groves of Klamath Land, under just such conditions as
> I might choose—I am dreadfully egoistic, I perceive; but
> you can practice your pardoning power upon me, thereby
> cultivating the grace of clemency and patience of which
> you stand in such urgent need.

Turning from the personal, France reported on the city news in which she was interested and already somewhat involved:

> Portland is just now in the midst of the Women's Crusade against intemperance. The Methodist Church building stands open all day, and prayers are going up morning, noon, and night for the success of the *Crusaders*. Every day bands of women go from saloon to saloon throughout the city praying, singing, and exhorting with various effects. They are often rudely addressed, and yet more often are treated respectfully. It remains to be seen whether they succeed in closing any saloons or liquor stores. But whether they do or not, they will have awakened a strong public sentiment on the side of reform, and vindicated women's ability to engage in the most arduous work of progress. I regard it, and so do many, as the best argument we have yet seen brought forward for enfranchising women. Every day some *man* says to me, "If women don't pray down this traffic, we shall have to give them the ballot and let them vote it down." This I think will be the end of it, and that it will be a *Province of God* none will deny. The women seem everywhere to be lifted out of themselves, their little vanities and sectarianisms, and to be moved with a very powerful influence . . . .

In concluding her comments, Frances declared: "I am not a crusader. I had my crusade in private, long ago, and the scars of it are not yet effaced. But I stand ready to help in other ways, and am willing that the glory should be given to others."[13]

While Frances was writing her letter to Oliver, cannon were booming, calling on townspeople to hear Governor Lafayette Grover speak on his own behalf as candidate for re-election. "One thing he can count on," Frances asserted,

> —the women who want suffrage will be against him, and will make him feel it, too. Some of you young men can begin now to fit yourselves for the suffrages of women. We

want earnest, firm, temperate, right-minded men, with
breadth of thought and purity of principle. We want such
men in office as we can approach without scandal, and trust
our public interests to, as we can our private reputations.
The old stack of politicians would scarcely suit us, and if
the places of honor are wanted, younger men and purer
men will know how to get them.

Frances then changed the subject to social life at Fort Vancouver:
Gen. Davis and his staff have kept up the dancing pretty
well all through the season, but owing to the lack of unmarried officers and ladies, the parties are said to be rather
stiff." She spoke only from "hearsay," as she did not attend
the dancing parties there, but she did have "a calling
acquaintance with the wives of the Military Set and liked
them for the most part very much.

A month later on April 23, Frances wrote Oliver that she was very
busy attending Temperance meetings, circulating petitions, and editing
The New Northwest during Mrs. Duniway's absence. She commented on the
"strong feeling" that exists with regard to the Crusaders.

I stand by the 'Crusaders.' But I do not regard their work as
effectual and *permanent*. They are a sort of 'John'—a voice
crying in the wilderness, 'Prepare ye the way' of the
Reform. The arrest and trial of the Crusaders was extremely
sensational. I was three days in the police court—my first
experience of this sort of thing. But it was very interesting,
as was shown by the crowds that stood patiently for hours
every day to hear evidence and pleadings. I made up her
mind that I did not want to be a lawyer, since I would be
bound to plead equally hard on either side of a case; and
one could not always be on the right side."

Frances also noted that she had gone to see Donald McKay and his
Warm Springs Indians perform their dances. "They do extremely well,"
she reported, "and I judge must draw crowded houses in the East. Sam
Parrish is to accompany them as agent; and Col. Meek as *historian* and
story-teller, I presume."

On May 6 Frances Fuller Victor was pleased to read in the *Morning Oregonian* that the Multnomah County Court had "ordered that she be permitted . . . to hold real and personal property, and to sue and be sued, without being joined by her said husband." Earlier that spring she had learned that Henry had returned to St. Helens. Perhaps to show her good will, she had requested him to improve a piece of wild land she owned in Columbia County. To perform the labor of clearing and ditching the property, Henry hired John Campbell of St. Helens. But when the work was completed, Henry failed to pay the charges; and Campbell brought suit against both Henry and Frances Victor.[14] The case of John Campbell vs. H. C. Victor and F. F. Victor came to trial during the June term of the Court. Campbell's complaint alleged that the defendants were husband and wife, and that at the express direction of F. F. Victor, the owner of the property, he had cleared and ditched the property. For his work he demanded $382 and court costs. During the trial, Frances challenged the truth of Campbell's complaint on a number of counts. For instance, she denied that she had authorized H. C. Victor to give directions to Campbell regarding the improvement of the property.

Both parties to the suit had stipulated that Raleigh Scott, a friend of Judge Deady, should sit as referee. In his decision, he first found against H. C. Victor for the entire sum Campbell had charged, and then $195 and court costs and ordered the property sold to pay that amount.[15] About this time, Henry took himself off to Washington Territory to pursue new ventures on his own behalf and that of his former San Francisco partner, Franklin Davis. Thus Frances, comfortably settled in her cousin's upper-class home, was free to record the background and current events of the burgeoning Women's Crusade against liquor.

The most aggressive opponent of the Crusaders was Walter Moffett, owner of the popular Webfoot Saloon, as Frances later stated in her *The Women's War with Whisky.*[16] On the afternoon of April 16, when the ladies had paid a second visit to his saloon, he had been ready for them. He had assembled a large crowd of spectators armed with a police whistle, drums, gongs, a hand-organ, and other noise-makers. The praying ladies, seated on camp stools along the outer edge of the sidewalk, continued to sing and pray in spite of the din. The following morning, 22 Crusaders again took up their vigil in front of Moffett's saloon. Mrs. Moffett was present with one of her children; and no disturbance took place. However, just before noon, the chief of police appeared with a warrant for the arrest of the ladies. A large crowd followed the police chief and the ladies, who were singing "All Hail the Power of Jesus' Name" as they entered the jail. Here they were charged with violating City of Portland Ordinance 475 by conducting themselves in a "violent an disorderly manner" on the corner of First and Morrison Streets. Walter Moffett testified that the complaint was true. The ladies pleaded "Not Guilty," and the case was postponed until the following day.

The court convened at 1:00 P.M. the next afternoon. Such a crowd had gathered that the defendants and their friends had to be admitted by a private door. After some preliminary legal skirmishing, six of the ladies being tried were required to take seats on one side of the courtroom. After the reading of the complaint, the ladies again pleaded "Not Guilty," and asked for a jury from the special list. Following the selection of the jury, the court adjourned until Monday. On that day, the courtroom was again packed. About 80 ladies were present, as was a great crowd of men, both inside and outside the courtroom. Following an argument for a jury of twelve, a jury of six, as ordered by the court, was selected. As first witness for the prosecution, Moffett presented his evidence. Then the three boys who had beat the drums testified, as did the organ-grinder, that they had been hired by Moffatt. Next several of the Crusaders as well as others were examined as to the nature of the disturbance. Finally, Judge Owen Denny charged the jury with finding from the evidence whether the ladies were guilty as charged. The jury departed about 4:00 P.M. to deliberate; but few of the audience stayed long enough to hear the verdict: "Guilty, but recommended to the merciful consideration of the Court." Judge Denny consented to stay sentencing until the next morning. At 11:00 A.M. the Crusaders and their friends arrived to find another trial in progress. While they waited, they agreed that they would go to jail rather than pay fines. When they were finally summoned, Judge Denny asked whether they had anything to say before he imposed sentence. One of the defendants read a letter that pointed out that the verdict was contrary to the testimony, as they had been "quiet and orderly in the midst of disorder and confusion." As Temperance women, they earnestly protested against being sentenced by a jury composed in part of liquor dealers, to which the embarrassed judge replied that the jury had been fairly and impartially selected in accordance with the law.

Then Judge Denny proceeded with what he termed the "most unpleasant part of his duty—pass sentence on Christian women for holding, or attempting to hold, religious exercises upon the sidewalk in front of a saloon. However, he made the penalty as light as he could—"a fine of $5.00 each, or one night in prison." The women refused the offers of gentlemen friends to pay their fines, electing instead to go to jail, where they sang hymns and were visited by friends. They were furnished with nightclothes and were about to retire for the night when the chief of police appeared and ordered them to leave the jail. Since their friends had departed, they offered to stay the night, but were rudely turned out to grope their way down the stairs to the street. Here they saw a crowd of men at the corner of the block. Being frightened, they returned to the jail and finally asked a stranger for his protection. This "good Samaritan" escorted them to the Methodist Church, where a Temperance meeting was in session. As the ladies walked up the aisles, the audience, realizing that they were free, began to cheer.

Despite these discouragements, the Crusaders continued their meetings and visits to saloons. On May 27, Frances' seven-stanza poem, entitled "Do You Hear the Women Praying?" was read at the meeting of that date. As she continued to chronicle the Crusaders' activities, she felt that they had chosen a favorable time during which to do their work –just prior to state and city elections, when liquor was freely used to influence voters, and when any move to form a new party would be opposed. Shortly before the state election, the Crusaders appealed to the Temperance men to field a Temperance ticket. On a Friday evening the Republicans held their primaries, nominating three men to whom the Temperance people could not object. The next day, the First Ward candidate withdrew, leaving the Republicans to find a suitable replacement on short notice—a task that proved insurmountable.

At this juncture there occurred, as Frances later stated in an article in the *Oregonian*, "one of those singular and fateful accidents which so often in history have changed the tide of battle."[17] On her way downtown that Saturday afternoon, she had chanced to call at the Methodist Church. There she had found a little knot of men and women, "talking over the rather gloomy prospect, still hoping against hope that a good man for their principles might be found. None of the ministers were present, and only four ladies who had ever worked with the Crusaders. There was no formality about the meeting, nor any person present who exercised any function of office or authority. Presently, a gentleman, well known to the Temperance people, and who has warmly sympathized with them, remarked that he had a draft of a circular to be used on election day. He then read it in an ordinary tone. I, for one, gave not much heed to it, presuming that, as men were accustomed to that sort of electioneering, the gentleman knew what he was about. Whether the other ladies present were more attentive, I cannot say; but from the fact that without more than a few minutes' deliberation as to "ways and means," it was informally agreed to print it, I presume that no one was detected anything very 'infamous' or 'blasphemous' about it. As I was going downtown with another lady, I offered to hand it in at Himes' printing office, and did so. Mr. Himes being absent, Mr. Turner of the *Temperance Star* took the manuscript [without] reading it."

Frances added that after having seen the circular in print, she could see that it was "unnecessarily irritating and in some portions unjust; but I think that I may say with certainty that zeal and not malice prompted it." She wanted to emphasize that "the Crusaders had nothing to do with the conception or publication of the "Voters' Book of Remembrance," as the circular was now titled. Nor would it have been written (certainly not so carelessly adopted) had not everything been thrown into confusion at the last moment, primarily by the neglect to put out a Temperance ticket as the ladies had desired . . . . The ladies, so much of whose toilsome effort has been countered by this blunder, and, it is hoped, all good Temperance people can learn a lesson from last Monday's experience." In closing she noted that "Wars, for principle, are always more bitter, longer, and harder to fight than wars for empire only. If women are to fight the Temperance battle, the necessity for which was brought upon them by men, it becomes every man worthy to be called such, to smooth the way for them as much as possible; and it becomes all women not actively engaged in it to lend their sympathy and assistance and that, too, without presuming to dictate to those who give their time freely, how they shall work."

Was this France Fuller Victor's warning to Abigail Scott Duniway and her followers who thought that woman's foremost fight should be for the ballot? Near the end of August, Frances' copyrighted pamphlet, *The Women's War with Whisky* came off the press of George H. Himes at Front and Washington streets, and was placed on sale at 50 cents a copy. Judge Deady, who was reading Thackery's *Henry Esmond* for his literary club, did not mention it in his diary. But a back page notice in the August 28 issue of *The New Northwest* indicated that Mrs. Duniway had a copy and would review it shortly. The September 11 issue of the paper carried her review.

Calling the pamphlet "a souvenir of the crusade," she noted that it was "a convenient compilation" of matter in a shape that those most interested would like to have. But on the whole, it was "remarkably one-sided." Claiming that she was just as much a friend of the Crusaders as Mrs. Victor, Mrs. Duniway took exception to Frances' statement that nobody answered the Reverend Medbury when he said that the Crusaders had done "great mischief" to the cause by meddling in politics. Mrs. Duniway asserted that the editor of *The New Northwest* had answered him "fully and forcibly" at the same meeting at which he had made the remark, as Mrs. Victor well knew. She further charged that "our historian" mistook "the public sentiment to which she tries to cater," as she would learn before she was done with the sale of her pamphlet.

Then Mrs. Duniway lashed out at opponents of her efforts to secure Woman Suffrage in the Pacific Northwest: "It is this ignoring of the Woman Movement and applying the gag law to its earnest advocates in the temperance work that has crippled the crusaders and caused the public lose confidence in their sincerity and leave off attending their meetings; and we are extremely pained to see so graceful a writer as our amiable and gifted friend engage in any sort of connivance or sympathy with a few proscriptive bigots who have been and are yet trying to carry on the war against whisky without consenting that national appeal be made at their meetings to the *voters* of the nation to empower women to work as law-makers where they can now only work as outlaws." There was nothing in the pamphlet that Mrs. Duniway could recommend "as an aid in breaking the political fetters that hold women subject to the power of the law-making rabble who vote regularly in the whisky interests."

Following this bristling review was a notice captioned, "Be Ye Ready," a reminder to members of the Oregon Woman Suffrage Association of the convention in Salem on September 22, to which Frances Fuller Victor was a delegate. In a lengthy letter to Bliwas, dated October 8 and written after her return from Salem, Frances did not mention the publication of her pamphlet; but she did note that Mrs.Duniway had given her "characteristic stabs" in *The New Northwest.*[18] She had not answered his letter of a month ago because she had not known her plans. The "poetical pilgrimage" by which she had expected to go overland to California by way of Ashland had been "broken up" by the departure of its "central attraction" on a business trip to the East. She had had a nice time in Salem. All her friends had been "flattering" and everything has been "satisfactory"—or would be if the legislature passed "a certain little bill" she had requested. She had also attended a Temperance meeting, held to prepare the legislature for upcoming legislation, as well as the Women's Suffrage Convention. Here Belle Cooke had read her address, at which Mrs. Duniway was "much annoyed" because in it she said she was "in no hurry" to vote, though claimed that to do so was as much her right as that of her father, brother, or husband. But because "women are so unaccustomed to act for themselves," she felt "some preparation to be necessary, and did not care to have the ballot thrust upon those who would repudiate it, instead of comprehending its best uses." Mrs. Duniway had retaliated by trying to weaken her influence at the convention. By such tactics, Frances noted, "she retards the cause by appearing as its leader in Oregon." As for herself, she had suffered "so much toil and turmoil" that all she asked of fate was "repose—not only from the discordant anxieties of life but from its passions and emotions of every kind;

— to sit aside and see the play go on; without any movement of responsive interest, love, fear, or ambition." She was glad that he was not compelled to live alone on his ranch. "Idiosyncracies, and one-sided views of things come from too much isolation," she counseled. "However, she had great faith in his power to keep his temper "sweet" and his mind "clear." After noting her "strong personal interest—almost a pride—in his success," she apologized for her "outspoken assurances." Then she added that she had missed an opportunity to send him the promised picture of herself and that when he received it she did not want him to frame it in dark wood. She meant it to be a "bit of brightness" when his eyes chanced to fall upon it. Reminding him that she was leaving for California within a fortnight, she directed him to address her next letter to her in Alameda, California. There she intended to spend the winter with a sister from the East.

In November, as duly reported in the *Oregonian*, Frances sailed from Portland by steamer to San Francisco. She doubtless knew then that House Memorial No. 2, introduced by Rep. Cyrus A. Reed of Marion County, had been referred to the Ways and Means Committee, where it would die at the end of the 1874 session[19] Upon her arrival in San Francisco, she stayed with friends at 130 Tyler Street while she surveyed the changing literary scene and enjoyed the cultural advantages of the city, as her February 9, 1875 letter to Oliver Applegate indicates.[20]

Her visit to the nearby Academy of Science, where she had shown her drawings of Klamath flowers to the resident botanist, had reminded her of Oliver. The botanist had identified most of the flowers, but needed the seeds and leaves of a specimen that Oliver had found near Agency Lake before he could identify it. If Mrs. Dyar could provide this evidence and if it was unknown to botanists, Frances said she would call it "Applegate Elegance." She also asked Oliver to send her a specimen of the gray rattlesnake they had seen at the Lava Beds. Then she noted that in visiting the Academy of Design, she had enjoyed Thomas Hill's "Heart of the Sierras" and wished that he could see and paint Crater Lake as no one in Oregon could. On a ruefully humorous note, she observed that "the mining excitement" in the city, through her inability to invest, has saved her "from making thousands of dollars." Asking to be remembered to his family and friends, she closed with a reference to "a funny production of our mutual friend [Joaquin] Miller" and signed herself, "Your Affectionate Friend, F. F. Victor."

More than two months later on April 21, she replied to Oliver's letter from New York City. If he returned to Oregon by way of San Francisco within a reasonable time, she told him, he would find her at the same address. She understood what had taken him East and approved of his course of action. Nor did she fear that he would fall from his "proper place because of uncongenial associates." She noted that his Uncle Jesse was frequently in the city because of his work for the surveyor general of California; and she hoped he would meet her sister, Mrs. Rayle, who was teaching grammar school in Alameda. Finally, she remarked that she would likely return to Oregon this summer for a month or two on business. Surprisingly, she did not mention that *The Overland Monthly* had accepted her short story, entitled "Miss Jorgensen," and that since February 22 her weekly column, entitled "Letters from a Sky Parlor," had been appearing in the *Sunday Morning Call* of San Francisco under her pen name, "Dorothy D." In fact, Dorothy D. was a mature version of the sparkling "Florence Fane" of *The Golden Era* who had earned Frances Fuller Victor a popular following in San Francisco a decade earlier.[21]

Dorothy D. established a rapport with her readers by discussing social issues raised in the national magazines or based on her own observations. They ranged from "the plight of helpless, professionless women . . . the need for better education for girls and boys" to "the differences between men and women as well as between popular literature and the narratives of Pacific Coast explorers. Her June 6 column, "WANTED, A DIVORCE," is a case in point. In the guise of Dorothy D., who interviews her friend, Belle Flibbertigibbet, Frances comments on the sensitive subjects of separation and divorce, both of which she had experienced. Belle admitted to having married an older man, not out of love, which she had never experienced, but because she thought marriage for a young woman was comparable to a young man's going into business. Though Belle loved her children, she felt imprisoned by her jealous husband and was thinking of seeking a separation or divorce—only to be thwarted at every turn. Dorothy D. counsels Belle that she must be honest with her husband or she would not only lose his love but his trust as well. She further notes that Byron had been right when he wrote: "Love is of man's life, a thing apart. 'Tis a woman's whole existence." Frances counsels her women readers along similar lines:

> If she has separated from her husband, she has thus
> declared that she has repudiated allegiance to him, and
> established the fact that there must be a reason. In justice to
> herself, if she determines to be divorced, she should make
> her reason known as justification of the step to be taken.
> Any attempt at secrecy suggests at least the presumption of
> unfairness in the complaint—a presumption that a pure
> and proud woman should not be willing to allow. A bad
> husband is a misfortune, and it is true that society has little
> tolerance for the unfortunate; yet most people do respect
> those unlucky ones who have the courage to own themselves
> worsted in the greatest ventures of their lives, and who
> frankly avow their determination to undo as far as possible
> what has been done wrong. Therefore, to all good women,
> with causes more legally serious than our friend Belle has at
> present, we say, Do not go near any secret divorce agencies,
> but state the matter candidly to a respectable and responsi-
> ble lawyer . . . .

> Dorothy D. wishes that young women, and young men
> as well, could give a reason for marrying above instinct or
> caprice. Until they can, and until both parties are educated
> to think on the subject, there will be plenty of cases like
> Belle's, and plenty more like those that have filled the news-
> papers with scandal from month to month—with desertion
> and murder cases—or with life-long suffering and bitter
> disappointment, in the endurance of which all that is best
> in man or woman is warped or wasted."

Dorothy D.'s final column, dated August 8, was titled "Etiquette and Manners of Street Cars and the Street." It touched upon the woman's rights issue by presenting an incident on a crowded streetcar in which a young woman, not wanting to "pose an inconvenience," declined the offer of a seat by a gentleman. An observant young woman seated nearby remarked to a fellow passenger, "We prefer standing to accepting a favor." He replied, "Well, in these days of woman's right, women have a right to stand, and I want 'em to use it." Dorothy D. pointed out that women "accepted the polite attention of men in exchange for legal rights." To which Frances, in the guise of Dorothy D., responded that she felt that the legal right to be assured a seat on a streetcar would surpass "the pleasure of accepting a seat that is given us as a favor after we paid for the one we failed to find."

Meanwhile, Frances had published occasional articles in the *Daily Morning Call*. On May 9, it carried two. Her article, "Under the Trees, A Botany Expedition to Angel's Island," was attributed to "An Amateur Botanist," presumably a young male reporter. A gentle satire on lady botanists and reporters, it may have been based on an actual expedition Frances had taken with botanists from the Academy of Sciences. The second was a reprint, under her own name, of her "A Stage Ride in Oregon and California," first published in Bliss' *American Publisher*. Late in June, Frances was saddened by word of the death of her faithful collaborator, Col. Joe Meek. On July 25, the *Call* published her signed three-column tribute to "An Oregon Pioneer," sub-titled "the Recent Death of Colonel Meek. One of the Most Notable 'Mountain Men' Amongst the Early Hunters and Trappers." After recounting his colorful life and how she had happened to write it up, she noted that Mrs. Fremont had recently conveyed her impressions of Kit Carson in the *New York Tribune*, adding that Carson and Meek, who had been friends, were representative of a class of men who had ceased to exist "with the circumstances that had called them forth." It was fitting that the people of the country they had explored "should do them reverence." It seems likely that Frances sent a copy of her tribute to her subscription-book publisher in Hartford, Connecticut, suggesting that a revised edition of *The River of the West* was in order.

While in San Francisco, Frances was increasingly concerned about the future of her most reliable market, the *Overland Monthly*, and interested in the rising fortunes of a one-time fellow Ohioan, Hubert Howe

Bancroft, head of Bancroft & Company, the leading book-seller and publisher of almanacs, school books, and law books on the Pacific Coast. In November, 1874 he was also known as a collector of historical materials on the western half of the North American continent, which were housed on an upper floor of his business establishment.

In the March and June numbers of the *Overland*, Frances Fuller Victor, Judge Deady, and other Portlanders had first learned of Bancroft's on-going collecting and his grandiose plan to recover part of the cost of collecting, by writing, and publishing a serialized history of the western half of America, beginning with that of its Native Races.[22] Former editor Avery having been appointed ambassador to China, the December, 1874 number of the *Overland* was under the joint editorship of Bancroft's former assistants, Britishers Walter Fisher and T. A. Harcourt. That issue carried the first review of Bancroft's Volume I of the *Native Races*. Henry Oak, Bancroft's assistant, later claimed that he had written it, "cribbing one or two elegant phrases" from a discarded review by President Daniel Gilman of the University of California, and that well-known California writer, J. Ross Browne, had permitted his name to be signed to it.[23]

Frances doubtless read the review upon her arrival in San Francisco late in 1874, and was pained to see another editorial change in the *Overland*, then on its last legs. She did not know until later that, while she was chronicling *The Women's War with Whisky* in Portland, Bancroft had been in the Eastern states, promoting his *Native Races* and looking for an Eastern publisher. But in the summer of 1875, she was impressed with his success as a Western publisher and bookseller and may well have realized that, with the demise of the *Overland*, she would be free to reprint, at her own expense, some, if not all, of her stories it had published—as her friend, Josephine Clifford, intended to do.[24]

Just what she meant when she referred to "her business in Oregon," in her letters to Oliver Applegate, is not clear. Did it concern her St. Helens property or Henry himself? She knew of his practice of spending the winter in San Francisco with his friend and erstwhile partner, Franklin A. Davis. One event that likely helped to prompt her return to Portland was the August debut of the *West Shore*, an illustrated literary monthly. On July 2, Judge Deady noted in his diary that he had promised

Under the command of Captain Wallace, the *Pacific* sank after minor collision
off Cape Flattery in November, 1875. Former naval colleague,
Henry Victor, and several hundred others drowned.
The two survivors reported a faulty passenger list.

its publisher and editor, Leopold Samuel, that he would write for the
new magazine.[25] A week later, he had finished his first article—an
account of how Portland had become "the Emporium of Oregon"—for
which Samuel had paid him $10.00.

After spending the month with her sister, Martha, then teaching at
the Alameda Grammar School, Frances on September 4 boarded the
steamer *John L. Stevens*, which docked safely in Portland three days later.
She again settled in quietly at the home of her Williams cousins, where
she was always welcome. On October 4, the *Morning Oregonian* noted with-

out fanfare that "Mrs. Frances Fuller Victor is now in the city visiting friends." A month later on November 9, the newspaper headlined "The Loss of the Str. Pacific." Reading the account in shocked horror, Frances learned that her husband had perished along with hundreds of others when the wooden sidewheeler, *Pacific*, sank within minutes on the evening of November 4 after colliding with the American ship, *Orpheus*, off Cape Flattery on the Washington coast.[26] Henry had boarded the ill-fated steamer at Tacoma, evidently en route to San Francisco, where he had intended to spend the winter.

The irony of Henry's death by drowning could not have been lost on Frances. He had survived the dangers of circumnavigating the globe while on a U. S. naval mission to Japan in the mid-1850s and distinguished himself as an officer in a Union blockading squadron during the Civil War only to lose his life aboard an outmoded commercial steamer, under the command of an incompetent Confederate with whom he had once served in the U. S. Navy. She must have also deemed it providential that she was in Oregon, living in the home of her highly respected Baptist cousins, when the tragedy struck. They were not only aware of the details of her 13-year marriage with the speculative, adventurous Henry but also were able to help her take the practical steps that the occasion demanded. Since Henry had not been "a believer," she could not, in good conscience, arrange a church memorial for him. But to establish "a justification" for having left him, she exhumed her poem, "A Reprimand," written shortly after their separation in 1868. After a decent interval, she published it in the *West Shore* for her friends and other women similarly situated to ponder. That was the kind of honesty that she demanded of herself and others. As his legal widow, she came to regard his death as a major turning point in her life, as indeed in some ways it was, and to view him in an increasingly favorable light. She had been delighted to sail with him to the Pacific Coast in the spring of 1863 and follow him to Oregon late in 1864. Since that time, he had provided her with a pen name that she used with pride, and she would continue to do so for the rest of her life.

At the time, Frances wired the New Jersey Victors of his sudden passing and invited her 21-year-old step-daughter, Mary Victor, then living with her mother's family in Ohio, to join her in Portland. As executrix of Henry's tangled estate, she engaged former Governor A. C. Gibbs, Henry's former employer, as legal counsel for herself and Mary. She was determined that they share equally in whatever was left of the property that Henry C. Victor has once owned in partnership with F. A. Davis in Multnomah and Columbia counties; and she was confident that Judge Deady would help her in this regard, which he did.

CHAPTER 11

WEST SHORE &
THE NEW PENELOPE
(1876-78)

The deaths of her former husband, Henry C. Victor, and her friends, Col. Joe Meek and Dr. James McBride in late 1875, and of Mrs. McBride—Mahala—in February, 1876, reshaped France Fuller Victor's personal world. During the next two years, she made a fair living by her pen and prepared herself for a greater challenge ahead.

While writing for Leopold Samuel's monthly magazine, the *West Shore*, more or less regularly in 1876, she also reduced her best-seller, *The River of the West*, by one third to provide space for Part II in a centennial edition of the volume, published and copyrights by the Columbia Book Company of Hartford, Connecticut, in 1877. Part I, entitled "Mountain Adventures and Frontier Life," and comprising 38 chapters, was attributed to Frances F. Victor. Authorship of Part II, "Our Centennial Indian War and the Life of General Custer," comprising 20 chapters, was not acknowledged. Frances doubtless read page proof on Part I and received royalties for her section of the volume, which likely enjoyed a good sale, as the massacre of the popular General George A. Custer and his troops was a matter of national interest. In introducing Part II, the editor noted: "The recent campaign against hostile Sioux was over the identical ground where the fur traders roamed intent on beaver skins and adventure; and it is believed that some account thereof, and a sketch of the renowned Indian fighter who perished on the Little Big Horn may appropriately supplement the story of the Mountain-men."

Frances also recycled nine of her short stories, published in or offered to the *Overland Monthly*, together with forty of her favorite poems, some written before her arrival on the Pacific Coast. Introduced by an unpublished story, "The New Penelope," based on the Greek myth of wifely devotion in a pioneer Pacific Coast setting, it was printed by A. L.Bancroft & Company in San Francisco at her own expense in 1877.

In addition to these publishing ventures, Frances, with the help of former Governor A. C. Gibbs and Judge Deady, tried to settle the complicated estate of Henry C. Victor, to which she and her stepdaughter, Mary, were sole heirs.

During these years, the Williams home on West Park between Taylor and Yamhill in downtown Portland provided Frances a comfortable haven. Here she enjoyed a sense of family but with the privacy she needed for research and writing. She also had easy access to the offices of the *Oregonian*, where her friend, W. Lair Hill was still editor, and to that of *The New Northwest*, mouthpiece of Abigail Duniway, with whom Frances had made peace. She was also well located to consult Judge Deady on literary and legal affairs, as she had done since her arrival in Portland in 1865. Doubtless, he asked her to contribute a biography of Col. Joseph L. Meek to *Transactions of the Third Annual Reunion of the Oregon Pioneer Association*, published by E. M. Waite in Salem in 1876. Deady may also have recommended her to Leopold Samuel, the German-Jewish publisher and editor of the *West Shore*. However, Frances was capable of speaking for herself; and the 28-year-old publisher must have been familiar with her work.

In introducing the *West Shore* to the public, Samuel had stated that it was to be "a family paper, devoted to the Literature, Science, Arts, and Resources of the Pacific Northwest." He intended to make it "the literary paper of the Pacific Northwest." To that end, he had secured "contributions from the brightest intellects and ablest writers of the state." That he had done so, Frances could see for herself. Among the poets he had published were Belle Cooke of Salem, Joaquin Miller, then traveling in Europe, and Samuel Simpson, poet and journalist, soon to author "The Beautiful Willamette." Among published essayists were distinguished Oregonians like Judge Deady, William L. Adams, and Thomas Condon.

Frances Fuller Victor's first contribution, whether invited or submitted, appeared in the January, 1876 number of the *West Shore*. It was an incomplete inventory of books and pamphlets written in and about the Oregon Country. In her opening paragraph, she asked: "Do we have a literature? Where are our historians, scientists, humorists, and poets? Let us see if we can find them!" In answering her question, she noted such diverse works as Abigail Duniway's first novel, *Captain Gray's Company* (1859) as well as her volume of poetry, *My Musings* (1875) and Joaquin Miller's *Specimens* and *Joaquin Etal* (1867–69), all published in Oregon. Then she listed chronologically works on Oregon, published both outside and inside the state. Beginning with the *Journals* of Lewis and Clark, published in 1808, it included Belle Cooke's *Tears and Victory*, self-published in Salem in 1871, and closed with Alfred B. Meacham's *Wigwam and Warpath*, published in the East, as well as Judge Deady's pamphlet, "Wallamet or Willamette." published in Portland, both in 1875.

In this inventory, Frances listed her own publications. For instance, for the year 1870, she listed Wiiliam Gray's *History of Oregon*, published in Oregon, before listing her *The River of the West*, published by a subscription-book publisher in Hartford, Connecticut later that year. For the year 1874, she listed William L. Adams' *Oregon As It Is* before listing her *The Women's War with Whisky*. She closed with this notice: "With this inventory of what the State has so far produced in literature and journalism, these observations close, indulgence being asked for any inaccuracies that may be discovered when the article has been subjected to the criticism of the readers at their leisure." In this article, Frances seemed to be advertising her qualifications for a position on the faculty of the University of Oregon, which, as Deady had advised her, would open its doors in Eugene in October, 1876.[1]

Just why or when Frances decided to turn teacher is not known. However, two of her sisters—Martha Rayle and their youngest sister, Marion Fuller—had long since demonstrated that teaching, even at the grammar school level, paid reasonably well and allowed time for research and writing. Further, Frances enjoyed sharing her knowledge with others, especially young people, and was well acquainted with the history of English and American literature, as she demonstrated when she responded to an invitation from the Portland Literary Society. Her "Remarks

Upon Poetry and the Poets," read at a meeting of the Society on the evening of January 25, 1876, was published at its request, according to a note in Frances' scrapbook.[2] Her thesis was simple: "Each civilization carries along with it as part of itself, the several higher kind of arts, such as are partly mechanical such as painting or wholly intellectual like poetry." She then characterized the work of the early major English poets, starting with Chaucer and Spencer, then progressing to Shakespeare and "the savage old rebel Milton." A discussion of the poetry of the 18th century classicists was followed by that of her favorite 19th century romanticists—Keats, Shelley, Byron, and Wordsworth—later Tennyson, Browning, Swinburne, "and our own Longfellow and Bryant." She concluded that "poetry is not after all so much an art as a gift. A poet only can write poetry."

These publications were apparently lost on the board of directors of the University of Oregon as was her article in the February, 1876 number of the *West Shore*, entitled "Women as Know Nothings," in which she predicted that women would not be any better off than the Know Nothing Party of the 1850s if they did not face up to political realities. On April 21, *The New Northwest* devoted nine columns to Frances' address, entitled "Women's Influence Over Society," which had been read at the fourth annual meeting of the Oregon Women Suffrage Association. It restated Frances' well-known position on women's rights. She had never written a word to prove that women did not have a right to the ballot. When it came to "the *rights* between men and women," she asked how men had acquired the authority to grant or withhold rights from women. Never having acknowledged the withholding, she had nothing to say about her right to express her wishes by the ballot if she chose to do so. Rather she had always tried to point out to women the obstacles they would have to overcome before they could make judicious use of the ballot when they got it, as she took for granted they would. One of the greatest obstacles, she noted, was women's "unfounded confidence in their moral influence." She had asked "candid women at the assembly" to show her "one thing in society" that was any better because of their influence. She urged women to stop arguing about their right to the ballot, study the social problems of the day, and use whatever influence they had to solve them. If the solution required the ballot, she promised that it would come into their hands so easily and naturally that they would "wonder that they had not always had it." In closing, she noted that men like women were "creatures of custom" and no more responsible for the prejudices of their forebears than women.

Her address won the applause of her Salem friends like Belle Cooke and Harriet Clarke. To the latter, she confided her "regret" at her widowhood. At least Mrs.Clarke reported as much to Jesse Applegate, as his reply to her, dated Mount Yoncalla, Feb., 1876 indicates:[3]

> Mrs. Victor you say seems to regret her husband: I think I
> can understand her feelings. When it is our duty to live in
> love and harmony, and for any reason we fail to do so, con-
> science must at times present to us our wrong doings in the
> premises. There are few differences among mankind where
> all the right is on one side and all the wrong on the other.
> —The greatest punishment we can suffer is the literal pun-
> ishment of a vindictive wish . . . .

Back in Portland, Frances wrote a poem, entitled "An Oregon Spring." It was published in the March number of the *West Shore*, while she waited the decision of the board of regents of the University of Oregon. On April 23, she replied to a letter from Oliver Applegate, who was visiting their common friends, "the Clarke ladies" in Salem. She welcomed his letter and his interest in her "plan." She regretted having brought it to his attention since she had just learned from Judge Deady that "certain parties" without his knowledge had met to elect a set of teachers for the new university at Eugene City. Getting the place that she wanted was the sister of Judge Reuben Boise.[4] It was just another of her "failures," which seemed to point the way out of Oregon to a greater sphere of operations where the pay for services rendered was better. She also noted that Judge Deady had visited his Uncle Jesse in Yoncalla and asked Oliver to jog the memory of J. Henry Brown, clerk of the Oregon Pioneer Association, to send her a copy of the "Pioneer pamphlet," for which she had written a commemorative biography of Joe Meek.

An early visitor to Crater Lake, Victor thought the timeless waters sublime
She subsequently memorialized this landmark with an article published in *West Shore*.
ORHI 15005

The May number of the *West Shore* carried Frances' article, "In the Matter of Culture." The July number carried her article, "Fact and Fiction," and the August number, her poem, "A Reprimand," written and addressed to Henry after their separation in 1868. That he and her step-daughter were very much on her mind is confirmed by the fact that on August 25, 1876, with the help of W. Lair Hill, she filed a petition for a

probate of Henry's will in the Multnomah County Courthouse in Port-land.[5] After stipulating the circumstances of his death, it noted that Vic-tor had been a resident of Tacoma, Washington Territory at the time of his death with assets in Multnomah County, Oregon and that no other Oregon county had jurisdiction. The petition further stipulated that these properties, "currently in litigation," were worth "over one thousand in the aggregate." Duly sworn, Frances F. Victor stated that she was the petitioner.

The pending petition plagued Frances but did not depress her. In mid-September, according to a notice in *The New Northwest*, she exhibited a painting of Mt. Hood, which she had recently finished. She also wrote an essay, entitkled "The Gem of the Cascades (Crater Lake)," which the *West Shore* published and illustrated with photographs in its November, 1876 number. Early in 1877, she was formally appointed executrix of Henry's tangled estate, as this notice, dated February 24, indicates:[6] "Frances F. Victor, with H. H. Scott and P. W. Gillette, as sureties under $2,000, two thousand bond, to act as executrix of the last will and testament of H. C. Victor."

Meanwhile from Astoria, where Frances had traveled to gather material for her proposed updating of *All Over Oregon and Washington*, she sent a letter dated February 6, 1877 to the Oregon Woman Suffrage Association, scheduled to convene in Albany. She urged the convention to discuss the formation of women's clubs for the study of political problems. She had just ordered a copy of a book titled *Probate Confiscation*, advertised in a California newspaper. The titled, she observed, "hit the nail on the head." If it arrived in time, she would send it to the assembly. "When a man dies," she complained, "the part that should go to his wife and children without delay or interference is seized by the courts and the officers of the law, each of which gets more or less of it—creditors perhaps what remains, and the estate is in fact *confiscated* so far as the man's wife is concerned." Frances' letter may not have been read at the convention; but Mrs. Duniway published it in the March 30, 1877 issue of *The New Northwest* with apologies for its lateness.

In a letter to "Dear Bliwas," dated Portland, March 18, 1877, Frances rhapsodized about the Oregon spring and warned him that she would be visiting him in Ashland as soon as it was "accessible by rail." She wished that she could settle down some place "in peace and quietness." Fortunately, she had "a good fund of hopefulness" and would go on "believing in the future." In the meantime, she hoped that her friends would help her with her new book. On a two-dollar book, she could not afford to pay an agent a commission. She would do the canvassing herself, but where the communities were small, she was inviting her friends to send in their names and additional ones if possible. However, she intended to print no more copies than she could sell. Enclosing Oliver's receipt for a subscription to the *West Shore*, she noted that Mr. Samuel deserved "credit and patronage" for his conduct of the magazine. She also observed that she might be asked to write promotional material for the new Immigration Office. In closing, she thanked him for his photograph and promised to respond in kind.

On April 20, 1877, the Vancouver *Independent* reported that: "Mrs. F. F. Victor is shortly to visit to canvass for subscriptions to her new book of poems and stories she is going to publish. Her well known ability and popularity recommend her wherever she goes, and we bespeak for her a cordial welcome in Vancouver." This notice suggests that Frances had already negotiated with A. L. Bancroft & Company to print it as it had Deady's *Law Reports*.[7] On May 17, Frances' cousin paid her $500 in gold for three lots and all the buildings on them in the city of St. Helens.[8] She doubtless used part, if not all, of this sum to finance publication of *The New Penelope*.

After a break of several months during which she canvassed for subscriptions to her new book, Frances resumed writing for the *West Shore*. The April, 1877 number carried her article, "Evils of Our Free School System." Under the title, "Look at This Picture, Then on That," the May number carried a shorter version of an essay she had published on how, if she were a painter, she would personify California as a girlish Cleopatra and Oregon as a young Anthony with the Columbia River at his feet and snow-covered Mt. Hood over one shoulder. A letter from her Williams cousins in Walla Walla, Washington Territory, may have inspired her June contribution, titled "Girls and Roses, A Letter to the Former." In it, she described her life-long love of gardening and urged the girls of Oregon to beautify their homes on farms and in towns with gardens as she had the Iowa farm home of her Uncle Almond Williams in 1858.

Later, in June, she replied to a letter from Oliver Applegate, now editor of the weekly *Ashland Tidings*.[9] His poem in the *West Shore* had reminded her of him. She enclosed "a pretty little lyric" for his paper and would send a prose piece later. Just now she was "very full of business." Within days she would know whether her book would be published. If so, she hoped his paper would carry an announcement. In any case, she would soon be traveling to the Sound. If she reached an agreement with Mr. Samuel, she would write a series of historical articles that would begin in the July, 1877 number of the *West Shore* and run for the rest of the year at least.

On July 17, the Seattle *Intelligencer* reported that "the authoress, Mrs. Frances Fuller Victor, who wrote *The River of the West*, is spending a few weeks in towns about the Sound. She wields a graceful pen and knows how to write very readable letters for any newspaper fortunate enough to secure her services." While in Olympia, Frances doubtless visited her friend Elwood Evans, to discuss her proposed historical series with him and make use of his extensive library.

The series is actually an expanded version of Frances' article, "The Search for Fretum Anian," which Bret Harte had published in the *Overland Monthly* in the fall of 1869. Samuel published the series, titled "Historical Adventures on the Pacific Coast," in the *West Shore* in the following eleven chronological installments: "The Spanish Discoveries," July, 1877; "The Spanish Discoveries," August, 1877; "The Search for the Passage to India," September, 1877; "The Spaniards Discover the Entrance to the Columbia," October, 1877; "Captain Cook's Voyage to the Northwest Coast," November, 1877; "A Considerable Flurry at Nootka," December, 1877; "Incidents of American Trade and Discovery," January, 1878; "Captain Gray's Discovery of the Columbia," February, 1878; "Explorations of Vancouver and Quadra," March, 1878; "Some Accounts of the British Fur Companies and Overland Explorers, English and American," April 1878; "The Struggle for the Possession of the Columbia River," May, 1878.

Notably, Samuel copyrighted the 1877 installments and offered them as a bonus to new subscribers. As Frances turned out each installment on schedule, she chronicled reliable historical information about the Pacific Northwest in every day terms—a fact not lost on the would-be historical publisher, Hubert Howe Bancroft, who was on the outlook for writers in his literary workshop in San Francisco. The last installment of "Historical Adventures on the Pacific Coast" was devoted to the Astor Expedition of 1811. In its final paragraph, Frances served notice that she considered herself a competent historian: "The history subsequent to the Astor Expedition is related by so many well-known authors that it would be superfluous to rewrite it for the columns of the *West Shore*. There are, however, some romantic incidents connected with it that deserve a special effort at preservation and which will make the subject of another series of articles in the not distant future."

Much had happened before Frances penned those lines in May, 1878. In August, 1877, she had written the preface for *The New Penelope*, in which she acknowledged that few of the poems therein could be called "peculiarly Western," but as such she dedicated them to her "friends on the Pacific Coast, most especially in Oregon." On September 14, Abigail Duniway's *New Northwest* pronounced the 349-page volume, bound in purple cloth with the title stamped in gold on the front cover, "a gem." The reviewer cited the title story as an example of how the author had preserved a part of Portland's pioneer past while alerting women to the vices to be overcome and how they could do so. Frances must have appreciated the final sentences of the review: "To be enjoyed it needs only to be read. The price is $2.00, and we predict for it a ready sale." Other Portland papers also published favorable notices, part of which Frances used to promote the volume. On October 9, the Oregonian reported that among the new books added to the Portland Library was *The New Penelope and Other Stories and Poems* by Mrs. Frances Fuller Victor. In her autobiographical sketch, written in 1895, Frances noted that she had printed only one thousand copies, which were "readily sold" and had netted her "a small profit."

About his time, on the advice of the law firm of former Governor A. C. Gibbs, Frances filed a Bill of Complaint against Frank R. Davis and Walter S. Davis of California in the U. S. Circuit Court of Oregon, Judge Deady presiding, on the joint-behalf of her and her stepdaughter.[10] Soon after, her Williams relatives in Walla Walla, Washington Territory, invited her to teach a course in literature while promoting her books in the region and gathering material for a revision of *All Over Oregon and Washington*. The December 22, 1877 issue of the Walla Walla *Weekly Statesman* carried this news item:

> Study of English Literature—A rare opportunity is now
> offered to our young ladies *or* ladies and gentlemen to

engage in the study of English literature. By English literature we mean its history and philosophy as well as its analysis—beginning with the Anglo-Saxons following down to the present time. Mrs. F. F. Victor, a lady whose achievements in the field of literature stamp her as a proper person for the task, will remain at Walla Walla during the winter and if proper inducements are offered will take charge of a class of the character indicated. Any further information can be had by applying to Mrs. Victor at her residence on Maine Street above the bridge.

The same issue carried a related item, perhaps at Mrs. Victor's expense or that of her relatives. Titled :"Mrs. Victor's Books," it read as follows:

It will be noticed that all three of Mrs. Victor's publications are at the Walla Walla bookstores. Her *River of the West* and *The New Penelope* have already been noticed approvingly in these columns. Her *All Over Oregon and Washington* is now before us, and after a hasty perusal we pronounce it a valuable publication. As a matter of course Oregon comes in for the lion's share, but still the writer has endeavored to do justice to the unrivalled resources of Washington Territory and has carefully compiled a great deal of information in relation to both sections of the territory. Eastern friends are constantly writing for information in regard to Washington Territory and Oregon, and we know of no better way in which these inquiries may be answered than by mailing to the correspondents a copy of Mrs. Victor's book. We understand that if sufficient inducement can be had Mrs. Victor will revise the publication and bring it down to date. As an advertisement of the country, its importance cannot be over-estimated, and we think the people of Walla Walla could profitably invest one thousand dollars to enable this industrious writer to revise her *All Over Oregon and Washington*. Those of our readers who wish to know the history of the country in which they live should purchase all three of Mrs. Victor's books.

Page 2 of the December 22, 1877 issue of the newspaper carried the following display:

For Sale at all Bookstores

———————

Mrs. Victor's Books
"The River of the West"
"All Over Oregon and Washington"
—and—
"The New Penelope"
"The New Penelope" is somewhat local in
its character, and displays a perfect knowledge
of the Pacific Coast and its people. It is decidedly
entertaining from the first page to the end
of the last chapter. Portland *Standard*.
It will be read with much interest both
East and West of the Rockies. Portland *Bee*.

———————

The literary merit of the book should
entitle it to a large sale.

That Frances Fuller Victor did teach literature in Walla Walla is confirmed by this notice in the December 28, 1877 issue of the *Daily Oregon Statesman* in Salem: "TEACHING. Mrs. F. F. Victor, the authoress, is at present engaged in teaching literature to the young ladies and gentlemen of Walla Walla." Who attended the class and where and how it was conducted are matters of speculation. Though Frances avoided the lecture platform, she was an animated conversationalist. Among class members must have been family members and their friends with whom she doubtless shared her on-going installments of

"Historical Adventures on the Pacific Coast," in the *West Shore*, which ended with the May, 1878 number.

Just when in 1878 Frances returned to Portland is not clear; but when she did she deserted the *West Shore* for a new Portland periodical, *The*

Resources of Oregon and Washington, edited by Dana C. Pearson.[11] In the August, 1878 number, Pearson announced that he had selected her as the "Associate-Corresponding Editor" and that she already had taken to the field "to visit every portion of Oregon and Washington reaching as far as possible, annually, every city, village, lumbering and mining section and settlement to gather facts and figures and write up the country." He added: Mrs. Victor is the only person authorized to travel for subscriptions, and we take pleasure in commending her to the confidence and kind attention of all, in her important work in their great field of labor . . . . We have been most flattered by the congratulations extended to us in the connection of Mrs. F. F. Victor with our paper." Frances doubtless felt herself well situated. As a paid correspondent for Pearson's paper, she could gather material with which to update *All Over Oregon and Washington* at his expense, as it were, and keep her name before the public.

If so, she figured without Hubert Howe Bancroft, already headed for the Pacific Northwest to collect documents and interview pioneers in preparation for writing up the histories of its states and territories. Frances Fuller Victor would be caught up in his dragnet just about the time that Judge Deady, who was interested in Bancroft's project, ruled in favor of Frances and her stepdaughter, Mary E. V. Sampson, in the case of F. F. Victor *et al. vs.* the Davis brothers of California, which involved the estate of Henry C. Victor.[12] In Chapter 22, "Historic Explorations Northward" in his *Literary Industries*, Bancroft recounts in detail how he and his wife, Mathilde, steamed from San Francisco to Victoria to Vancouver Island to search for historical documents and interview pioneer informants in the Pacific Northwest much as his corps of researchers in San Francisco had already done in Mexico and California. After explaining how he had gained access to the records of British Columbia and the papers of Sir James Douglas and other notables, Bancroft notes that he hired Amos Bowman of Anacortes, Fidalgo Island, "scientific adventurer," who took dictations in short-hand and returned with the Bancrofts to San Francisco, where Bowman took a place in the Bancroft library—"a good stenographer but not successful at literary work."

Upon his arrival in Olympia, Washington Territory, Bancroft met Elwood Evans, "historian of this section," who spent two days with him and placed all his material at Bancroft's disposal. Bancroft quotes Evans as saying that he had hoped to write Washington's history himself but that Bancroft's "advantages" were superior to his that he "cheerfully" turned over the information he had been gathering during the last thirty years because he was confident that it would be properly used in Bancroft's hands. At the Portland stop, Bancroft also "met many warm friends," among whom were Judge Deady, Mrs.Abernethy, widow of the first provisional governor of Oregon, and Mrs. Harvey, daughter of Dr .John McLoughlin, as well as the editors, W. Lair Hill and Harvey W. Scott of the *Oregonian*. With regard to "Mrs. F. F. Victor, whose writings on Oregon were by far the best extant, and whom I much wished to see, was absent on the southern coast gathering information for the revision of her *All Over Oregon and Washington*. On my return to San Francisco I wrote her offering her an engagement in my library, which she accepted, and for years proved one of my most faithful and efficient assistants.[13]

At this point Bancroft was informed that the annual meeting of the Oregon Pioneer Association was convening in Salem. Proceeding at once to the capital city, his party "entered upon the most profitable five days labor of the entire trip, for there were congregated from the remotest corners of the state the very men and women we most wanted to see, those who entered it when it was a wilderness and had contributed the most important share toward making the society and government what it was. Thus six months of ordinary travel and research were compressed within these five days."

Among Frances Fuller Victor's friends, Bancroft mentions "John Minto, eloquent as a speaker and writer and with a wife but little his inferior. The women, indeed, spoke as freely as the men when gathered round the camp fires of the Oregon Pioneer Association." J. Henry Brown, clerk of the Association made appointments faster than the Bancrofts and Amos Bowman could keep them and promised to make transcripts of documents in the state archives. Other local people to whom the Bancrofts were indebted for "a profitable and pleasant stay" were the Samuel A. Clarke family. Mrs. Clarke had "a merry view of everything and called crossing the plains in 1851a grand picnic." In a letter to Oliver Applegate in Ashland, dated June 16, 1878, Mrs. Clarke indicated that they were equally impressed with Bancroft's grand scheme to write and publish a serialized history of the Pacific states.[14]

Before returning to Portland to finish their work there, the Bancrofts stopped at Oregon City to take "recitals" from A. L. Lovejoy, co-founder of Portland, and S. W. Moss, pioneer author and merchant, and arranged to get copies of documents in the city's archives. In Portland, they took dictations from Judge Deady and Judge William Strong. Bancroft notes that these dictations, together with their writings already in print, constituted "a history of Oregon." After a trip to The Dalles by steamer, Bancroft planned a leisurely overland journey from Portland to San Francisco in "a private conveyance"—a trip he had long contemplated. Along the way, the Bancrofts "stopped at many places, saw many men and gathered much new material." For instance, they spent most of a day with Jesse Applegate, "the foremost man in Oregon for a period of twenty years." Bancroft writes that he never forgot that day and the friendship that grew out of it. At Roseburg, General Joseph Lane, first governor of the Oregon Territory, was interviewed for the second time. Though Lane's son, Lafayette, "promised everything and performed nothing," Bancroft later got all that he wanted from the 78-year-old general by letters. At Jacksonville, while waiting for a conveyance to take his party to Ashland, he met Lindsay Applegate. In Ashland, he met Oliver Applegate, whom he mentions by name only.

By July, Bancroft was back at his desk in his library to take stock of what he had collected on his tour of the Pacific Northwest and to write up the history of British Columbia, with that of Washington Territory and the state of Oregon to follow. At this time, according to Mrs. Victor's friend and student, William Morris, Bancroft estimated that his serialized history of the Pacific Northwest would total some fourteen volumes.[15] The first volume would be devoted to the histories of Panama, Mexico, and California. The next two or three to Oregon and the Northwest Coast, and one to Alaska. He explained that the history of Oregon would include that of the territories of Washington , Idaho, and Montana, and that they could be written in a year's time in his library. Then Bancroft outlined how the histories would be written after he had determined the geographical divisions: "When all the material I have on a

Salem supporter, the Hon. John Minto, won Victor's regard with his
Horatio Alger-like rise from boy-miner in England via the coal fields
of Pennsylvania and thence to many Oregon achievements.
ORHI 104250

given division is gone over and notes taken according to the general plan, I shall give one person one thing or part to write, and another person another part . . . ."

He was even more forthright in stating his assistants' rights:

> The work is wholly mine. I do what I can myself, and pay
> for what I have done over that; but I father the whole of it
> and it goes out under my name. All who work in the library
> do so simply as my assistants. Their work is mine to print,
> scratch, or throw in the fire. I have no secrets, yet I do not
> tell everybody just what each does. I do not pretend to do
> all the work myself, that is to prepare for the printer all that
> goes out under my name. I have three or four now who can
> write for the printer after a fashion; none of them can suit
> me as well as I can suit myself. One or two will write with
> very little change from me. All the rest require sometimes
> almost rewriting.

He added that he liked to acknowledge his obligations to his assistants, but such acknowledgments were his to give and not to be claimed as a right. Nor was he sure of mentioning certain persons in connection with certain parts of the work, as he had done in the introduction to the *Native Races*. The only mention he promised was a biographical notice in the final volume of the projected series.[16]

Just when and where Frances received Bancroft's letter and what she thought of it at the time are not known. But in her autobiographical sketch written in 1895, she recalled her response as follows:

> Soon after the publication of 'The New Penelope,' Mr.
> Bancroft advertised his plan of publishing a series of Pacific
> Coast histories. As I had prepared by a long study of my
> subject to write a history of Oregon that should be stan-
> dard, I felt a good deal cut up by having my field invaded by
> another not so well prepared, but with a plump exchequer
> and an array of assistants. It was useless to compete against
> forces, and on being solicited by Mr. Bancroft to become
> one of his collaborators, rather than have my previous work

lost, I consented to join his corps of writers, taking for my division Oregon History. In this I put all my material, doing my work as conscientiously as if I had been writing with the hope of making fame and fortune for myself, at first in the ardor of my occupation, thinking little on that matter.

Late in the summer of 1878, Frances consulted Judge Deady, not only on Bancroft's offer but also on her Bill of Complaint, pending since December, 1877. On October 7, the U. S. Circuit Court of Oregon, Judge Deady presiding, handed down a ruling favorable to Frances Fuller Victor and Mary Edwards V. Sampson. At the hearing, they were represented by A. C. Gibbs. The defendants, Frank A. Davis and Walter S. Davis of California, were not present nor were they represented by counsel. Plainly stated, Deady ruled that the complainants owned two-thirds of the disputed property in Columbia and Multnomah counties and that within 60 days the defendants should convey title to the undivided one-half of the properties claimed. Deady's decree would fester until 1885, when it was overturned by the Oregon Supreme Court in Salem. In 1878, however, it permitted Victor to accept Bancroft's offer.

On Sunday, October 20, 52-year-old Frances Fuller Victor departed Portland—one of 127 cabin passengers aboard the steamer *Great Republic*. The same evening the first meeting of the recently organized Oregon Press Association was held in the Salem home of Samuel A. Clarke. Here Frances' departure for Bancroft's library must have been a topic of interest while members enjoyed "an elegant collation," served by Mrs. Clarke and her daughters. Afterwards, literary works were read and speeches made by several members, including Abigail Duniway and Mrs. John Minto. The latter inspired "intense merriment" by her comments on "Bohemian journalists," who had recently called her "a crowing hen" and were now coming out on "the side of newspaper courtesy."

The next morning the *Oregonian* reported both on the press party and on Mrs. Victor's departure. Prior to leaving, she had granted Leopold Samuel the right to reprint in the December, 1878 number of the *West Shore* her poem, "I Only Wished to Know," published in *The New*

Penelope. That she did not advise Oliver Applegate of her plans by letter is not surprising. On Christmas Day, 1878, he was married to Ella Anderson, daughter of a Methodist minister and pioneer of 1853, in Ashland.[17]

Arriving in San Francisco in time to spend the winter holidays with her sister, Martha, and friends, Frances did not know how long she would be engaged at the Bancroft Library or what would be expected of her there. However, she must have been looking forward to threshing the harvest of documents and dictations that the Bancroft party had gathered during its sweep of the Pacific Northwest. In any event, she was confident that she was better prepared than he or anyone else in his library to write up its history. She also was well aware that she was leaving behind unfinished business. The final settlement of Henry's labyrinthine estate she could leave in the hands of her lawyer, A. C. Gibbs, at her expense. Updating, renaming, and republishing her *All Over Oregon and Washington* she would have to do on her own, though she was hopeful that the settlement of Henry's estate would finance a sparkling revision of one of her favorite books—and essential part of her larger legacy to the Pacific Northwest.

CHAPTER 12

HOLDING HER OWN IN THE BANCROFT LITERARY WORKSHOP
(1879-84)

During the first half of the eleven years that Frances Fuller Victor spent as the only woman in the Bancroft Literary Workshop, she won the respect of her employer and her colleagues, most of whom were her juniors. During these six-day weeks and ten-hour days, she turned out a tremendous amount of work for Bancroft.[1] On her own time and under her own name, she wrote an occasional article for a California, Oregon, or Washington publication, based on her research in the Bancroft Library. Thus she kept her name before the public and supplemented her weekly salary of $23.10.[2] She also profited from the re-issue of her Beadle dime novels, first published by her brother-in-law, Orville Victor, in New York City in 1862. This additional income helped her fund her attempt to settle her claim and that of her stepdaughter, Mary V. Sampson, to the disputed estate of her late husband, Henry C. Victor, in St. Helens, Oregon.

Prior to her arrival in San Francisco, the August 31, 1878 issue of the weekly *Argonaut* carried a reprint of her poem, "Waiting," under the heading, "California Poets, VIII." It was prefaced by a brief account of her literary background from the publication of her first poem in Ohio in the early 1840s to her most recent book, *The New Penelope and Other Stories and Poems*, 1877. It did not mention her engagement at the Bancroft Library. It apparently was read by Kate Bancroft, then living at the home of her uncle, Alfred L. Bancroft, titular head of A. L. Bancroft & Co.[3] On September 1, Kate wrote her father that she was glad that Mrs. Victor was going to write for him. "Probably now," she mused, "she'll be able to save and pay the three or four dollars she owes the firm."[4] Except for his second wife, Mathilda, and his daughter, Kate, by his first wife, both of whom had accompanied him on collecting expeditions, Bancroft had yet to find a woman writer who had the physical and intellectual stamina that he demanded of himself and his male writers.[5]

Frances was no stranger to the wood and brick, five-story Bancroft Building at 721 Market Street. Ever since her arrival in San Francisco in the spring of 1863, she had followed the fortunes of the Bancroft firm under different names and at different locations. After settling in a boarding house at 218 Eddy Street, she set out to explore Bancroft's paper world—a beehive of activity from the basement to the fifth floor.[6] In addition to a display of large musical instruments like organs and pianos, the basement housed the receiving, packing, and shipping departments as well as a steam engine that powered the manufacturing devices on the upper floors and an artesian well that provided water for the building. The first floor was occupied by the most public and profitable departments. Among them was the music department proper, with Charles Bancroft, a nephew, in charge. Headed by E. P. Stone, the law department which published and sold legal digests and documents, also was located on this floor. So was the stationery department, offering items ranging from blank labels for salmon factories to official forms for business, bank, and law firms—all printed on the premises.

On the second floor, the subscription department fielded an army of agents, who canvassed the Western half of North America from Panama to Alaska and as far west as Australia and Japan. At the rear were the business offices, chief of which was that of A. L. Bancroft, who owned less than half of the business and no part of the site or the building on it. Nearby were the offices of the chief cashier, the bookkeeper, and correspondents—all loyal and long-time employees. Up front was the education department, in charge of Harlow P. Bancroft, another nephew. It offered everything for "the fitting out of a school, academy, or college," and maintained a free teacher-placement bureau. Under the direction of E. G. Sanborn, this department also published a series of readers and spellers for elementary schools, adopted by several Western states, including Oregon.

The general location of the Fremont cottage. Fort Point lies beneath the present Golden Gate Bridge. This view looks over the fort, across the Golden Gate to the headlands of Marin County.

ORHI 27854-A

The third, fourth, and fifth floors were off limits to the public. The third floor was occupied by the printing department, under the direction of William Bancroft, yet another nephew; and the fourth floor by the bindery with an equally dedicated staff. The fifth floor was devoted solely to H. H. Bancroft's ever-increasing library and his literary workshop. On the morning that Frances mounted the stairs with documents of her own, she doubtless saw it much as Bancroft described it in his *Literary Industries.*[7]

The sky-lighted room ran the full length of the 170-foot building, which narrowed in width from 50 feet in the south to 35 feet in the north. The narrower end housed the library, then numbering over 20,000 items. Bales of newspapers were stored on the floor. The larger, better-lighted south end provided working space for Bancroft and his assistants, who varied from fifty to a dozen, depending on the nature of the work in progress. Along the west wall was a high table at which several indexers and note takers could stand at the same time. Others at more advanced stages of the writing process sat at small tables. Thus indexers, note takers, and writers all had easy access to the library.

Frances likely found Bancroft in his office, the first of four along the east wall of the building. He may have been standing at his ingenious writing machine—a revolving table, some eight feet in diameter. After an assistant arranged relevant source materials on the table, he could turn it to bring them up as he needed them. The walls of his office were hung with historical maps and portraits as well as certificates of honor awarded him as the founder of the library and author of *Native Races*. Among them was an honorary membership in the Massachusetts Historical Society and an honorary Master of Arts degree from Yale University.

Bancroft assigned Frances an empty office next to his and advised her that the two next to hers were the working and sleeping quarters of his two ablest assistants—Henry L. Oak, chief librarian, and foreign-born William Nemos, both bearded young bachelors. She soon ferreted out their backgrounds and, more importantly, their positions in the workshop. Another stalwart in Bancroft's stable of writers was Thomas Savage. In *Literary Industries*, Bancroft named Savage as his third most valuable assistant, just ahead of Frances Fuller Victor.[8]

The impression that Frances made on the men in the workshop can only be imagined. After she left his employ, Bancroft wrote: "I found Frances Fuller Victor during her arduous labor for a period of ten years in my library, a lady of cultivated mind, of ability, and singular application, likewise her physical endurance was remarkable."[9] In his estimate of her work after they both left the workshop, Henry Oak stated that she had been the only published writer in the workshop. "Of her ability and faithfulness," he wrote, "hardly too much can be said in praise." He added that she had the advantage of "literary experience and an intimate acquaintance with the history of the Oregon Territory." However, he faulted her for "lack of drill in the library method of presentation, especially her failure to use notes prepared by library assistants. He also faulted her "enthusiasm," wherein she often exceeded the space allotted to her. So he and others had been forced to condense her work by using smaller type or transferring parts of it to other volumes.[10]

Indeed, Frances used her own historical collection, did her own research in the library, and wrote for information she did not find there. Soon after her arrival, she took over Bancroft's on-going correspondence with General Joseph Lane and that of the critical Jesse Applegate. In a letter to Bancroft, dated Roseburg, Oregon, November 12, 1878, the General reported that he had received a letter from Mrs. Victor, asking for information which he had given Bancroft in June of that year. On the 20th, the General replied to Frances' letter of the 15th. He enclosed an eight-page letter, describing his arrival in Oregon as its first territorial governor and his service as its delegate to the U. S. Congress until it achieved statehood in 1859.[11]

On December 8, 1878, Frances wrote Judge Deady from her home address.[12] She had not yet seen the dictation that he had given Mr. Bancroft in Portland because of "the mass of matter" through which she must wade. Much was "comparatively useless and not to the point," and much of the rest "had to be proved." She needed someone to go through the state archives from the beginning of the formation of state government and comment on the significant legislative acts, especially "the motives and circumstances" that had prompted their enactment. She also wanted biographies of "men of mark," such as he had written for the San Francisco *Evening Bulletin*, including his own. Her final paragraph was for his eyes alone:

> Write *ME* of these things. Of course, this is Mr. Bancroft's
> book. But I am getting everything in shape as he never
> could—not being familiar with the ground, and if we agree
> about it when I am ready to begin I shall probably write it.

In any case, it is my conscientious desire to do my work faithfully.

In this postscript, she addressed one of Deady's major concerns:

By the way, Mr. B. will not allow Wallamet—says custom rules. It cuts me to the quick to write Willamette.

By February, 1879, *Oregon I* was well underway. It covered the years 1834-1848 about which Frances had written in her *River of the West*. In her library research, she found a file of the *Oregon Argus* in a bale of Oregon newspapers. Finding items that needed clarification, she wrote its former editor, D. W. Craig.[13] She asked for a sketch of this and other Salem newspapers—everything from their beginnings and politics to their rates to his biography. In a letter, dated March 20, she thanked Craig for his detailed reply and asked him for a list of notable Oregon women about whom she hoped to write at a later date.

Correspondence between Judge Deady in Portland and Mr. Bancroft in San Francisco is equally revealing.[14] In a letter to Bancroft, Deady suggested that he send his Salem agent, J. Henry Brown, to Portland to take notes from the file of the *Oregonian* because its board of directors would not send the file to Salem as Brown had requested. In response, Bancroft noted that Mrs. Victor had taken notes from the *Oregon Argus* and doubted that Mr. Brown would know what notes to take out.

By this time, Bancroft had told Frances that he did not intend to put the names of assistants on the title pages of volumes that they helped write, but he would give his estimate of the work of each in the final volume of the series. As she was happily executing an undertaking she had long planned, she set aside the question of authorship at the time. Her immediate concerns were how to structure a state history without a model and to write a documented monograph on the name Oregon.[15] In her eight-page monograph, she credited the American explorer, Jonathan Carver, with having been the first to use the word in print in referring to the "Oregon or River of the West," as one of "the four most capital rivers in the continent of North America." The first American writer to use the word had been the poet, William Cullen Bryant in his poem, "Thanatopsis," written in 1817, which had made the word immortal. It finally had been fastened on the Columbia River territory by Hall J. Kelley through his memorials to Congress. In a word, the term Oregon has been invented by Carver, made famous by Bryant, and given currency by the visionary Kelley.

She also digested Jesse Applegate's notes on her *River of the West*, which he had forwarded to H. H. Bancroft, Esq. Historian.[16] Applegate had written, in part:

> Mrs. F. F. Victor began to collect material for a readable book to be called "The History of Oregon." When her material was sorted, arranged, and put together, as it fell below the dignity of history, she thought it best to call it a biography of Joe Meek. But her publisher overruled her in the matter of title, and christened the child of her brain, "The River of the West."

Applegate further noted that Mrs. Victor had spent a week or more at his home in Southern Oregon, where she asked "some thousands of questions." He had given her all the knowledge he possessed "on the early history of the country," little of which he had found in her finished work. He added that he took no pleasure in reviewing incidents of half a century ago. Oregon had no history worth recording. However, to the extent that Mrs. Victor had used "the annals of Oregon" in connection with the incidents in the life of her hero, Joe Meek, she had taken pains to ascertain the facts and had stated them impartially. So the shortest way by which he could give Bancroft the benefit of his knowledge of Oregon history was to comment on her *River of the West* page by page.

In an undated note, scribbled on page 23 of Applegate's "Views of Oregon History," Frances stated that he was "slightly in error" as to her purpose in writing about Oregon. She explained how she had come to write first, *The River of the West* and then, *All Over Oregon and Washington*, in neither of which she had "aimed" at writing history. That she had told it in part was shown by the fact that most Oregonians called the former, "Mrs. Victor's History of Oregon."

By November, 1879, Frances had finished the 26 chapters of Bancroft's *Oregon, I*; and Bancroft submitted them to Jesse Applegate for comment. In a letter, dated Yoncalla, Ogn, November 24, 1879 and addressed to H. H. Bancroft and Mrs. F. F. Victor, Historians, Applegate stated that he had read the manuscipt of their forthcoming "History of Oregon" and appreciated the honor that they had done him in asking him to criticize a work that would "stand through the centuries as the highest if not the only authority on the subject it treated." In suiting style to substance, they had equaled Washington Irving and excelled "all living historians." But he could not resist chiding them for wasting their labor and talent "on savages and uncivilized Oregonians." As their "humblest friend," he was tired of trying to help them make something out of what at best could be to the world of no more importance than "a tempest in a teapot." However, on December 8, 1879, he wrote Bancroft that he had just answered a letter from Mrs. Victor, presumably on his behalf, and hoped that Bancroft would be "a good master" and that Mrs. Victor would "render good service."[17] So ended Jesse Applegate's reluctant contributions to Bancroft's *History of the Pacific States.*

By year's end, Frances was writing the final chapter of *Oregon, I.* In it she narrated the "Journey of Thornton" and the "Adventures of Meek," whom she characterized as "The Pious Lawyer and the Profane Trapper." Her letters to Elwood Evans and Judge Deady indicate that they had replaced the feisty Jesse Applegate as her informants. In a letter to Evans, dated December 9, she wrote that she wished he could read the chapter in which she had "entirely and completely unraveled the tangles" that had troubled her at that time. "The whole story is as plain as A. B. C." she continued. "You would enjoy the unfolding." Then she confided that Dr. W. T. Tolmie of British Columbia and Judge James Swan of Washington Territory had written Bancroft that they had heard that she was writing the history of Washington Territory and did not think that she was as competent as others, including Evans. Conceding Evans' "superior personal knowledge of events and full literary ability," she contended that she was just as able as anyone else to write according to Mr. Bancroft's plan—to get all the material together and extract the truth." "It is the material we want," she added. "The writing is easy enough."

As for Dr. Gray's current campaign to erect a monument to Dr. Whitman as "the man who had saved Oregon for the United States," her research showed that he was wrong and would make "Oregon the laughing-stock of future generations." She had read all the diplomatic correspondence on the subject. The Ashburton Treaty, which Whitman was said to have influenced, related only to the boundary of Maine and had been signed before Whitman had journeyed east on mission business in the winter of 1742. She suggested that Evans advise Gray of those facts "privately by letter." Gray would suspect her of "not holding a missionary in sufficient veneration." She respected Whitman "as a man and a missionary" and was confident that he would not want to be misrepresented."[18]

In a letter to Judge Deady, dated December 21, Frances asked him for the date of Dr. McLoughlin's conversion to Catholicism among other matters. Then she asked him to secure for her, without mentioning her name, a copy of the *Pacific Christian Advocate*, in which Thornton had attacked views that she had expressed in her *River of the West*—views which she now recognized had been "too mild." Thornton had gone to Washington, D.C. "as a tool" of the governor of the provisional government of Oregon, George Abernethy (1845-1849). Failing where the appointed delegate, Samuel R. Thurston, had succeeded, Thornton had returned to Oregon to attach himself to Dr. McLoughlin as his professional adviser. "It is a just disputation of Providence," Frances observed, "that Abernethy died poor and that Thornton is as he is. But, of course, in history, we do not go into that view of the subject, just hard facts."

On January 7, 1880, Frances received a flattering letter from Elwood Evans.[19] In her reply, she noted that she enjoyed being praised by her friends, but had not used it to impress Mr. Bancroft, who had said he was pleased with her work. Though she was sure that Evans could do "justice" to the history of the Washington Territory, she doubted that he had the "patience to work as one of his [Bancroft's] assistants." During the past year, she had worked from Monday through Saturday for fifty-one weeks. She was also writing letters concerning her work that "put into Mr. B's and under his name much that would not otherwise be in his library." This material was her "stock in trade," which she could not reuse and for which she was paid "a very modest salary." If she died before she had a chance to "refurbish" her own reputation, she hoped a friend or two would give her "a decent obituary." As for Evans' materials in "Mr. B's hands," she would need them for the next few weeks while she wrote up the Cayuse Indian War. She had everything she needed to write "a complete history of how the Methodist missionaries had saved Oregon for the United States while they were trying to stuff it down the throat of the Methodist church." If she did not overturn Gray's position now, "future historians would point to evidence that Bancroft had overlooked." She added that in Bancroft's history of Oregon, "Mr.Gray is set right." She also thanked Evans for having mentioned the Boston *Missionary Herald* for 1841–42. It wold help her determine why Whitman has gone East in the winter of 1842. The *Herald* was not in the Bancroft Library, but she would write for relevant copies. In this connection, she noted that she had written a poem of a thousand lines, entitled The Poppies of Waiilatpu." She would like "to set it afloat in a pretty little book." And should there by any profit after the bills were paid, she would offer it toward "a suitable monument to Dr. and Mrs. Whitman." Finding out all these things has been "intensely interesting and laborious," she wrote. "Nobody else in the library could have found it out because they had not the clue, but knowing what I did about the men themselves, I put that to that, and had the whole story." She was sending him "the desired books" for which she was charging him half-price. She apologized for the condition of her *All Over Oregon and Washington*, her last copy. She wanted to revise it, but there was no money in it, and she as still in debt "for trying to do impossible things."

Soon after, perhaps to prove that she was competent to write the history of Washington Territory, Frances wrote an article entitled "Nomenclature of Puget Sound." It appeared as the lead article in the May 1, 1880 issue of *North Pacific Coast*, a new semi-monthly journal published in New Tacoma. She started with the exploration of Juan de Fuca and his discovery of the strait that bears his name. This was followed by Spanish, British, and American explorers who had named geographic features in their search for the fabled Northwest Passage. Last came the map-makers—Captain George Vancouver in 1792–94 and the American naval officer, Lt. Charles Wilkes, in 1841. Together they had bestowed hundreds of names on strategic geographic features in the Puget Sound area. In closing Frances noted that, more or less, history is brought out by giving the origins of names.

In the meantime, her letters to Judge Deady, dated April 10 and June 17, indicate that she was working in *Oregon, II* in the summer of 1880.[20] In the first, after thanking him for information on the Portland Library Association, she noted that she often wished that she were doing her work in Portland. She needed someone to give her the history of the improvements at Willamette Falls—"from Dr. McLoughlin down." In the second letter, she asked about "all the important land cases under the Donation Law." As for "Wallamet," she again explained that it vexed her to use "the Frenchified spelling," but Mr. Bancroft would not change it without "some special authority—for instance, a legislative act."

The July, 1880 number of the *Californian*, which had replaced the defunct *Overland Monthly* in San Francisco, presented a challenge that Frances could not resist. It was a four-page article, entitled "How Whitman Saved Oregon," written by her former Salem friend, Samuel A. Clarke. Its closing paragraph suggests that Clarke's romantic account of how Whitman had "saved" Oregon was a promotional piece for the Villard Railroad Company, headquartered in Portland:[21]

> The work of development has just begun. It is to be regretted that Dr. Whitman did not live long enough to see this day, and receive from a grateful country the plaudits he so well earned . . . . The pioneer missionary of 1836 could not dream that the settler of 1880 would find all the modern conveniences and civilized usages at his command and possess the means, by telegraph, to communicate with the uttermost parts of the world.

Frances' rebuttal, entitled "Did Whitman Save Oregon?," was published in the September number of the *Californian*. It focused on Clarke's ignorance of the history of diplomatic relations between Great Britain and the United States, available to her in Bancroft's Library. She summarized the treaties and conventions negotiated by the two nations from the end of the Revolutionary War to the Ashburton Treaty, signed in August,

1842. She explained that Ashburton had come to Washington, D.C. earlier that summer to negotiate a number of issues. Here she paused to remark: "That a private citizen like Dr. Whitman would have had any influence on questions that had baffled the skills of great diplomats for half a century is not susceptible of belief." Next she addressed "the romantic and foundationless story of Dr. Whitman's journey for a political purpose." Ashburton had returned to London, where negotiations over the Oregon Question had continued. Further, James K. Polk, who had used the Oregon Question as an issue in his presidential campaign, had "cheerfully" signed the Oregon Treaty in June 1846. It had made the 49th parallel the northern boundary of the United States west as well as east of the Rocky Mountains.

Frances addressed her closing remarks to her colleagues in the Bancroft Literary Workshop as well as to the Clarke family:

> "no similar question was ever clothed with the real romance
> that has clung to and colored the Oregon Question. It less
> needs the adventitious aids of invention than any modern
> history . . . . That Dr. Whitman was, while a soldier of the
> cross, equally fit to be a soldier of the sword there is no
> doubt. He was a valiant and true man, and would have
> scorned to claim for himself honors he had never won. It,
> therefore, is no kindness to his memory to place him in a
> false position, from which the reader of encyclopedias
> could easily route him. The author of "How Whitman
> Saved Oregon" is only one of the number who have given
> credence to this well-invented historical romance, without
> taking the trouble to look up his authorities. He is too
> good a writer to be so careless of his facts, and too sensible
> a gentleman not to be glad of being set right.

Frances' airing of this prickly historical incident was not lost on Bancroft. He asked her to interview representatives of the Mormon Church, when he invited them to the literary workshop to present church documents relative to the history of Utah.

Frances also continued to publish in Oregon. The December, 1880 number of the *West Shore* carried a letter in which she took her reader on a tour of Oregon mountains, forests, and rivers. A second letter addressed the Whitman controversy. This she mailed to her friend, D. C. Ireland, then owner-editor of the *Daily Astorian*. He published it after the holidays, according to a letter she wrote Elwood Evans, dated February 17, 1881in which she thanked him for sending her a copy of Archibald McKinley's review of his address on Whitman. It convinced her that "the Whitman we have been taught to regard as a patriot, a saint, and a martyr is a fraud, and it would be a fraud on the country to erect a monument to *that* Whitman."

In the spring of 1881, H. H. Bancroft started publishing the first volume of his history of the Pacific states under the imprint of A. L. Bancroft & Co. However, relocating the ever-increasing library had preceded the ambitious publishing program. According to Bancroft, his nephew, William, head of the printing department, regarded the space on the fifth floor occupied by the library as essential to the publishing program. Further, during the decade that the library had occupied the fifth floor, Bancroft and Oak had "trembled for its safety," especially after smoke from a fire in the basement had driven library workers out on the roof. Thereafter, they had discussed relocating the library in a separate, fireproof building as distant as Sonoma. Finally, Bancroft selected a more convenient site on Valencia Street—an easy street-car ride from the firm's publishing and subscription departments.

The two-story brick building in the center of the 120 x 126-foot lot was carefully constructed.[22] All openings were closed with iron covers, and a high fence was built on two sides of the lot to protect the building from winds that might fan a fire. The grounds were planted with trees, grass, and flowers—"a little Eden," according to Bancroft. The glass over the doorway displayed the number 1518; and the door bore the nameplate, "The Bancroft Library," in plain script. Before the move on October 9, Oak and his assistants weeded out duplicates and re-catalogued the 35,000-volume library before dividing it into convenient classes. Some 16,000 volumes were arranged along the walls of the first floor of the well-lighted building. They included accounts of early voyages, legislative and other public papers of the federal government as well as those of states and territories on the Pacific Slope; scrapbooks, directories, pamphlets, and cumbersome folios. This floor also accommodated a huge case of maps as well as several smaller ones for the new card index and paper envelopes filled with notes on given subjects. Shelving extended across the floor was loaded with bales of Pacific Coast newspapers.

The top floor, reached by a stairway rising from the center of the main floor, housed the heart of the library and provided working space for Bancroft and his assistants, Some 12,000 volumes, arranged alphabetically by author, constituted the major share. Over 400 rare and irreplaceable volumes constituted a second class. A third class of volumes related to the four geographic divisions of the history—Central America and Mexico, California and the Northwest Coast, Oregon and the interior territories, and British Columbia and Alaska. Most of Bancroft's assistants sat at small tables, each doing his own work. Bancroft's "private apartment" was located at one end of the second floor and "the rooms of Mrs. Victor, Mr. Oak, and Mr. Nemo at the other." The empty wall space on both floors was covered with portraits, engravings, and unique specimens," all having reference to the territories covered by the collection.

On October 10, 1881, the typesetting began on Bancroft's *History of the Pacific States*. At the time, he estimated that he had the equivalent of 15 volumes in manuscript and that three-fourths of the remainder "had been accomplished in note-taking." The first volumes he gave to the printers were *Central America, I (1501–1521)* and *Mexico, I (1515–1521)*. In defending his decision to publish his historical series under the imprint of the family firm, he wrote: "The world may call it making merchandise of literature if they choose . . . .I knew it was not. There was no money in my books to the business, hence the business did not specially want them."[23] After engaging Nathan Stone, a former employee, who had just returned from Japan, to direct the publication and sale of his historical series, he invited the governor of California and the mayor of San Francisco "to inspect the work" and give him a certificate that it would be completed "at the rate of three or four volumes a year." Finally, he revised his will to provide for its completion in the event of his death.

Among other manuscripts ready for the printers was Frances Fuller Victor's *Oregon, I (1834—1848)*, though not as she had written it. Among other changes, Bancroft had transferred her account of the Oregon Question to *Northwest Coast II (1800–1846)* on which he and Oak had worked.

On December 1, 1881 Frances was living at 3 Glen Park Avenue within walking distance of the new library. From here she forwarded to Elwood Evans relevant parts of a letter, dated Richmond, Missouri, September 12, 1842, written by Philip Edwards. A lay member of the Methodist Mission in the Willamette Valley, he had returned to the East with Jason Lee in 1838. In his letter, Edwards had advised against using wagons in crossing the plains. Clear evidence, Frances advised Evans, that before Dr. Whitman had headed East in the winter of 1842 a project for colonizing Oregon had been "on foot." She intended to write an article in which she would credit Dr. Elijah White with having raised an immigration party on the advice of the federal government when it returned him to Oregon as an Indian agent in 1842. Though she did not mention the new library, she reported that she was busy, apparently on *Oregon, II*.

For Frances, 1882 was an eventful year. In April her first Beadle dime novel was re-issued in New York City. She also met Helen Hunt Jackson when she visited the Bancroft Library. In the fall of 1881, the *Century Magazine* had engaged her to write a series of articles on the missions strung along Father Junipero Serra's Camino Real. The well-financed Mrs. Jackson, wife of a Colorado railroad magnate, has caused quite a stir when she visited the library and prompted Frances to dash off a three-part series, obviously with Bancroft's permission, which she entitled "Studies of the California Missions" and submitted to Charles Phelps, editor of the *Californian*. At Bancroft's request, Frances also wrote a promotional piece on his library for the same magazine.

Bancroft's undated letters to Clarence Bagley, a publisher and historian of Washington Territory, document the progress of Bancroft's historical series and his methods of dealing with contributors.[24] In the first, Bancroft assured Bagley that his librarians would check on all of his papers in the Bancroft Library, where they were perfectly safe. He also noted that much of the *Northwest Coast* and *British Columbia* as well as *Oregon, I* were in print. In a follow-up letter, Bancroft noted that, except for Bagley and Evans, the history of Washington Territory would have "gone in with Oregon." As for Mrs. Victor, she was going to Portland for an absence of six weeks.

Two memoranda that Bancroft wrote Nemos during Frances' absence are equally revealing.[25] In the first Bancroft noted that he was reading the galleys of Chapter II, "Some of My Assistants," of the final volume of the series, *Literary Industries,* which he would leave to his assistants to finish, In the second memo, Bancroft asked Nemos to write up his "system for training assistants in getting out and arranging materials for history." The matter had come to mind while he had been going over Mrs. Victor's *Oregon, I.* He admitted that "she is a good magazine writer and knows something about Oregon, but knows nothing about writing history or our method." His aim was to give "the simple story in the text and provide explanations, elucidations, and discussions in its notes." She mixed the two "indiscriminately." Her statements and dates were sometimes inaccurate, and her conclusions were too often "from the heart." Her chapter on life at Fort Vancouver belonged in the *Northwest Coast,* where he had put it. "Yet," he conceded, "she is a good, honest, and hardworking woman. What are we going to do about it?" Perhaps Nemos could help arrange her material and present it to him in the proper form. He had said nothing to her, but it shouldn't take more than two years to make a good history of Oregon, and she had been at it for almost four.

While staying at the home of her cousin, Douglas Williams, in Portland, Frances called on Judge Deady for historical information and legal advice. There is no evidence that her stepdaughter, Mary, and her husband, Albert Sampson, joined her in Portland, but they authorized her to act on their behalf with respect to the estate of Henry C. Victor in St. Helens. During the week of June 10-17, Deady noted in his diary that he had subscribed to Bancroft's *History of the Pacific States* for "4\frac{1}{2}$ a volume in cloth, perhaps 25 volumes." On the 30th, Deady wrote James Nesmith in Salem, enclosing a card from Mrs. Victor, asking for information. Deady asked Nesmith to answer her query and help "write the best history of Oregon yet published."

In San Francisco, Charles Phelps serialized Frances Fuller Victor's "Studies of the California Missions" in the May, June, and July numbers of the *Californian* and accepted her essay, "Up the Columbia River— Rose and I," for the September number. It was based on a real or imaginary steamboat trip from Astoria to The Dalles. By the end of June, William Marshall, a popular lecturer of Fitchburg, Massachusetts, had tracked Frances down at the Bancroft workshop and enlisted her aid in unraveling the Whitman story.[26] She responded with a series of letters, beginning in July. In the first, she explained Whitman's purpose in going East in the winter of 1842, and the limited role he had played in the Oregon immigration in the summer of 1843. In the second, she noted that Mr. Bancroft had all the evidence in his library, but was unwilling to share it until his history of Oregon was published. She also warned Marshall against the current testimony of Perrin Whitman, Dr. Marcus Whitman's nephew, and that of the Rev. Myron Eells, as they both had been children "when the events described had occurred."

On November 1, 1882, Frances wrote Deady about discrepancies between laws published in the *Oregon Blue Book* and the *Oregon Spectator*, a newspaper.[27] With respect to Mr. Bancroft's history, "a fortune would be spent on advertising it." She had written an article about the library for the *Californian* "by the desire of Mr. Bancroft." He had wanted it "in a hurry to its detriment," and then had put off printing it until the December number. Later that month, Bancroft felt the sting of the *Wasp*, a satirical San Francisco weekly. In his column, "Prattle," Ambrose Bierce charged among other things that Bancroft was hiring "hack writers" to do his work for him. They collected and digested the data, which he transcribed so that he could call it his own. Bancroft ignored this attack as did Frances' signed article, "The Bancroft Historical Library," published in the December, 1882 number of the *Californian and Overland Monthly*.

After ranking the Bancroft Library with that of the Alexandrian, now lost to civilization, Frances lauded Bancroft's ambition and enterprise in assembling the authorities on the history of California with a view to writing its history. He had gathered these materials in California and Eastern states, and Europe, where his agents continued to apprise him of relevant items. He had followed the same system in collecting materials for other Pacific states. Ivan Petroff and others had brought

Russian collections to the library that were of great value to the history of Alaska. During his visit to British Columbia in the spring and summer of 1878, Bancroft has obtained a copy of every book on the subject as well as the manuscripts of many gentlemen connected with the Hudson's Bay Company.

With regard to her own interests, she wrote:

> For the history of Oregon and Washington Territory, he
> secured the collection of the Hon. Elwood Evans, the most
> comprehensive yet made of the historical data of that
> region, the extensive correspondence of Mrs. Victor with
> Oregon pioneers, a partial collection by United States
> Judge M. P. Deady, manuscript contributions of Judge
> William Strong, Judge P. P. Prim, Judge J. Q. Thornton,
> General Joseph Lane, Hon. Jesse Applegate, Hon. J. W.
> Nesmith, and sixty other of the earliest settlers and men of
> affairs in that portion of the Pacific Coast. Even Idaho and
> Montana have furnished some original matters, but that
> territory is not thoroughly explored.

She added that the history of Utah was complete, thanks to the cooperation of representatives of the Church of the Latter Day Saints. Estimating that the library on Valencia Street contained some 35,000 items, she mentioned Mr. Bancroft's "special study" and that of "the only lady assistant" as well as "the apartments of the two gentlemen who reside on the premises." She also referred to Mr. Bancroft's "associates," who did the indexing and note taking. "From this point of view," she observed, "too much importance can not be attached to this library which Mr. Bancroft has collected nor the work to which he is devoting his life together with his faithful co-workers who deserve well of the public for conscientious application to a really serious, long-continued, and laborious task, albeit it is to Mr. Bancroft and his assistants a labor of love." In closing, she noted that "this special historical collection is proof of the vigor and intellectuality of the citizens of California, eminent among whom will always be the name of the founder of the library."

Doubtless pleased with Frances' article on his library, Bancroft prevailed on the editor of the first number of the *Overland Monthly*, 2nd series, January 1883 to run a article on him and review his *Central America, I (1501–1530)* and *Mexico, I (1516–1521)* in the February and April numbers of the magazine.

Writing to Judge Deady at home on "whimsical flowered" stationery on December 7, 1882, Frances thanked him for his "lucid answers" to her questions "on law, etc.," in return for which she would be glad "to overlook" his biography if permitted to do so. Her main concern was with her "legal griefs," though she knew that she should not discuss them with the judge of whose bar she was complaining. She pointed out the discrepancies between the land description in her original complaint and that in his favorable 1878 decree. Her lawyer had taken a fee for correcting the error, but he had failed to do so. Now that she wanted to sell the land, what was she to do? "Mr. D. W. Williams," she wrote, "will assist me in any way he can, and if you can give him a hint on how to proceed it will probably help me out of my trouble . . . . For all this presumption," she begged the Judge's pardon.

On January 29, 1883, Charles Phelps, former editor of the *Californian*, referred to Frances in a letter critical of Bancroft. It was published in the *Nation*, a weekly supplement of the *New York Post*. A week earlier the *Nation* had published a review of Bancroft's *Central America, I*. Phelps responded with the charge that Bancroft had not written it. He noted that in his preface to his *Native Races* Bancroft had admitted that he had been assisted in producing the five ponderous volumes in a relatively short time. As one interested in literary affairs on the Pacific Coast, Phelps further reported that he had recently learned that Bancroft not only paid for favorable reviews of his books, but he also misrepresented their authorship. In fact, "two or three gentlemen and one lady" were currently engaged in writing the volumes that bore Bancroft's name; and four or five histories on different sections of the Pacific Coast such as Oregon, Utah, and California were "in the course of simultaneous production with each section taken by a different writer." Phelps added that "the only magazine on the Pacific coast" had recently published a long article lauding Mr. Bancroft. It had been from the pen of "a lady employed in his bureau." While piously allowing that Bancroft had established a valuable collection "by fair means," Phelps lashed out at him for being "so lustful of renown as to adopt unfair means to obtain" recognition.

The February 15 issue of the *Nation* carried Bancroft's reply. Admitting that he had used assistants because the work was too much for one man, he claimed to have written half of the finished manuscripts. He did not rewrite satisfactory work, as he could make better use of his time. However, he denied Phelps' "silly charge" that he paid for "favorable publicity."

Frances rose above the fray by writing "Mountaineering in Oregon," for the March, 1883 number of the revived *Overland Monthly*. Addressed to Californians, it described the usual ascents of Mt. St. Helens and Mt. Rainier north of the Columbia River and closed with an account of her journey over the southern Cascades and her visit to Crater Lake with members of the Applegate family in the summer of 1873. For Frances, writing about mountain climbing was the next best thing to doing it and it kept her name before the public eye.

On April 3 she was in Portland at the home of her cousin, Douglas Williams. Her main mission was to confer with the Oregon Land Commission about the ownership of a strip of land in front of her St. Helens property over which the Columbia River ebbed and flowed. On that day, she answered a letter from the Rev. Myron Eells, forwarded from San Francisco.[28] She advised him that he could get a copy of her article on Whitman by writing the office of the *Overland Monthly* on 409 California Street. She had written it in response to Mr. Clarke's "rehash of Mr. Gray's historical statements." When "a pure historian arose," he would find that her research has discovered that Gray's account of Whitman was "a fiction of his lively imagination." In her article she had sketched the treaties concerning Oregon to point out to Gray and others that they should "retreat from their false position while there was yet time."

Correspondence between Bancroft and Deady during the months of May and June, 1883 reveal the role that the latter played in editing the Oregon volumes and promoting Bancroft's *History of the Pacific States*, On

May 15, Bancroft wrote Deady that his agent, L. Leadbetter, would submit to him all of *Oregon, I* that was ready. On June 1, Deady replied that he had given Leadbetter a letter recommending Bancroft's history and the names of 40 Portlanders. He was relieved that Bancroft was finally approaching Oregon, for he was beginning to fear that its annals would go "unhonored and unsung for another half century." He was also concerned that Bancroft would publish the volume with "the orthographic abomination and historical falsehood—Willamette." He argued: "The history of a country is largely contained in its geographic names, and can best be preserved by giving them correctly."

Within days, Deady reported to Bancroft that he had received proof sheets of *Oregon, I.* He thought the work "invaluable." The notes, which "bore on the most interesting and controversial points," he likened to "a cloud of witnesses." They were what one expected from "an eye witness." He also enclosed a biography of Mrs. Deady's parents, Robert and Rhoda Henderson, who deserved "a niche" in Bancroft's "Pantheon of Oregon Worthies." He wanted his own name printed as he wrote it— "Mathew P. Deady." The self-centered Deady also referred to Selim E. Woodworth, mentioned in a footnote on page 589 of *Oregon, I.* In his letter to Bancroft, Deady observed that in 1866–67 he had met Woodworth, then a distinguished Civil War veteran, in San Francisco, and that Woodworth has told him that in 1846 he had been a midshipman with orders to proceed west with the annual migration to carry word of the treaty ending the war with Mexico. Traveling ahead of the migration and having been trained as a printer, Woodworth had gone to the office of the *Oregon Spectator* in Oregon City and set the announcement in type.

In a letter, dated June 12, Bancroft promised to give Deady's every request "careful attention," except changing the spelling of "Willamette." He explained that he had used the spelling in the *Native Races* and that "the books would go out in one set."

Six days later, Frances wrote Deady that Bancroft had handed her the biographical notes on Mrs. Deady's parents, for which she had found a place. She was pleased that he was reading the page proof of *Oregon, I,* and hoped that he would read that of *Oregon, II,* in which he would find "more frequent occasions for corrections." She urged him to watch for passages in which Mr. Bancroft had inserted "disparaging remarks" about prominent men for the wrong reasons. For instance, he had called Judge O. C. Pratt, then living in San Francisco, "infamous," because he would not contribute to the history—"a piece of personal malice," she observed. On the other hand, he praised J. Quinn Thornton, who furnished material "with the object being immortalized." Fortunately, she had detected Thornton's misstatements "about being the author of the land law." Bancroft had also called General Lane "an Indian butcher," which was not "historically true." But Lane was dead and would never buy a set of the histories. She further noted, "Mr. Bancroft will regard your remarks, knowing that he is under obligation to you, besides having a high opinion of your knowledge and attainments." Her closing query as to whether the case of the Vancouver town site had been settled indicates that she was working on the history of the Washington Territory.

The publication of Bancroft's historical series was on schedule. *Mexico, II (1521–1600)* and *Central America, II (1530–1800)* had been issued in April and July, 1883, and *Mexico, III (1600–1803)* was scheduled for October. In an effort to promote the sale of these volumes and gather material for the remaining volumes of the region, Bancroft, his 23-year-old daughter, Kate, and a Spanish-speaking stenographer set out for Mexico City. So Bancroft missed Judge Deady while he was in San Francisco for a fortnight for the celebrated Debris case. According to his diary, on September 29 Deady visited the Bancroft Library. Henry Oak showed him "a large collection of historical material relating to this coast." He also had the pleasure of "correcting some provoking but not material errors in some of Mrs. V.'s notes to the History of Oregon" concerning himself.

By March, Bancroft was back in the workshop for the release of Oak's *California, I (1542–1800)* in April and those of *Northwest Coast, I (1543–1800)* in July and October.[29] March 5 had been a red-letter day for Frances. On that day she attended the wedding of her sister, Martha Rayle, and the widower, Sebastian C. Adams of Salem, Oregon. That the widowed Martha had been attracted to the scholarly Adams is not surprising. Since her arrival in Alameda from the East in 1875, she had been engaged in teaching, first as a grammar school teacher, then as a high school instructor, and finally as the principal of a private academy. Frances must have been pleased when Martha agreed to spend the rest of her life in Oregon, sight unseen.

Within two months, Frances joined the newly-weds in Oregon temporarily, on her own behalf and that of her stepdaughter. Through their attorney, Erasmus Shattuck, Frances and Mary had asked the Columbia County Court to affirm Judge Deady's decree of 1878 that they owned one half—one quarter each—of the disputed property in St. Helens and that the remainder belonged to Walter Davis of California and his Oregon attorney, Columbia Lancaster. They had also asked the court to appoint a referee to partition the property accordingly and assess legal costs. The defendants, Davis and Lancaster, had countered that their claim, based on proceedings of the United States District Court for Oregon, which did not have jurisdiction, was invalid. On May 6, 1884, the Columbia County Court upheld the defendants' arguments and dismissed the complaint that Frances and Mary had filed.

After learning of the dismissal, Frances wrote Judge Deady:[30] "If the fates are propitious, I shall leave for Portland on the 14th when I hope to see you and thank you in person for historical enclosures . . . . If I try your good nature with my personal or literary wants at any time, please say so frankly, but if I ask you about the former when I see you, let me know that there will be no impropriety in it." In his diary entry for June 14, Deady noted that Mrs. Victor had called and that he had spent an hour answering her questions "about Oregon's early days."

Late in July, Frances wrote William Marshall from San Francisco that she was writing another article on Whitman for inclusion in a book, the publication date of which she would advise him. On October 2, in a reply to Marshall, she stated that her article would not be published because she had not been paid for it.[31]

During the months of September, October, and November, she began writing the histories of Nevada, Colorado, and Wyoming under instructions by letter from Bancroft. Headquartered in Salt Lake City and Denver, Bancroft and his family were gathering material for the histories of Utah and Colorado. In early letters, Bancroft advised Frances to acquaint herself with the histories of Colorado and Wyoming as he had done with Nevada before drawing up a plan for the volume that would give each territory its due proportion. From Colorado Springs, he cautioned Frances against using the views of Helen Hunt Jackson on the Colorado Indian Wars. Not only were they unpopular with potential readers in the region, but she had not credited the Bancroft Library in her series on the California missions in the *Century* magazine.[32]

In the meantime, Frances had submitted her unpublished, well-documented article on Whitman to Harvey W. Scott, editor of the Portland *Morning Oregonian*, He published it on November 6, 1884 under the tripledeck headline: "DR. MARCUS WHITMAN—An Estimate of Services Rendered to Oregon by the Pioneer and Martyr—An Exhaustive Examination by Mrs. Frances Fuller Victor of All Points to the So-Called Whitman Controversy." It provoked immediate rebuttal from Edward C. Ross of Prescott, Washington Territory in the form of a letter, dated November 29, 1884—the 35th anniversary of the Whitman Massacre. Ross' attack brought Elwood Evans to Frances' defense. His letter, published on December 16, was entitled "WHITMAN'S WINTER JOURNEY—Hon. Elwood Evans on a Disputed Point in Early Oregon History—Proof that the Whitman Journey had no political significance—History separate from romance."

At the end of the 1884, though her personal prospects were uncertain, Frances was holding her own in the Pacific Northwest and in Bancroft's Literary Workshop.

CHAPTER 13

THE HISTORY
COMPANY
(1879–84)

A QUARTER MILLION PEOPLE in San Francisco, Frances Fuller Victor among them, reportedly watched the conflagration that consumed the A. L. Bancroft & Co. building on April 30–May 1, 1886. Water from the firemen's hoses turned the blaze into a lurid rainbow in the setting sun—a dramatic exclamation point in Frances' last five years at the Bancroft literary workshop on Valencia Street.

Hubert Howe Bancroft, titular head and manager, rebuilt the company's five-story headquarters on Market Street and named it the History Building, as a monument to his life's work. Further, he organized a new company devoted primarily to the publication of the Bancroft Historical Works, which eventually numbered thirty-nine volumes. As the final volumes were being published and sold by subscription, Bancroft launched a companion series, the highly controversial, seven-volume *Chronicles of the Kings.* These were biographies of successful "Builders of the Commonwealth," who were enticed to pay handsomely for inclusion. At this turn of events, Bancroft's most able assistants deserted him— first, the disillusioned Henry L. Oak; next foreign-born William Nemos for reasons of his own, and then overworked and underpaid Frances. For her, the April fire in San Francisco was yet another setback in these trying years as she sought to maintain her literary reputation apart from her work at the Bancroft workshop, and to cope with family and property losses.

On January 29, 1885, the case of Frances Fuller Victor and M. E. V. Sampson *vs.* W. S. Davis had been argued by opposing attorneys in the

Oregon Supreme Court.[1] The justices affirmed the judgment of the Columbia County Circuit Court, which had dismissed the women's claims against Davis. Frances' friend, George McBride, then secretary of state and living in Salem, noted the outcome. On March 6, he quit-claimed to Frances, in consideration of one dollar, his interest in twelve lots in Columbia City.[2] Her spring correspondence reveals that her disappointment in her personal affairs did not affect her work at the Bancroft literary workshop. A letter dated Dayton, Nevada, March 8, 1885 from an old Pony Express rider indicates that she had written him for information about the Pony Express—"its inception with its incidents, accidents, and adventures."[3] Her correspondent agreed that its history was worth preserving in a manner more reliable than that published in a sketch in *Harper's Monthly* a year or two ago. In a few succinct paragraphs he outlined the rise and fall of the Pony Express with the help of the secretary of war from 1860 until the "lightening of the telegraph killed the little horse."

On April 25 1855, in a reply to a letter from Judge Deady, Frances referred to her literary work and the outcome of her appeal to the Oregon Supreme Court.[4] She thanked him for having spoken to Harvey W. Scott about her article on Oregon school lands. Since she had not yet received a copy of the *Oregonian*, she did not know whether he had published it. With regard to the Oregon Supreme Court decision, she wrote:

> You know, of course, that I have lost my case, my property, and all the hard-earned money I ventured in an attempt to save it. Had Gibbs in the first case attended to his duty properly the point on which the decision turned could not have been made and had Lancaster not laid a plot to work himself into my place through that error, the case would have remained where it came from your court. Such is a woman's chance in a man's world. I am dreadfully vexed, and must add dreadfully discouraged. But this is neither here nor there to you.

She added that at the library she was "rusticating" her wits "among the sagebrush just now on paper, of course." She would soon "take up

Colorado." The year would probably bring her labors to an end when she must "seek new fields and pastures," In this connection, she noted that a lady correspondent from Cleveland, Ohio had asked her for a letter of introduction to someone in Portland, which she hoped to visit this summer. Frances also noted that the Bancrofts were presently "traveling overland in a private conveyance from the south end of the state (San Diego) and camping."

The April 23, 1885 *Oregonian* had published Frances Fuller Victor's four-column article headlined "THE OREGON LANDS—Who Secured the Thirty-Sixth Section for the Schools? Rockwell of Connecticut. Hon. S. R. Thurston and Judge Thornton of Oregon. A Review and Critique."[5] With access to federal documents, Frances had demonstrated that "no man from Oregon" had anything to do with framing the federal land bill that had designated the thirty-sixth section of every township in Oregon as land to be used to support public schools. Three weeks later, in the May 14 *Oregonian*, Harvey Scott ran: "JUDGE THORNTON'S REPLY TO MRS. VICTOR," in which the 75-year-old Thornton charged: "Following her love of notoriety, she never loses an opportunity to rush into print and display her name as full as the alphabet permits." In refuting the charges of this "vampire-like woman," who was trying "to suck dry the fountain" of his reputation, Thornton stated that he was glad that she had struck while he was still alive.

Scott gave Mrs. Victor the last word on the subject in the June 16 Oregonian under the caption, "MRS. F. F. VICTOR—Replies to Judge Thornton Respecting His Claim to the Early Land Grants." Dismissing Thornton as "chief of scolds," Frances rehearsed the circumstances under which she had written *The River of the West* in which she had given "so flattering an account of Mr. Thornton's service to Oregon." Having since discovered that "everything he claims to have done was conceived and accomplished by others," she was persuaded that he shared "the love of notoriety" that he attributed to her. She did not intend to continue the controversy. But as a student of history, she had long since discovered "the hollow pretenses" on which Thornton based his claims. She might have held her "peace," but she was confident that "future students of history" would thank her for not having done so.

On June 20, 1885 Frances responded to a suggestion from William Marshall that she publish her research on Dr. Marcus Whitman in pamphlet form.[6] If he published such a pamphlet, she asked that she be credited with having been "the pioneer in the study of historical *questions* in Oregon." Elwood Evans had preceded her in gathering material on Whitman, but he had followed Gray and Spalding as she had done in *The River of the West*, written "within six weeks without study." However, when she had called Evans' attention to the evidence, he had joined in the examination. Thus Evans' publications on the subject should be included in the pamphlet together with her article and Gray's reply in the *Astorian*. In closing, she noted that she had come to see Dr. Whitman as "a big, good-hearted, shrewd, and rather coarse-grained man—sometimes stubborn and imprudent." At least, such was the impression of one of the woman immigrants who had survived the massacre. However, Frances cautioned against going into the matter, as it would only bring up controversy.

Mrs. Victor's pen was otherwise occupied on the weekend of June 27-28, 1885. On the 27th she dashed off a letter of introduction for Mrs. Emma Adams to present to the Deadys upon her arrival in Portland.[7] Noting that Mrs. Adams, a journalist from Ohio, wanted to pick up interesting facts about the country and its people, Frances predicted that she would write "a very good letter" about the Deadys in exchange for introductions to other persons. Then, within hours, Frances learned, by telegraph, of the death of her beloved younger sister Metta, at The Terraces in New Jersey, and her burial there the following Sunday.[8] In view of their closeness, Frances must have known of Metta's lingering illness, and she relieved her own grief by writing comforting letters to Metta's immediate family, especially to her husband, Orville.

During the winter of 1885 and spring of 1886, Frances was writing the history of Wyoming from data assembled for her by T. M. Copperthwaite and Edward Newkirk, clerical assistants, and Nathan Stone, in charge of the subscription department [9] She was looking forward to the publication of *Oregon I (1834–1848)* sometime in 1886 after a final scrutiny by Judge Deady.[10]

In April, 1886, the Bancroft family was living temporarily at the Florence Hotel in San Diego where they owned considerable investment property. The main purpose of their visit was to oversee the construction of a summer home in nearby Spring Valley. With half the historical series issued or scheduled for publication, Bancroft hoped to close the library for general work by January, 1887. Though he saw many years ahead on the proposed *Chronicles of the Kings*, he felt that by reducing library expenses, ranging from one to two thousand dollars a month, he could "take life easier with less nervous haste and strain."[11] He had left to his wife, Matilda, their two small sons and his daughter Kate, by his first wife, the task of overseeing the home-building operation at Helix Farms, a 500-acre tract of land a few miles south of San Diego. In purchasing the tract with a romantic history of its own, Hubert Howe Bancroft, Alfred's older brother, had realized a boyhood dream. In the meantime, he was directing the operations of both the library and the history department In an April 24 letter to William Nemos, he wrote that he wanted to see "Mrs. Victor's Wyoming" and all that was ready on the Northern Mexican states and *Texas II*.[12]

He may have been working on one of these manuscripts when his wife drove up in her phaeton with an "important" telegram.[13] Sent by Nathan J. Stone, head of the history department, it read: "Store burning. Little hope of saving it." A half hour later a second telegram confirmed that nothing had been saved "except the account books." For Bancroft it meant thirty years of "headaches and heartaches eaten up by fire in an hour." Though the blow laid him low, it seemed "to strike softly, as if coming from a gloved hand." He completed "the duties of the day" before boarding the northbound train with his daughter for the night trip to San Francisco, where the flames had lit up the sky.[14]

The fire had broken out about 3:30 P.M. in the basement of the Market Street building in an area leased by a furniture company. In the panic resulting from the fire roaring up the wooden elevator shafts to the fifth floor, two mattress workers were killed and a fireman and others were injured. However, all of the three hundred or more employees of A. L. Bancroft & Co. survived the ordeal. Within hours the building was gutted and everything in it, including five or six sets of plates for the Pacific states historical series. Among them were those of *Oregon I.* Fortunately, Frances had two of the treasured volumes in her study at the library. From the May morning editions of the city's newspapers, she learned that the estimated loss of the building and stock was over a half million dollars after payment of the insurance coverage, which A.L. Bancroft had recently reduced by $40,000. Adjoining shops and hotels had also suffered considerable property losses. The press, often critical of the unending volumes of the Bancroft Works, extended its sympathy. The *Chronicle* editorialized on the lessons to be learned from the fire—the need for a revised building code and better equipped fire districts. It also lamented the loss of the facilities that the Bancroft Company had provided the citizens of the state for many years. The *Alta Californian* encouraged "the rehabilitation of this San Francisco institution, for the Bancrofts are as much a part of California as the mountains that keep solemn guard upon our boundaries."

That the Bancroft Library had been spared was cause for rejoicing. Henry Oak reduced his salary as a token of his concern. But for the next few weeks questions haunted the staff. If the publication of the history of the Pacific states was to continue, under what circumstances? The only person who could answer that question was H. H. Bancroft, who, by his own testimony, could hardly bring himself to view the charred remains at 721 Market Street.[15]

During the devastating night of April 30-May 1, A. L. Bancroft, together with department heads of the company, made decisions that saved a good part of the business and left the major losses to H. H. Bancroft.[16] The May 1issue of the *Chronicle* carried an announcement that A. L. Bancroft & Co. had rented temporary quarters on Geary Street and that duplicates of orders and instructions could be sent to the company's warehouse at Sacramento and Davis, where a supplementary printing press was maintained. A L. Bancroft also leased a nearby store on Market Street to receive goods in transit. Nathan Stone was equally aggressive on behalf of the history department; on May 3, he issued a circular to subscribers announcing that the Bancroft historical series would "positively proceed to conclusion" and requested "immediate remittance."[17] It was May 4 before H. H. Bancroft left his hotel room and joined his subordi-

The continuing attraction of San Francisco and Telegraph Hill foreever distracted
Victor during her protracted forays to the north country;
but she wanted more park space.
ORHI 27856

nates on Geary Street. On the 5th, a notice under the name of A. L Bancroft & Co. was sent nation-wide to correspondents. It read in part:

"You are aware of the great loss we suffered by the destruction of our publishing house and stock on April 30. We have been clearing away the ruin in order to resume business. Though the shock was severe, we are on our feet again. The first branch of the business to be resumed will be the publication of the Bancroft Historical Works. The publication will be delayed a few weeks, but after that it will go to completion. . . . strictly according to the original design."

On May 6, the Bancroft-Whitney Company, a merger of Bancroft with a small competitive legal publishing firm, filed papers of incorporation with the approval of H. H. Bancroft. As chief shareholder, he assigned most of his shares to his daughter, Kate. Albert L. Bancroft was named president of the new company and Sumner Whitney, treasurer. The older Bancroft later noted that the officers voted themselves larger salaries, thus diminishing dividends to shareholders.[18]

On May 7, Nathan Stone sent a second circular to subscribers, noting that the manuscripts of the histories had been saved and that the material for their manufacture had been ordered from the East by telegram. By now, the break-up of the A. L. Bancroft Company was well underway.[19] Various family members opened their own businesses, widening the rift between Hubert and Albert, and leaving the former to consider how he could best protect his remaining assets and complete publication of his Historical Works. After deeding his revenue-producing property in San Diego to his wife, his chief assets were the seven burned-out lots on Market Street and the library on Valencia Street. On May 10, in a reply to a sympathetic letter from Judge Deady, he wrote that the fire might force him to sell the library, which he valued at $250.000.[20] He had not formally offered it for sale, but he believed that if the people of Portland or San Francisco would come forward and save the collection for the West Coast they would perform an act for which posterity and the world would forever honor them.

In the meantime, sympathetic subscribers had responded to Nathan Stone's request for remittances. In order the protect these funds from creditors of the old A. L. Bancroft & Co., H. H. Bancroft formed a new corporation—the History Company. On May 18, 1886, Nathan Stone opened a bank account in that name.[21] However, papers of incorporation were not filed until September 13, then Albert Bancroft was in New York City on a purchasing trip. The corporation was capitalized at $500,000, divided into 10,000 shares. Of these, H. H. Bancroft held 8,900 shares; Nathan Stone, manager, 1,000; Matilda and Kate Bancroft as well as Olive Stone, ten shares each.[22] In later years, H. H. Bancroft explained that after the fire it had seemed best "to organize an independent company having for its purpose primarily the publishing of my books together with general book publishing and acting as agent for strictly first-class eastern publications."[23] The sale of Bancroft's library was still an option, and on May 21 a representative of the California Historical Society inquired about its sale.[24] On June 11, Bancroft replied to Judge Deady on the stationery of the new History Company.[25] He thanked Deady for having spoken about the library to Judge Lorenzo Sawyer an associate of Deady on the Ninth Circuit bench, and writing to Senator Leland Stanford. Bancroft also promised to send Deady copies of the enclosure "for the use of the committee of ten wealthy Oregonians who will subscribe $25,000 each to secure the library for Portland."

Soon after this, Nathan Stone issued another notice to subscribers. It announced that the History Company would release *California V (1846–1848)* in August, 1886, replacing *Oregon I (1834–1848)*. The *Oregon* plates having been destroyed by the fire, its release would be delayed until October. Stone's decision to restart the stalled historical series with a California volume under the imprint of the new company was sound. The California volume had popular appeal and assured subscribers and reviewers alike that the series would be completed on schedule. Concurrent with Stone's circular was H. H. Bancroft's announcement that he had let contracts for construction of the new History Building on Market Street.[26] No one had offered Bancroft a fair price for his burned-out lots, and savings banks were eager to lend him money with which to rebuild.

Advised that the publication of *Oregon I* was scheduled for October, Frances Fuller Victor took steps to assure that her authorship of the volume was known in the Pacific Northwest. On September 22, she sought the help of Elwood Evans.[27] "Within a very short time," she wrote, "the first volume of Mr. Bancroft's *Oregon* will be issued." Of course, she thought of it as hers. Though Eastern publishers persisted in giving Mr. Bancroft "the sole credit for the histories written in his library and under his name," she hoped that on this coast she would receive more than simply a mention in the last volume of the series "as one of the several who have done 'nobody knows what.'" She only asked that "a fluid pen" like Evans' would "without disparaging Mr. Bancroft's ability, enterprise, ambition, or deserts," mention her name in a review, "as having had an important place in the corps of writers on Bancroft Works," particularly on Oregon and, of course, Washington." This, she felt, was due her for her "continued study of and labor for the region," and to give her a position whereby she could secure other work, as she expected that her library work would close during the coming winter. It had been her "wish and judgment" that Washington have "a volume to herself." However, after she had written it, Mr. Bancroft had cut it down and put Idaho and Montana into the volume. She was also disappointed that he had taken out her chapters on "the San Juan difficulty" and "the Puget Sound Agriculture Association" and put them into his volumes on the Northwest Coast. He had also changed her estimate of I. I. Stevens, first Territorial governor of Washington. She wanted Evans to know all this before he read her volume on the Washington Territory.

Frances also sought the collaboration of Mrs. Emma Adams, after she returned to San Francisco from Portland. Together the women crafted a letter, signed "Emma Adams." It appeared in the October 5, 1886 issue of the Oregonian under this headline: "FROM SAN FRANCIS-CO—Mrs. Frances Fuller Victor and Her Latest Literary Work—Her Ability as a Historian Thoroughly Appreciated by Mr. Hubert Howe Bancroft—The Forthcoming Volume on Oregon." The letter lauded Bancroft's history of the Pacific states before commenting on his volume on Oregon:

> The most remarkable thing about it is that a woman has
> performed a larger part of the best labor on it than any
> other individual unless it be the author himself. That
> woman is Frances Fuller Victor, whom Oregonians well
> know and whose warm interest in Oregon was evinced in
> two volumes from her pen (*The River of the West and All Over
> Oregon and Washington*) ere Mr. Bancroft invited her to devote
> it to his colossal scheme. Eight years of thoughtful, unre-
> lenting, discerning toil Mrs. Victor has given to bringing
> out of obscurity the past of our vast Northwestern
> domain. I take all the more pleasure in mentioning this
> because this gifted woman is of my own state Ohio, and in

the columns of its journals began her literary career. Indeed the Buckeye state claims not Mrs. Victor only, for Mr. Bancroft himself was born there and spent his early years on its soil.

The History Company's eagle-eyed canvassers doubtless singled out the following paragraph:

"The approaching volume is from Mrs. Victor's pen. In the book she very properly strives to give notice to the well-known founders of the Oregon colony, territory, and state but likewise to all, both men and women, who since contributed to the upbuilding of the commonwealth. The writer's acquaintance with and interest in some of the parties makes it a pleasure to state that among the parties deserving to be numbered for their faithful advocacy of the rights of women are mentioned Mrs. Duniway, Mrs. Coburn, and Mrs. Minto . . . . Merited praise is also bestowed on Jesse Applegate, as upon many other pioneers, to whom the state owes a debt that it can never cancel."

To illustrate Mrs. Victor's knowledge of Oregon history, Mrs. Adams described an episode during a recent Grand Army encampment in San Francisco. She and Mrs. Victor had been seated on a platform to watch the formation of the Grand Army parade. When a Portland detachment took its position in front of them, Mrs. Victor was certain that "the small edition of the Stars and Stripes" they carried had a history. Descending the steps, she confirmed her hunch that the flag had been carried during the Rogue River Indian wars and had been hand-sewn by Mrs. Tabitha Brown, who had helped found the Tualatin Academy in the Willamette Valley.

The Adams' letter reflected what many Oregonians knew about the authorship of Bancroft's *Oregon I*; but Bancroft challenged it in a notice published in the *Oregonian*, in which he asserted that no entire volume in the series had been written by Mrs. Victor. [28] In a note to her dated October 16, Bancroft explained his denial of her authorship in these words: "I do not want for myself the credit due to my assistants. At the same time, I don't deem it necessary to explain to the public just what part of my work was done by each. Everybody knows that you have been at work on

Oregon, and that is all right, although I have done considerable work on your manuscript for better or worse, or at all events to make it conform to the general plan."

By this time, the writing corps knew that the History Company intended to reissue all the volumes published by A. L. Bancroft & Co.; they also knew that name had been removed from H. H. Bancroft's *Literary Industries.* Sometime in 1886, Henry Oak drew up an estimate of the aggregate number of volumes written by each member of the corps.[29] This he shared with Nemos, who approved of it in general, though both agreed that it was difficult to determine what constituted the equivalent of a volume and that in some instances authorship could not accurately be assigned.

At the library, Frances was delighted with the favorable review of *Oregon I (1834–1848).* On October 23, the San Francisco *Argonaut* published the first. It was followed by reviews in the Sacramento *Union* on the 25th and in the Portland *Oregonian* on the following day. Typical was the lead review in the column, "Current Literature," in the November issue of the San Francisco *Bulletin.* The reviewer pointed out that heretofore in the history of the Pacific states, Oregon had been included in that of the Northwest Coast, whereas the present volume "recited" Oregon's settlement by Americans and ended with the discovery of gold in California. "A plain and unromantic story," it was told "with great but not wearisome detail." There were incidents enough to make it interesting and doubly so because the chief actors—men like Peter Burnett, Jesse Applegate, Marcus Whitman, Dr. McLoughlin, and Sir James Douglas—were those who did much to colonize Oregon. He concluded that the Cayuse Indian War, "the most notable feature in the early annals of Oregon," was described with spirit and that the Provisional Government with its "makeshift" legislature was "admirably preserved for history."

Late in October, 1886, Judge Deady noted in his diary that he had just received from Bancroft the first volume of the Oregon history.[30] It was a worthy monument to the pioneers of Oregon and contained a notice of Mrs. Deady's family, which he had furnished. On November 3, Frances thanked Deady for his criticism of the volume.[31] She explained that the practice of which he complained—that of "tailing" at the end of the volume the biography of anyone who subscribed to the series—had not been her plan but that of Mr. Bancroft to ensure the financial success of the series. Her plan was to "include everybody on the migrations, and whoever made himself notable afterwards was duly mentioned in the place where he did something to signalize himself." In reducing her manuscript, Bancroft did not always understand the value of certain matters; and as it sometimes "overran terribly," he often "slashed in the wrong places." Of this she knew nothing until the galleys came back and could be changed only slightly. In spite of these things, she believed it "more nearly <u>correct</u> than any original history" to which he could point; and she was glad to have his "favorable judgment upon it." She was presently writing "California politics—nauseating subject"—which she would finish in a few weeks before going East. She closed with a plea for "Poor Jesse Applegate! He must be forgiven for his eccentricities now," and with "Kind Regards" to Mrs. Deady.

During the last two weeks of November, Bancroft continued to write Deady about the sale of his library.[32] On the 19th, he wrote the judge that he was offering it for sale to the state at the legislative meeting on January 1, 1887 and asked that the "chief state and federal officers of Oregon" sign the enclosed memorial to the legislature and governor of California, starting with the names of Judge Deady and Governor Zenas Moody. Ten days later Bancroft acknowledged Deady's assurance that he would do all he could in the disposal of the library and noted that he had received the *Oregonian* with Mr. Scott's review of *Oregon I*. "It is very fine," he wrote, "All that any man on earth could ask!

Frances Fuller Victor was even more pleased with Harvey W. Scott's review of *Oregon I* in the November 26 issue of the New York *Tribune*, under the heading of "OREGON—American Capacity Tested." In his opening paragraph. Scott designated the theme of the volume in these words: "The genesis of a State must always be a study of deep interest, and of all the many possible beginnings none possesses more attraction than that in which a new country is colonized by men advanced in civilization who are brought in direct contact with nature and are forced to learn again the primitive lessons of the pioneer." In her copy of Scott's article in one of her scrapbooks, Frances penned these comments on the margins: "I took particular pride in this part of my work" and "Mr. Scott being himself a pioneer speaks intelligently of my work."[33]

Worksheets at the Bancroft Library and Frances' letters indicate that she spent the winter of 1886–87 at The Terraces in New Jersey. Here she could share Scott's glowing review of *Oregon I (1834–1848)* with Metta's family. On March 14, she was back in San Francisco at her old address, 611 Nineteenth Street. On that date, she wrote to Ben W. Austin, secretary of the Trinity Historical Society in Dallas, Texas, who had invited her to accept an honorary membership in the society.[34] Austin's invitation, addressed to Mrs. Barritt, had been forwarded to Frances from New Jersey. In sketching her literary career and name changes, she started with the publication of *Poems of Sentiment and Imagination*, in which she combined the poetry of her sister, Metta Victor Fuller, with her own sentimental poetry. In 1853 she had married Barritt and written under his name "in a desultory manner." About a decade later she had married Mr. H. C. Victor, brother of O. J. Victor, to whom her sister was married, and "removed" with him to the Pacific slope. Thus her name was Victor, not Barritt. Here she paused to exclaim: "What an awkward thing it is for literary women to be deprived of their own names! I furnished my biography to an encyclopedia the other day under the F or Fuller heading, believing that Fuller is my rightful name." She added that the Pacific slope had "incited" her to industry and besides "much miscellaneous matter," she had published *The River of the West, All Over Oregon and Washington,* and *The New Penelope.* She would send him a copy of the last, but had no copies left of the former. For the last eight and one-half years her "severest labor" had been on Bancroft's "Pacific State histories" which she had helped to write "in his historical library," During the coming year, she expected to write articles on statesmen she had studied in her "historical researches," and would be happy to forward copies for his collection.

Later that month, Judge Deady received a brief progress report, dated March 26, 1887, from H. H. Bancroft, in which he noted that the state legislature had not purchased his library, or, as he put it, "the boys do not appear to hanker after my books. . . It takes money 'to fix things,' as Huntington says.[35] All this publicity about the sale of the library had an unsettling effect on the writing corps, especially Henry Oak. After finishing his last volume, he resigned in 1887 because of ill health[36]

Having decided to conduct a book store and publishing business in addition to operating the History Company, Bancroft filed papers of incorporation on June 21, 1887.[37] Directors included H. H. Bancroft, his daughter, Kate, and his nephew, William Bancroft, as well as N. J. Stone and F. A. Colley [both formerly associated with the old Bancroft organization.

This new corporation was capitalized at $500,000, apparently the value of the Market Street site, together with the History Building and its stock. The 5,500 shares, valued at $1.00 each, were disproportionately divided among the directors. Bancroft and his daughter each owned 2,746 shares. The salaried directors each owned only two shares, thus reducing their exposure to financial risk. On June 30, Bancroft wrote Deady a brief note on the stationery of the History Company. Making no mention of the revival of his fortunes, he thanked Deady for his "fine testimonial." It was of special value just when the History Company was trying to interest the people of Oregon more fully in its Works—clearly a reference to the *Chronicles of the Kings*, then underway.

The writing corps saw little of Bancroft, who spent most of his time in his office in the History Building, which he had opened to the public in August.[38] In July and October, the History Company interrupted the parade of state histories with the first two of six supplemental volumes of Bancroft's Works—*Popular Tribunal II (1856)*, which Bancroft had written a decade earlier. Deady, for one, found them "fascinating." On December 15, Bancroft wrote Nemos that he would be at the library the coming week to help get out *California VI (1848–1859)* and *California VII (1860–1890)*—a collaborative effort, in which Frances Fuller Victor had written the political chapters, in addition to the volume on Nevada, Colorado, and Wyoming.[39] He cautioned Nemos against letting "Mrs. V." spend too much time on "preliminary matters," and mentioned another pair of supplementary volumes: *California Pastoral (1769–1848)*, written by the Bancroft family with assistance from Thomas Savage, and *California Inter Pocula (1848-1856)*, also written by them, except for 115 pages on the Modoc Indian War, which Mrs. Victor had written for *Oregon II*.[40]

Bancroft shepherded the last volumes of his Works through the History Company press from his retreat at Helix Farm in the spring of 1888. At the same time, he promoted the *Chronicles of the Kings*, as his letters to Nemos indicate.[41]

In the first, Bancroft invited Nemos to make himself at home on the farm whenever he chose. At the time, Bancroft himself was working on the literature of Central America, Mexico, and California for a fifth supplementary volume entitled *Essays*. He asked Nemos to edit his chapters carefully, especially the spelling of foreign names and technical terms. In a postscript, dated May 25, Bancroft noted that Stone and his agents has taken the first *Kings* order; and in a letter sent four days later he gave his view of the *Chronicles*:

> Your analysis of the character of Brigham Young is very
> good, short, simple, and individual, no indiscriminate and
> lavish praise and no great blame, but the truth. This is the
> most interesting kind of reading to me since the man has
> done something, and all our men have done something—
> everyone of them has an interesting biography. Carried out
> on the present plan, I do not think I exaggerate when I say
> that the *Chronicles* will prove to be one of the most interest-
> ing books of the kind that has ever been written, and that it
> will last throughout all time. And I believe as men see and
> understand the work they will be more & more glad to
> come in.

Frances Fuller Victor, according to William Morris, saw the *Chronicles*, published under the title, *Chronicles of the Builders of the Commonwealth*, in quite a different light.[42] Its purpose, he wrote: "was to present in detail the lives of wealthy and influential men who had borne a prominent part in the affairs of the various Pacific Coast States. For such notice they were charged from a thousand to ten thousand dollars according to the length of the published sketch . . . . This included also the printing of a portrait engraved on steel. The attempt to burden the prestige gained by the histories and their projector with such a load could result only in crippling both. The volumes printed subsequent to the inauguration of the scheme could not be received with the same open-mindedness as the former works. The information subsequently made public that money was accepted for notice in the *Chronicles* lost for Mr. Bancroft the regard of the press of the Coast, caused grave doubts to be expressed concerning his disinterestedness as a historian, called out an expression of many bitter—in some cases utterly false—statements concerning his work, and sadly damaged the literary reputation he had for nearly twenty years building on the work done under his direction.

Morris added that, though the *Chronicles* were "a type of parasite upon history," one should recognize that "the labors of the writers upon both works were not a whit less conscientious and painstaking than they had always been."

Among the wealthy and influential Portlanders who "came into" the *Chronicles* were Henry W. Corbett, Henry Failing, William S. Ladd, and Cicero H. Lewis—all of whom entered into contracts with the History Company. Judge Deady came in at no expense to himself—evidently as a reward for his work on and promotion of both the historical and biographical series. In addition to editing the biographies of his Portland friends for Bancroft's *Chronicles* and performing his judicial and civic obligations, Deady decided to air the Whitman myth as set forth in an address by Seymour Condon at the annual meeting of the Oregon Pioneer Association. In a letter to the *Oregonian*, dated June 21, he questioned "Dr. Whitman's agency" in organizing the immigration of 1843 and piloting it to Oregon. On July 2, the *Oregonian* published a letter from Perrin Whitman, in which he claimed that his uncle had "set in motion the agitation" that had resulted in the migration, which he had led to Oregon.

Later in the month, Deady sent Frances Fuller Victor a copy of his letter to the *Oregonian* and a complaint about his biography in *Oregon II*. From her home address, on July 12, she acknowledged receipt of the enclosure and thanked him for "speaking out so plainly." No one had done so except Elwood Evans. Once convinced, he had become "a working ally" and had furnished her with valuable evidence. Then she confided:[43]

> I am just finishing the last of my work at the Bancroft
> Library. I have some part of the *Chronicle of the Kings* to
> write. Are you going to be a *King*? If you are I would like to
> write you up. I suppose there will be a chapter on the judi-
> ciary. Don't think it is vanity if I say that I am not fairly
> treated by the History Company, which sends all of the
> most difficult work to my desk and never advances my pay!

She added that she had gone East last summer but had suffered from the heat and had been seriously ill in Los Angeles. A week later, she replied to Deady's second complaint about his biography in *Oregon II*. [44] She patiently explained that she had rewritten "the objectionable note" and sent it to the History Company with a request to alter the plate.

By this time, Nemos had written the first few chapters of the first volume of the *Chronicles*—his last contributions to the publications of the History Company. Though grateful to Bancroft for having employed him at a good salary and providing him with living quarters for the past 15 years, he evidently had little interest in visiting the family farm and even less in directing the writing of the biographies of wealthy western-ers willing and able to pay a handsome sum to be entombed as *"Kings."*[45] In a notarized statement that Nemos signed in San Francisco on July 31, 1888, he did not reveal his reason for resigning. The affidavit began with the declaration that William Nemos—*"nom de plume"* under which he had been known for the past 16 years—had been engaged since April, 1873 as a writer on Bancroft's History of the Pacific States. Since 1882, he had been recognized as "chief of the historical and library staffs," and his salary had been double that of every other staff member but one. With Bancroft's frequent absences for extended periods of time, he alone "engaged and discharged three classes of workers—indexers, compilers, and advanced writers." They all followed methods of "extraction, com-piling, and finishing" which he had originated. Together with Mr. Ban-croft, he did the rewriting and editing. The only writer not subordinate to him was "the first holder of the librarianship," who, lacking writing skills, was entrusted with "inferior sections." Nemos further stated that he had written "the leading parts" of this writer's field, though his "quickness of eye" made him one of their best proofreaders.

These lines from the final paragraph of the affadavit suggest that Nemos may have made a compact with Bancroft:

> Having accepted the consideration offered by Mr. Bancroft
> for my services, I have properly no right to enumerate my
> share in the written text, which is his property. Suffice it
> here to say that I assumed, in joint collaboration with Mr.
> Bancroft, the most important parts of the historic groups,
> notably early Central America and Mexico, and the princi-
> pal portion of the all-interesting modern California, after
> the entry of the Americans, and the true birth of the
> region. My contributions cover in fact a wider political area
> than those of any other writer on the staff, embracing
> moreover essays and reflective chapters on all the fields, and
> in the odd, or so-called private volumes. The performance
> of so large a task required aid, and indeed, of all the mem-
> bers, I alone employed subordinate writers to prepare mate-
> rial for my pen, for my restudy and rewriting. This however
> only for certain sections; for important parts I performed
> the research as well as the writing.[46]

None of his colleagues in the literary workshop ever saw a copy of Nemos' affidavit. He did not release it until after H. H. Bancroft's death in 1918—and then in the Swedish language.

Nemos' resignation forced Bancroft to spend more time at the library, as Frances' letters to Deady, dated July 31and August 15, 1888 attest.[47] In the first she explained that in comparing biographies in *Oregon I* and *Oregon II*, she found two for Mrs. Deady's father, Robert Hender-son. If she took out the one in *Oregon II*, she would have more space for Deady's biography in that volume and suggested that he submit addi-tional material—perhaps a legal decision that affected the welfare of the state. In her August letter, she regretted that his expanded biography would not fit the place where it belonged in *Oregon II*, page 144. Rather than cut it, she would put it in the appendix. On September 4, Bancroft resolved the matter. He wrote the judge that he had told Mrs. Victor to make room for his biography in its proper place. He would not think of putting it in the appendix. "We feel," he states, "that you are entitled to all & more than we can ever do for you." Then he asked Deady to provide them "a line to Judge Sawyer" by noting that he had looked into the biographical companion to the historical series, and examined some of the biographies, and was taking an active part in its success in Portland.[48]

According to entries in his diary, Deady corrected the page proof for *Oregon II* and revised the biographies of his Portland friends for the *Chronicle of the Kings*.[49] During the week of September 8-14, while on holiday at Grimes House on Clatsop Beach, he worked on both. Bancroft sent him the page proof pasted on blank leaves with margins for notes. On these Deady made corrections of fact and would have liked to have made some of opinion. Rather he cautioned Bancroft "against Mrs. Victor's prejudices and predilections." After revising the biographies of Corbett, Failing, and Ladd, he commenced on his own. Not knowing what to put in or leave out, he decided to let Bancroft do the weeding.

During the rest of 1888, Bancroft and the judge corresponded, sometimes on a weekly basis. On September 19, Bancroft advised Deady that he had received the revised Portland biographies. As for his own, Deady should make it "exactly" as he wanted it. With regard to "scrapbook *Oregon II*," he was going over it with Mrs. Victor. A month later Deady noted in his diary that he had revised the biography of Cicero Lewis and received a copy of the steel engraving of his portrait that was to accompany his biography in the *Kings*. This he returned for altering. On the 23rd, writing from the History Building, Bancroft assured Deady that the engraving would receive "careful attention" and that no one would charge him "a dollar."[50]

Writing from the library on November 26, Bancroft notified Deady that after having eliminated "the less important parts" of his "very perfect" biography, he had handed it in to the printer. Upon receipt of the page proof, the judge could make any changes or additions he liked. Deady was pleased with the amended engraving, but not with his biography. Further, Cicero Lewis had written him, asking for legal advice on how to cancel his contract with the History Company! On December 7,

Deady addressed these matters in separate letters to Bancroft, who answered them both three days later. At the library, he wrote: "Mr. Lewis is strictly in error with respect to the facts." He would have to pay for his biography in the *Kings*," according to his written obligation." Though he would "do anything in the world" for the judge, if he released Lewis from his contract, he would have to pay thousands of dollars to the History Company, which already had spent considerable on agent commissions and other expenses. A few hours later at the History Building, Bancroft answered Deady's complaint about his own biography. He reminded the judge that he had told him to write his biography "exactly" as he wanted it and that he had cut out only a few unimportant parts like the quotation from Socrates. He advised Deady to have his biography redone in Portland unless he preferred to have Mrs. Victor do it, though she might not please him. In closing, he stated that he would rather spend the rest of his life on Deady's biography rather than see Deady give up on it. However, Bancroft stood equally firm on the question of Lewis' contract with the History Company. On December 18, he wrote Deady that the History Company could not continue to do business "if subscribers are permitted to cancel their contracts at their pleasure." Nor could be submit himself to the humiliation of accepting Lewis' proposal of settlement. He had done much for Oregon and received little in return. If all Oregonians were like Lewis, he did not want anything more to do with them.

Frances Fuller Victor was aware of this and other controversies at the History Company. On Christmas Eve, 1888, in response to Deady's comment on his biography in Oregon II, she penned another confidential letter. In it she explained that she was no part of "the muddle" over the *Kings*. Before she had gone East last year, Bancroft had spoken to her about working on them at "better pay," she had understood.[51] Upon her return, she discovered that Bancroft had started different sections and had assigned her the section on transportation. However, when the subject of pay came up, Bancroft told Nemos that she had gone East "to get a better position and *failed*," so he would not increase her pay. With her funds exhausted, she had been forced to resume work for the History

Company. Besides she had left her part of the California history incomplete and felt obliged to finish it. When agents brought in biographies written in the field, she had written up a few at their request. They had been satisfied with her work, but she told them that since the *Kings* was "a money-making scheme," she would not continue to write up biographies "without proper pay." This had "raised a tempest with Mr. B.," because the agents were on her side. Soon after, he removed all biographical dictations from her desk, leaving her only the work on transportation, which she would finish in a few months. Bancroft had also written her that Judge Deady had given him "a terrible raking down" about his biography in the *Chronicles of the Kings*. This she took as a hint that her services might be required. While it would give her great pleasure to put Deady "in the third person," she must hold to her point that she would not write biographies "without proper pay." If Deady wanted her to do the work, he should "say *so* to Mr. B." on any grounds he liked. Before closing with the compliments of the season to the Deady family, Frances noted "the very great loss of her sister, Mrs. Adams of Salem. She was "one of whom it may be truly said 'None knew her but to love her. Nor name her but to praise.'"[52]

Despite this personal loss, Frances could take satisfaction in the fact that *Oregon II (1848–88)* headed the quarterly parade of Bancroft books published in 1899. But not for long. Complaints were soon launched by Judge Deady and his long-time friend, O. C. Pratt, a former Supreme Court justice for the Oregon Territory, now living in San Francisco. At the History Building, Bancroft and Nathan Stone were trying to placate them both. On January 10, 1889, Bancroft promised Deady that he had thrown out other material in order to fit his biography into its proper place in *Oregon II* and had never spared money or labor to please him. At the same time, Stone was dealing with Pratt. A candidate for the *Kings*, he had protested the treatment of his judicial career in *Oregon II.*

Entries in Deady's diary during the spring of 1889 reveal his involvement in both matters.[53] On February 22, he mailed Stone a sketch of the 1850-1852 conrtroversy over the location of the state capital, in which Pratt had been "a principal figure." He asked Stone to show it to Pratt before using it in the corrected edition of *Oregon II*. In a March 5 entry,

Deady noted that he had received a corrected copy of *Oregon II*, which carried a new account of the trial of the alleged Whitman murderers before Judge Pratt. The substitution treated the subject in a much more dignified and complimentary way than the original.

On February 13, Deady had complained to Frances Fuller Victor about the error in his biography in Oregon II. It was April 5 before she answered him at her home address.[54] She asked Deady to reread her Christmas letter in which she had discussed "the biography business" and he would see that she was not responsible "for the blunders in the biographies in the *Kings*," because she had refused to write them "for the niggardly pay offered." After Mr. Stone told her about the treatment that Deady had received, she had volunteered to write his biography "entirely without pay," but the notes had not been put into her hands. As for his biography in *Oregon II*, "Mr. B" had put in a note with which she had nothing to do. As it had been done at the History Building, she had not seen it until after it had been printed. Deady's patience had doubtless been tried, but that did not justify his being "rude and impatient" with her. To forfeit his "good opinion" would be a great loss. So she was making these explanations, which "under the same provocation" she would not make to everyone.

Her last paragraph suggests that her resignation from the Library was art hand:

> Mr. Bancroft is in Colorado drumming up the *Kings* and I have not seen him for two months. He had asked me if I would remain in service—in connection with a scheme he has in hand at the same salary and the same hours as now, and I have said *No*, so I shall be free in a few weeks to follow my own devices. I rather long to see my name in print once more.[55]

On June 24, Deady wrote Frances again to complain of her "notice" of him in *Oregon II*. This message was forwarded to her at Santa Cruz, where she had been vacationing with her niece Lillian, Metta's oldest daughter, since May.

In her reply, dated July 9, she noted that she had twice explained why she was not responsible for the errors in his biography.[56] She felt she had put him "up front as much as proper in a general history." Stone had told her he was rectifying the unfair treatment that Deady had suffered in the *Kings* as well as how Bancroft had insulted Mr. Lewis by refusing to see him when he visited the History Building. That was why she had declined "any further connection with the work," except on her own terms. This she did not expect to get. She had hoped to be in Portland by August or September "to look over the ground in view of some work." Until she was settled, her mail should be addressed to Station C, San Francisco.

On August 8, her cousin by marriage, Harriet Williams died in Portland. Frances did not attend her funeral, for she was living at her former address, 611 Nineteenth Street, San Francisco.[57] Here she replied to a letter from William Marshall, forwarded to her by the Bancroft Library. In it Marshall had requested information relative to Nathaniel Wyeth's sale of Fort Hall on the Oregon Trail to the Hudson's Bay Company, treated in *Oregon I*. Frances noted that Dr. McLoughlin had mentioned the sale in his private papers, some of which were in her possession.

She did not mention that she had resigned from the Bancroft Library and was returning to the Pacific Northwest to update her out-of-print *All Over Oregon and Washington* or that she had prevailed upon J. B. Lippincott Company of Philadelphia to publish it at her expense. That Frances did not return to The Terraces in New Jersey, where she would have been welcome, suggests that she felt that she had not finished her work in the Pacific Northwest. Whether she collaborated with her niece on a popular novel entitled *Can Love Sin?* by Mark Douglas, published in Philadelphia in 1889, is questionable. It features the love life of a wealthy Oregon federal senator, and Frances was doubtless familiar with related facts. However, the novel adds no luster to her literary legacy and remains one of the lesser legends attached to her name.[58]

In any event, now in her sixty-third year, Frances Fuller Victor knew enough about the publishing business to pursue a fourth publishing venture in the Pacific Northwest under her own name and at her own expense.

CHAPTER 14

THE PACIFIC
NORTHWEST
REVISITED
(1890-94)

FRANCES FULLER VICTOR spent the year-end holidays of 1889 in San Francisco and Alameda. Her sister, Martha Rayle Adams of Salem, now deceased, had willed her an unimproved lot in Alameda. Frances now mortgaged this property to help finance her next literary venture in the Pacific Northwest.[1] She evidently did not depart San Francisco until her last two Bancroft volumes were published: *Nevada, Colorado, and Wyoming* and *Washington, Idaho, and Montana* in January and April, 1890, respectively.[2]

During this time, Judge and Mrs. Deady had stopped in San Francisco prior to embarking for Honolulu.[3] Upon their return in mid-March, 1890, the Judge had received the latest version of his biography for Bancroft's *Chronicles of the Kings*, before boarding the through train to Portland. In early April, Frances took the same train north, stopping in Salem to visit her erstwhile brother-in-law, Sebastian C. Adams, who had recently married another widow, Sarah Babcock. She had a widowed sister, Ellen M. White, who lived in Salem and would, in due course, become Frances' landlady. Adams' daughter by his first marriage was the wife of Major George Williams, apparently a distant cousin of Frances Fuller Victor and president of the Salem banking firm of Williams and England. Another member of this extended family was 36-year-old George McBride, a friend of Frances and her long-time real-estate adviser, now secretary of state in the administration of Governor Sylvester Pennoyer.

From her long-time Salem friend, the poet Belle Cooke, Frances was saddened to learn that their mutual friend, Harriet Clarke, had died in

January at the family residence, Gaiety Hill, once a synonym for hospitality.[4] She advised her friends that her first task was to update and publish at her own expense her out-of-print *All Over Oregon and Washington* in an illustrated subscription-book volume, entitled *Atlantis Arisen: Talks of a Tourist About Oregon and Washington.* If they asked her about its arresting title, she explained that the ancient Greek myth of a submerged continent occupying that part of the world now covered by the Atlantic Ocean was "scientific truth." If one continent had sunk, another, now known as America, must have arisen to balance it. Geology proved that the Pacific Coast had risen first. Last to be developed, she observed that it was the pioneer's last view out over the ocean that encircles the known world. Henceforth, she noted, "man's efforts will be to restore to earth on this favored soil the glories of the buried continent and to substitute for Atlantis Lost, *Atlantis Arisen.*"[5]

When Frances returned to Portland, she found a partially bridged city. Electric cars moved people across the Willamette River to East Portland and into the West Hills above the city.[6] Her widowed cousin, Douglas W. Williams, was confined to his home under care, so she took temporary lodgings elsewhere. Certainly she called on Harvey Scott in the new seven-story Oregonian Building and on Judge Deady in his chambers to assure him that she would use his spelling of "Wallamet" in her forthcoming book.[7] At J. K. Gill's bookstore, she and her business partner, E. H. Kilham, arranged for canvassers to take subscriptions for it. Here she doubtless thumbed through Elwood Evans' two-volume *History of the Pacific Northwest,* published in 1889 by the Northwest History Company of Portland.

Frances also found that Abigail Duniway had sold her newspaper, *The New Northwest,* in 1887 and joined her husband and sons in Idaho, where they hoped to make a fortune by buying cheap land where the proposed railroad would pass.[8] The magazine, the *West Shore,* to which Frances had contributed in her pre-Bancroft days, was being published every Saturday in Portland and Spokane by a reorganized company. But it would cease publication in May, 1891.[9] Her chief critics had joined "the silent majority"—J. Quinn Thornton in 1888 and W. H. Gray in late 1889.[10]

On May 2, 1890, she boarded a car of the Portland branch of the Northern Pacific Railroad.[11] Twelve miles below St. Helens, where she still owned a few lots, the train was ferried across the Columbia River to the town of Kalama, a few miles from the mouth of the Cowlitz River. Proceeding by rail to Olympia, capital of the new state of Washington, as it had been of Washington Territory, she doubtless met with Elwood Evans to discuss their respective histories of the Pacific Northwest and her travel plans. As the state's leading historian and about to become the first president of its historical society, he may have suggested that she steam down the Chehalis River to the Pacific Coast to visit the new towns on Gray's Harbor, discovered by Captain Robert Gray almost one hundred years ago.[12] She was impressed by the coastal towns like Hoquiam, being developed by Eastern capitalists as railroad terminals. She reported new information on Shoalwater Bay to the south and gathered "gossip" about the Olympic Peninsula—a "club-shaped piece of territory north of the mouth of Chehalis River."[13]

Returning to Olympia, she steamed down the Sound to Tacoma, which she called "The City of Destiny," because the Northern Pacific Railroad had selected it as its major terminus on the Sound and was promoting the development of the surrounding area. This she saw as she proceeded by rail from Tacoma to Seattle. Despite the fire of 1889, "The Queen City," as Frances called it, was a flourishing commercial center of over 40,000.[14] Its streets spread over the slopes that faced the Sound and clanged with cable and electric cars. In recounting the history of the region, Frances noted "the want of women in territorial times."[15]

n 1890, Frances found 43 church organizations with over 8,000 communicants, most of whom were women. Sermons were preached in English, German, Swedish, Norwegian, and Welsh, representing 16 denominations. Seattle had four daily and several weekly newspapers, of which the *Post Intelligencer* and the *Seattle Press* were the principal ones. The state university was located in the heart of the city, and the Chautauqua Society owned property on Vashon Island, near Tacoma. From Seattle, Frances proceeded by train to Port Townsend, which she called "The Key City," the original port of entry to Washington Territory. It faced the Sound and backed on the Strait of Juan de Fuca.

To the north lay the San Juan archipelago. Frances had a special interest in two of the islands lying east of Haro Strait, the international boundary between British Columbia and the state of Washington. Foremost was San Juan Island. As a historian, she knew that British and American encampments had faced each other on this island from 1860 to 1872 while its ownership had been arbitrated.[16] The other island was Fidalgo, lying east of Rosario Strait and belonging to Skagit County, Washington. France noted that she had heard "wonderful things" from its founder, Amos Bowman, about the town of Anacortes on the northeast corner of the island.[17] In her account of her visit to Anacortes, which she called "the Venice of the Pacific," Frances did not reveal that she had first met Bowman during his brief stay at the Bancroft literary workshop late in 1878.[18] She simply described him as a British subject, trained in engineering. While surveying for the Canadian Pacific Railroad in 1876, he had purchased a quarter section of land on Fidalgo and founded a town, which he had named after his wife. Here he had set up a trade house, soon designated a post office, and published a newspaper as well as a set of maps, designed to demonstrate that a route through Anacortes was the shortest and quickest between Great Britian and Asia—by way of New York, the Great Lakes, Chicago, and Spokane, Washington. By distributing his maps to newspaper subscribers and exchanges, Bowman had attracted the attention of land developers and railroad magnates. In February, 1890 when the Oregon Improvement Association advertised that it would sell lots on the island, some 3,000 persons converged on the island. By the time Frances visited the Bowmans in June, steamers connected the island with ports on the Sound and in British Columbia.

After steaming north to Bellingham Bay on the Washington mainland, she returned to Seattle. She then caught glimpses of the Inland Empire as the Northern Pacific Railroad whisked her east from Seattle to Pasco on the upper Columbia near its confluence with the Yakima and Snake rivers.[19] The railroad crossed the Cascades by way of the two-mile Stampede Tunnel, and came down into the Yakima Basin. The town of Ellensburg, though "not a creature of the railroad," controlled the trade of the basin by means of the railroad, and another branch of the Northern Pacific would soon connect it with the Columbia River to the south. Upon reaching Pasco, the division point for railroads in the region, Frances noted that it should have been called Ainsworth in honor of J. D. Ainsworth, father of a number of transportation systems in the Pacific Northwest.[20]

At Pasco, passengers bound for Walla Walla, as she was, were detached from the through train to Spokane and switched to a line that crossed the Snake River over a handsome bridge to the town of Wallula, once the site of the Hudson's Bay Company's Fort Walla Walla. Here she boarded a car of the Oregon Railway and Navigation Company for the 30-mile run to Walla Walla. There her relatives included her youngest first cousin Jane Williams Wilson, her husband, Oscar, and their two sons, as well as Jane's mother-in-law and her own mother, Zilpha Williams, and her younger siblings who had joined the Wilsons during the mid-1870s. During Frances' 1890 visit, the cousins evidently discussed compiling a family genealogy.[21]

In her book, Frances included statistics on the production of fruit, vegetables, and cereals in the Walla Walla Valley. She noted that Walla Walla, with a population of over 7,000, had a handsome courthouse and "a collegiate institution, Whitman College." She also mentioned the Presbyterian Mission at Waiilatpu, where Dr. and Mrs. Whitman and a dozen others had perished at the hands of the Cayuse Indians in 1847. A movement was afoot to erect a monument to the memory of Dr. Whitman. She thought that "the most suitable monument would be an endowment for the college that bears his name."[22]

A branch of the Northern Pacific Railroad took her north through the Palouse country to the falls of the Spokane River. Here, in spite of the fire of 1889, she found a western metropolis of over 30,000. With the Missouri River on the east and Puget Sound on the west, it controlled much of the trade of northern Idaho and eastern Washington.[23] By interviewing well-informed surveyors, miners, and editors, she learned of the city's spectacular growth that sprang from the mining and agricultural resources of the region and the network of railroads that brought them to market. In an interview with a reporter for the *Spokane Spokesman*, reprinted in the June 13, 1890 issue of the *Oregonian*, she stated that with so much to see she was behind her schedule, but intended to have her manuscript ready for publication by fall.

The final chapter concluded with a table of the population and valuation of the 34 counties, ranging from Adams to Yakima, of "the younger brother of Oregon" who would not "be content with the younger brother's portion."[24] The product of library research, it was probably written in Portland. In any event, by July Frances was back in Portland, sharing the home of an acquaintance. On the 16th, the *Oregonian* published her reply to Bancroft's letter of a week or two earlier in which he had charged that the editor had been in error "in stating that Mrs. Victor had written several volumes" for his history of the Pacific states. He admitted that she had given him "much raw material," which he had put into suitable condition for publishing, but denied that she had done "any finished work" for him.[25]

In her reply, Frances noted that at first she had ignored Bancroft's charges, as the people of Oregon knew her well enough from her earlier writings. On second thought, she decided to explain some things in connection with her volumes on Oregon. Mr. Bancroft had not allowed her to "polish" her work. "The first writing had to go," she wrote. She did not object to his selecting the subject matter. He had excerpted her account of the Oregon Question and placed it elsewhere in the series. He had devoted seven volumes to California, but would have restricted the history of Oregon and Washington to one volume, had she not persuaded him to devote two volumes to Oregon and a third to Washington, Idaho, and Montana. In much the same way, she had written the histories of Nevada, Colorado, and Wyoming. Further, Mr. Bancroft had thrown in passages "to add chic to the style." Some she found amusing or downright contradictory, especially in passages on the missions and Indian wars, about which they disagreed. However, she was grateful that he had acknowledged that she had furnished him valuable material and agreed that "not everybody can be a historian." But it grieved her that "too much editing" had thwarted her purpose "in performing a long and serious labor."

On September 5, Frances wrote Judge Deady from "Miss Thompson's," noting that she had paid another woman several weeks' rent at the rate of seven dollars a week and that Mr. John Gill was trying to get a "canvasser" for her new book. She also enclosed receipts for two $100 checks which Deady had collected from Henry Failing and S. G. Reed, according to his diary.[26] However, the Judge failed to give her a promised letter of introduction to Asahel Bush, a Salem banker. In two letters to Bush, dated September 11 and 16, Frances noted the oversight.[27] In the first, she asked for an appointment, explaining that she had a book on Oregon "to be brought out by a good Eastern house." She had received several $100 contributions and some of smaller amounts, but the work would cost $1,500 before it paid anything. In the second letter, written in San Francisco, she noted that during her visit to his Salem office with Major George Williams, she had, "as a woman of refined habits," not allowed herself to appear "as a solicitor." The Major had later told her that she had "no business" about her. She asked Bush to "make Salem pay something towards publishing to the world the attractions of the state" and invited him to send her anything he thought deserved "particular mention." She would be in San Francisco another week or two before heading East to see her "Tourist Talks" through the press.

There is no evidence that Frances stopped in Ohio to see her step-daughter, now Mary Robinson, or her two remaining sisters, Celia Van Bearse and Marion Fuller in Marysville. However, later in the year these women helped her document a petition for a Navy widow's pension. In Philadelphia she delivered her manuscript of *Atlantis Arisen*, together with the illustrations, to J. B. Lippincott Company. She doubtless designed the dark green cloth cover at the top of which was imprinted in gold "ATLANTIS ARISEN" and at the right-hand bottom corner in smaller type "Frances Fuller Victor." Numbering 412 pages, it carried an undated Preface, a Table of Contents, and a List of Illustrations and sold for $3.00. Frances copyrighted it in 1891, the year it was printed.[28]

She was back in San Francisco in time to pick up copies of the last two volumes of Bancroft's Works, written largely by Bancroft and his family, *Essays and Miscellany* and *Literary Industries*. They were published in October and November, 1890.[29] In the section on California Literature in *Essays and Miscellany*, Frances Fuller Victor's work prior to entering the Bancroft Library was treated favorably and in detail. She was listed among the early and frequent contributors to the *Overland Monthly*, under the editorship of Bret Harte. With respect to descriptive writing, her work on Oregon and Washington "impart a special charm." The section on historical writing stated: "*The River of the West* by that versatile writer, Mrs. F. F. Victor, belongs to Oregen, but deserves special mention here for its attractive weft of mountain and trapper incidents with descriptive and anecdotal matter." The section on fiction noted that in her short stories she "invests her characters and incidents with a vividness of tone." Her apparent preference for Oregon topics had risen from the discovery of "a fresh field in opposition to California, which has so often been depicted." In closing, the essayist noted that previous references to Mrs. Victor gave evidence of "her rare versatility in heavy as well as light branches of literature." In this regard, she stood "unapproached among female authors of the Pacific Coast."

In *Literary Industries*, Bancroft had singled out Frances as the sole exception to his observation that the labor in his literary workshop had been that of men, "not the play at work of women."[30] He was glad, he wrote, to testify to the abilities of one woman, Frances Fuller Victor, if for no other reason than "to escape the charge of prejudice." Following her two-page biography, written by Frances herself, Bancroft noted: "In 1878 she accepted a hint from me and readily came to my assistance with greater enthusiasm than one less acquainted with her subject could be expected to feel. In ability, conscientiousness, never-ceasing interest, and faithfulness, she was surpassed by none."

By January 27, 1891 Frances had returned to Salem and was visiting friends and the extended family of Sebastian and Sarah Adams, according to the diary of Ellen M. White, sister-in-law of Sebastian.[31] [Sebastian was the widower of Frances' deceased sister Martha.] Whether planned or accidental, Frances' arrival in Salem was timely. In view of her partial research on early Indian wars, in Portland in 1874 and later at the Bancroft Library, she was the logical person to write up the causes and conduct of these interrelated wars. She agreed to move to Salem when

Secretary of State George McBride needed her services in compiling records of the wars. In the meantime, she had important business in Portland: canvassing for and distributing copies of her new book, *Atlantis Arisen*, and documenting her petition for a Navy widow's pension for which she had just become eligible.[32] To accomplish these tasks, she took up residence in the East Portland home of her friends, E. H. Kilham and his wife. Headquartered at the J. K. Gill bookstore in downtown Portland, Kilham oversaw the canvassing for and sale of *Atlantis Arisen*. At the same time, Frances began to document her petition for her badly needed pension with the help of family and friends and her own devices. Her stepdaughter, Mary Robinson, was among the first to furnish an essential document. Dated February 4, 1891, it stated that she was the only child of the late Henry C. Victor, and that her mother, Jane Edwards Victor, had died on October 4, 1861.

The documenting process was temporarily interrupted by the death on March 7, 1891 of Frances' widowed cousin, Deacon Douglas W. Williams, at his home in Portland. Though not a member of the Baptist Church, Frances was asked to write an In Memoriam on his behalf.[33] It began with this simple statement: "This day has just passed over to the silent majority a true gentleman, true friend, and true Christian." After placing him in the Williams genealogy, Frances lauded his "generosity, patience, modesty, and firmness in the right."

According to Ellen White's diary, Frances spent the weekend of May 3, 1891 in Salem. Together they attended Sunday services at the Unity Church, of which Mrs. White and other family members were regular attendants. Returning to Portland on Monday, Frances received a copy of the annulment of her marriage to Jackson Barritt, rendered by the Fairfield County Court, Ohio, in the March term, 1862. Later that month, a Portland attorney summarized the facts of the marriage certificate of Henry C. Victor and Frances Fuller of Philadelphia, dated May 14, 1862. On June, 1891, at the Multnomah County Courthouse, Frances granted power of attorney to Charles M. Carter of Washington, D. C to represent her at the Pension Office there. In an affidavit, dated Washington, D.C. June 27, 1891, Carter detailed his knowledge of the case. While living in Portland in 1865 he had known H. C. Victor and Mrs. F. F. Victor as husband and wife and had filed and collected for the former a prize claim for service performed during the Civil War. He had also been in Portland when Victor was lost at sea. Had Mrs. Victor remarried, he would have heard of it. Further, he knew that she was "very poor" and supported herself by her pen.

In Salem, Secretary of State McBride and B. F. Giltner, his brother-in-law and chief clerk of the office, executed similar affidavits. McBride added that Mrs. Victor often consulted him about her property in Columbia County, which had little present value. At the same time, Frances' agent in Alameda, California executed an affidavit stating that her unimproved lot valued at $950 was encumbered by a $450 mortgage and that as far as he knew her only income came from her writing.

From the Kilham home, Frances continued to document her petition for a federal pension and to promote her books in San Francisco, especially *Atlantis Arisen* and the volumes she had written for the Bancroft History Company. In August, she wrote Ella Sterling Cummins of San Francisco that she would have to be patient with her, for she was ill and forbidden to do things that she loved to do. She would, however, send to the *Wasp* a copy of her new book in which she would find something of note on pages 180 and 183.[34] By mid-November, Frances had sent the Wasp Publishing Company a copy of *Atlantis Arisen* and asked for "a few kind words" about it. She would like them to write a biography of her, but before assigning her a place in fiction she asked that they read her "The New Penelope," of which Mrs. Parkhurst had a copy.[35]

On October 2, Frances wrote Judge Deady, asking him to return her family genealogy to Gill's bookstore, in care of Mr. Kilham.[36] She had been ill but was doing some writing that required its use. She was likely referring to a joint biography of her deceased sister, Metta Victoria Victor, and herself.[37] On November 9, she replied to a letter from Deady. She wondered whether he had carried the genealogy to the coast, where he often vacationed. If so, her "patent of nobility" had gone with it and she regretted its loss. She added that she would send him a complimentary copy of *Atlantis Arisen* as soon as it arrived in quantity and asked him not to buy copies for the library until the city had been canvassed. She needed every subscription she could get. Until she had money with which to pay publishing costs, she could not take proper measures to restore her health. On November 7, the *Oregonian* had reviewed the volume, lauding Frances' "rare discernment" of the valuable and interesting as well as her familiarity with "every scrap of history or legend pertaining to the two great Northwest states." The editor advised that "the author should receive [compensation] through subscriptions to the volume, for which an active canvass will be made. It is a duty our people owe to her intelligence and painstaking efforts on behalf of the Northwest."

On January 13, 1892, Frances wrote Deady again.[38] She was distressed that he had not received his copy of *Atlantis Arisen*. Neither Mr. Kilham nor her agent had been able to deliver it and she could not do so. In accordance with his instructions, she had ordered two copies for the library, which had not been picked up. However, Frances continued to receive regional recognition. At the April, 1892 meeting of the Oregon State Board of Horticulture in Grants Pass, Oregon, Dr. J. B. Pilkington of Portland praised the work of "the woman explorer and writer, the Cleo (goddess of history) of the Northwest. Her recently published *Atlantis Arisen* should be in every library in the Northwest."[39]

During that spring, Frances completed the documentation of her petition for a Navy widow's pension. In her letter of April 17 to the Pension Commissioner in Washington, D.C., she noted that it had been nearly two years since she had submitted her declaration, Subsequently, she had submitted all the evidence called for. Since then she had read newspaper lists of men who had secured claims, "but only now and then a woman's name." She asked the Commissioner to make an exception in her case and "allow a non-political applicant to see her name on the lists of pensions granted." On May 31, she executed a final affidavit at the Multnomah County Courthouse in which she stated that she had made no application prior to July, 1890. On June 17, in Washington, D.C., Charles Carter paid a $10.00 fee; and Frances Fuller Victor was notified that she had been granted a monthly pension of $8.00, commencing July 23, 1890.[40] Though only a pittance, it was a moral victory, and back payments constituted a small windfall that financed her move to Salem to begin work on the history associated with the Cayuse, Rogue River, and Yakima Indian wars.

In her cryptic diary entry for June 22, Ellen White noted that Mrs. Victor had called to engage a room and that she had gone downtown and bought a carpet for "the front chamber." Three days later Frances moved in, and Mrs. White's sister, Sarah, and her husband, Sebastian, spent the evening with them. Thereafter, Mrs. White made regular but abbreviated diary notes on their joint social and church activities as well as on Frances' payments for room, board, and wood and her occasional trips to Portland, San Francisco, and the Oregon Coast.

Entries for July 18–22 indicate that Frances returned briefly to the Kilham home in East Portland. Here on July 18, she penned a reply to a new and much younger friend, Mrs. Eva Emery Dye.[41] Frances' letter indicates that the women had met at the home of Mary Gillette in Portland and that Frances was trying to set the newcomer straight on the complicated affairs of Dr. John McLoughlin of the Hudson's Bay Company and Dr. Marcus Whitman, the massacred Presbyterian missionary, two of her favorite subjects. With respect to "The Annals of California," about which Mrs. Dye had asked, Frances noted that Mr. Kilham had a copy in his library. After giving her directions to the Kilham home, Frances suggested that she go to East Portland to see the book herself; the Kilhams would welcome her. She explained that she was returning to Salem. In closing, she asked Mrs. Dye how she was getting along with her first Oregon novel.

Upon returning to Salem, Frances paid Mrs. White $8.00 for lodgings, and went to the statehouse to begin her research. According to Mrs. White, the women established a pleasant routine, taking walks, visiting family members and friends to take tea, have dinner, or play cards. After the summer vacation, they attended the Unity Church, sometimes morning and evening. Frances dined regularly at the McBride-Giltner residence on Sundays. However, Mrs. White made no reference to Frances' historical writing. On September 15, Mrs. White noted that she had gone downtown to the bank to get some money for Mrs. Victor, who left on the train to California and returned on October 11. During her absence, the women exchanged letters, and Frances sent Ellen a package to deliver to a mutual friend.[42]

Frances Fuller Victor never made an aimless trip. In California, she evidently called on her Prussian-born friend, Josephine Clifford McCracken, now married to a wealthy Arizona mine owner and living in a "rose embowered cottage" in the Santa Cruz mountains. At the suggestion of Ella Sterling Cummins, she may have called on the editor of the rejuvenated *Overland Monthly* and joined the recently founded Pacific Coast Women's Press Association, headquartered in San Francisco.

In the fall, Frances returned to Portland, as noted by Mrs. White in an October 23 diary entry. On November 2, Frances had gone to the statehouse; on the 5th she paid $21.50 for board and winter wood; on the 12th she began paying $5.00 a week for room and board. The two women attended a winter flower show at the Reed Opera House as well as lectures at Willamette University. On occasion they dined at Channing Hall. Thanksgiving and Christmas were celebrated in the traditional way with feasting and gift exchanges, in which Frances participated. Mrs. White also noted Mrs. Victor's guests, especially Major George Williams, who drove her to the statehouse and brought her books.

While Frances worked on her history of the early Oregon Indian wars, she kept up with the times. On January 6, 1893, she wrote Mrs. M. M. Ewer of San Francisco a letter about including copies of her Bancroft volumes to which she had affixed a "special preface," announcing her authorship of them. Together with other examples of her writing, they were displayed at exhibits in San Francisco and at the 1893 world's fair in Chicago.[43] The January, 1893 number of the *Impress*, official publication of the Pacific Coast Women's Press Association, carried her signed biography of her friend, Josephine Clifford McCracken. Its publication put Frances at the mercy of fellow members.

On February 25, Frances replied to a query from Miss Nellie M. Hill of Palo Alto, California.[44] She began by summarizing her work on the Pacific Northwest from *The River of the West* to *Atlantis Arisen*, including her Bancroft volumes. Copies of these books could be found in the public libraries of California, the Bancroft Library, and the San Francisco Women's Literary Exhibit, to which she had donated her last copies. She regretted that she was too busy to assist in historical research that might "yield valuable results or become a source of error." In March, Frances also responded to two letters from Mary Sheldon Barnes, who was privileged to use the Bancroft Library.[45] In the first, she detailed her historical writing prior and during her engagement at the library. In closing, she noted that within a few months a new work of hers on "the causes and conduct" of the early Indian wars of Oregon would interest "students of history." In the second letter, Frances noted that she could not give the present addresses of all of Bancroft's workers, but she did give the address of Henry L. Oak and the approximate whereabouts of Thomas Savage, Alfred bates, J. J. Peatfield, and William Nemos. She warned Mrs. Barnes that her undertaking would require "much hard study" and promised to see her if she got to San Francisco later that year.

In the meantime, Judge Deady, after a demanding trip to Washington, D. C., where he had been honored by members of the United States Supreme Court, was struggling to open the March term of the U. S. District Court of Oregon. On March 24, with his family and doctor at his bedside, he died peacefully at home and was buried in the family plot in Riverview Cemetery, which he had helped to found.[46] Three days later, Frances wrote Mrs. Deady the following letter of condolence:[47]

Dear Mrs. Deady –

You have been much in my thoughts since the news of your bereavement. I can, through a rather intimate acquaintance with the mind and character of the Judge measurably appreciate your loss.

The dearest friend of all your life, and while a masterly intellect at the same time your warm admirer and tender lover—all this is your loss irreparable on this side that gate through which he has passed to immortality.

I write these few words to assure you of my deep sympathy and that those of us who were only privileged to enjoy an ordinary friendship, mourn with and for you.

Very Sincerely Yours,

Frances F. Victor

On April 14, 1893, the Salt Lake City *Tribune* carried Mrs. Victor's signed reply to a derogatory article on the Bancroft histories published in the February 16 issue of the newspaper. Except for the underlined words, she had no quarrel with the following paragraph: "Mr. H. H. Bancroft is an intellectual fraud . . . . that is, he palms off as his own what purports to be history when he knows that it is not history, but merely a partisan statement *written by infernal rogues*, and to which he attaches his name for money." She also wanted to correct a statement in a San Francisco newspaper that the Mormon Church had agreed to buy a large number of Bancroft's *History of Utah* if Franklin Richards, a Mormon, were permitted to write it. As one of Bancroft's writers, Mrs. Victor asserted that she knew "a great deal about the methods practiced in Bancroft's library." To her knowledge, his writers, including herself, were honest and set down the facts as they found them. The history of Utah had been written by the "scholarly" Alfred Bates. First assigned to her, she had interviewed Richards and his wife when they visited the library. However, when Utah came up, she was engaged in writing the history of Oregon and Utah had been assigned to Mr. Bates. Mr. Bancroft had edited it, as he did all the histories. He would have been wiser, Frances noted, had he aspired to less and been satisfied with publishing other people's books. Clearly, he could not have written all the books that bore his name. With the assistance of Oak, Nemo, Bates, and herself, and others, who had done over 80 years of work on the series, Mr. Bancroft's claim that he had done 100 years of work in 20 disproved itself and was not worth discussing. Her main contention was with bringing discredit "on honest historians." In commenting on Mrs. Victor's letter, the editor of the *Tribune* concluded: "Mrs. Victor, who shrank from certain things in the Utah story, had been spared. Mr. Bates had written it. Mr. Bancroft had improved on it for money."

Frances must have been pleased with this response to her letter, for she hoped to attend the 1893 World's Columbian Exposition in Chicago, scheduled to open May 1. By this time she had sent to the Pacific Coast Women's Press Association for their booths at the Mechanic's Fair in San Francisco and the Chicago world's fair copies of her writings. In addition to her "Florence Fane" columns written for the San Francisco *Golden Era* between August, 1863 and January, 1865, she had sent four volumes of the Bancroft historical series to which she had affixed her name. Each carried a copy of this "Special Preface:"

> It is well known, Mr. Bancroft having set it forth in his *Literary Industries,* that the series of the Pacific coast histories employed the talents and labors of a number of writers beside himself. As one of those writers whose individual work is not acknowledged, being called on to state what literary work I have done for the Pacific Coast, it seems not only just but necessary to affix my name to at least four volumes of the *History of the Pacific States,* although this does not cover all the work done on the *History* by myself. The four volumes referred to comprise the states of Oregon, Washington, Idaho, Montana, Colorado, Wyoming, and Nevada. My name is therefore placed on the backs of these volumes without displacing that of Mr. Bancroft.

On the opening day of the 1893 Chicago world's fair, Frances Fuller Victor was honored by an acquaintance from California, according to the *City Argus* of San Francisco, which reported that Mrs. Mary E. Hart, custodian of the State Historical Exhibit, had read Mrs. Victor's account of how she would personify the states of California and Oregon if she were a painter—the former as a dark-eyed, girlish Cleopatra; the latter as a golden-bearded young giant, Anthony. A month later, Abigail Scott Duniway, long-time advocate of women's rights in the Pacific Northwest and sometimes critic of Mrs. Victor, addressed the World's Auxiliary Congress of Women at the fair. In describing the discovery of the Columbia River by Captain Robert Gray, she quoted an entry in his log book, dated May 11 1792. After crossing the perilous bar and finding a river of fresh water, Gray had closed with the familiar phrase, "So end." Here Mrs. Duniway remarked: "To this Mrs. Frances Fuller Victor, Oregon's eminent historian and author of *Atlantis Risen* [*sic*] adds 'No not so ends, modest captain of the good ship *Columbia*. The end is not yet nor will be until all of the vast territory rich with every possible production which is drained by the waters of the new found river have yet yielded up illimitable wealth to distant generations."[48]

Back in Oregon, according to Ellen White's diary, Frances was in Portland from May 8 to 22, visiting friends. On the 29th, she wrote Mrs. Dye in Salem that she had failed to see George Himes, a collector of historical items, about a Whitman letter,[49] She asked Mrs, Dye to help her get possession of it as she needed it to "enlarge" her poem, "The Poppies of Waiilatpu," which she intended to publish and would show her. Her party had enjoyed their visit with her in Oregon City and she hoped to hear more about the Whitman letter.

That she was included in *Women of the Century*, edited by Frances E. Willard and Mary A. Livermore, which Charles Wells Moulton published and released in New York City, Buffalo, and Chicago in 1893, must have pleased Frances.[50] In fact, she doubtless wrote it. Only a page in length, the biographical information noted that her father was of "an old Colonial family,"some of whom were among the founders of Plymouth, Massachusetts. On her mother's side, she was descended through thirty-nine generations from Egbert, the first king of England. Her great-grandmother, Lucy Walworth, had been a granddaughter of William Walworth and a cousin of Chancellor Walworth, the last chancellor of New York. At the age of nine, Frances Fuller had written verses on her slate at school and arranged plays from her imagination, assigning parts to her mates to whom she explained the significance. At the age of fourteen, she had published verses that had received "favorable comment." At age eighteen, some of her poems had been "copied in English journals." Her biography also noted the "two pairs of poet sisters, the Carys and the Fullers," in the state of Ohio, to which the Fuller family had "removed." It did not mention Frances' first marriage to Jackson Barritt in 1863, but did note that the Fuller sisters had married brothers. The younger sister, Metta, had remained in the East, while Frances had followed her husband, then an officer in the United States Navy, to California. At the close of the Civil War, he had resigned his commission and settled in Oregon. In that new world she had studied the country and its history from every point of view. She had written

stories, poems, and essays for California publications, which, if collected, would make several volumes. At the death of her husband in 1875,
she had returned to California to assist Mr. H. H. Bancroft on his series
of Pacific histories, writing in all six volumes of that work, on which
she was engaged for about eleven years. Her home was listed as "Portland, Ore."

At the end of June, Mrs. White noted in her diary that Mrs. Victor
departed for a three-week trip to the Oregon coast, apparently to gather
material for an essay on seaside resorts for the *Overland Monthly*. She
returned to find a previously submitted essay, "A Province of California,"
in the July number of that magazine. It was an account of the settlement
and Indian wars of "the southwest corner of Oregon," which present-
day residents called "A Province of California." She had likely uncovered
the facts while researching the history of the early Indian wars on the
Southern Oregon coast—a good example of Frances' ability to find
more than one market for new information

But Frances' chief task at the time continued to be her "history of
the early wars of the white race with the Indians of the Northwest," as
she stated in the unsigned Preface to *The Early Indian Wars of Oregon*, dated
Salem, July 30, 1893. In setting forth "the causes in detail which led to
these race conflicts," she had "endeavored to 'nothing extenuate, nor set
down aught in malice,' but rather to give a philosophical view of the
events recorded." This was important because "fiction and sentimental-
ism on one hand and vengeful hatred on the other" had "perverted the
truth of history." She further noted:

> The Indian is a wild man; it would only be a fact of evolu-
> tion to call him a wild animal on his way to be a man, pro-
> vided the proper environments were furnished him. While
> the instincts and perceptions are acute, the ethical part of
> him is undeveloped and his exhibitions of a moral nature
> are whimsical and without motive. Brought into contact
> with white men, whether of the lowest or of the highest, he
> is always at a disadvantage which is irritating, and subject to
> temptations which are dangerous. On the other hand, the
> white man is subject to the more subtle temptation to abuse

The diary of pioneer George Himes, a founder of the Oregon Historical Society
and the Oregon Pioneer Association, will eventually resurface.
Among countless entries through eighty-plus years,
it may tell us why he and Victor were incompatible.

ORHI 101849

his superiority for selfish purposes; he being in selfishness
often but little, if at all, removed from the wild man.

In setting forth the causes of the Indian wars, Frances added:
One point to be brought out in these pages is the accounta-
bility of the government in our Indian wars, and its indebtedness to the pioneers of every part of the country: first, in
inviting settlement, and then in not properly protecting settlers. The policy of the government for a hundred years has
been to throw out a vanguard of immigration, and when
these have fallen to savage cupidity or hatred, to follow with
a tardy army and "punish" when it should have prevented.
The Spaniards did better than this, for they sent a garrison
out with every colony and "reduced" the native population
with comparatively little bloodshed.

If this record of the first ten years of Indian warfare in Oregon presents this subject fairly to the reader, it will have achieved the purpose for which it was written.

On August 10, the Salem *Oregon Statesman* reported that Mrs. Frances Fuller Victor, who was living at the home of Mrs. E. M. White on State Street, would soon complete her work on "the causes and conduct of the early Indian wars of Oregon." Thereafter, "being one of Oregon's gifted authors," she would devote her attention to other compositions. According to Mrs. White's diary, on September 7, Frances learned of the death of her youngest sister, Marion Fuller, in Marysville, Ohio. On the 18th, in a reply to Eva Emery Dye, Frances wrote that she was starting for the Chicago world's fair within the week and asked whether there was anything she could do for her as she was going "among the publishers."

In a diary entry of the same date, Mrs. White noted—without complaint—that Mrs. Victor was three weeks behind in her board payments. There is no evidence that the women had come to an agreement about deferred payments for board. In the past, Frances often had been a nonpaying guest in the home of a friend or family member. In 1893, except for her $8.00 monthly pension, royalties on *Atlantis Arisen*, and payment for occasional articles in the *Overland Monthly*, her income was limited. Just when she was paid the $1,306.13 for her work on *The Early Indian Wars of Oregon*, as noted in state legislative records, is not clear.[51]

In any event, from September, 1893 forward Mrs. Victor did not pay board, though she doubtless helped with the housework, sewing, gardening, and entertaining. She also knew that Ellen White loaned money to others. On October 11, according to Mrs. White, Frances learned that her banker, Major George Williams, could not send her "to C——." On the 23rd, Mrs. White noted that she and Mrs. Victor had met Sebastian and Sarah Adams at the depot upon their return from the world's fair. She also noted that she and Mrs. Victor joined the literary section of the Unity Club that met in the church parlors on Wednesday evenings. On November 10, according to the Salem *Statesman,* each member gave the titles of five of their favorite novels and their reasons for selecting them, and Mrs. F. F. Victor read "an interesting and valuable paper on The Evolution of the Novel."

Publication of Frances Fuller Victor's illustrated article, "Northwest Seaside Resorts," in the February, 1894 number of the *Overland Monthly* suggests that she was looking forward to returning to San Francisco. On February 6, she used the columns of the Salem *Statesman* to advertise a new venture that would occupy her for the rest of the spring. She announced that she had been appointed a member of the Advisory Council of the Women's Auxiliary Congress, meeting in San Francisco for a week, commencing April 30. She appealed to the women of the Willamette Valley who would like to say something at the meeting, where questions pertaining to the education, employment, and advancement of women on the Pacific Coast would be discussed. It was expected that a discussion of such "vital questions" would produce a lasting impression upon society as to "the value of woman's thought on the world." She invited any woman in the state who wanted to read or have a paper read at the meeting to notify her of her subject and home address.

At long last, at the age of 68, Frances was in a position to invite the women of Oregon to reflect upon their status and what they had accomplished as women. Her chief targets were her friends in Salem and Eva Emery Dye in Oregon City. To the latter, she wrote three letters and as many postcards.[52] On February 5, she advised Mrs. Dye of her appointment to the Advisory Council and invited her to submit a suitable subject. On the 8th, in reply to Mrs. Dye, she urged her to send in "a strong paper," even if she could not attend. She noted that Mrs. Dye had "an unlimited choice of subjects," as only a half dozen women had responded. Though the railroad company had "shut down on passes," she was going to ask for one. Her own subject was going to be, "The Evolution of Women, Past and Present." She would welcome Mrs. Dye's company and asked for her academic degrees. Then she listed the subjects submitted by other Oregon women: "Hygiene and Scientific Temperance" by Mrs. Kinney of Astoria; "The Social Unrest of the Times" by Mrs. Dolan of St. Helens; "Medical Science" by Dr. Emma J. Welty of Portland; "Women's Part in University Founding" by Mrs. England of Salem. Frances was uncertain when she would "go below." It depended on "proofreading, etc." When she saw her way clear, she would let Mrs. Dye know.

On February 24, Frances wrote Mrs. Dye that she had sent in her subject, "Woman's Part in the Drama of the Northwest;" and on March 12 she wrote her to ask whether her paper would interfere with a monologue that Frances might present on the women of the Presbyterian missions. She had proposed that "a Pioneer Day be held." But the management had given her only one evening, and they wanted her to read a paper that evening, which she did not want to do.

Meanwhile, Ellen White continued to detail Mrs. Victor's activities—a card party, which they had jointly hosted; Frances' joining the Unity Church on Easter morning; Frances attending a physical culture class at Willamette University, perhaps to research her subject for the Women's Congress in San Francisco. On April 24, now 34 weeks behind in her board payments, Frances paid her landlady $13.00 for winter wood.

On April 25, the Salem *Statesman* reported that among the 27 delegates to the Women's Congress in San Francisco were Mrs. England and Mrs. Victor of Salem and Mrs. Dye of Oregon City. On the 27th, Mrs. White noted in her diary that "S and SC" came by to bid "Mrs. V." goodbye and that she and a roomer had gone to the depot to see Mrs. Victor and Mrs. England "off on the train to C——." Mrs. White's last entry for that date was: "Mrs. V. owes me one hundred and seventy-three dol."

That Mrs. Victor departed the state before it published her latest book did not concern her. She knew that she would be well paid for having written it and that she would not have to promote its sale nor canvass for subscriptions. But she could not have imagined that it would be another six years before she would return to her adopted state.

CHAPTER 15

SANCTUARY IN
SAN FRANCISCO
(1895-99)

Frances fuller victor found a sanctuary in the Pacific Coast Women's Press Association during the last years of the 19th century. As an officer of this organization, with its membership of more than 200 women journalists and authors, she was able to cement friendships with women who helped her earn her living by her pen, while she defended her reputation and worked on unfinished historical ventures that eventually took her back to Oregon. Meanwhile, she had always preferred, especially during the winter months, the sophisticated, go-ahead spirit of San Francisco to the rainy provincialism of Portland, despite her many friends there.

After spending a week with friends in Santa Cruz, California in August of 1894, Frances evidently attended the third annual Women's Press Association convention in San Francisco in September. An active member, she was fourth vice-president on the 1894-1895 ticket.[1] By January, 1895, she was comfortably settled at No. 234 on Haight Street, which terminated at Golden Gate Park. Her address was also within walking distance of the office, library, reception rooms, and press of the Women's Press Association at 20 Ellis Street. There she had opportunities to meet the organization's leaders, but the library and the program and press committees were her primary interests.

The January, 1895 number of *The Impress*, the official publication of the Women's Press Association, introduced her to her sister members in an article aptly titled "A Literary Pioneer," written by Charlotte Perkins Stetson, the current president of the Women's Press Association (and a niece of Harriet Beecher Stowe.)[2] It emphasized the variety of Frances Fuller Victor's Pacific Coast publications, from her Florence Fane column in the *Golden Era* in 1863-1865 to her *Early Indian Wars* in Oregon in 1894, as well as the volumes she had written for Bancroft in the intervening years. Mrs. Stetson also commented on Frances' New England ancestry, "from names high on the colonial records up to royalty itself." Since her husband's loss at sea, Mrs. Victor had been doing admirable work, "meeting the usual recognition awarded to a fine but unpretentious ability by a rude, young country." She was now in San Francisco again, where she would continue to contribute to the literature of the Pacific Coast

Though the State of Oregon had not yet published her history of the early Indian wars, Frances had added it to her credits. However, a story in the *Oregon Statesman,* Salem, must have given her pause. It reported a controversy that threatened publication of her book. Her friend, John Minto of Salem, had publicly recommended that her manuscript be published as written, but he had been opposed by self-appointed lobbyists for the veterans of the Indians wars. They claimed that the history did not deserve the patronage of the state because "the authoress" had not sought the counsel of many who had been available and "willing and anxious to assist by giving the facts." It would be "a great injustice to the veterans" if the book were published without first submitting it to a committee accredited by the veterans organization.

On February 24, 1895, the *Statesman* carried Frances' reply under the headlines: "THE WEBFOOT HISTORY—Mrs. Victor's Rational Defense of Her Oregon Indian War History—She Deems Authenticated State Archives Better Data than Ambiguous Personal Narratives." Frances contended that she had talked and corresponded with veterans, but had used their testimony only when she could verify it with documentary evidence. She further stated that, since 1865, she had sunk more money into trying to get books about Oregon before the public than she had ever gotten out of them. It had been her love of the subject, not avarice, that had prompted her writings. She further claimed that, despite the shortcomings of her Bancroft histories, she had done more than any other writer to preserve the records of "Oregon's first families." She thanked John Minto for his support and urged that the printing and binding go forward as ordered. Her forthright defense of her work and the support of her Salem friends evidently insured the publication of the volume, now under the direction of Harrison Kinkaid, secretary of state during the administration of Governor William Lord.[3] There the matter rested for the next two years while Frances made her presence felt in San Francisco.

In April, 1895, Frances responded to receipt of a copy of the first issue of the Oakland *Blade*, which reminded her of the journalism of Horace Greeley and Samuel Bowes of the Atlantic states. "Bright little *Blade*," she urged, "perform your mission. Cut away imposture and imposition." The editor proudly acknowledged her letter by headlining it: "FROM FRANCES FULLER VICTOR—The Eminent Historian of the New Northwest." By this time, she was preparing her address to be read at the second annual Women's Congress, sponsored by the Women's Press Association and attended by Susan B. Anthony and Anna H. Shaw, president and vice –president of the National Woman Suffrage Association, headquartered in the East.[4]

The topic for the May, 1895 Congress was how the home could promote virtue in the community. Frances Fuller Victor continued to shun the platform, and her address, "Errors of Our Ignorance," apparently read by Mrs. Stetson at the Congress, was published in *The Impress*. It raised the sensitive issue of the need for sex education in the home. Marshalling the testimony of literary giants like Carlyle, Dr. Johnson, Hawthorne, and Hugo, Mrs. Victor drew a distinction between "ignorance," which is always a "sin," and "innocence," which is freedom from sin but not from knowledge. She argued that the most virtuous person was one who had knowledge of sin and yet, through choice, pursued a path of virtue. Knowledge barred such a person from falling into evil, whereas a person who is virtuous through innocence that comes from ignorance is always at peril. How the home could help dispel "popular errors in some of the things we need to know and perhaps do not" was the message of her address.

"The attraction of the sexes for each other," she states, "comprises the history and the poetry of the world." In view of this fact, a girl should be prepared for the physical life ahead of her. It was unfair to leave her in ignorance of anything that so vitally concerned her as a knowledge of physiology, especially topics that relate to marriage. The phrase, "maidenly purity," usually implied "complete ignorance." If mothers did right by their daughters, the motive for "the prurient curiosity" which has resulted in false and injurious beliefs would not exist. A boy, even more than a girl, needed to be educated about the law of his being. "What chance for health and happiness," Frances asked, could an ignorant wife have with "an equally ignorant husband?"

In ignoring their responsibilities, parents were helping to destroy "the sanctity and beauty of the passion that rules the world," debasing it to the level of "an obscene joke." Whatever the form of service, Frances observed that every marriage "is meant to be a link in the endless chain of human life." The only persons vitally concerned are the man and the woman, who alone can bestow herself in marriage. In today's society, much that is wrong is traced to "ill-conceived unions." But marriage itself is "a blessing," France insisted. "Women do not hate men. They cannot. They only want recognition and brotherly aid. They feel their own importance in the world and want it admitted." Though the "bachelor girl of the era" loses her balance sometimes, she is never "dangerous." Rather, she "is understandable, but a better knowledge of the physical facts will lead a woman to look beyond herself and consider the sociological relations between the sexes." In conclusion, she noted that marriage, "which changes both husband and wife, is one of the most beautiful secrets of nature." She advised women to make society better by studying themselves. "Woman," she contended, "is nature's most wonderful production. Her name should be Love, and the names of her children, Truth and Reason."

One can only wonder what those in attendance made of Frances Fuller Victor's forthright pronouncements. In her account of the session, Susan B. Anthony wrote: "No meeting ever held was more beautiful or inspiring. The best speakers of the state, both men and women, participated, and every honor, public and social, were conferred on the Eastern guests."[5]

In June, Frances received a circular from the editor of the Salem *Statesman* addressed to "Dear Sir." Its request for "anything personal" about pioneers provided her with an opportunity to comment on her associations with several of Oregon's best-known pioneers and to re-introduce herself to Oregonians. She began by clarifying her marital status as the widow of Henry Clay Victor, whom she had followed to Oregon in 1865 and who had been lost at sea a decade later. Then she detailed her writing career on the Pacific Coast, beginning with her first two years in San Francisco as a columnist for *The Golden Era*, followed by her first voyage from San Francisco to Portland via Victoria, Vancouver Island. Then she described her 1865 meetings with Governor Addison C. Gibbs and Judge Mathew P. Deady in Portland; J. Quinn Thornton and the Montieth brothers, founders of Albany; Mrs. Joseph Avery of Corvallis; and Jesse Applegate of Yoncalla. Later that year she had also met William L. Adams and W. H Gray in Astoria, where Gray's *History of Oregon* was being serialized in the local newspaper. Soon after, Judge Deady had introduced her to Joseph L. Meek, hero of her *The River of the West*, in which she mistakenly incorporated Gray's account of the Whitman myth.

In the meantime, she had written a handbook on Oregon, for which Albert D. Richardson of New York City had failed to find an Eastern publisher. This she later published as *All Over Oregon and Washington* in San Francisco at her own expense after the Oregon state legislature had refused to fund its publication as an advertisement for Oregon. Abigail Duniway had opposed her efforts because she had not been "radical enough on the suffrage question." However, in writing the histories of Oregon and Washington in the Bancroft Library, she had given Mrs. Duniway "the credit she deserved for her work in the field of women's rights."

In her review of her career to date, Frances did not mention her visits in 1873 with the Applegates to the sites of the Modoc Indian War nor her account of the women's crusade against whiskey in Portland in 1874. But she did refer to her popular column, "Dorothy D.," in the San Francisco *Daily Morning Call* in 1875 as an example of writing opportunity there as opposed to the lack thereof in Portland. The loss of Frances' husband by drowning in 1875 was noted, as was her publication, again in San Francisco and at her own expense, of a collection of her short stories written for the *Overland Monthly*, together with selected poems she had written earlier. Shortly after this, Mr. Bancroft had asked Frances to become one of his collaborators. After she had written the aggregate of six volumes, he had accorded her only eight lines in his book, *Literary Industries*, except for her biography, which she had written herself. After resigning from the Bancroft Library, she had returned to Oregon to write *Atlantis Arisen* and *Early Indian Wars in Oregon*. Except for the last, all her work, including four of her Bancroft volumes, had been exhibited at the 1893 Chicago World's Fair.

This autobiographical sketch appeared in the June 16, 1875 issue of the Salem *Daily Oregon Statesman*. Frances' Salem friend, Ellen White, did not comment on it in her diary; but Sebastian C. Adams, her former brother-in-law, acknowledged receipt of her card of the 13th and noted that he had picked up three copies of her "meritorious" article. He was glad she had written it, he said, for it carried information about which many Oregonians were ignorant.[6]

On July 7, the San Francisco *Daily Morning Call* published a similar account in the form of an interview, titled "THE WOMAN HISTORIAN—Interesting Passages in the Life of Frances Fuller Victor— HER WORK IN THE WEST—Chosen by the Oregon Legislature to Write a History of the Indian Wars." The two-column interview was illustrated with a half-page photographic study of Mrs. Victor by Portland's leading photographer, Isaac Taber. Noting that "a woman historian is a *rare avis* in the field of literature," the interviewer, L. P. F., likely a member of the Women's Press Association, introduced Frances Fuller Victor as "a woman with the faculty for removing the mantle of tradition from the skeletons of the past and giving to the world the interesting results of her discoveries." The interviewer also noted Mrs. Victor's "bright career" in Ohio and New York City, where, before the Civil War, she had met celebrities in the artistic and literary worlds, among whom had been Alice and Phoebe Cary. The publication of her *Youth's History of America* had been prevented by the outbreak of the war, during which she had married Mr. Victor, a naval officer, with whom she had come to San Francisco in 1863. Here she had been part of "early coast newspaperdom." Her stories had taken on "the western coloring" and when they appeared unsigned in the San Francisco and Chicago press, they were credited to Bret Harte, then at the height of his popularity. In detailing Mrs. Victor's "life labors as a historian," the interviewer mentioned her *Atlantis Arisen* and her yet unpublished *Early Indian Wars in Oregon*. Her most popular book had been *The River of the West*, another edition of which would be brought out in the near future. A long paragraph was devoted to Frances' aristocratic ancestors, one of whom, Sir William Walworth, Lord Mayor of London, had been knighted by Richard II. The interview closed with an account of Frances' labors in the Bancroft Library, where her identity had been lost "in the shadow of the publisher's name." She had emerged with her health impaired, her name remembered by friends of her early journalistic days, but unfamiliar to later newspaper workers. After her husband had drowned at sea, the way had not been easy for her; but her book-making days were far from over, and she was now engaged "in accumulating material for ultimate publications."

Among the thousands who saw the photograph of the handsomely coiffed Frances Fuller Victor and read her story was Mrs. W. B. Bancroft, a would-be playwright and member of the Women's Press Association. Her husband, Will B. Bancroft, had sued his uncle, H. H. Bancroft, for alleged libel in 1893; and on February 4, 1894, the latter's name had been removed from honorary membership in the Society of California Pioneers due to offensive passages in his history of California.[7]

The July 28, 1895 issue of the San Francisco *Daily Morning Call* featured a book review by Frances, which indicated she was indeed a veteran historian. In June, her Walla Walla, Washington cousins may have advised her that a delegation of publishers from the Chicago region had been touring Eastern Washington on a special car of the Northern Pacific Railroad. Among them had been Dr. O. W. Nixon, president of the *Inter Ocean*, a Chicago periodical. He had written a book entitled *How Marcus Whitman Saved Oregon. A True Romance*. When he visited Whitman's grave near Walla Walla, Nixon had proclaimed that Whitman performed a great service in saving Oregon for the Union[8] Upon securing a copy of his book, Frances discovered that he had named her one of Whitman's chief defamers. She so stated in her review of his book, first published in the San Francisco *Daily Morning Call* and reprinted in the *Oregon Statesman* on August 18 under the headline: THE TRUTH PERVERTED—Revival of the Whitman Myth—An Old, Old Story in a New Dress—Attempt to Make Sentiment at Expense of History—Mrs. Fuller [*sic*] to the Rescue." [9] In her review, Frances Fuller Victor stated that it struck her, "a conscientious 19th century historian," as curious that anyone would try "to foist upon an intelligent public, history constructed on the plan of King Arthur's round table." This was what Dr. Nixon had done in his book, properly subtitled *A True Romance*. The real author of Nixon's *A True Romance* was W. H. Gray, one of Whitman's assistants at his mission in the Walla Walla Valley. In writing *The River of the West*, she had mistakenly followed Gray's narrative. But once she had discovered her errors, she had corrected them in her own writings and pointed them out to others. Her findings had been attacked in the press and from the pulpit, but they had not been overturned. Then Victor once again skillfully undermined the Gray-Nixon claim that Whitman had promoted the 1843 immigration to Oregon by establishing that his winter ride East in 1842 had been prompted by affairs at the Presbyterian missions in Eastern Washington and by granting that on his return to Oregon he had overtaken the 1843 immigration and served it well.

Late in August, the San Francisco *Morning Call* published Nixon's reply, titled, "HOW DR. MARCUS WHITMAN SAVED OREGON VS. MRS. FRANCES FULLER VICTOR by Dr. O. W. Nixon of Chicago." It attracted public attention because of Nixon's vindictive style. Naming Mrs. Victor as among the most persistent of defamers of Whitman, Nixon charged that she had "sailed into Oregon after traveling was easy and soon found she had a mission, *viz.* to teach ignorant Oregonians pioneer history." Her "pretended history" had been disproved, yet she continued "to dress up her dolls stuffed with sawdust and palm them off as creatures of life." He did not hope to convert her, as her mission now was "to dance on the grave of Dr. Marcus Whitman and his noble wife and make faces." Noting that she was the author of "the quirks and fables called history in Bancroft's *Oregon*," Nixon credited Bancroft "in lucid moments," with having changed some of the things that Mrs. Victor had written. He deemed himself competent to question

"Mrs. Victor's truthfulness" on the grounds that in 1850 he had taught school in Oregon. Here he had heard history "direct from the men and women who made it." Later, as a purser on a Columbia River steamer, he had met "another class of the makers of Oregon history." He also quoted, out of context, statements by Jesse Applegate, Narcissa Whitman, and "General" Asa L. Lovejoy, who had accompanied Whitman on his winter ride, as Mrs. Victor had not. In closing, he asked only that Whitman be recognized as the man who, more than all others, had awakened the nation. "The world will always be full of doubters," he lamented, "and very sure we will have Mrs. Victor standing in the middle of the road, throwing mud at the old pioneers of Oregon."

These harsh remarks prompted the Oakland *Times* to report that the San Francisco *Morning Call* had just published "a fierce attack" from Dr. Nixon of Chicago on Mrs. Frances Fuller Victor of Portland, Oregon. Persons acquainted with her literary ability were looking forward to her reply. It came in the September 8 issue of the *Call* under the headline: "MRS. FRANCES FULLER VICTOR vs. Dr. O. W. Nixon of Chicago." After disposing of Nixon's "school-boy name calling," Frances proceeded to state the facts with "strong hopes of converting him." His mistake lay in assuming that something was true because a person who ought to know had said it was true. At the beginning of her "Oregon studies," she had made the same mistake; but "once caught in the act," had been enough for her. As for Bancroft's *Oregon*, she had taught him all that he knew about Oregon. She was not going to say that Mr. Bancroft or Dr. Nixon printed falsehoods. Whatever her convictions, she had better manners. Then, as "the real author" of Bancroft's *Oregon*, she corrected Nixon's account of Whitman's winter ride East by quoting from letters of Archibald McKinley of the Hudson's Bay Company, a friend of Whitman, who had given him a company outfit to wear on his trip East. She further noted that the testimony of Whitman's guide, Lovejoy, had been taken years after the journey when he was infirm of brain and body." Finally, she contended that if Whitman had been a politician at the time, the *Oregon Spectator* would have mentioned it. A veteran of the Cayuse Indian War had told her that at the site of the Whitman massacre letters from Dr. John McLoughlin urging Whitman to leave the country had been found. She was sorry that he "had pitifully died when he could have lived." But she could not "deify him in consequence."

Frances found the controversy stimulating. On September 10, she reached out "across the yawning distance and accumulating years" to bring Captain Oliver Applegate up to date." [10] She had been in San Francisco for the past eighteen months and was still alive, though her struggle would not go into history. Talking of history, Californians were now calling her "a historian." When she said that she would rather be praised for her "imaginative works," a friend reminded her that she was "an authority on Pacific history." This, in turn, had reminded her to ask him to return the copy of Bancroft's *California Inter Pocula*, which she had sent him for comment on her coverage of the Modoc Indian War, contained in the volume. Then she asked whether he had seen her recent book review in the San Francisco *Morning Call*. In his book on Whitman, Dr. Nixon had labeled her "a false historian." Of course, she had answered him—to little purpose. Still the controversy served to keep an interest in historical matters alive and to advertise the book that she was writing on the subject. The rest of her letter was more personal. She enjoyed her activities at the Women's Press Association, though they paid nothing. If she had enough money, she would be pleased to settle down somewhere for the rest of her life. After counseling Oliver to re-enter "the race of life" for himself and his children, she noted that her own health was better than it had been last year when excitement would throw her "into a hysterical condition." She still had to have her papers for the Women's Congress delivered by a reader, though she had recently managed to read a page or two about Crater Lake before the Women's Press Association.

The upcoming campaign to amend the California state constitution by deleting the word *male* from the suffrage clause was not a burning issue with Frances Fuller Victor, as it was with a small majority of the Women's Press Association. Other members like Mrs. Florence Matheson took exception to the proselytizing suffragists in their midst. In the December, 1895 number of the *American Magazine of Civics*, she stated her objections in an article entitled "Women's Disbarment to Political Service." [11] Mrs. Matheson noted that at the May, 1895 Women's Congress, devoted to the subject of Home, she had sat among "the silent majority," which had been stigmatized by suffragist speakers for not agreeing with them that women should enter the field of politics. Branded as a "traitor" to her sex, she had been moved "to talk back." The majority of women whom she knew did not want the vote nor did they want to attract attention to themselves by expressing themselves in public. Of the 150,000 women in San Francisco, fewer than 800 were active suffragists. Yet they arrogated to themselves the right to speak for all women and demanded in their names something they did not want. Among the active minority were a few noble women who were acting in accordance with their convictions. But this also included "many disappointed women alone in the world who were attracted by the suffrage agitation."

Mrs. Matheson then described a third class of women who had "a mania for notoriety" and were doing the cause more harm than good. She granted that some day equal suffrage would be the rule, for a nagging woman always got her way, but "something previous would be lost in the process." She added that she would be more sympathetic with her "struggling sisters if their goal were not office-holding." Only in exceptional cases should women take on the duties of public office with the prospect of doing themselves or the office credit. Mrs. Matheson based her conclusion on the facts of "women's physical organization." Plainly, women were intended by nature to be wives and mothers—to bear and rear the children of the world. The "advanced woman" might be displeased to learn that what she scornfully called "the animal function of motherhood" was really the only reason she had been included "in the plan of creation." Maternity was solely "a woman's business." It involved "a gestation period, often attended by suffering, as were other periods of physical change such as menstruation and menopause." During such periods, no woman should attempt "serious physical or mental work." The "governing mind" should be free from "petty prejudice or sickly sentimentality."

Mrs. Matheson also noted that nature revenged herself on unmarried women as demonstrated by "the irritability and general thorniness" of some of the most gifted "women bachelors." Suffragists should talk to "ignorant and sinful women" as individuals, If women did secure the vote, she hoped that "an age qualification" would be imposed so that no woman under fifty could be appointed or elected to an important position unless a physician certified that her female functions had ceased.

Not surprisingly, Frances Fuller Victor, whose address on the need for sex education in the home, was read to the May, 1895 Women's Congress, volunteered or was asked to pen a polite but pertinent reply, entitled "Does Maternity Preclude Politics?" In answering her "frank and friendly opponent," Frances stated, "the real reasons" that many women did not want the vote. Some were ignorant of the benefits of voting. Other dreaded ridicule or accepted the religious superstition that men were naturally superior to women. Lastly, a few asked, "What is the use of contending for something we will never get?" As for Mrs. Matheson's charge that a few suffragists had arrogated to themselves the right to speak for all, Frances noted that no one could be forced to avail herself of the ballot once it had been secured. The noble few who were speaking their convictions were among the most intelligent of the women in the platform; and if "disappointed women" had an incentive to study politics, they would make "a strong reserve whenever social or political wrongs needed to be corrected." In this connection, her opponent had overlooked the fact that many women wanted the ballot with which "to right the habit of public drinking."

Then Mrs. Victor addressed Mrs. Matheson's argument that women under fifty should be barred from politics because of their "physical organization." She noted that her opponent was "not an evolutionist." She did not understand "the scientific view" that we make ourselves in accordance with our environment. Frances agreed that nature intended motherhood to be "an almost mechanical function," but civilized women had followed a different line. "Let us return to nature," Frances urged. She also scoffed at Mrs. Mathewson's view that women should be barred from entering politics until they are beyond the age of bearing children.

"Women between the ages of twenty and fifty are in the thick of the battle of life as much as men though they are seldom paid for it. If maternity is honorable," Frances added, "it should not deter them from exercising the privileges of belonging to humanity." She was persuaded that "to be a mother brings a woman into close relationship with humanity and thereby enriches her nature. The care of children, even other people's, does that. Motherhood is, however, to be intelligently entered into, and there may be reasons why it should never be undertaken." As for putting a ballot in the hands of "sinful women," Frances noted that they, more than any other class, needed the ballot with which to protect themselves from "sinful men who legislate against them."

When Mrs. Frances Fuller Victor's spirited response appeared in the May, 1896 number of the *American Civics Magazine*, she must have felt that she was serving the suffragist cause in California with the veteran suffragists, Susan B. Anthony and the Rev. Anna H. Shaw.[12]

Since early 1896, Frances had been working on a sketch of Dr. John McLoughlin, one of her Oregon heroes. Needing illustrations, she had written Capt. Theodore Wygant, husband of Margaret Rae, Mcloughlin's granddaughter, for photographs of him as well as of the old Hudson's Bay Company fort in Vancouver and the family home in Oregon City.[13] On February 13, Wygant, a real estate agent with an office in the Portland Chamber of Commerce building, mailed her two photographs of the Doctor. He explained that his wife appreciated Frances' interest in her grandfather, but they could do nothing more. A month later, Wygant acknowledged Frances' second letter. Times were "tight" in Portland, he wrote, "with no opportunity in the line of mere glory." He enclosed the address of Mrs. Myrick, one of whose daughters was an amateur photographer, but asked Frances not to mention their name if she wrote her.

By this time, illustrated articles by Mrs. Victor were appearing in the San Francisco press. For instance, an article titled "The Boundary Dispute over San Juan Island—Tail Twisting by the Pioneers of Puget Sound—How Haro Archipelago was Secured" appeared in the February 16 issue of the *San Francisco Chronicle*. She had simply rewritten her account of the dispute as published in Bancroft's *British Columbia*. Now serving as librarian for the Women's Press Association, she was also in a position to scan national publications. Imagine her delight when in the February 6 number of Dr. Nixon's *Inter Ocean*, she spotted errors in an item titled "Bret Harte's Calamity Jane." It stated that Harte had patterned the heroine of his famous story, "Luck of Roaring Camp" after the semi-fictionalized Calamity Jane, born Martha Jane Canary in 1852. The February 23 issue of the San Francisco *Morning Call*, in a section titled

"California Literature," carried a contribution from Mrs. Victor. In it she pointed out that Calamity Jane could not have been the mother of the babe, Luck, born in a mining camp in 1851– the setting for Harte's story, published in 1868, as Frances well remembered. Harte had called his heroine Cherokee Sal, who had not been an Indian fighter like Calamity Jane, but rather "a very sinful woman, though not too sinful to be crowned with motherhood."

Then Frances noted that such "irresponsible reporting" reminded her of "some forgotten facts of our own literature." She had once conversed with Mrs. Clappe, who had published a series of letters on California mining camps in 1851–52. Signed "Shirley," they had been published in the short-lived *Pioneer Magazine*, edited by F. C. Ewer between 1854–56. Mrs. Clappe had lent Mrs. Victor bound volumes of her published letters and after reading them she was satisfied that they were "the foundations" on which Harte had built his stories, "Luck of Roaring Camp" and "The Outcast of Poker Flat." Quoting from parallel passages in *Shirley Letters* and Harte's stories, Frances had also found mention of Joaquin Murrietta from which Joaquin Miller had obtained his pen name. In another place, she had found a hint of Mark Twain's "Jumping Frog." Upon returning her letters to Mrs. Clappe, Frances had told her that "the so-called early writers of California should acknowledge their indebtedness" to her, but she only smiled. On another occasion when the conversation had turned to poetry, Frances had complained to Mrs. Clappe that Harte had failed to include any of her poems in his volume, *Outcroppings*, which he had presumably collected. Whereupon Mrs. Clappe had explained that a writer known as Ridinghood and herself had compiled the volume before Frances had arrived in San Francisco. They had placed it in the hands of Anton Roman, founder of the *Overland Monthly*. After Harte had achieved prominence in San Francisco, Roman had asked him to edit it without consulting the original compilers. Mrs. Clappe supposed that the sale of the controversial volume had merely paid the cost of its publication.

In this same article, Frances also took exception to Ella S. Cummins' statement in her *The Story of the Files* that *The Golden Era*, to which Frances had contributed from 1863–65, had been "killed" by permitting women to contribute to it. Frances pointed out that of its over 200 contrbutors only 78 had been women. Its decline, she argued, had been due to a change of conditions. Men like Bret Harte, Mark Twain, and Joaquin Miller, whose abilities had fostered it, had found "wider and more remunerative fields." Further, the overland railroad had brought in Eastern publications; and the *Era* had become "a sealed book," not because women had written for it, but because "the world had changed."

On April 1, the *California Review* carried Mrs. Victor's "A Study of Victor Hugo," likely presented at a literary program for the Women's Press Association. Her purpose was to show that in order to understand an author's work one must understand the man, especially if he had been the most influential figure in nineteenth century French literature. In this scholarly exercise, Frances revealed her interest in French literature and history. On the 19th, the *Morning Call* published her follow-up on her article on Bret Harte. It was illustrated with a line drawing of Mrs. Mary Tingley-Lawrence, a charter member of the Women's Press Association and the former columnist, "Ridinghood" She had introduced herself to Frances and assured her that the inferences she had drawn from Mrs. Clappe's *Shirley Letters* had been correct. She had also told Frances something about herself and her part in the publication of *Outcroppings*. Daughter of a distinguished member of the California bar, Col. George Tingley, she had lived in hotels, sliding down sand hills with Lily Hitchcock and exchanging "*bon mots*" with the young gentlemen of San Francisco. A student of Mrs. Clappe, she soon emulated her teacher. At age 17, with the encouragement of the Reverend Thomas Starr King and the Reverend F. C. Ewer, she had been preserving "fragmentary California literature." She had sent letters to authors throughout the state, requesting copies of their best contributions to California periodicals—poetry or prose. Had her book been published as compiled by her, revised by Mrs. Clappe, and approved by King and Ewer, Frances noted, it would have formed "a part of the intellectual history of California." However, being young and shy, Mary Tingley had placed her manuscript into the hands of Anton Roman. In the meantime, Bret Harte had won "the approbation and money" of the literary elite like Starr King and Jesse Benton Fremont. So Roman had asked Harte to edit the manuscript. He tossed away all the prose and illustrations and failed to include any work by Mrs. Clappe or herself, though in his preface Harte had acknowledged Miss Tingley's help; and Roman had retained her title *Outcroppings*. However, Mary Tingley had found her "true place in journalism" when she wrote for the *Sacramento Union* under the *nom de plume* of "Ridinghood" and became the toast of the mining camps with offers of gifts and marriage. In June, 1870 she had married Senator James Henry Lawrence, publisher of the *Mariposa Gazette*, for which she wrote. Spending her summers "at the big trees" and in Yosemite Valley, she met distinguished tourists. At this time, she wrote *A Summer with a Countess*. The biography of Lady Avonmore, it was read before the New York State Historical Society and published in book form. She also wrote articles for the *Overland Monthly* such "College Charlemagne," a sketch about a French college she had attended in 1860. Frances also mentioned an unfinished book based on the experiences of the wife of the minister to the kingdom of Korea. Why, Frances asked, had so little attention been paid to women writers like Mrs. Lawrence?

Frances Fuller Victor's spirited defense of California women writers won her the friendship of Mary Tingley-Lawrence and other wealthy and prominent members of the Women's Press Association. Through them she apparently learned of the present accomplishments of the Prince sisters, former residents of San Francisco, now in Japan. On April 26, the *Morning Call* published an unsigned letter, dated Tokyo, March 15, 1896.[14] The headline, superimposed on a sketch of the Japanese landscape, read: "TWO SAN FRANCISCO WOMEN Who Have Achieved Fame in JAPAN." The letter was illustrated with a line drawing of Isabella and Mary Prince. Teachers of young ladies in San Francisco, the sisters had been engaged by the wife of the Japanese consul in San Francisco to instruct the ladies of the Japanese court in American customs, dress, language, and literature. The nameless correspondent indicated that she had been a member of the Prince household in San Francisco prior to their appointment and asked her readers to imagine that they were being entertained by the Prince sisters as they had entertained her in Japan. This bogus introduction was followed by an account of the sisters' life "inside and outside the court." Frances further noted that the names of the Prince sisters, descendants of Miles Standish, deserved "to go into history" as the first American women to be offered appointments in a foreign court. She was posting this letter without the knowledge of the Prince sisters as a courtesy to their former students and acquaintances in California.

Frances also had commitments closer to home, as a full-page story, headlined "A Gathering of Prominent Women," in the May 2 issue of the San Francisco *Evening Post* indicates. Announcing that the theme for the 1896 Women's Congress was "Women and Government," it was illustrated with photographs of state officers; France Fuller Victor was listed as a member of the San Francisco advisory council. Her address, "Tribal Government," read at an early session, was published in the May 6 issue of the San Francisco *Morning Call*. She began by comparing "tribal government" to the folded-up tree in the pod of a maple tree. Within "the tribal pod," she explained, was enclosed all that evolution had brought to light along the lines of government since the birth of mankind. The tribe had preceded the family. It evolved from the experiences of the governed. Every race had started at the same place and followed similar processes, though at different times, under different conditions, and with different results. In the nomadic age, woman's part in tribal affairs had been important, as it was in the natural world, where she had to defend and feed herself as well as her offspring. During this period, descent was necessarily reckoned through the female line. Later, when the stronger male acquired and defended property rights, descent was traced through the male line. This shift changed the lot of women and children. They suffered abuse at the hands of some males. On the other hand, they often were protected and provided for. Noting many similarities between the earliest government of the Greeks and tribal governments of the aborigines on the North American continent, Mrs. Victor concluded:

> There is a remarkable resemblance in the origin and growth
> of governmental ideas all over the globe. When we meet
> with a race very much lower in the scale of mental develop-
> ment, we must not say that their origin is lower than ours,
> but only that they have been hindered in their growth by
> conditions they have been unable to overcome. Neither can

we be permitted to judge them by our standard of morality
for the same reason.

By this time, Frances was corresponding with 38-year-old Captain
Hiram M. Chittenden of the U.S. Corps of Engineers, located in St.
Louis, Missouri, about some of Col. Joe Meek's statements in her *River of
the West*.[15] This correspondence, in turn, revived her correspondence with
Oliver C. Applegate. In September, 1896 she wrote him three letters
about Captain Chittenden and other matters.[16] On the fifth, on stationery of the Women's Press Association, listing her as Librarian, she
scribbled a question that had arisen between herself and Chittenden,
author of a book on Yellowstone Park. It concerned the year in which the
fur trader, J. H. Ashley, had first entered the Rocky Mountains. Frances
noted that Oliver's father, Lindsey Applegate, had once written her that
he had been a member of the Ashley expedition of 1823, and asked for
details of that expedition at the earliest date.

Oliver replied immediately, enclosing articles on the proposed Crater
Lake National Park. One indicated that the name Victor had been
retained for a rock he had named after her in the summer of 1873. On
September 10, she acknowledged the honor. Like Helen Hunt Jackson,
author of *Ramona*, who was buried in the "Garden of the Gods" in Colorado, she would like to be buried with a rock for a monument "beside
the lovely and awe inspiring Lake." Then she urged Oliver to answer
Chittenden's question. Differing with her *River of the West* "in minor matters," Oliver had written her several times. In his last letter, after having
reread her book, he stated that it would 'always stand not only as the pioneer but also as one of the best examples in the historical work of the
fur-trading era." She was going to revise and re-issue it, for she thought it
would enjoy a better sale now than it had in the past. So she needed all
the help she could get.

She also noted that he had not returned her copy of Bancroft's *California Inter Pocula*, which she had sent him for his comments on her
account of the Modoc Indian War, contained in that volume. She added
that sets and odd volumes of Bancroft Works were available in San Francisco bookstores at reduced prices. She explained, in a letter dated the
27th, that she had suggested he return her copy of *California Inter Pocula*

because she thought it would have his hand-written comments on the margins. Now she asked him to accept the volume as a gift and send her his comments in a separate letter. She further explained that since the first of the month she had been the treasurer, rather than the librarian, of the Women's Press Association. She was still corresponding with Chittenden about "the history and topography of the Yellowstone country." In her *River of the West*, he had found mention of a lake that Joe Meek had said was the source of the Madison River, but he had yet to find the lake. She had written Meek's son, Courtney, "as a forlorn hope." But she was confident that the mountain men had been "infallible topographers," and she would "pit them against Govt. expeditions every time."

As treasurer, Frances doubtless helped plan the 1896 *Christmas Souvenir* published by the Women's Press Association. It carried a brief history of the Association together with a statement of purpose and an invitation to women interested in the literary and artistic worlds of the Pacific Coast to join. Most of the pamphlet was devoted to photographs, biographies, and samples of the literary and art work of the members. Frances' photograph appeared on a double-spread reserved for officers. Another double-spread carried a brief biography and her poem, "He and She," written while she was touring Modoc land with Oliver Applegate[17]

December 30, 1896 was a red-letter day for Frances Fuller Victor. On that date, Captain Chittenden reported to the major of the U. S. Army Corps of Engineers in San Francisco. Mrs. Victor visited him and they talked for three hours—a visit he would have enjoyed had he not been suffering from a severe cold.[18]

Early in 1897, Mrs. Victor learned that 1,300 copies of her *Early Indian Wars of Oregon* had finally been printed by the state printer in Salem, and priced at $3.00 a copy. Having copyrighted the volume in 1894, she evidently expected to receive a modest royalty. In any event, she wrote to Governor William Lord and her friend, John Minto, secretary of the State Board of Horticulture, to that effect. In response to her letter of February 13, Minto wrote that it would give him great pleasure if she were to receive the $500 that the governor had recommended after he read her "statement," but in view of the "Senatorial imbroglio," there was nothing that he or the governor could do to see that she and others got their "just dues." [19] He complimented her on having set Oregonians straight on Dr. Gray's writings and noted that Jesse Applegate (now deceased) had done "the work of a patriotic American" when he had surveyed "the Southern road" in 1846.

On March 15, Mrs. Victor wrote Harrison Kincaid, secretary of state, to thank him for sending her copies of his 1895–96 report and that of his predecessor. Had she not done such thorough work when she was writing Bancroft's *Oregon II*, it would have been better; she still saw work to do if "pecuniary aid" was at hand. To the *Early Indian Wars of Oregon*, she would like to add the campaign of the First Oregon Cavalry, the Modoc Indian War, and that part of the Nez Pierce Indian War that had taken place in Oregon. Her letter, published in the Salem press, carried this editorial comment: "Mr. Minto fears that Mrs. Victor's historical undertaking will not receive remuneration in proportion to the labor involved. . . . The truthful historian, in his own generation, is the hardest worked, most roundly abused, and poorest paid of individuals." [20]

On the day that Frances wrote Kincaid, the *Morning Oregonian* published a review of "MRS. VICTOR'S WORK—Her Book on the Early Indians Wars of Oregon." It was written by the Reverend Horace S. Lyman, 42-year-old superintendent of schools for Clatsop County and would-be historian, then living in Astoria. [21] He explained that he had been asked to review the volume because its high price would limit circulation. This was unfortunate because Mrs. Victor, "the most prolific historical writer on this coast," had presented the Indian part in Oregon history in a concise and connected way. She had exhibited the courage of the early pioneers and illustrated "the essential service of the Oregon volunteers." Among the book's "imperfections," Lyman listed her reliance on Jesse Applegate's letter recounting his journey to California during the Cayuse Indian War; her statement that Chief Tipsey had been hostile to Whites; and her down-playing of Colonel Cornelius' campaign in the Yakima country. Never a friend of Whitman, she implied that his massacre and the Cayuse War were the results of trying to convert the Cayuse Indians to Protestantism. These "personal idiosyncrasies" were to be expected. Mrs. Victor had written the history of Oregon "with the Roman steel." This had been a great service even when her conclusions had been prejudiced. Her "destructive criticism" had dealt a blow to "sentimentality." Now the materials of "constructive history" were being assembled as never before—thanks to those who combated her as well as to herself.

On March 19, the *Daily Morning Oregonian* ran John Minto's response to Lyman's review. He contended that though $3.00 might seem a high price for a 720-page book, it was the cheapest for any treating the same subject. Mrs. Victor had written it "in her best style." She had not availed herself of "personal narratives," because the legislature has restricted her sources. According to a letter from Frances to Minto, she had received only between $225 and $300 for her work. However, like the Rev. Lyman, Minto differed with Mrs. Victor's evaluation of Dr. Whitman and even more with her use of Jesse Applegate's letter, in which he had robbed himself of the honor due him and by which he had misled Mrs. Victor.

Frances Fuller Victor responded to Lyman's review before she read Minto's response. On March 21, the *Oregonian* published it under the headline, "REVIEW OF A CRITICISM—Mrs. Victor Replies to Mr. Lyman's Remarks on Her 'Early Indian Wars of Oregon'". In it she said that she was "tired" of having Whitman made "the *piece de resistance*" of all Oregon reviews of her work. She would defend her views of Whitman later and in a different forum. Now she challenged Lyman to show where she had defamed Whitman, and she took him to task for not touching on the question he had raised—that the high price of her book would limit its circulation. She noted that it had been intended to be "a monument" to the veterans of all the Indian wars of Oregon, with each to be given a copy. In dismissing specific charges, she explained that she had copied Jesse Applegate's letter together with that of John Minto so that her readers would have the same evidence that she did. With respect to the character of Chief Tipsey, she had relied on the testimony of veterans who had lived near his territory. When she wrote up Colonel Cornelius' campaign in the Yakima country, she discovered that he had been a better fighter than a writer. When he failed to respond to her request for details, she had been forced to rely on his official report. After reading Minto's reply to Lyman's review, Frances mailed the *Oregonian* a note. She admitted that she had "blundered" in her estimate of the compensation she had received for her work. However, the secretary of state's report showed "the official figures, which were not in dispute."

On March 27, the *Oregonian* gave Lyman the last word. By quoting from her published writings, he endeavored to show that Mrs. Victor did not consider Dr. Whitman a great patriot. But Lyman did approve of her recommendation that every veteran of the Indian wars be given a copy of her book. The legislature had already acted on her recommendation on March 26, according to a news clipping of that date.[22]

Frances Fuller Victor doubtless savored this small victory as she performed her duties as treasurer and chairman of the program committee for the Women's Press Association in San Francisco. The April 14 issue of the San Francisco *Daily Morning Call* announced that the association was giving a public entertainment at the California Theater to raise funds for a clubhouse. In recounting the seven-year history of the association, the reporter named "Mrs. Frances Fuller Victor, historian of the Northwest, and Miss Ina D. Coolbrith, poet laureate of California" among the "gifted women" who had directed its affairs of late. Another newspaper clipping credited Frances with directing the rehearsal of a children's play for the occasion.[23]

During the summer and fall of 1897, Frances was writing initialed and unsigned items for a new weekly, the *Olympic*. Topics ranged from the national crazes for cycling and photography to the effect of advertising on business. In August alone, the weekly published a dozen items from her pen. Titles were as diverse as "A Road for Wheels Across the Continent" and "One of the Wonders of the World," illustrated by a photograph of Crater Lake, When filing these published pieces, Frances signed and dated a few.

During this time, she also pursued her historical interests. On August 24, she wrote her acquaintance, Eva Emery Dye of Oregon City, asking for photographs and sketches she needed for her unfinished article on Dr. McLoughlin.[24] Rather than asking for the names of photographers and artists who might supply her needs, she left it up to Mrs. Dye to ferret them out. This closing paragraph is more reminiscent than revealing:

I wish we might meet and talk over literary matters. Did
you get out that book you were working on in 1893? Please
tell me about it and your plans for the future. I have nothing to tell worth relating. My time has been occupied writing short articles and participating in Press Association
affairs, etc., etc. Next year I mean to work for myself. I am
quite well as I trust you are. Do you still like Oregon and
are you ever coming down here again?

About this time, *The British-Californian*, printed at the same address as
the Women's Press Association's *Impress*, provided Frances Fuller Victor
with a new monthly market. The July-August number carried a letter
from London about Queen Victoria's 1897 jubilee and a provocative essay
entitled, "Are Women Brighter than Men?" by Arthur Inkersley, a prominent member of the British community of San Francisco. The September number carried his biography and Mrs. Victor's spirited reply, titled
"Arthur Inkersley and the New Woman." In it, she charged that "this
old-fashioned young man" had mounted a hobby horse "old enough and
lame enough to be put out to grass." She recommended that he attend a
convention where both men and women were speakers. He would
observe that a man uses much of the allotted time to arrange his
thoughts, whereas a woman addresses her subject at once. If that was
what Mr. Inkersley called "intuition," women should claim it. It often
overcomes a man's "reason." Therefore, it should be assumed to be equal
if not superior to reason. The December, 1897 number carried Mrs. Victor's "In Re Climate," in which she discussed the effect of climate on
race. The April, 1898 number ran her "A Timely Word" to Californians
about "too much self-applause."

While she was writing these witty "potboilers" to pay her board bill,
her interest in Oregon history had been spurred by an unexpected correspondent—Professor Frederic George Young at the University of Oregon at Eugene.[25] In her September 20, 1897 reply on Women's Press
Association stationery, Frances said that his letter and its enclosures had
been a pleasant surprise.[26] She called his historical series, the first of
which he had enclosed, an excellent way to preserve history; but she did

Prof. Frederick Young of the University of Oregon was secretary of the recently incorporated state historical society. As the century turned, this firm and admiring friend of Victor had enormous demands on his time concerning bold planning for the Lewis and Clark centennial celebration,
ORHI38559

not know how she could aid in the enterprise. As "a hard-working author," she had little money to spare. Her work, not her income, had always been her chief concern, and it was too late to change now. She noted that she still had "unfinished and pressing work to do." She did counsel Young against preserving "hearsay testimony" unless it was documented with "contemporaneous history." Her whole effort had been " to weed out worthless authorities and stamp out prejudices." She added that no one could "gainsay a plain statement made at the time and on the spot by a sensible witness," as were the documents he had enclosed for her perusal. Yet in the first number of his series—*The Journal of Lt. Lawrence Kip*—the *Indian Council at Walla Walla, May-June, 1855*—she found two errors. One by Kip, the other by the editor. She explained each in detail and corrected it, supplying Young with authorities

The winter of 1897–98 was a time of condolences for Frances Fuller Victor. On January 5, her former brother-in-law, Sebastian C. Adams, died after a brief illness at his home in Salem.[27] On the 28th, the Honorable Elwood Evans, as Frances always addressed him, fell to his death while boarding a streetcar in Olympia, Washington.[28] On February 15, the Spanish-American War broke out with the sinking of the battleship USS *Maine* in the Cuban harbor of Havana. From March through May, the battleship USS *Oregon* made the 15,000-mile voyage from San Francisco around Cape Horn to the leading part of the battle of Santiago on July 3, 1898.[29] As a historian and free-lance writer, Frances followed the course of the war as she forged ahead on her book on Dr. Marcus Whitman. At the same time, she was moving from Haight Street to 312 Fillmore Street, as her April 12 note to the Reverend Myron Eells of Washington state indicates.[30] She asked him for the maiden names of his mother and of Mrs. Elkanah Walker and Mrs. William Gray, all members of the Presbyterian mission east of the Cascade Mountains. "You will see," she wrote, "that I am still inquiring into the things of history." She added that "right or wrong" her investigations had done more "to bring out the bottom facts of Northwest history" than any other writer had. She complimented him on his fairness in fielding undisputed facts and noted that Tennyson's Welsh motto "Truth against the world," was also her own. In closing, she asked him what he thought of Nixon's book on Whitman.

Within a few months, she learned that William I. Marshall, a one-time correspondent, also was writing a book on Whitman. This information came from Dr. Elliott Coues in Santa Fe, New Mexico, where he had been researching the Jacob Fowler and Francisco Garces story.[31]

Whereupon Mrs. Victor wrote Marshall that she had learned of his writing project from Coues and, diplomatically, reminded him of their former correspondence, in which she brought "the facts of the case" to his attention. She then noted that, spurred by Dr. Nixon's book, she had just completed a 400-page book, which she was trying to place with "different classes of publishers." She did not want to "silence" Marshall, "an adherent of the cause of truth," she said; but she could not sacrifice her "long digested effort." She asked him to write to her about the matter.

Soon after, Frances forwarded her manuscript to Dr. Coues, and, informed Professor Young that she had done so in a December 5 reply to his earlier letter. [32] She began by thanking him for the bulletin he had enclosed. It would bring to light much of interest in the history of the Northwest. Her interest was more "profound" than most contributors, she said, because of her continuous investigations of "every branch of Oregon history." She also noted that her work in the Bancroft Library had been hampered by her distance from Oregon. Then she revealed that she had just completed and offered for publication "a final statement of the Whitman case." In it, she had given the history of the Presbyterian missions as the missionaries had never done; and she had settled forever the questions as to the motives and deeds of Dr. Whitman in his journey East in the winter of 1842. Here she noted that Dr. Elliott Coues, "the eminent literateur and historian," to whom she had submitted her manuscript, had written that he had read every word of it and judged it "entirely favorable." He thought it should be published "in justice to the truth of history" and that it would be "a good business venture." She would appreciate a similar endorsement from "scholars and historians in Oregon." Everyone knew her general views of Whitman, but they did not know "the new facts and interpretations" that her book would furnish. If the faculty or president of the University of Oregon would give her a letter that she could use in a publisher's circular, she would count it "a special favor." It need not express an opinion of the book, but only what the author had done or could be expected to do. Stanford University would doubtless furnish such a letter, as the professor of history there had complimented her on her earlier work. Her final ploy was to offer Professor

Young some original "letters from pioneers on historical subjects." She suggested that he have typewritten copies of them made from which he could strike "personal matters."

On December 17, 1898, the Oregon Historical Society was incorporated in Portland, not in Salem, the capital city, nor Eugene, the home of the University of Oregon.[33] At the initial meeting, held in the Portland Library building, Harvey W. Scott, publisher and editor of the *Oregonian*, was elected president. Professor Young was elected secretary and editor of a projected quarterly periodical. George H. Himes, long-time secretary of the Oregon Pioneer Association and living in Portland, was elected assistant secretary. In view of the declining membership of the Oregon Pioneer Association, a merger of these two organizations was generally recommended.

In the meantime, a third, non-political, short-lived organization known as the Native Sons of Oregon, with its headquarters in Portland, had established "cabins" throughout the state. On February 23, 1899, Grand Secretary Eugene D. White announced that a monthly magazine — *Oregon Native Son*, published by the Native Son Company located in the Oregonian building—would be the official organ of the organization.[34] All pioneers, native sons, and citizens were invited to subscribe and contribute to the magazine, devoted to pioneer history, the resources and industries of Oregon, and other items of interest. The first number appeared in May, 1899 and featured Secretary White's article, "Native Sons of Oregon," and George Himes' article, "The Oregon Pioneer Association." The Native Sons found no financial support.

Frances Fuller Victor had already responded to two letters from the magazine's first editor, 45-year-old William Gladstone Steel.[35] She had known him as an adventurous newspaperman, who had traveled to Washington, D.C. in 1885–86 to promote the creation of Crater Lake National Park. In her first reply, Frances heralded the publication of *Oregon Native Son*, but predicted that maintaining its publication would be "a struggle." She warned Steel against relying on the tales of "old pioneers" and detailed her experiences with J. Quinn Thornton, who had falsely claimed that he authored the Oregon school land law, and with Dr.

William Gray, who had spread the Whitman myth. She had written a book which, if some "public-spirited Oregonians" would help her publish, would "settle that myth forever." She also observed that an editor of a historical journal assumed heavy responsibilities. If he printed everything that pioneers sent in, he could keep it going until his readers perceived the errors. Then it would come to an untimely end. On the other hand, if he demanded "good articles," he would have to pay for them. After having studied Oregon history for a quarter of a century, she was now an authority on both coasts, but poorer than when she started. Presently she was writing for her "bread and butter" and would send him her biography and photograph. She mentioned her pioneer letters and noted that she thought him "a good choice as editor," if he could afford to do the work.

In her second response, dated February 20, 1899, she advised Steel that he could get a photograph of Dr. Elijah White by writing the Howard Street Methodist Church in San Francisco, where White had once been a member. She had met White at the Bancroft Library in 1879, shortly before he died. As for her pioneer letters, she intended to give them to the Oregon Historical Society—or to him, if he became the permanent editor of *Oregon Native Son*. She was very busy writing "potboilers," but would send him bits of writing for his approval. Finally, she asked him whether he wanted a photograph of her taken in 1879 or one taken 20 years earlier.

Steel did not write for her photograph; and Frances discovered that he was "a good mountain climber, but not a good historian." In an early number of *Oregon Native Son*, she found mention of Thornton as author of the Oregon land law—a claim that she had long since discredited. In the June, 1899 number she found an account of the Whitman massacre by Mrs. Denny of Portland, who had been a child at the time. Before publishing it, Steel should have compared it with the sworn testimony of adults given at the time, Frances noted in a letter to Professor Young, dated August 24.[36] Frances first thanked Young for having proposed her name as an honorary member of the Oregon Historical Society—the first public recognition of her work on "Oregon, historical or otherwise." In return, she pledged to help the Society "bring out the truth of history." Then she cited instances in *Oregon Native Son* in which the editor, a friend of hers, had printed pioneer tales as history. She mentioned them, not in "a carping spirit," but rather to illustrate what she thought "a historian's duty to be." Then she thanked Young for sending her a copy of his edition of the journal and letters of the merchant-adventurer, Nathaniel J. Wyeth. She could use this material in some work she was doing and it would allow her to help "an army man" who often applied to her for "information on western subjects." In answering Young's questions about the Bancroft Library, she noted that it was closed to all, including those who had written Bancroft's histories for him. She feared that he would not permit copying, but she would send Bancroft's California address to Young so that he could write him directly. As for the McLoughlin papers in her possession, she had contemplated writing an article for an Eastern magazine. But she had been unable to secure photographs—even from McLoughlin's heirs. She was willing to turn them over to Young, if he would write them up properly.

During September and November, 1899, Frances Fuller Victor interrupted her work on another "potboiler," a book titled *Campaigning in the Philippines*, to correspond with Professor Young.[37] In her letter of September 23, she asked him to propose the name of Dr. Elliott Coues for honorary membership in the Oregon Historical Society and enclosed a publisher's prospectus of his work pertaining to Oregon. She also asked Young to send Coues a copy of his Wyeth material and bill her for any expense incurred. She listed his Washington, D.C. address as well as those of Capt. Hiram M. Chittenden and Col. William Bracett, both of whom could use the Wyeth material in their work. By contacting them, she said, the Society could bring the state "into notice." On November 13, she sent Young a bulky envelope, containing the originals of all of Thornton's 1865 letters to her, together with copies in her more readable handwriting. She trusted that Young would have time to read them. If he found them helpful in his university work or his plans for the Society, she would put similar material in her possession in like shape as fast as time permitted. A week later, on November 21, she dashed off a follow-up note about Dr.

Coues. He had written her from Washington, D.C. that he had not received the Wyeth material and that he wanted her "to attend" to the matter of the honorary membership in the Oregon Historical Society. She added that Dr. Coues had just returned from the Southwest, where he had contracted "a serious illness," but was now at his desk again.

On this same rainy afternoon that reminded her of Oregon, Frances also wrote her old friend, Oliver C. Applegate.[38] She said that "in overhauling some old letters the other day" she had reread those that he sent her after her return to Portland, following her six-week trip to the Klamath-Modoc country in the summer of 1873. She had relived every memorable experience from crossing the Cascades and attending the Modoc Indian trial at Fort Klamath to visiting Crater Lake. "It would make a novel, would it not?" she asked. Then she suggested that he write up the Indian lore of that region for the "Ethnological Bureau at Washington." They had asked her for a copy of her *Early Indian Wars of Oregon*; and the head of the Geographical Department had sent her maps of Crater Lake with Victor Rock properly placed. In thanking the official for the compliment, she had written that the name Applegate should be applied to a prominent point on the rim, for no one had done more to bring it "into notice" than Oliver C. Applegate. She also agreed that her *River of the West* should be re-issued. She was sorry that they had not been able to fix the dates of the Ashley expeditions. Captain Chittenden's book on the fur trade would fix dates that differed from hers. In any event, she expected to visit Montana next summer. She had been promised a trip through Yellowstone Park, and "a sight of the camping grounds occupied by Bridger and Meek in 1833!" Her health would never be better, but she kept on "doing." The only way to enjoy life was to "use" it. He could be assured that "one of the most agreeable episodes" of her rather "eventful" life had been her visit to Klamath Land with him "as the central figure."

On Christmas Day, 1899, Dr. Elliott Coues died in Johns Hopkins Hospital in Baltimore, Maryland without knowing that he had been elected an honorary member of the Oregon Historical Society and before he was able to find an Eastern publisher for Frances Fuller Victor's book on Whitman.[39]

Over the holidays that marked the end of the decade and of a century, Frances moved to yet another San Francisco address—908 Van Ness Avenue—for reasons unknown. On January 23, 1900, in her reply to Professor Young's letter of the 20th, she asked that he use that address until further notice.[40] The subject of Dr. Coues was "a sore one," she said. Why had he and not some useless man been taken, she wondered. He had been as a kind of brother to her. She regretted that he had died without knowing that the State of Oregon had honored him—not that he needed recognition, but that Oregon needed to acknowledge it "for its own credit." She hoped that the Historical Society would take notice of his works pertaining to Oregon and the fact that he had wished to be placed on "the roll of honorary members."

Then she turned to more practical matters. She thought that Young's proposed *Quarterly* was a dignified way of teaching history and its lessons. Before promising her cooperation, she listed "the discouragements" she had faced in Oregon. Most Oregonians did not appreciate, as he did, that she had given the best years of her life to writing Oregon history. They were always looking for opportunities to overthrow her hard-earned conclusions. Not because they knew better than she did, but because they would not admit that she knew better than they did. In their opinion "any pioneer is a better historian than the most painstaking student of history." Nor did they accord her work any commercial value. After ticking off her publications, most of which she had undertaken at her own risk, she stated that she felt entitled to "some profit and privileges above the ordinary."

Such was the practice in other communities. For two decades, ever since 1870, she had furnished *The Oregonian* with historical articles for which she never received a dollar. Yet when she had asked to be taken on in some capacity that would assure her a weekly income, her request had been denied. This preamble did not imply that she was refusing the professor's request. She had intended to write an article on the Oregon land laws for an Eastern magazine "for the pay that was in it." Now she was inclined to make the school land law into a separate article for the *Oregon Historical Quarterly*. If so, she needed to know the size and style of the periodical, and when her manuscript would be required.

Her final paragraph indicates that her return to Oregon, at least on a trial basis, was at hand:

> I have it in mind at present to visit Oregon in the spring. Should I do so, it might be profitable to both of us if, en route, I could spend a day or two in Eugene for the discussion of matters of interest to both in this connection. In the meantime, any information you may convey to me will be appreciated.

She did not reveal that some of her Portland friends had agreed to help her publish an author's edition of a small volume of her selected poems. It would feature one unpublished poem, "Poppies of Waii-lat-pu," dedicated to the memory of Narcissa Whitman. Nor did she confide that, also with the help of friends, she hoped to secure from the state legislature a monthly or annual stipend for her past and future services to the state. Should she fail, after an absence of six years, she might still get a glimpse of Yellowstone Park, courtesy of Captain Chittenden; and she could always return to her sanctuary in San Francisco.

Most important of all were the several possibilities residing in the great and increasing expectations related to the grand scheme for an "appropriate centennial celebration in recognition of the Lewis and Clark Expedition to the Pacific Ocean." Meat and drink for Mrs. Victor.

EPILOGUE

So now we are left to fathom one of the formidable historians of the nineteenth century. Historian Ralph Gabriel first registered Victor's name with me at Yale; and then Prof. Vernon Carstensen at the University of Wisconsin placed her name on a list of notables whom graduate historians should ponder. Later I made editorial association with Frederick Young (Jung) and Joseph Schaefer who had built strong relationships between Wisconsin and Oregon earlier at the century's end. Returning once more from Wisconsin to Oregon in the summer of 1902 they had decided to take their bicycles west along the Oregon Trail made famous fifty years before their time. My thought fifty years later with a young family and intrepid wife was to hew as close as possible to the same trail, but also to parts of the Lewis and Clark route now 150 years in the past. The big event for Young and Schaefer was the forthcoming 1904 centennial fair to celebrate the Lewis and Clark crossing from St. Louis to the Columbia River mouth. Young was a new commissioner and forceful proponent of the trade fair.

The year 1954 was the 150th anniversary of the land and water crossing by the legendary Lewis and Clark. At certain points my "expedition" split off in Montana and Idaho to examine their early camp sites. In Oregon the famous learned society I was bound for had in 1900 purchased the endangered winter site of the renowned explorers—Fort Clatsop. Elizabeth and I were building up insights into the localities the explorers and pioneers had traversed. Localities provide, as Baron von Humboldt regarding the Khyber Pass in 1832 opined, "the only surviving reality for historic events long ago passed by."

So it was with us and the young traveling scholars who preceded us. And it surely was so for Frances Fuller who had preceded them. Without doubt the young historians bound for the university at the upper end of the Willamette Valley discussed the well-known historical writings of Frances Fuller Victor. Being young men of sensibility and discernment they might well have been in awe of this great chronicler. She had personally known and interviewed many of the personages they were now reading about from earlier generations. She was full of ideas and advice for their discussions in Eugene and Portland, especially ideas for the newly incorporated state historical society, and for the big fair which the society's earlier leaders had first suggested.

In May 1900, at the beginning of the bright new century, Frances Fuller Victor boarded "the cars" in San Francisco, bound once more for Portland, Oregon. She was a nationally respected author of books and magazine articles on history and travel, newspaper columns, novels, short stories, and poetry. She was also 76, tired, and almost penniless; this would be our intrepid chronicler's last journey.

She had never kept diaries or daybooks. Her countless news columns and letters served that purpose. Nor have I found much to reveal her interest in "current events," though the Spanish-American War was just over. Hero and western historian, New York Governor Theodore Roosevelt had "taken the veil" as Mr. McKinley's vice-president. A new age was dawning. Mrs. Victor hoped to see "a proper celebration" of the much-discussed centenary of the epic round trip by Lewis and Clark trekking across the unmapped reaches of the trans-Mississippi West (1804-06). In her usual no-nonsense manner, Victor had pinned much hope on her professional association with the as yet undeveloped plans. She continued to bombard her new historian friend Frederick G. Young with endless ideas, observations, and entreaties. Young, earlier the Portland High School principal, had been recently appointed professor at the University of Oregon in Eugene far up the Willamette Valley. He represented the new, formally trained German historical school that Victor admired. Young also was an aggressive founder and leader of the newly formed Oregon Historical Society. The invaluable chronicles of the faltering Oregon Pioneer Association (1873) and the member's interests

Portrait of Frances Fuller Victor, from her publication *Poems*.
This photograph was taken about 1900, two years before her death.
orhi 104262

gradually were being fused into the new Society's larger holdings. The Oregon Trail, Cape Horn and Isthmus heroes were swiftly fading away and the "new historians" carried on their more formal pursuits and evaluations of how the Oregon Country had come to be. Wonderful folk tales were being reevaluated—great technological changes were transforming Americans and their attitudes.

Victor had not stopped in Eugene en route to Portland since her young friend and ally was somewhere back along "the Trail" with his Midwest colleague Schaefer. Professor Young would have known too well that Mrs. Victor, who been away from Portland and Oregon for six years, was—in every sense—carrying a significant amount of baggage. There is no doubt that they and others, both keepers of flames and legends and progressive analysts of the new scientific school of recording history, would have recognized Mrs. Victor's work as estimable, formidable, and of a value beyond price. Hers were often the personally recorded stories of nineteenth century American expansion and occupation, taken at the rheumatic knees of many early participants as they recalled their pioneering adventures for an avid listener. From San Francisco and Half Moon Bay to Victoria in the north, there was much praise and public notice of her writings. There was sincere commendation, but some was fulsome praise; and there was also rage and censure. Important legends had been weighed in the balance by Frances Fuller Victor and found to be wanting. Sacred cows had been not only gored, but dropped in their tracks. Frances Fuller Victor, in her fearless desire for the fact and truth of history, had sometimes been too tactless, too frank—brilliant, yes, but maybe a little too headstrong. As suggested by her friends, she did not know quite when to stop, or how, nor did they understand her deep intelligence.

Victor had more than once offended some pioneers or descendants who tended the sacred altars. Some had died gravely offended; others, such as George Himes, an indefatigable chronicler, were still very much alive. Since 1873 the solid wagon master of the Oregon Pioneer Association, Himes was now also assistant secretary of the energetic Oregon Historical Society in Portland and a professional printer, as well. Furthermore, as a boy of 12, he had walked across the Trail. So also had Harvey W. Scott, now head of Portland's *Oregonian* newspaper, new president of the Oregon Historical Society, and key planner of the Lewis and Clark Exposition and Agricultural Trade Fair, which the Society was now refining.

Frances Fuller Victor agreed with Frederick Young that the one palpable gift of the Fair should be a "permanent substantial building" for the Oregon Historical Society. Young also wished to buy the Bancroft library now up for sale in San Francisco. Victor agreed. Himes was pretty much ignoring them both. Victor had arrived in the Far West by steamship in the middle of the Civil War. The year 1859 had been established by Himes and others as the cut-off year for true pioneers. Victor was a twice-married, upstart woman whom not just a few in the proud city on the Willamette River might—during her earlier progresses through Portland, with her abundance of auburn hair, and uncompromising hazel eyes—have regarded as a spoiler and adventuress. And too late to be a true pioneer.

Victor had also, perhaps unwisely, taken on among other perilous assignments, a re-evaluation of the thorny Rev. Marcus Whitman legend. In reassessing the massacre at the Waiilatpu Mission in Washington and possible reasons for it, she had riled Methodists, Presbyterians, Roman Catholics, army men, and militia, hoary pioneers, and some of the few remaining American Indians. Murky events of two generations ago had been pored over by the woman fact-finder; and recollections of some ancient pioneers had been rendered suspect, to put it mildly. The passage of time seldom serves recollections of things past very faithfully. When Victor arrived in Portland there were fewer persons to greet her. Judge Matthew Deady had died, but Victor arranged temporary lodging with her friends, the Edward Kilhams. The June 3 *Oregonian* reported that she was residing at 475 Washington Street while working on a volume of poems and a revision of her big book *River of the West*. In friendly fashion, the news reporter included an imposing list of Mrs. Victor's publications on Western and Pacific Northwest history. He stated "The Mother of Oregon History would commence new labors in the historical field." Ancient teeth no doubt ground as some readers of Oregon's leading newspaper thought about just what she might turn her too energetic mind and pen to; but neither they nor the reporter could know that the celebrity was faded in health and fortune. She had reached Portland safely, but her uncertain income from writing since 1863 always had been inadequate. The Civil War pension from her husband Henry Clay Victor, who had drowned off Cape Flattery in the *Pacific* twenty-five years earlier, was still less than ten dollars a month. In earlier years she had remarked to the eminent Oregon jurist Deady how "she wished to be carried out from her own house." Even that was not be.

As always Victor made a meager best of things, occasionally selling a prized book from her library or soliciting orders for research volumes as yet unfinished. In earlier years she had tried to find a library position in Portland for her younger sister, and now she sought steady work for herself. There was nothing. To Young she reported, "All work and no pay." She stated that unless she could find her services "worth something to someone" she would have to "quit Oregon." "One can not live on some green trees, and some peaks . . . not even a poet." And the fact was her poetry had never been financially rewarding.

Happily Oregon's junior senator, Joseph Simon, a member of the federal Veteran's Pension Committee, had earlier introduced a bill on behalf of "the widow of Henry C. Victor, Assistant First Engineer in the United States Navy, 71 (actually 75) years of age , poor and incapacitated by age and physical infirmities from earning a living by physical or mental labor." When the bill was finally approved March 21, 1902, the pension was fixed at $20 a month, but in the meantime Victor struggled with many problems.

As autumn came Victor continued to savor the small circle of new friends she always made among men and women of every age; something to do perhaps with her inn-keeping parents' early example. In general, she ignored critics such as Horace S. Lyman, Eva Emery Dye, and testy George Himes. Lyman had not included Victor in his broad study of Oregon literature. In a *Pacific Monthly* article Eva Emery Dye of Oregon City had included Victor in an afterthought, merely and meanly identifying her as "industrious." She certainly was that. Ignoring these hostile slights as best she could, she buoyed herself with plans for future articles, books, and several poems. She earnestly solicited criticism of her work from Frederick Young in his position as editor of the new *Oregon Historical Quarterly* (1900). In a series of proposals she offered:

1. A broad review of Hiram Chittenden's two-volume work on the fur trade "in extenso." He had praised and used her extensive fur trade writings.

2. Long notes for an article on Astoria.

3. References on the Oregon Boundary Question, from the British point of view. The negotiations had gone on for years and she had mastered them.

4. A novel underway and half done.

5. Materials gathered for an article on Oregon literature. (She would have revenge on Lyman.)

6. A book on the Reverend Marcus Whitman, half done. (Young would surely have shuddered.)

7. And the famous Newberry Library in Chicago wanted assistance with a book list.

Victor was in correspondence with "many Eastern literary people" on a variety of questions, including Prof. Edward G. Bourne, who much admired her work while he condemned the views of the Oregon historian Samuel H. Clarke, now in Washington, D.C.

She mentioned work on an article on the First Oregon Cavalry. She would do a "snap shot" of this "neglected subject which should find reader interest in *OHQ*." "Lest we forget" was her eventual subtitle. She reported to Young that she had received a copy of Adj. Gen. Cyrus Reed's report for the Civil War regiment of Oregon volunteers. Although she had completed her Whitman manuscript, she wanted her friends to realize that she was interested in aspects of regional history beyond the Reverend Whitman and Dr. John McLoughlin. While requesting payment of Young, Victor stated that she hoped some time "to spare him reference to these personal matters." Shortly after her Chittenden review was sent in with a bill for $25.00, just "half of what an Eastern periodical would pay her." It would appear that Victor supposed the Oregon Historical Society was in a strong financial position. The grim truth was that the institution, with all its great intentions, short history and competing interests, was scarcely better off than the "Mother of Oregon History," now plotting in her boarding house.

She further reported to editor Young that she was feeling "pretty well" and would have the cavalry article completed by May 1. She hoped that she "would not annoy him" by asking whether he had a little money on hand. Her aim was to line up articles for the September and December *OHQ* numbers; then she would leave for California. "Simply stated, Oregon winters are too long at both ends." And Victor mentioned once again to Young that "the Stanford man" (a graduate originally from McMinnville, Oregon) who resided at her boarding house with another Stanford student, often sat with her, learning something of Oregon history and state affairs and something of the historical methods that she employed.

She plowed on through the summer of 1902 working on several projects, including the very substantial cavalry article that showed her undiminished brilliance in matters historical. Again, she advised Professor Young "the Exposition should be more than a trade fair." When all was over, a substantial building should remain to house "a state institution," a proper historical society. She discussed with Young his idea to purchase the famous H.H. Bancroft library and manuscripts. Further she agreed with Young and Bancroft the library should be available for the Lewis and Clark Exposition. The collection was valued at $500,000; Mrs. Victor said it could be purchased for $300,000; and Bancroft wrote that he could give $50,000. It was not to be; and certainly it was a regrettable loss since Bancroft had carried so much of the Oregon Country history back to his San Francisco history mill where Victor had earlier toiled hard and long. She averred that Harvey Scott, who had also walked the Trail, should give space in *The Oregonian* to publicize the new *Quarterly*. ". . . everything has to be advertised nowadays."

Young responded to all these missives from Victor; yet he must have groaned over his letter-strewn desk because so many of her ideas were strong and logical, revealing insights into the many-fissured chambers of Oregon history and culture. But money and philanthropy were thin prospects. Victor had preceded Young in Portland by many years and knew more of the pathways through "Stumptown's" social thickets. She sent Young a clipping from Col. George B. Currey's *La Grande Observer* which stated that much of early Oregon politics had been "infamous" and it had not improved much. "Look at the way the Centennial Fair site hangs fire. It is the same grudging spirit. The fear that some man will gain a point."

Her last contributions to the *Oregon Historical Quarterly* (Vol. 2), should be noted here. The "First Oregon Cavalry" (No. 2) and a review of "The American Fur Trade in the Far West" (No. 3) were her substantial offerings. The forty-page article and the ten-page review of Chittenden's two-volume study of the American fur trade are superb realizations. Her practiced, even-handed style were there for all to see.

With the news of Bret Harte's death in London, Victor recalled for Young that forty years earlier Harte had published her first historical article "Manifest Destiny in the West," in his *Overland Monthly*. He had inculcated in her a sense of responsibility for "writing for all time." Her "fugitive pieces" were the foundation of all concrete history of the Northwest Coast. Long before she joined Bancroft's staff, she "had tried to elevate the character of the state, or assist its friends in their upbuilding projects." Through Young she hoped to realize "the proper estimation and recognition of what she did to build up the history and literature of the Oregon Country."

In the midst of all this activity, Victor had moved from her "remote" boarding home on Washington Street to "a more downtown location," 501 Yamhill Street. After the Society's quarterly board meeting in September, Young took time to visit the Society's honorary member; it would appear they both savored the long session of anecdotes, gossip, and future plans. Naturally, a long, chatty letter followed Young to Eugene, and he wrote to encourage her completion of an article on early Oregon transportation in association with Joseph Gaston.

Joseph Gaston, pioneer railroad builder and journalist, had become a fellow boarder. He was supportive of Victor and looked forward to this new partnership with a person with a mind of her own, devoted to truth and justice. They made great plans together. Her demanding workload still demonstrated vigor and intellectual rigor, but she seemed unaware that death was closing in. (She did, however, ask her Portland adviser and friend, Edward Kilham, to care for her assorted manuscript papers and modest estate. She was also concerned for some details of her eventual funeral ceremony. This seems as much as she gave to any consideration of her own mortality.)

On November 10, Victor sent a brief unsigned note of apology to Young to say that she was ill and that her Oregon transportation article remained unfinished. She hoped to meet the deadline for the December number (No. 4) of the *Quarterly*. Her room was comfortable, her desk filled with letters and plans; there was much to occupy her mind and time. She hoped that Young and others would stop by. In the meantime, she was snugged down with Mrs. Gilmore, the housekeeper, watching the famous winter rains outside her cozy room.

On November 13, Mrs. Gilmore spent several hours with Victor. Around midnight, Victor called out to her companion to say that death was near. About 3 A.M. on the 14th, Victor slipped away. She was, alas, not "to be carried from her own house."

Mr. and Mrs. Kilham quickly discharged their responsibilities, sending a telegram to her relatives in Walla Walla. The first news story, a final touch of irony, appeared in the *Evening Statesman*, deep in the heart of Washington's Marcus Whitman country. The Walla Walla newspaper more specifically identified Mrs. Victor's employment with the Bancroft publishers in San Francisco, her association with prominent historians in the West, and her many brilliant attainments. But Victor, a high-energy personality of notable reputation, was not going to receive the honors one might reasonably expect.

The Kilhams conferred with the reverend minister of Portland's First Unitarian Church, Thomas Lamb Elliot. Victor was not a member there, but she had been associated in Salem and San Francisco with Elliot's Unitarian colleagues. He was pleased to be of service.

On Saturday, November 15, the *Oregonian* ran a four-tiered headline, "End of a Well-Known Historian." A somewhat condescending story buried in the *Journal* was followed by two obituary editorials, the least acceptable written by would-be historian Catherine Scott Coburn, a younger sister of Abigail Scott Duniway and Harvey Scott. She stated that Mrs. Victor had been "a pioneer in the literature of the Northwest" and "one of the earliest compilers of Northwest history," but that she had not always been accurate. Although editor Harvey Scott admired Mrs. Victor, faint praise was the overall tenor of Mrs. Coburn's *Oregonian* evaluation. Her estimate, while not unfair, was hardly of a pitch or tone any blueblood would welcome, certainly not Victor who despised conde-scension.

William A. Morris, "the Stanford man," turned in a tribute, as his opening sentence reveals: "By the death, on November 14th, of Frances Fuller Victor there was removed the most versatile figure in Pacific Coast literature, a literary pioneer on the coast, and a woman to whom Orego-nians owe much."

On December 2, 1902, the Sacramento *Wednesday Press* ran a lengthy article, captioned, "FRANCES FULLER VICTOR—Death of a Tal-ented Pacific Coast Poet and Historian." Her death, Winfield J. Davis noted, deserved more than a passing notice, for she had been one of "the most vigorous and industrious of California writers." The biographical sketch mentioned the work of Metta Victor, her younger sister, and Vic-tor's marriage to Jackson Barritt in 1853. In listing her major Pacific Coast publications, it focused on her work as a columnist for *The Golden Era*, an essayist and short story writer for the *Overland Monthly*, and a historian at Bancroft's library. It described her as a woman of strong character, "loyal to her friends and just to her enemies." The article closed with a reprint of her poem, "El Palo Santo," first published in the San Francisco *Bulletin* in 1863—thus bringing her literary career in California to full circle.

Despite the increasing support of Frederick Young and now her new young friends in Portland, there was a cool reserve and a whiff of smol-dering resentment clouding issues. So how did this singular chronicler and scholar, this forceful and determined observer of so many American frontiers end up in an unmarked hillside grave above the Willamette River south of Portland? True, the descendant of kings and colonists was nestled in Portland's smartest new cemetery, but she lay beneath a tem-porary wooden marker. Just as Frances Fuller Victor did, we ask the ever-constant questions in history: How did this happen? And, why?

She deserved more.

Forty years after Frances Fuller Victor sailed to California, Edward Kil-ham might well have pondered some of these mysteries and ephemera as he tried to establish the value of Frances' papers. On July 8, 1903, he wrote William I. Marshall in Chicago as to the value of documents in her collection relative to the British view of Oregon affairs. It was September 22, 1904 before he filed an appraisal of her estate, which he valued at $294, with the Multnomah County Court. During 1904-05 Professor Young was fully engaged as a commissioner of the Lewis and Clark Exposition in Portland. Among other events, "the Fair" celebrated the arrival of the winner of a two-car transcontinental race from New York City to Portland on June 21, 1905. More important for the cultural world, the Exposition showcased Oregon's nationally known figures such as poet Joaquin Miller, suffragist Abigail Scott Duniway, and novelist Eva Emery Dye. The latter promoted a national campaign to raise funds for a statue of the Shoshone Indian woman, Sacajawea. It was unveiled at the Exposition on July 6 as a symbol of "womanhood" and served the purposes of suffragists nationally. Frances, who had faded from view, would have viewed this exploitation of the faithful Sacajawea as unhistorical.

In 1906, Frances' cousin, Mrs. Mary William Ingram, published, apparently at her own expense, *The Williams-Walworth Genealogy*, in Walla Walla, Washington; and in Chicago, A.C. McClurg published Eva Emery Dye's third historical novel, *McDonald of Oregon—A Tale of Two Shores*. It was based on the diary of this mixed-blood Indian, who had been shipwrecked in Japan and had returned to the Pacific Northwest to claim his native heritage.

In March of this year, Professor Young, as secretary of the Oregon Historical Society, moved that the board of directors acquire the papers of Frances Fuller Victor. He was appointed chairman of a three-man committee, composed of himself, George Himes, and J. R. Wilson, to investigate the situation. At the December board meeting, Young moved that William I. Marshall of Chicago be elected an honorary member of the Society and that the papers of the Salem historian, J. Henry Brown, be acquired together with those of Mrs. Victor. In his 1906 report to the membership, he noted that he would soon announce that the collections of two Oregon historians—Frances Fuller Victor and J. Henry Brown— would "at last be placed in charge of the Society, where their preservation will be sure."

In the meantime, Young had been communicating with Kilham about acquiring Mrs. Victor's papers and erecting a monument in her memory. On October 6, 1906, Young wrote Kilham from Eugene City, suggesting that Mrs. Victor's Portland friends raise funds for the memorial by public subscription. Kilham responded the next day from his place of business at 109-111 Second Street. After consulting with Miss Gaston, he thought Young's suggestion was "inadvisable." The people of Oregon had not appreciated Mrs. Victor during her lifetime and were not likely to respond now that she was dead. "It puts it in the shape of a beggar proposition," Kilham declared.

In the spring of 1907, Young called on Kilham at his place of business in Portland and authorized Mrs. Victor's friends to select a stone for a monument. On April 11, Kilham wrote Young that they had found "a modest stone suitable for that purpose." It would cost $500. In a brief, unsigned letter dated April 16 and delivered after he had attended a quarterly board meeting in Portland, Young noted that he had not been commissioned to use any of the Society's funds for "the Victor memorial." He explained that when he first talked with Kilham about the matter, he had thought that "the way had been clear because increased appropriations had provided a surplus."

However, at the meeting, he had learned that a motion had been worked up to give the men at headquarters in Portland (George Himes and his assistant) increases in their meager salaries. Young was not sure that the funds of the Society would "suffice" for the purpose they both had "at heart." In his reply two days later, Kilham expressed disappointment. Now it was incumbent upon him, as administrator of Mrs. Victor's estate, "to seek a market in some other direction." On July 7, 1907 Kilham made his final offer to Young. He stated that he had been corresponding with Eastern collectors with regard to Mrs. Victor's papers. After consulting with Mr. Gaston, he agreed to turn them over to Professor Young for $250.

Here the Kilham-Young correspondence ends. Why Young did not formally present Kilham's offer to the board or buy the papers himself one can only speculate. Having visited Victor in her Portland boarding houses, he was familiar with the extent and value of her collection. She had already consigned many important historical documents to the Society's archives.

In the following years, others kept her memory alive. Among them was her friend Joseph Gaston. During the last years of his life, he published seven illustrated historical volumes—three on the history of Portland and four on a centennial history of the state. In the first, he placed her portrait in the middle of a circle of five contemporary male historians—William H. Carey, George Himes, J. Henry Brown, Horace Lyman, and Harvey K. Hines. His coverage of her work was more effusive in his history of the state. He observed that she had filled a "large page in Oregon history not only as a historian but also as a poet of merit." He added that "Harvey Scott once being asked who was the most reliable historian in Oregon had replied, 'Oregon has but one historian—Mrs. F.F. Victor'." High praise, Gaston noted, from a competent judge. In Gaston's view, her work as a writer of Oregon history was "greater than that of all others combined," and as a collector of Oregon history, she was "second only to George Himes."

In November 1912, Kilham finally settled Mrs. Victor's estate. He sent the remaining funds and perhaps a few papers and manuscripts to her only surviving sibling, her next youngest sister, the widowed Celia Pearse, who signed a receipt for the same at Marysville, Ohio, where she died soon after.

The News and Comment section in the March, 1918 *Oregon Historical Quarterly* carried a notice of the death of Hubert Howe Bancroft on March 2 at the age of 86. It was written by Leslie Scott, son of the deceased Harvey Scott and a former student of Professor Young. The first two paragraphs remarked on Bancroft's contributions to the history of the Pacific states. But the third and longest paragraph focussed on the work of "his able assistant," Oregon author and historian Frances Fuller Victor. Scott noted that according to William Morris (whom he incorrectly identified as a Bancroft editor) she had written at least six volumes that had carried Bancroft's name. Thus the *Oregon Historical Quarterly*, in recording "the great and indispensable service of Mr. Bancroft," thought it "fitting to remember the work of Mrs. Victor."

Eight years later on May 23, 1923, an *Oregonian* editorial commemorated the centenary of Mrs. Victor's birth, paying tribute to her part in the Bancroft histories in these terms:

She united exceptionally the qualities of literary craftsman-
ship with delicate and intuitive appreciation of the
grandeur of pioneer achievement. More keenly, perhaps,
than the participants in early events themselves, she com-
prehended the type of people and institutions entirely new
to Eastern experience. The original conception of such a
history of Oregon was hers; she had already collected a rich
store of material for the purpose when Bancroft appeared
on the scene. In doing this, she performed a service of ines-
timable value to the state, since its builders were then nearly
all alive, and the facts concerning the beginnings of the
commonwealth were well known to them, and had it not
been for Mrs. Victor would have been lost to posterity.

Two years later, Fred Lockley, who had been on the editorial staff of
the *Oregon Journal* since 1910, published his *History of the Columbia River from
The Dalles to the Sea*. A teller of folk tales, he noted that while he had been
living in Salem in the 1890's he had met Mrs. Victor, who had just
resigned from her Bancroft work. He added incorrectly that she had been
living at the house of E.M. Waite, an old-time Salem printer, and was
selling cosmetics from door to door to make ends meet. Lockley's misinformation gave rise to a legend that persists to this day. As Mrs. Waite's
diary reveals, Mrs. Victor was living with her during these years. They
both knew the Waite family; and on occasion Frances may have visited
the ladies of the household to deliver cosmetic orders as a courtesy but
not as a livelihood.

Such was the general view of Frances Fuller Victor's legacy and legends associated with her name in 1935. That year Alfred Powers, professor
of creative writing and editorial adviser to Binsford and Mort, Portland
publishers, copyrighted his mammoth *History of Oregon Literature*, printed
at the Metropolitan Press. In his introduction to his 809-page opus,
Powers acknowledged the help of librarians at the Oregon Historical
Society, the Oregon State Library at Salem, and The Bancroft Library at
Berkeley, California. His purpose was to provide a convenient, bird's eye
view of Oregon literature from the legends, songs, and pictographs of
native Indian tribes to the work of contemporary Oregon historians,

poets, essayists, short story writers, and novelists. His eleven-page essay on Mrs. Victor places her in the mainstream of Oregon literature. Observing that she had labored longest and hardest of all Oregon writers, especially in gathering and writing its history, Oregon historians had taken her work for granted and neglected her. Later in the volume, Powers credited her with being among the first to research the history of Oregon literature, though her work was greatly expanded by J. B. Horner, professor of literature of Oregon State College at Corvallis.

In his history, Powers perpetuates the views of Morris, Gaston, and Lockley. But his interest in Mrs. Victor persisted. The December 1941 *Oregon Historical Quarterly* carried an article based on his own research, entitled "Scrapbook of a Historian—Frances Fuller Victor." It was a reflective account of the contents of her Scrapbook No. 120, which he had located in the library of the Oregon Historical Society together with letters she had written to Judge Deady. Powers quoted from newspaper clippings of her writing. He was intrigued with clippings that hinted at the Victor-Bancroft controversy, which needed more study. He concluded that these "headlights" in this scrapbook revealed Frances Fuller Victor as "one of the most brilliant of Oregon women and one of the greatest in her benefactions, whose lack of suitable recognition has continued for two score years since her death."

On January 31, 1946, the *Salem Capital Journal* ran an article headlined: "Noted Oregon Historian Lies in Unmarked Grave." Written by Ben Maxwell, it reported some of the facts and legends circulated by Fred Lockley and Don H. Upjohn. The latter believed that Mrs. Victor had written much of The *River of the West* at the home of the poet, Belle Cooke. Maxwell also reported that Mrs. Victor's sister, Mrs. S.C. Adams, had lived at 256 State Street, Salem, in 1891 and had died there. Actually her sister, Martha Rayle, married Sebastian C. Adams of Salem in San Francisco in 1884 and died in Salem in 1888 while Frances was still working for Bancroft. However, Maxwell was correct as to the time and place of Mrs. Victor's death and the site of her burial—Lot 4, Section 15, unmarked grave No. 3, Riverview Cemetery, Portland. In closing, Maxwell noted that Mrs. Victor had been a member of the Daughters of the American Revolution. Though she had the required credentials, there is

A view down the Willamette River across the burgeoning east bank
and beyond to Mt. St. Helens in Washington, taken from Riverview Cemetery
six years before the Victor interment in 1902.
ORHI 89202

presently no evidence she was a member. In any event, this public
announcement prompted the Portland chapter of the D.A.R. to place a
bronze plaque on the grave in 1947. In addition to this recognition, in the
late 1940s, the superintendent of Crater Lake National Park designated a
new point on the east rim "Victor View".

Specific note should also be given a Victor facet much reflected upon
by Hazel Mills, Constance Bordwell, and Dorothy O. Johansen. The
phrase "the historian as chained poet" frequently surfaced in my conversations with all three historians through the years. We all agreed: There
was simply no one like Frances Fuller Victor, who was, in the very best
sense, unique. She did to the end suffer privately her feeling of meager
praise as a poet; but today we may judge not a few of her lines and
images sublime. As a historian she would have firmly seized the sense of
Robert Frost's sentence later crafted: "The fact is the sweetest dream that
labor knows." How she loved them! Facts kept her traveling over many
lonely roads. They were the meat and drink she savored.

Then there were those "chaps" in the Oregon Pioneer Association
and the Oregon Historical Society early on, leaders who treated her

shabbily or casually at best. After all, she had not crossed the Oregon Trail. Frances had traveled across the Isthmus *by train*—an upstart woman of inadequate credentials, whatever they were. So many of those "chaps" are pretty much forgotten now, but Mrs. Victor lives on regally in the manner of her encrusted royal ancestors. And so many other men and women in the West owe their enduring memory to her tireless discipline and industry. Let's think. What if she had not come "out West"?

So now, at last in the centenary year of her death her steadfast and perceptive biographers have returned her to us as a full-bodied Victorian presence—no longer unhonored, no longer unsung. And in their perceptive study we will see that Frances Fuller Victor was a richly endowed frontiers historian as well as a celebrated poet and biographer of nineteenth-century America on the move. Clio would do nothing but praise.

Her "circularity" comes into focus all along the way West; from days on the Erie and other canals, to the turnpikes and wayside inns of early Ohio and Illinois to the prairie's edge in Nebraska—a sweeping, oceanic landscape that enthralled later generations of American observers. It is the young historian Frances Victor (Barritt) whom I shall always remember perched in a church steeple high above Council Bluffs recording her impressions of the lumbering wagon trains moving slowly west away from the village streets beneath her. She had a rendezvous with their destinies. Clio would do not but praise.

Truly, so much of her abides. There is nothing so permanent as facts in print, as Mrs. Victor knew. They are somehow "the sweetest dreams." We all together hope our volume devoted to this exalted personage conveys a sense of profound gratitude and admiration to the best of our early Western historians: Frances Fuller Victor, *Prima inter pares.*

Thomas Vaughan
Oregon Historian Laureate

ACKNOWLEDGMENTS

Now the end has come at last and I list myself as editor together with my extraordinarily skillful and perceptive associate editor, Marguerite Wittwer Wright. I express deep admiration for the frankly dazzling and puzzling Frances Fuller Victor; and a profound obligation to biographers Hazel Mills and Constance Bordwell. As well we ardently thank Priscilla Knuth. Special mention must be given to Constance's friend and professional associate at Seattle University, Prof. June J. Bube, to Rick Harmon, former editor of the *Oregon Historical Quarterly*, and Professor Dorothy Johansen, recently deceased. Librarian Louis Flannery, Adair Law and Chet Orloff, long-time associates at the Oregon Historical Society, were early supporters of Professor Bordwell, as were Robert Clark, George Belknap, and Josephine Baumgartner and David Duniway. Authors Mills and Bordwell conferred with a host of Victor admirers who I know will understand the complexities of my now seeking to recover their names. We sincerely appreciate their special constructions, their insights, and their strong loyalties to Mrs. Victor.

Special recognition must be given to the photo expertise of Susan Seyl and of Mrs. Scott (Sieglinde) Smith of the Oregon Historical Society Library and Miss Caroline Hixson, my former assistant there. Last the recent important assistance of Cameron Vaughan Tyler and Monique Coleman of the Multnomah County Library staff is happily recognized. Finally, a salute to Bruce Taylor Hamilton as an editorial advisor, but more importantly as the designer of this book.

Thomas Vaughan

Dedicated with thanks and esteem

THE AUTHORS

For almost fifty years I speculated how Frances Fuller Victor acquired such acute focus, energy and drive. During this same half century, I have watched this present biography of her grow, taking on saga status, almost like the subject herself. In the following chapters, the authors have fashioned a compelling story, one that tells at last the larger Victor life. This straightforward, engrossing account also reveals not a little about two women she would have much admired, librarian and archivist Mrs. Hazel Emery Mills and Professor Constance Bordwell. Because of their curiosity, discipline, intellectual rigor and sense of fair play, the "Mother of Oregon History" has been returned to vibrant life.

In 1951, Randall Mills, an assistant professor of Oregon literature at the University of Oregon, began to muse about the author of *River of the West*, Frances Fuller Victor. He was joined by his wife Hazel, who had studied with Herbert Bolton at Berkeley and had secured an M.A. in literary studies there. As they prepared their preliminary Victor research findings in the library of the Oregon Historical Society, Professor Mills suddenly died. Mrs. Mills then won her library degree at the University of Washington subsequently serving in important positions at the state libraries in Oregon (Salem) and Washington (Olympia). She was well positioned to continue her Victor researches.

Articles and lectures followed and the alerted American Association for State and Local History awarded her a travel grant to study Victor and Jackson Barritt archives in Eastern repositories.

After her retirement from the Washington State Library, Mills completed a draft of the Victor biography for the years up to 1878, when Victor, a recent widow (nationally recognized for her historical writings), left Portland to return to San Francisco and a staff position with Hubert Howe Bancroft, the publishing titan. She was returning "home."

To complete the biography, Hazel Mills asked her long-time friend Prof. Constance Bordwell for editorial assistance. Just retired from the University of Oregon, Bordwell had written her own narrative works and she perceived that a strict historical line must be imposed on the Mills work. A comparison exists with Victor's work: "an exhaustive compilation of facts from the best collection[s] of the time with the minimum of theory." The two busy biographers thus continued harmoniously until the late 1980s.

Hazel Emery Mills had come to see me shortly after the death of her gifted, energetic husband Randall. Even then, in the winter of 1954–55, Mills had completed a generous sketch for a Victor biography. She had come to my crowded little Society office in the old Market Street site where, since 1917, the Oregon Historical Society existed in a warren of stuffed and scruffy little "rooms" of the City Auditorium. I was keen to hear about this half-forgotten paragon, but Mrs. Mills informed me that much, much more research had to be done before she could let her manuscript go. Then, through of the sixties, seventies, and eighties, as we held our many editorial meetings, her ever-heavier notebook became more tightly embraced. Of concern to me was the fact that Mills, as often happens, became ever more captivated by the search for one last source, one more tiny footnote for her doughty heroine.

By 1990 Mills' health had seriously declined. She wrote that November requesting Bordwell, now living in Portland, to continue "writing and revising to make a more readable narrative of the life of this remarkably talented woman." As Mills continued her decline in Eugene, Bordwell pressed on alone. During the last decade Priscilla Knuth and then Bruce Taylor Hamilton provided important insights and editorial support to Bordwell in their capacity as "stout friends" of all three historians involved.

My very long association with this Victor saga should be now revealed. My singular editorial associate at the Oregon Historical Society, Priscilla Knuth, telephoned me just before her death in the fall of 1999. Throughout our long thirty-five years together we had worked on every variety of publication from the *Oregon Historical Quarterly* and massive books down through pamphlets and broadsides. There was never a negative exchange, and our congenial partnership produced much print of permanent value.

This gray afternoon, however, Ms. Knuth called from her bed to say that she could no longer assist Constance Bordwell with the long-aborning Francis Fuller Victor biography. Bruce Taylor Hamilton had just departed the Society's publication office bound eventually for new landscapes and printing projects in Santa Fe. Since there would now be no one to assist Miss Bordwell, they had together conferred with Mills and decided that I must now come forward to work with Bordwell on "the final chapters." A few weeks later I spoke at Priscilla's memorial service and in a few days responded to Bordwell's cheery telephone call suggesting a "manuscript review."

"I tried to look you up in the *Dictionary of Oregon History*, said I. "Well, I'm not in there yet, and neither is Frances Fuller Victor, if you can imagine, " said the tiny scholar.

"So, you and I are going to fix that," said I grandly. We got on famously, with a quick recognition that irony and good humor would be major themes in our undertaking.

Rather than dwell on my later consternation upon probing the labyrinthine workbook, I would here note that Bordwell's loyal and attentive nephew, Douglas, soon accepted my analysis of the plight overwhelming his nonagenarian aunt. The manuscript had become so huge it had taken on a primal existence of its own. Entering the ninth decade of her illustrious life Professor Bordwell could not grapple this monster alone. It had to be cut down, reduced, pruned, synthesized, in some way brought down to a reasonable book size—one that would be finished by the forthcoming centenary of our historian-heroine's death late in 2002. I decided that we would together erase the irony that Victor, Oregon's questing historian, was not listed in the dictionary of Oregon luminaries. We would persevere.

In close analysis of our *oeuvre* it became too obvious that I might never discharge my casually accepted responsibility as editor of this biography. As the months and then two years elapsed Bordwell insisted that I must sign on as co-author with Mills and herself. That I could not do. They had given years of devotion and discipline. For them this restoration of Mrs. Victor to life was more than an author's quest; this had become a trust to which they had bonded.

What grand luck it was for me when Marguerite Wittwer Wright, my long-time administrative-public affairs colleague at Oregon's state historical society at last consented to help us in the completion of this manuscript. Wright had been one of the most illustrious editors of the *Oregon Daily Emerald* at the University in Eugene, as well as the first editorial assistant to Publisher/Editor Charles A. Sprague of Salem's daily *Oregon Statesman*. Wright and I reworked the early chapters while Bordwell and I slowly moved through the last years of Victor's life.

In the first week of August 2001 Bordwell and I were enmeshed in Victor's final Portland years. There was much to do, seemingly insurmountable since Bordwell was ever more attached to Victor in the manner of Mills, now recently deceased. We at last concluded that I must change my schedule from volunteer afternoons during the week to a daily conference. Bordwell urged this even as I sensed a substantial subsiding of her energies. On Monday, August sixth I arrived at her apartment to find a grieving Douglas Bordwell. With deep sorrow, I accepted that a very exceptional person, Commander Bordwell, had shipped out some time that morning. A thought from Thomas Hobbes' *Leviathan* came to me. These three great women, and Knuth too, believed that life is like a race. There was no finishing post to distract them. The joy was being in the race, in the van if possible, but essentially in motion "to make our world somehow a better place." They had reflected this strength all the years I had known and worked with them.

Professor Bordwell would here wish me to give special note to the tireless hunts undertaken by her partners. Working in the pre-computer decades, Hazel Mills preserved key documents, arranged chronologically, in over thirty loose-leaf notebooks that fill a wall bookcase. Her hand-written notes on scores of related topics—large and small—are filed in desktop cabinets. These form the core of her Frances Fuller Victor Collection, which she donated to the Oregon Historical Society. Since then, the library staff has reorganized and expanded the Collection for the use of qualified researchers. The fact is Victor left very little of her own person behind. No diary and few letters. Mills relentlessly unearthed so many long buried facts important to this story.

Thomas Vaughan

NOTES

Chapter 1
Voyage to the Golden Gate (1863)

1. John Haskell Kemble, *The Panama Route, 1848–1869* (Berkeley: University of California Press, 1943) p. 46, 95–96.

2. Kemble, *op. cit.* p. 122.

3. Fessenden, Otis N., *Illustrated History of the Panama Railroad* (New York: Harpers & Bros., 1861) p. 115.

4. Frances Fuller Victor, "Florence Fane in San Francisco," *Golden Era.* XI, No. 35, August 9, 1863, p. 5.

5. Victor, "A Short Stay in Acapulco," *Overland Monthly*, VI (March, 1871) p. 214.

6. Kemble, *The Panama Route, op. cit.* pp. 147–148; Otis, The Panama Railroad, pp. 146–147.

7. Herbert Howe Bancroft, *History of Mexico*, Vol. III. 1600–1803 (San Francisco: A. Bancroft & Co., 1883), pp. 259, 419, 460–461, 622–635.

8. *Ibid.* Vol. VI. 1861–1887 (San Francisco: The History Company, 1888) pp. 60, 75, 77.

9. *Poetry of the Pacific: Selections and Original Poems from the Poets of the Pacific States.* May Wentworth, Ed. (San Francisco: Pacific Publishing Co., 1867) pp. 291–293.

10. Victor, "El Palo Santo," *Ibid*, pp. 294–295. She reprinted both poems, with variations, in her *The New Penelope and Other Stories and Poems* (San Francisco: A. L. Bancroft and Company, 1877), pp. 305–306; 314–315; and *Poems* (Portland: Author's edition, 1900) pp. 72–72; 76–78.

11. Charles Henry Webb, *John Paul's Book* (Hartford, Conn.: Columbia Book Co., 1874 pp. 388–389.

12. Published in Washington, D.C., 1848.

13. James A. Hart, *A Companion to California* (New York: Oxford University Press, 1978) p. 146.

14. Bayard Taylor, *El Dorado: or, Adventure in the Path of Empire* (New York: 1850). Horace Greeley, *An Overland Journey from New York to San Francisco in the Summer of 1859*. Edited by Charles T. Duncan (New York: Knopf, 1964) pp. 307–308.

15. Feral Egen, *Fremont: Explorer for a Restless Nation* (New York: Doubleday & Co., 1977) p. 511.

16. Hubert Howe Bancroft, *History of California*, Vol. VII, 1860–1890. (San Francisco: The History Company, 1890) p. 291.

17. Victor, "Florence Fane in San Francisco, *Golden Era*, October 25, 1863.

18. Victor, "Florence Fane in San Francisco, *Golden Era*, October 25, 1863.

19. "The Pacific Squadron," *Bancroft's Almanac for the Pacific States*, edited by William H. Knight, 1864.

20. Frances Fuller Victor, "Mrs. F.F. Victor," *Salem Daily Oregon Statesman*, June 1, 1895. A five-column article, she wrote it at the request of the editor, as one in a series of sketches of notable Oregonians.

21. "The Late James Nisbet of 'The Bulletin'," San Francisco *Bulletin*, Aug. 3, 1865.

22. "Charles Henry Webb," *Dictionary of American Biography* XIX, pp. 572–573. An item in the San Francisco *Evening Bulletin*, May 11, 1863 states that Webb "is now permanently connected with the *Bulletin*, one of its editorial corps."

23. "Arrivals at the Russ House, June 8th," *Evening Bulletin*, June 9, 1863.

24. Oscar Lewis, *San Francisco: Mission to Metropolis* (Berkeley, California Howell North Books, 1966), pp. 110–112; John S. Hittell, *City of San Francisco* (San Francisco: A. L. Bancroft & Co., 1878) pp. 333–334.

25. Herbert H. Bancroft, "The House of H. H. Bancroft and Company," *Literary Industries* (San Francisco: History Company, 1890) pp. 142–167.

26. Oscar Lewis, *op. cit.* pp. 108–109, 120.

27. Flora Haines Apponyi, *Libraries in California* (San Francisco: A. L. Bancroft and Company, 1878) pp. 261–262, 269, 277.

28. Victor, "Florence Fane," *Golden Era*, Sept. 13, 1863.

29. *Ibid*, August 9, 1863.

Chapter 2
Florence Fane in San Francisco (1863–64)

1. James C. Derby, *Fifty Years Among Authors, Books, and Publishers* (New York: G.W. Carleton & Company, 1884) pp. 402–405.

2. Frances Fuller Victor, "Florence Fane in San Francisco," *Golden Era*, Nov. 1, 1863.

3. Franklin Walker, *San Francisco's Literary Frontier* (Seattle: University of Washington Press, 1969) p. 119.

4. *Ibid.* pp. 153–154.

5. George R. Stewart, *Bret Harte, Argonaut and Exile* (Boston: Houghton Mifflin Company, 1931) pp. 84–115.

6. Fitz Hugh Ludlow, *The Heart of the Continent* (New York: Hurd and Houghton, 1870) pp. 408–445; Gordon Hendricks, *Albert Bierstadt, Painter of the American West* (New York: Harry N. Abrams, in association with Amon Carter Museum of Western Art, 1973) pp. 129–132.

7. Ludlow, *The Heart of the Continent, op. cit.* pp. 445–501.

8. Walker, *San Francisco's Literary Frontier, op. cit.* pp. 169–170.

9. *Ibid*, p. 86.

10. *Ibid*, pp. 146–151.

11. Doris Muscatine, *Old San Francisco: The Biography of a City from Early Days to the Earthquake* (New York: G. P. Putnam's Sons, 1975) pp. 359–370.

12. Frances Fuller Victor, "Mrs. F. F. Victor," Salem *Daily Oregon Statesman*, June 16, 1895. A five-column autobiography, it was written at the request of the editor as one of a series of sketches of notable Oregonians.

13. "Arrival of the U.S. Steamer Narragansett," San Francisco *Evening Bulletin*, October 26, 1863.

14. In *San Francisco's Literary Frontier, op. cit.*, p. 179, Walker ignores Frances Fuller Victor's involvement in planning a new literary journal, except to note that Florence Fane would furnish the money.

15. *Ibid.* pp. 160–162.

16. "Letter from New York. Honor to the Officers of the Russian Fleet," *San Francisco Evening Bulletin*, November 4, 1863.

17. "The Russian Ball Last Night," San Francisco *Evening Bulletin*, November 18, 1863.

18. Material on Half Moon Bay is found in *Bancroft's Hand-Book and Almanac of the Pacific States. . .for the Year 1863*, edited by William H. Knight (San Francisco: Bancroft & Company, 1864) p. 223; Mel Scott, *The San Francisco Bay Area: A Metropolis In Perspective* (Berkeley: University of California Press, 1959) pp. 45–49.

19. Mildred Brooks Hoover, Hero Eugene Rensch and Ethel Grace Rensch, *Historic Spots in California* (Stanford, California: Stanford University Press, 1966) "Maps of the Silver Mountain Mining Region" p. 5.

20. Henry Victor, "The Silver Mountain Mining Region," San Francisco *Evening Bulletin*, May 13, 1864; "The Big Trees Road Across the Sierra Nevada," June 3, 1864; Frances Fuller Victor, "A Prospecting Tour," *Sacramento Daily Union*, May 18, May 27, June 1, 1864.

21. William H. Brewer, *Up and Down California in 1860–1864*, edited by Francis P. Farquar, 3rd edition (Berkeley: University Press, 1974) pp. 431–432.

22. Hoover, Rensch, and Rensch, *op. cit.*, pp. 24, 26.

23. Wilbur H. Hoffman, *Sagas of Old Western Stage Travel and Transport* (San Diego: Howell-North, 1980) pp. 110–115.

24. Walker, *op. cit.*, pp. 179–182.

25. "Thomas Jefferson Farnham." *Dictionary of Oregon History*, edited by Howard M. Corning (Portland, Oregon: Binfords & Mort, 1956) p. 83.

26. Victor, "Autobiographical Sketch" in Salem *Oregon Statesman, op. cit.*

27. Roy E. Held, "The Odd Fellows' Library Associations of California," *The Library Quarterly*, XXXII, No. 2 (April, 1962) pp. 150–151.

28. On December 29, 1864, The Portland *Daily Oregonian* carried an advertisement for the Oregon Iron Works, Henry's future employer—short-term.

Chapter 3
Prospects & Pioneers in Oregon (1865)

1. "Brother Jonathan." *Dictionary of Oregon History*, edited by H. M. Corning, (Portland, Oregon: Binfords & Mort, 1956) p. 35.

2. Frances Fuller Victor, "A Winter Trip to Victoria and Portland" San Francisco *Bulletin*, January 20, 1865. p. 2.

3. C. C. Elliott "Legitimate Theatre in Early Victoria" British Columbia Historical *News* Vol. 3, No. 3, 13.

4. W. G. Carson, *Letters of Mr. And Mrs. Charles Kean Relating to American Tours* (Washington University, St. Louis, 1945) pp. 103–104.

5. Victor, *op. cit.* January 20, 1865. p. 2.

6. *Ibid.* p. 2.

7. "The Keans Again," Portland *Oregonian*, December 28, 1864.

8. C. W. Burage, Surveyor "A Map of the City of Portland," 1866. OHS collections.

9. "Hudson's Bay Company" and "Portland." *Dictionary of Oregon History*, edited by H. M. Corning, (Portland, Oregon: Binfords & Mort, 1956) pp. 120, 200–201.

10. *Ibid. op. cit.* p. 62.

11. *Ibid. op. cit.* p. 206.

12. *Ibid. op. cit.* p. 64.

13. *Ibid. op. cit.* p. 195.

14. *Ibid. op. cit.* pp. 63, 138, 209.

15. Portland *Oregonian*, January 2, 1865. 3.

16. Victor, "Autobiographical Sketch." *Oregon Daily Statesman*, June 16, 1895. 7.

17. *Oregonian*, January 2, 1865.

18. Malcolm Clark, Jr., *Pharisee Among Philistines: The Diary of Judge Matthew P. Deady, 1871–92.* Oregon Historical Society, 1975. See Deady Frontispiece portraits, especially. One regrets the Diary does not reflect the substantial time Deady and Victor spent together.

19. K. E. Andersen, "Historical Sketch of the Library Association of Portland" 1964, pp. 5–7.

20. *Dictionary of Oregon History*, p. 218.

21. Alfred Powers, *History of Oregon Literature* (Metropolitan Press, Portland, 1935), pp. 713–714.

22. Mrs. D.W. Williams was the cousin of Victor's mother. "In Memoriam" (Portland, March 15, 1891) O.H.S. Collections.

23. Frank B. Gill, "An Unfinished History of Transport in Washington and Oregon" OHS MSS Collections.

24. "Canyon Road," *Dictionary of Oregon History*, p. 43.

25. Arthur Throckmorton, *Oregon Argonauts: Merchants Adventurers on the Western Frontier* (Oregon Historical Society, 1961) pp. 269ff.

26. "Samuel Clarke." *Dictionary of Oregon History*, p. 55.

27. Frances Fuller Victor, *River of the West*. R. W. Bliss and Co. (Hartford, 1870) Introduction, p. 1.

28. "People's Transportation Company," *Dictionary of Oregon History*, p. 195.

29. Lewis A. McArthur, *Oregon Geographic Names*. Oregon Historical Society, 6th Edition. Revised and Enlarged by L. L. McArthur, Portland, 1992, p. 30.

30. *Ibid. op. cit.* p. 641.

31. *Ibid. op. cit.* p. 135.

32. Frances Fuller Victor, "Wayside Pictures from Oregon," San Francisco *Evening Bulletin*, July 14, 1865, pp. 1–2.

33. *Ibid.*

34. *Ibid.*

35. *Ibid.*

36. *Ibid.*

37. *Ibid.*

38. June Applegate to Elwood Evans, October 13, 1867. MSS 603, Oregon Historical Society.

39. Frances Fuller Victor, San Francisco *Evening Bulletin*, July 14, 1865.

40. "Applegates et al.," *Dictionary of Oregon History*.

41. San Francisco *Evening Bulletin*, July 14, 1865.

42. *Ibid.*

43. *Oregon Historical Quarterly* (*OHQ*), Vol. 27, pp. 179ff.

44. *Ibid.* Vol. 27, p. 442.

45. *Dictionary American Biography*, Vol. 325–326, *OHQ*, Vol. 1, 371,383.

46. *OHQ*, Vol. 13, 115: 77, 57.

47. *OHQ*, Vol. 1, 371, 83.

48. *Ibid.* Vol. 6, 412.

49. *Ibid.* Vol. 6, 412.

50. *OHQ*, Vol. 16, 165–166.

51. A. L. Throckmorton, *Oregon Argonauts, op. cit.* 303.

Chapter 4
A Time of Good Fortune (1865–68)

1. Frances Fuller Victor, "A Voyage Up the Columbia River" (From a Lady Correspondent), San Francisco *Bulletin*, Sept. 2, 1865, p.1, c. 1–3.

2. *Ibid.*

3. George S. Turnbull, *History of Oregon Newspapers* (Portland: Binfords & Mort. 1939), p. 302.

4. "A Floating Palace," Portland *Morning Oregonian*, July 24, 1865

5. For an account of the journey, see Samuel Bowles, *Across the Continent* (Springfield, Mass: Samuel Bowles, 1865); Albert D. Richardson, *Beyond the Mississippi*. (Hartford, Connecticut: American Publishing Co., 1867), pp. 367–547.

6. In September, 1890, Frederick Homer Balch's novel, *The Bridge of the Gods*, was first published by A. C. McClure, Chacago. It portrays the life and lore of Columbia River Indians prior to white settlement. In the 1930s, a Portland publisher obtained title rights.

7. Frances Fuller Victor, "A Voyage Up the Columbia River," *op. cit.*

8. Among them was missionary John Smith Griffin, whose views seldom squared with those of other informants. See Steven W. Richardson, "The Two Lives of John Smith Griffin," *OHQ*, Winter, 1990, pp. 340–370.

9. J. Quinn Thornton, born in August 1810, would prove to be "a thorn" in Frances' side in the years ahead. His letters with her comments on them are in the MSS Collections at OHS.

10. Frances Fuller Victor, "The Late Eruption of Mount Hood," San Francisco *Evening Bulletin*, October 28, 1865.

11. Frances Fuller Victor, "Autobiographical Sketch," *op. cit.* Harvey T. Tobie, *No Man Like Joe* (Binfords & Mort for the Oregon Historical Society, 1949) pp. 271–272.

12. Jesse Applegate's letters to Frances Fuller Victor, dated October 15, 29, and November 12, 1865 and his letter to Judge Deady, dated November 13, 1865. In MSS Collection, OHS.

13. Frances Fuller Victor's letter to Elwood Evans, November 15, 1865, in Elwood Evans' correspondence and papers, 1843–1894, Western American Collection, Yale University.

14. After the Civil War, a business slump struck Portland as well as the rest of the nation. After the federal government introduced greenbacks or paper money, Portland businessmen maintained gold as the standard. By purchasing with greenbacks, which were subject to change, and selling for gold, they managed to stay in business and even make money. However, debts were paid in gold. A. L. Throckmorton, *Oregon Argonauts*, published by the Oregon Historical Society Press, 1959, pp. 263–264.

15. The second of three brothers, Henry had circumnavigated the globe as a naval officer and was used to working with and for others.

16. Henry's checkered career with the Company is documented by their papers, MSS. 993, Box 3, OHS MSS. Collections.

17. The National Archives, Record Group 217; Records of the General Accounting Office, Fourth Auditor's Office, Abstract of Payment Accounts, April–June, 1866.

18. J. C. Chapman to J. B. Underwood, Portland, October 23, 1865. O. C. M. R. Company papers, OHS.

19. Deed, Elizabeth J. Knighton to H. C. Victor November 20, 1865. Entered in Deed Record Book B, Columbia County Courthouse, St. Helens, Oregon.

20. Richardson's letter to Judge Deady, dated December 6, 1865 in Matthew P. Deady Mss. Collection, OHS. His book was published in Hartford, Conn. By the subscriber book publisher, American Publishing Company.

21. The day after Christmas the Davises appointed Henry to handle their business affairs in Oregon.

22. Deed Record Book B, pp. 155–156 (new book), Columbia County Courthouse, St. Helens, Oregon.

23. Frances Fuller Victor's letter to Elwood Evans, Feb. 5, 1866, in Elwood Evans correspondence and paper, *op. cit.*

24. "Heavy Robbery of Government Lands," San Francisco *Evening Bulletin*, Feb. 12, 1866.

25. The titles of paintings are recorded in Henry Victor's will. See also B. F. Avery, "Art Beginnings on the Pacific," *Overland Monthly*, July 1868, pp. 33–34.

26. Mary Edwards Victor was born in 1855 and so was eleven when her father's will was drawn up and twenty–one the year he was drowned in the wreck of the *Pacific*.

27. Frances Fuller Victor's letter to Judge Deady, dated March 17, 1866. Deady MSS Collection, OHS.

28. Portland *Morning Oregonian*, April 23, 1866, "Marine Intelligence."

Chapter 5
Fortune is a Fickle Gypsy (1866–68))

1. Frances Fuller Victor, "Mr. Ela's Story," *The Overland Monthly*, December, 1870, pp.556–564.

2. San Francisco *Evening Bulletin,* April 16, 1866.

3. "Marine Intelligence," Portland *Oregonian*, April 23, 1866.

4. Salem, *Oregon Statesman*, December 25, 1865.

5. Columbia County, Deed Book B, p. 338 (old book).

6. Thomas Vaughan, ed. & Virginia Guest Ferriday, assoc. ed., *Space, Style and Structure; Building in Northwest America* (Portland, Oregon Historical Society, 1974), I. p.64.

7. Frances Fuller Victor, "Autobiographical Sketch" in Salem, Oregon *The Statesman*, June 16, 1895.

8. Written in Astoria in 1865, "Sunset at the Mouth of the Columbia" was first published in the December 6 issue of the San Francisco *Evening Bulletin*.

9. *Oregonian*, May 21, 1866, p. 3.

10. *Oregonian*, May 22, 1866, p. 3.

11. L.A. Ingersoll, *Ingersoll's Century Annals of San Bernardino County, 1769–1904* (Los Angeles, California, L.A. Ingersoll, 1904), p. 825. Victorville, California was named for Jacob N. Victor. He concluded his railroad career with the California Southern Railway. In 1881, he was appointed superintendent of the line, a position he held until 1887–1888.

12. George A. Ladd to J.B. Underwood, Letter, Portland, June 7, 1866, O.C.M.R. Military Road Company Papers, 1864–1877, MSS 933, OHS.

13. J.A. Chapman to J.B. Underwood, Letter, July 23, 1866 in O.C.M.R. Company Papers, *Ibid.*

14. H.C. Victor to J.B. Underwood, Letter, July 23, 1866, in O.C.M.R. Company Papers, *Ibid.*

15. Columbia County Deed Book C, (old book) p. 66.

16. Biographical sketch of Benjamin J. Giltner in Joseph Gaston, *Portland, Oregon: Its History and Builders* (Chicago & Portland: S.J. Clarke Publishing Company, 1911) II. p. 733.

17. National Archives, Records of the Fourth Auditor's Office, Appropriation—"Prize Money," sheet 295. H.C. Victor entries are dated August 25 and September 13, 1866. No evidence was found by the National Archives staff that Henry Victor ever received any prize money for helping to bring the *Princess Royal* to the Philadelphia Navy Yard.

18. Columbia County, Deed Book C., p. 81, (Old Book).

19. Columbia County, Miscellaneous Records, Book B. pp. 56–57.

20. Columbia County Deed Book C., p. 91(Old Book)).

21. *Oregonian*, November 12, 1866.

22. "Marine Intelligence," San Francisco *Bulletin*, Jan. 3, 1867.

23. Underwood to Victor, Letter, Jan. 14. 1867.

24. Columbia County Deed Book B, p. 71(New Book)).

25. *Oregonian*, February 21, 1867.

26. Harvey K. Hines, *An Illustrated History of the State of Oregon* (Chicago: Lewis Publishing Co, 1893), pp. 1152–1153.

27. See Bancroft, *History of Oregon II*, pp. 735–736. In a paragraph on salt manufacture, Frances Fuller Victor worked in a brief biographical account of Henry C. Victor and facts about his salt works. A sample of salt was displayed at the Paris Exhibition in 1867.

28. Multnomah County Circuit Court Journal, 1855–1911. *State of Oregon v. H.C. Victor*, June term, 1867.

29. Whatever the cause of his destructive rampage, Henry Victor learned that the trial of the case of *Enoch G. Adams v. H.C. Victor* was also scheduled for the June, 1867 term of the Court.

30. H.C. Victor to Underwood, Letter, April 16, 1867, in O.M.C.R. Company Papers. *op. cit.*

31. Columbia County Deed Book C. pp. 218–219.

32. *Ibid.*

33. Columbia County Miscellaneous Record, 1856–67, Book B. p. 91.

34. *Ibid.*

35. H.C. Victor to Underwood, Letter, June 18, 1867, O.C.M.R. Company Papers, OHS.

36. *Oregonian*, June 18, 1867, p. 3.

37. Multnomah County Court Journal, *State of Oregon v. H.C. Victor*, June Term, 1867.

38. *Oregonian*, June 18, 1867, p. 3.

39. Frances Fuller Victor to Deady, Letter, June 28, 1867, Deady MSS., OHS.

40. Columbia County Deed Book C. p. 256.

41. Gibbs & Parrish to Underwood, Letter, July 18, 1867. O.C.M.R. Company Papers, OHS.

42. Multnomah County Circuit Court Journal, *Enoch G. Adams v. H.C. Victor.*

43. Gibbs & Parrish to Underwood, Letter, July 18, 1867. O.C.M.R. Company Papers, OHS.

44. Parrish to Underwood, July 22, 1867.

45. H.C. Victor to Gibbs, Letter, September 26, 1867. Gibbs Papers, Folder V, MSS, OHS.

46. J.N. Victor to Gibbs, Letter, October 14, 1867. O.C.M.R. Company Papers, OHS.

47. Gibbs & Parrish to Underwood, October 24, 1867. *Ibid.*

48. Benjamin P. Avery, "Art Beginnings on the Pacific," *The Overland Monthly*, No. 1 (July, 1868) pp. 33–34. Avery would have known Frances Victor, for he was the editor of the San Francisco *Bulletin* in the late 1860s. He states that Butman's "Mount

Hood" was his best work, and that the 78x52–inch painting "was originally sold to an Oregonian, but had been lately bought by parties in this city, and is valued at $2,000."

49. May Wentworth, ed. *Poetry of the Pacific: Selections and Original Poems from the Poets of the Pacific* States (San Francisco, Pacific Publishing Company, 1867), pp. 291–299.

50. "Marine Intelligence," *Oregonian*, December 2, 1867, p. 3.

51. *Oregonian*, December 9, 1867, p. 4.

52. "From St. Helens," *Oregonian*, December 9, 1867, p. 3.

53. "Passengers for San Francisco," *Oregonian*, December 28, 1867. p. 3

54. Weather items, *Oregonian*, January 14, 16, 17, 20, 25, 1868.

55. Apparently adverse weather delayed Underwood in conferring with Pengra about the action to be taken against Henry Victor.

56. Columbia County Deed Book D, p. 69.

57. E.D. Shattuck to Underwood, Letters, April 26 and May 11, 1868 in O.C.M.R. Company Papers, OHS.

58. Multnomah County Circuit Court Journal, June Term, 1867, *Enoch G. Adams* v. *H.C. Victor.*

59. Columbia County Miscellaneous Records, Book B. p.170. The receipt was not entered until April 6, 1869.

60. H.C. Victor to Pengra, Letter, July 18, 1868. Gibbs Papers, Folder I, OHS.

61. Pengra to Gibbs, Letter, July 25, 1868, Gibbs Papers, Folder V, OHS.

62. Columbia County, Miscellaneous Records, Book B, p. 93.

63. Mary Williams Ingram, compiler, *Williams–Walworth Genealogy* (Walla Walla, Washington, n.d.) p. 62.

64. Frances Fuller Victor to Deady, Letter, July 30, 1868, Deady MSS, OHS.

65. Matthew P. Deady, "Portland–on–Wallamet," *The Overland Monthly*, I. No. 1 (July, 1868) pp. 34–43.

66. Frances Fuller Victor to Deady, Letter, August 5, 1868, Deady MSS, OHS.

67. *Oregonian*, August 19, 1868, p. 3.

68. *Oregonian*, August 20, 1868; *San Francisco Bulletin*, August 24, 1868.

69. San Francisco *Evening Bulletin*, July 1, 1868, p.1, c. 2–3.

70. Stewart, *Bret Harte, Argonaut and Exile, op.cit.* p. 169.

71. Albert Bigelow Paine, *Mark Twain, A Biography. The Personal and Literary Life of Samuel Langhorne Clemens* (New York: Harper and Brothers, 1912) I, 360–363. The book was eventually titled *The Innocents Abroad.*

72. San Francisco *Evening Bulletin*, August 29, 1868.

73. John Haskell Kemble, *The Panama Route, 1848–1869, op.cit.* p. 147.

74. Frances Fuller Victor, "A Short Stay in Acapulco," *The Overland Monthly*, VI, no. 3 (March, 1871) pp. 214–222.

75. Frances Fuller Victor did not publish "A Reprimand" until after Henry was lost at sea in the wreck of the steamship *Pacific* in November, 1875. First published in *The West Shore* in Portland in August, 1876, it was reprinted in her *The New Penelope and Other Stories and Poems* in San Francisco in 1877, and finally in her author's edition of *Poems* in Portland in 1900.

Chapter 6
The River of the West (1868–70)

1. *New York Times*, September 21, 1868, steamship *Arizona* passenger list.

2. Junius H.Browne, *The Great Metropolis. A Mirror of New York* (Hartford: American Publishing Company, 1869) pp. 59–60.

3. Ingram, *Williams—Walworth Genealogy, op. cit.*

4. Johannsen, *The House of Beadle and Adams, op. cit.* V. II, p. 286.

5. *Ibid.* p. 280.

6. B. J. Pengra letter to Governor Gibbs, Oct. 6, 1868, Gibbs Papers, MSS, OHS.

7. Browne, *The Great Metropolis. A Mirror of New York, op. cit.* A full–page engraving of Printing House Square faces p. 310.

8. Johannsen, *The House of Beadle and Adams, op. cit.* Photograph of Richardson, V. II, p.240.

9. Richardson was Bliss' first "star" author. All three of his books were best sellers. See Hamlin Hill, *Mark Twain and Elisha Bliss* (Columbia, Missouri: University of Missouri Press, 1964), pp. 11–17.

10. F.F. Victor's interviews with Bliss are based on Mark Twain's negotiations with him earlier that same year.

11. Metta Victoria Victor, *The Figure Eight; or, The Mystery of Meredith Place* (by Seeley Regester (Pseud.) New York: Beadle & Company, 1869; *The Betrayed Bride; or Wedded But Not Won* (by Eleanor Lee Edwards (pseud.). New York. Starr & Company, 1869.

12. Ames, Alice and Phoebe Cary, *op. cit.* pp. 134–135.

13. Frances Fuller Victor, *All Over Oregon and Washington*, Preface. 1.

14. Ingram, *Williams—Walworth Genealogy, op. cit.* p. 51; 57–58.

15. William Fraser Rae, *Westward by Rail* (London, 1871) p. 70. The year of the journey was 1869 and serves as the basis for Frances Fuller Victor's trip that same year.

16. Names of passengers arriving in San Francisco on the daily overland train traveling west of Promontory Point were not furnished by the railroad to San Francisco newspapers until mid–1871. See Louis J. Rasmussen, *Railway Passenger Lists to San Francisco and the West*. V. I (Colma, California: San Francisco Historic Records, 1966), Preface.

17. Account of Money Paid Contributors to *Overland Monthly*, 1869–1875 in Overland Monthly Papers, MSS Cu–B, Bancroft Library.

18. Advertisement for the firm of D.W. Williams and George T. Myers in the *Portland City Directory*, 1869, p. 60.

19. Information given by a descendant of Giltner to David C. Duniway, then Oregon Sate Archivist.

20. Salem *Weekly Statesman*, October 22, 1869.

21. See biographical note on Margaret McBride Woods in Bancroft, Oregon I, p. 628 and George S. Turnbull, *Governors of Oregon* (Binfords & Mort, 1959) pp. 34–35.

22. "Sebastian C. Adams," *Dictionary of Oregon History, op. cit.* p. 2.

23. Frances Fuller Victor, "Trail–Making in the Oregon Mountains," *Overland Monthly*, March, 1870.

24. Portland *Oregonian*, November 27 and December 3, 1869.

25. Harvey R. Tobie, *No Man Like Joe. The Life and Times of Joseph L. Meek*, (Binfords & Mort for Oregon Historical Society, 1949). The stabbing occurred on December 6, 1869, but the case did not come to trial until October, 1873.

26. Malcolm H. Clark, Jr. of Portland advised us of the law case of *Julius Mack v. H. C. Victor*, which he obtained from the court records in the Multnomah County Courthouse. The trial number of the case was Multnomah County No.33568.

27. San Francisco *Bulletin*, February 26, 1870.

28. Portland *Oregonian*, March 8, 1870.

29. See S. A. Clarke's Scrapbook, 226d, p. 177, OHS.

30. Jesse Applegate to Frances Fuller Victor, March 23, 1870. Quoted by Victor in a two–page printed enclosure titled, "Private Testimonials," which she sent to Professor Young, editor of the *OHQ* in a letter, dated Portland, January, 1870.

31. F. F. Victor letter to M. P. Deady, dated Salem, March 25, 1870, Deady Papers, MSS, OHS.

32. M. P. Deady letter to F. F. Victor, March 29, 1870, quoted by Victor in the 1901 "Private Testimonials" concerning his view of her The River of the West.

33. F. F. Victor letter to M. P. Deady, dated Salem, April 5, 1870, Deady Papers, MSS, OHS.

Chapter 7
All Over Oregon & Washington (1870–72)

1.   Portland *Oregonian*, May 19, 1870.

2.   U.S. Census, Multnomah County, City of Portland, The enumerator was DeWitt C. Ireland, Asst. Marshall.

3.   Frances Fuller Victor to the Rev. H. H. Spalding, May 11, 1870, in Eells Northwest Collection. Whitman College Library, Walla Walla, Washington.

4.   The Rev. Harmon Spalding, *Dictionary of Oregon History, op.cit.* p. 229.

5.   San Francisco *Bulletin*, March 12, 1870.

6.   Portland *Oregonian*, March 19, 1870.

7.   F. F. Victor's 12 "Summer Wanderings" articles were published in the *Oregonian* between June 21 and August 10, 1870. Five describe her Columbia River trip and her overland journey to Walla Walla, Lewiston, and the Indian reservation at Lapwai. Two narrate her July steamboat trip up the Willamette River and her visit in Salem. The last five are detailed accounts of her travels to Olympia, then around Puget Sound and to Victoria, B.C. by wagon, steamboat, and steamship.

8.   Frances Fuller Victor, "Summer Wanderings," Portland *Oregonian*, June 21, 1870, p.1.

9.   F. F. Victor, "Summer Wanderings," Portland *Oregonian*, June 22, 1870, p. 1.

10. *Ibid.*

11. *Ibid.*

12. Cushing Eels, *Diary*, May 1, 1859–1863, MSS.Eells Northwest Collection, Penrose Memorial Library, Whitman College.

13. Frances Fuller Victor, "Summer Wanderings," Portland *Oregonian*, July 2, 1870, p.1.

14. *Ibid.*

15. Frances Fuller Victor, "Summer Wanderings," *op. cit.*

16. *Ibid.*

17. *Ibid.*

18. *Ibid.*

19. Frances Fuller Victor, "Summer Wanderings," Portland *Oregonian*, July 7, 1870, p.1.

20. *Ibid.*

21. *Ibid.*

22. *Ibid.*

23. Mrs. Levi Ankeny was evidently the hostess.

24. Portland *Oregonian*, June 16, 1870.

25. Frances Fuller Victor, "Summer Wanderings," Portland, *Oregonian*, July 12, 1870. Miller had published his first two books, *Specimens* and *Joaquin et al* in Portland in 1868 and 1869, respectively.

26. Governor Woods remained in Salem until President Grant appointed him governor of Utah Territory in 1871.

27. Frances Fuller Victor, "Summer Wanderings," Portland *Oregonian*, July 12, 1870.

28. *Ibid.*

29. Frances Fuller Victor, "*The River of the West* Vindicated," Portland *Oregonian*, July 14, 15, p.1.

30. Frances Fuller Victor, "Summer Wanderings," Portland *Oregonian*, August 6, 1870.

31. *Ibid.*

32. Portland *Oregonian*, August 1, 1870, p.3, "Arrival of the Victoria Steamer."

33. Frances Fuller Victor, "A Stage Ride in Oregon and Washington," *The American Publisher*, Hartford, Conn., August, 1871, Vol. 1, No. 5.

34. *Ibid.*

35. *Ibid.*

36. Frances Fuller Victor, "Mr. Ela's Story," *Overland Monthly*, December, 1870; Overland Monthly Papers, UC–B. MS, C–H97.

37. George R. Stewart, Jr., *Bret Harte, Argonaut and Exile* (Boston, and New York, 1931), p. 184.

Chapter 8
A Venture in Publishing

1. Helen Krebs Smith, *The Presumptuous Dreamers* (Smith, Smith, Smith Publications, Lake Oswego, Oregon, 1974) p. 143. Belle Cooke was one of the most active suffragists in Oregon, according to Samuel Clarke's *History of the Willamette Valley*.

2. San Francisco *Bulletin*, January 25–28, 1871.

3. Sherilyn Cox Bennion, "The Pioneer: The First Voice for Women's Suffrage in the West," *The Pacific Historian*, Winter, 1981, v. 25, no. 4, p. 15–16.

4. *History of Woman Suffrage* (Rochester, New York), III, 1876–1885, p. 753–756.

5. Abigail Scott Duniway, *Path Breaking: An Autobiographical History of the Equal Suffrage Movement in Pacific Coast States* (New York: Schoken Books, 1971) p. 68.

6. Stewart, *Bret Harte, op. cit.* p. 184–185, 189.

7. Ella Sterling Cummins, *The Story of the Files*, San Francisco, 1893, "The Overland School," pp. 158–159; Pacific Coast Women's Press Association, *The Impress*, December 25, 1896, Special Christmas Number, "Josephine Clifford McCrackin," p. 45.

8. The only changes made in the 1871 reprint was to substitute 1871 for 1870 and Union Publishing Co., Chicago, IL. for Bliss & Co., Newark, NJ on the title page.

9. Hamlin Hill, *Mark Twain and Elisha Bliss, op. cit.* p. 16.

10. Portland *Oregonian*, January 15, February 2, and April 11, 1871.

11. Portland *Oregonian*, May 5, 1871 carried an editorial by Harvey W. Scott heralding the first number of the *New Northwest*.

12. F. F. Victor, "The Romance and Poetry of Oregon," *Democratic Era*, May 12, clipping in Mrs. Victor's Scrapbook No. 120, Oregon Historical Society.

13. In this editorial, Mrs. Duniway reveals her admiration for the older and better known Mrs. Victor

14. F. F. Victor, "About the Mouth of the Columbia," *Overland Monthly*, VIII (January, 1872), p. 74.

15. F. F. Victor to Matthew P. Deady, Portland, Oregon, August 19, 1871, Deady Papers MSS, Oregon Historical Society.

16. Beverly Beaton and C. Thomas Edwards, "Susan B. Anthony's Woman Suffrage Crusade in the American West," *Journal of the West* (April, 1972), p. 9.

17. *Ibid.*

18. F. F. Victor, "A Rocky Mountain Story," *The American Publisher*, Vol. I, No. 7 (October, 1871).

19. F. F. Victor, *All Over Oregon and Washington*, Preface.

20. Portland *Oregonian*, October 23, 1871.

21. F. F. Victor, "About the Mouth of the Columbia," *Overland Monthly* (January, 1872); "From Astoria to the Cascades," *Overland Monthly* (February, 1872); "The Gorge of the Columbia," *Overland Monthly* (March, 1872).

22. F. F. Victor, Letter to Elwood Evans, San Francisco, December 15, 1871 in Correspondence and Papers of Elwood Evans, 1843–1874, Western Americana Collection, Yale University Library.

23. Portland *Oregonian*, April 8, 1872.

24. Portland *Oregonian*, April 27, 1872.

25. Malcolm H. Clark, Jr., ed., *Pharisee Among the Philistines: The Story of Matthew P. Deady, 1871–1892*, I. p. 76.

26. F. F. Victor, "Autobiographical Sketch," Salem *Statesman*, June 16, 1895, p. 2.

27. *New Northwest*, May 3, 1872, p. 2.

28. F. F. Victor, Letter to Col. Meek, San Francisco, May 3, 1872.

29. F. F. Victor's letters to Matthew P. Deady, F. G. Young, and Others, 1866–1902. Originals in MSS, OHS.

30. U.S. Census, Hohokus Township, Bergen County, New Jersey, July 12, 1870, p. 395.

31. F. F. Victor's *Life of Joseph L. Meek: Record of Early Times in the Rocky Mountains and Oregon* is listed in F. Leypoldt, *The American Catalog, Author and Title Entries in Books in Print and for Sale . . .* July 1, 1876.

32. *All Over Oregon and Washington, op. cit.*

33. See Note No. 31 (above).

34. F. F. Victor, "On the Sands," Lakeside Monthly, VI., 1872. Reprinted in Victor's *The New Penelope and Other Stories and Poems*, 1877.

Chapter 9
Aftermath of the Modoc Indian War (1873)

1. Louis J. Rasmussen, *Railway Passenger Lists of Overland Trains to San Francisco and the West*, (Colma, California, San Francisco Historic Records, 1966), II. p. 247.

2. San Francisco *Bulletin*, April 12, 1873. See "The Modoc War, 1864–1873," in Bancroft, *History of Oregon*, II., 555–636, for a readable account of the causes, events, and conclusion of the conflict.

3. San Francisco *Bulletin*, April 14, 1873.

4. Victor, "An Old Fool," *Overland Monthly*, (June, 1873), (July, 1873).

5. Victor, Letter to Oliver C. Applegate, Alameda, California, May 11, 1873. MSS, OrU.

6. Portland *Oregonian*, May 23, 1873.

7. Upon Victor's return to Portland after her six–week visit to the Klamath County with members of the Applegate family, Abigail Duniway prevailed upon her to write a letter describing her adventures there for the *New Northwest,* published on September 5, 1873.

8. *Ibid.*

9. *Ibid.*

10. See "Captain Oliver Cromwell Applegate" in *History of Klamath County Oregon— Its Resources and Its People*, Klamath Falls, Oregon, 1941, pp. 196–197.

11. Victor, *Atlantis Arisen* (Philadelphia: J. B. Lippincott Company, 1891), pp. 178–179.

12. 43rd Cong. 1st sess. House Exec. Doc. 122, *Trial of the Modoc Prisoners* v. 1607.

13. *Ibid.*

14. A. B. Meacham, *Wigwams and Warpath* (Boston: John P. Dale & Company, 1875).

15. Victor, Bancroft, *History of Oregon*, II, *op. cit.* pp. 630–631.

16. Victor, *Atlantis Arisen*, p. 179.

17. Victor, Bancroft, *History of Oregon*, II, *op. cit.* p. 636.

18. Victor, Letter to O. C. Applegate, Portland, April 23, 1874, MSS, OrU.

19. Barry V. Sproull, *Modoc Indian War*, Lava Beds Natural History Association, 1969. This pamphlet of 30 unnumbered pages is illustrated with photographs of Capt. Jack's Stronghold in full color, portraits, and maps of battles. A photo of Canby's Cross implanted in a rock cairn, on the site, as near as can be determined, of the murders of the Peace Commissioners.

20. Keith and Donna Clark, eds. *Daring Donald McKay or the Last War Trail of the Modocs* (Portland: Oregon Historical Society, 1971).

21. Gorman, M. W. "The Discovery and Early History of Crater Lake." *Mazamas*, I. no. 2. (1897). See also the Jacksonville *Oregon Sentinel*, August 21 and 28, 1869.

22. Victor, *Atlantis Arisen*, *op. cit.* 181–182.

23. *Ibid.*

24. Victor, Letter to O. C. Applegate, Portland, August 27, 1873. MSS, OrU. "Poems and Letters of Samuel A. Clarke," Scrapbook OHS 226d. Description of Mrs. S. A. (Harriet) Clarke and her home on Gaiety Hill in Salem.

25. Victor, Letter to O. C. Applegate, Portland, September 17, 1873, OrU.

26. O. C. Applegate to F. F. Victor, September 9, 1873, OrU.

27. Victor, Letter to Lindsay Applegate, Portland, December 17, 1873, OrU.

28. Victor, Letter to O. C. Applegate, Portland, December 22, 1873, MSS, OrU.

Chapter 10
Historian & Journalist (1874–75)

1. Victor to B. F. Avery, Portland, Jan. 3, 1874 in *Overland Monthly* Papers, Bancroft Library, University of California.

2. Victor to B. F. Avery, Jan. 21, 1874 in *Overland Monthly* Papers, Bancroft Library.

3. *Ibid.*

4. Victor to Capt. J. M. McCall, Portland, Jan. 12, 1874—the original in McCall Letters in Oregon State Archives, Salem.

5. Victor in her *Early Indian Wars of Oregon*, published by the state in 1894, states on page 343 that Major J. A. Lupton was killed in an unprovoked attack on local Indians by his militia.

6. Victor to Oliver Applegate, Portland, Jan. 18, 1874 in Victor–Applegate Correspondence, OrU.

7. Jesse Applegate had suffered a severe reversal of his fortunes in the loss of his Yoncalla homestead because he had signed a bond for a state official who had absconded with state funds.

8. *The New Northwest*, Jan. 16, 30, 1874.

9. Victor to B. F. Avery, Portland, Feb. 12, 1874. The opening paragraph of Part I of "The Pioneers of Oregon" reveals her deep interest in Oregon and its history.

10. See *Journal* of the House of Representatives of the 8th Biennial Session of the Legislative Assembly of the State of Oregon, 1874, pp. 195, 283.

11. The two–day session was held in the Reed Opera House in Salem on February 12 and 13, 1874.

12. Victor to Oliver Applegate, Portland, Feb. 19, 1874, 4 pp. Victor–Applegate Correspondence, OrU.

13. Both of Victor's husbands had been addicted to drink, for which she had left them.

14. Multnomah County Court, June term, 1874, Case of John Campbell *vs.* H. C. Victor and F. F. Victor.

15. We are indebted to Malcolm H. Clark, Jr. of Portland for a summary of the proceedings of this land case. No record of F. F. Victor's response to Scott's decision has been found.

16. Victor, *The Women's War with Whisky; or Crusading in Portland*. She copyrighted this 60–page pamphlet, printed by George H. Himes late in August, 1874. Our treatment of the crusade is based primarily on Victor's pamphlet and Abigail Duniway's review of it, published in *The New Northwest*.

17. Victor, "A Word in Defense of the Crusaders," *Morning Oregonian*, June 19, 1874, p. 1.

18. Victor to Oliver Applegate, Portland, October 8, 1874, Victor–Applegate Correspondence, OrU.

19. See note, No. 10.

20. Victor to Oliver Applegate, San Francisco, February 9, 1875. Victor–Applegate Correspondence, OrU.

21. Victor, "Letters from a Sky Parlor" appeared in the *Sunday Morning Call* from February 21 to August 8, 1875. Clippings of the column are preserved in Victor's Scrapbook 120 at OHS.

22. The March, 1874 number of the *Overland Monthly* carried an article describing the elaborate indexing system of the Bancroft Library and stated that "the mass was to be sifted and the results given to the world in some form." The June number carried an article, titled "Some Rare Books about California," which alluded to "Mr. Bancroft's self–imposed life work on condensing his material into a series of standard works on . . . a territory he terms the Pacific States."

23. Henry L. Oak, *"Literary Industries" in a New Light* (San Francisco, Bacon Printing Co., 1891) p. 57.

24. George W. Jones in his "The Romantic History of Josephine Clifford McCrackin," printed in *National Magazine*, Boston, Mass., noted that in 1877 Clifford published a collection of her "Overland Tales." It seems likely that in 1875 F. F. Victor was in touch with her poet friend, Ina D. Coolbrith, who had accepted the office of librarian of the Free Library of Oakland, California to make ends meet.

25. J. D. Cleaver, "L. Samuel and the *West Shore*: Images of a Changing Pacific Northwest." *OHQ* (Summer–Fall, 1993) pp. 167–224.

26. The loss of the steamship *Pacific* and the tragic fate of all but two of its passengers and crew is described in Lewis & Dryden, *Marine History of the Pacific Northwest*, pp. 224–227.

Chapter 11
The West Shore & The New Penelope (1876–78)

1. In his diary entry of August 12, 1876, Judge Deady notes that he had gone to Eugene to attend several sessions of the University of Oregon board of directors, of which he was chairman. *The Diary of Mathew P. Deady, 1871–1892, Pharisee Among Philistines*, edited by Malcolm Clarke, Jr. (Portland, Or,: Oregon Historical Society, 1975) Vol. I, p. 216.

2. On May 25, Deady and his wife attended a meeting of the Portland Literary Association on that date, according to his diary, p. 213. A copy of Mrs. Victor's address is in her scrapbook in the OHS library.

3. Jesse Applegate's letter to Mrs. Clarke in an S. A. Clarke envelope in OHS library.

4. Mary Boise Spiller (1829–1901), sister of Judge Reuben Boise, had been chosen principal of the Preparatory Department of the University of Oregon, according to Deady's diary, Vol. I, p. 224, No. 21.

5. Malcolm H. Clark, Jr., now deceased, provided this information.

6. This notice is a part of the above file.

7. An entry in Deady's Diary, dated Jan, 24, 1871, reads: "Received a letter from Bancroft & Co. containing proposal to publish volume one of Deady's Rep. The proposition is well enough, except I will not consent to pay for making index."

8. This transaction, dated May 17, 1877, is recorded in Deed Book F in the Columbia County Courthouse in St. Helens, Ore.

9. George S. Turnbull, *History of Oregon Newspapers* (Portland, Ore.: Binfords & Mort, 1939) p. 260. F. F. Victor's letter to Oliver C. Applegate, June 29, 1877, OrU.

10. This statement is based on Malcolm H. Clark Jr.'s research.

11. On July 8, 1878, the *Oregonian* reported that F. F. Victor had made an engagement with Pearson as his "corresponding, traveling editor." An original of page 4 of *The Resources of Oregon and Washington*, Vol. I. August, 1878, is held by the OHS Library.

12. See Chapter XXII. "Historic Exploration Northward," pp 530–561 in *Literary Industries in the Works of Hubert Howe Bancroft*, Vol. XXXIX (San Francisco: The History Company, 1890).

13. *Ibid.* p. 543.

14. Mrs. Clarke's letter to Oliver C. Applegate, dated June 26, 1878, O. C. A. Correspondence, OrU.

15. William A. Morris, "Authorship of the Pacific States Publications: A History Within a History," *OHQ*, December, 1903, p. 335.

16. *Ibid.* p. 340.

17. "Captain Oliver Cromwell Applegate," in *History of Klamath County, Oregon* (Klamath Falls, Or., 1941) p. 196.

Chapter 12
Holding Her Own in the Bancroft Literary Workshop (1879–84)

1. Michael Perman, Introduction, *A Perspective on the American Past* (D. C. Heath, 1996), pp. xiii–xxi, discusses the what, why, how, and so–what questions that confronted Frances Fuller Victor in the Bancroft Literary Workshop.

2. Harry Clark, *A Venture in History—The Production, Publication, and Sale of the Works of Hubert Howe Bancroft* (University of California Press, 1973) p. 33.

3. Henry R. Wagner, "Albert Little Bancroft, His Diaries and Account Books," in the *California Historical Quarterly*, June, September, December, 1950.

4. Kate Bancroft's letter to H. H. Bancroft, dated September 1, 1878, in the Bancroft Family papers.

5. *Literary Industries*, Vol. XXXIX of *The Works of H. H. Bancroft* (San Francisco: The History Company, 1890) pp. 236–237.

6. According to the San Francisco *Directory* for the year 1879, Frances Fuller Victor lived at this address. The description of Bancroft's paper world is based on John H. Caughey's Chapter 6, "The House of Bancroft" in his *Hubert Howe Bancroft, Historian of the West* (University of California Press, 1946) pp. 57–66.

7. H. H. Bancroft, *Literary Industries, op. cit.* pp. 198–200.

8. *Ibid.*, pp. 255–259.

9. *Ibid.*, pp. 337–238.

10. Henry L. Oak, *"Literary Industries" in a New Light* (San Francisco: Bacon Printing Co., 1893) pp. 37–38.

11. The autobiography of General Joseph Lane, 1878 is in the Bancroft Library and OHS.

12. F. F. Victor's letter to Judge Deady, OHS.

13. F. F. Victor's letters to D. W. Craig, OHS.

14. Deady's letters to H. H. Bancroft in the Bancroft Library and Bancroft's letters to Deady in the Deady Collection at OHS.

15. F. F. Victor's monograph on the name Oregon appears at the end of Chapter I, "Oregon in 1834," of Bancroft's *Oregon*, I, pp. 17–25.

16. Jesse Applegate, "Views of Oregon History," dated Yoncalla, 1878 is in the Bancroft Library.

17. *Ibid.*

18. F. F. Victor's correspondence with Elwood Evans is in his papers and correspondence in the Western America Collection at Yale University Library.

19. *Ibid.*

20. F. F. Victor's letter to Deady, OHS.

21. "Samuel Asahel Clarke," *Dictionary of Oregon History, op. cit.*, p. 55.

22. H.H. Bancroft, *Literary Industries, op. cit.* pp. 201ff.

23. *Ibid.* pp. 586–587.

24. The Bagley Collection is in the library of the University of Washington, Seattle.

25. These memos are in the Bancroft Library.

26. The William Marshall Collection is in the library of the University of Washington, Seattle.

27. F. F. Victor's letter to Judge Deady, OHS.

28. Eells' letter to F. F. Victor in the Eells' Collection in the library of the University of Washington, Seattle.

29. Henry Clark, "Table I, Publication Order of Bancroft's Work," *A Venture in History, op. cit.,* p. 59.

30. F. F. Victor's Letter to Deady, OHS.

31. F. F. Victor's letter to William Marshall, library of the University of Washington, Seattle.

32. William A. Morris, "The Origins and Authorship of Bancroft's Pacific States Publication; A History of a History," in *OHQ* (December, 1903), pp. 294, 331, 337.

Chapter 13
The History Company (1879–84)

1. Oregon Supreme Court Verdict, No. 01524. *Frances Fuller Victor et al.* vs. *Walter S. Davis.*

2. Columbia County Deed Book H, March 6, 1885.

3. Fi 47,209, OHS.

4. Frances Fuller Victor, Letter to Deady, No. 20, OHS.

5. In Jesse Q. Thornton's Scrapbook, MSS, 371, OHS.

6. William Marshall Collection, University of Washington.

7. Frances Fuller Victor, Letter to Deady, No. 21, OHS.

8. According to the *Williams–Walworth Genealogy,* pp. 49–50, Metta died on June 26, 1885 at The Terraces, and her remains were laid to rest in a nearby cemetery.

9. History Company Records, Box 4, Bancroft Library, University of California, Berkeley.

10. H. H. Bancroft, *Literary Industries, op. cit.* p. 772.

11. History Company Records, *op. cit.*

12. H. H. Bancroft, *Literary Industries, op. cit.*

13. J.W. Caughey, *Hubert Howe Bancroft, op. cit.* pp. 301–311.

14. H. H. Bancroft, *Literary Industries, op. cit.* p. 773.

15. *Ibid.* pp. 775–787.

16. Harry Clark, *A Venture in History, op. cit.* pp. 110–112.

17. H. H. Bancroft, *Literary Industries, op. cit.* pp. 788–789.

18. J. W. Caughey, *Hubert Howe Bancroft, op. cit.* pp. 311–312.

19. Harry Clark, *A Venture in History, op. cit.* p. 114.

20. H. H. Bancroft, Letter to Deady, Deady Collection, OHS.

21. Harry Clark, *A Venture in History, op. cit.* p. 114.

22. *Ibid.*

23. H. H. Bancroft, *Literary Industries, op. cit.* p. 790.

24. A letter to this effect, dated May 21, 1886, is in the Bancroft Library.

25. Bancroft's letter to Deady, dated May 10, 1886, in Deady Collection, B214, OHS.

26. San Francisco *Chronicle,* August 2, 1886.

27. Frances Fuller Victor's letter to Elwood Evans in Evans' Collection, Yale University Library.

28. William Alfred Morris, "The Origin and Authorship of the Bancroft Pacific States Publications: A History of a History, " *OHQ,* December, 1903, p. 342.

29. *Ibid.*

30. Henry L. Oak, *"Literary Industries" in a New Light* (San Francisco: Bacon Printing Co., 1893) p. 33.

31. Deady, *Diary,* Vol. II, 502.

32. Frances Fuller Victor, Letter to Deady, No. 22, OHS.

33. During the last years of his life, Jesse Applegate was confined to the state asylum.

34. Bancroft's letters to Deady, Deady Collection, OHS.

35. F. F. Victor's copy of Scott's review is in one of her scrapbooks in OHS.

36. Hist. Soc. of Penn. MSS Collection, Simon Gratz Autograph Coll. Am. Poets.

37. Bancroft's letter to Deady, Deady Collection, OHS.

38. Henry L. Oak, *"Literary Industries" in a New Light, op. cit.* p. 54.

39. Harry Clark, *A Venture in History, op. cit.* pp. 115–116.

40. Bancroft's letter to Deady, Deady Collection, OHS.

41. H. H. Bancroft, *Literary Industries, op. cit.* p. 655.

42. Deady's *Diary,* Vol. II, p. 525.

43. In the History Company's Records, *op. cit.*

44. William Alfred Morris, "The Origin and Authorship of the Bancroft Pacific States Publications: A History of a History," *op. cit.* p. 334.

45. Frances Fuller Victor, Letter to Deady, No. 23, OHS.

46. A microfilm copy of Nemos' affidavit is in the Bancroft Library, U.C. Berkeley, a Swedish version is included in the microfilm.

47. Frances Fuller Victor's letters to Deady, No. 24, 26, OHS.

48. H. H. Bancroft, Letter dated September 4, 1888, Deady Collection, OHS.

49. Deady, *Diary*, Vol. II, p. 539.

50. Bancroft's letter to Deady in Deady Collection, OHS; and Deady's letters to H. H. Bancroft, in the Bancroft Library, U.C., Berkeley.

51. Frances Fuller Victor, Letter to Deady, No. 27, OHS.

52. Bancroft to Deady, January 10, 1889, OHS.

53. Deady, *Diary*, Vol. II, pp. 543, 551.

54. Frances Fuller Victor, Letter to Deady, No. 28, OHS.

55. Frances Fuller Victor, Letter to Deady, No. 29, OHS.

56. See Victor's "In Memoriam for Douglas Williams", OHS.

57. Victor's letter to William Marshall in the Marshall Collection, University of Washington Library.

58. A copy of *Can Love Sin?* by Mark Douglas at OHS.

Chapter 14
The Pacific Northwest Revisited (1890–94)

1. This lot shows up on the inventory of Frances Fuller Victor's property in her petition for a Navy widow's pension.

2. The New York *Sun* of Feb. 17, 1890 and the New York *Tribune* published favorable reviews. Copies are filed in Scrapbook No. 197, OHS.

3. Deady's *Diary II*, pp. 576–593.

4. Samuel L. Clarke Scrapbook, No. 226, OHS.

5. *Atlantis Arisen* (Philadelphia: J. B. Lippincott, 1891), p. 412.

6. Terence O'Donnell & Thomas Vaughan, *Portland, An Informal History and Guide* (Portland: Oregon Historical Society Press, Second Edition, 1989), pp. 35

7. *Atlantis Arisen, op. cit.*, p. 83.

8. Dorothy N. Morrison, *Ladies Were Not Expected* (Portland: Oregon Historical Society Press, 1985), p. 117.

9. J. D. Cleaver, "L. Samuels and the *West Shore*: Images of a Changing Northwest," *OHQ*, Summer–Fall, 1993, p. 216.

10. *Dictionary of Oregon History, op. cit.*, p. 243, 103.

11.   *Atlantis Arisen, op. cit.,* p. 262.

12.   *Washington Historical Magazine,* Vol. I, Oct. 1893.

13.   *Atlantis Arisen , op. cit.,* p. 236.

14.   *Ibid.,* p. 306.

15.   *Ibid.,* p. 314.

16.   *Ibid.,* p. 328–330.

17.   *Ibid,,* p. 336–339.

18.   Caughey, *H. H. Bancroft, op. cit.,* p. 263.

19.   *Atlantis Arisen, op. cit.,* pp. 346 ff.

20.   *Ibid,* pp. 352–353.

21.   *Williams–Walworth Genealogy,* compiled by Mrs. Mary J. Williams Ingram, Walla Walla, Wa. Circa 1906.

22.   *Atlantis Arisen, op. cit.,* p. 362.

23.   *Ibid.,* p. 365–366.

24.   *Ibid.,* p. 412.

25.   Scrapbook 226c, OHS.

26.   Deady's *Diary, Vol. II,* p. 600.

27.   Oregon State Library, Salem, Oregon.

28.   A copy is in the Frances Fuller Victor Collection, OHS.

29.   Harry Clark, *A Venture in History, op. cit.,* p. 59.

30.   *Literary Industries,* pp. 237; 259–261.

31.   White's diary is in the Oregon State Library, Salem. White noted that Victor called on her on January 27, 28, and 29 as well as on February 2 and 3. She did not explain her relationship to Victor nor the fact that the 1891 state legislature, then in session, was considering a resolution to authorize Secretary of State George McBride to compile from materials in the state archives "a complete record" of the early Indian wars of Oregon as well as a sketch of the pioneer history preceding these wars. He was authorized to spend no more than $1,500 on the work to be done under his supervision, according to House Resolution No. 22 of the 20th session of the legislature, passed on February 13. The Senate passed a concurring resolution on the 14th.

32.   Navy Pension File No. 7962, National Archives.

33.   A copy of the Williams *In Memoriam* may be found at OHS.

34.   Post card in Information File at California State Library. Pages 180–181 recount Victor's trip to Crater Lake with the Applegate party in the summer of 1873. The

last paragraph on page 183 records how Victor would personify "the young giant Oregon" if she were a painter. ". . . with empire written on his brow, and power tempered by mildness beaming from his eyes. Of fair complexion he with tawny blonde hair and curling golden beard." His purple robe would be "embroidered with wheat ears. . . .His throne should be among the rugged mountains . . . . On his right should roll the magnificent Columbia, to which ships in the distance should seek entrance; and over his shoulder the white crest of Mount Hood stood blushing in a rosy sunset."

35. Post card in Information File at California State Library.

36. Victor's letters to Deady, No. 32, No. 33, OHS.

37. Such a biographical sketch, illustrated with photographs of the sisters, appeared in the 1892 number of the Charles Wells Moulton *Magazine of Poetry*. A year later, the magazine carried a similar biography of Frances as well as several of her early poems.

38. Victor's letter to Deady, no. 34, OHS.

39. Second Biennial Report of the Oregon State Board of Horticulture to the Legislative Assembly, 1893, Appendix, pp. 208–209.

40. Navy Pension File No. 7962, National Archives.

41. Victor's letter to Deady, No. 35, OHS.

42. This entry may be the source of the legend that during these years in Salem, Victor had sold cosmetics to make a living.

43. Victor's Jan. 6, 1893 letter to Mrs. Ewer in Information File, California State Library.

44. The original of Victor's letter to Hill is in the Oregon Collection at the University of Oregon Library.

45. Victor's letters to Mary Sheldon Barnes are in the Bancroft Library.

46. Deady's *Diary, I,* p. 320.

47. Victor's letter to Mrs. Deady, Mss 687 B, OHS.

48. Duniway's address appears in her scrapbook No. 2 in the David C. Duniway papers, courtesy of Harriet L. Smith in February, 1971.

49. Victor's letter to Dye, No. 37, OHS.

50. *Women of the Century*, p.734.

51. Jim Martin, *A Bit of a "Blue"* (Salem, Or: Deep Well Publishing Company, 1992) p. 185 states that on April 24, 1894 Victor received her final payment from the state.

52. Victor's letters and cards to Eva Emery Dye, OHS.

Chapter 15
Sanctuary in San Francisco (1895–99)

1. In the September, 1894 number of *The Impress*, Frances Fuller Victor was listed as the fourth vice–president on the 1894–1895 ticket.

2. Gary Scharnhorst, "Making Her Fame—Charlotte Perkins Stetson in California," *California History*, Summer, 1985, pp. 192–243.

3. "William P. Lord," *Dictionary of Oregon History, op. cit.*, p. 152

4. *The History of Women's Suffrage*, edited by Susan B. Anthony & Ida H. Harper, published by Susan B. Anthony, Rochester, N. Y. Vol. III (1883–1900) Chapter XXVI-II, "California," pp. 480–481.

5. *Ibid*

6. Adams' card to Mrs. Victor is in one of her scrapbooks, OHS

7. John W. Caughey, *Hubert Howe Bancroft, op. cit.*, pp. 337–339; 341–346.

8. Walla Walla *Gazette*, June 1, 1895.

9. Myron Eells Collection, Penrose Memorial Library, Whitman College, Walla Walla, WA.

10. Frances Fuller Victor—Oliver C. Applegate correspondence, Letter No. 20, OrU.

11. *American Magazine of Civics*, Vol. VII. Pp. 591–598. New York: Civics Publishing Co.

12. Mrs. Victor doubtless knew that Susan B. Anthony was the keynote speaker at the Pacific Northwest Congress of Women, held June 8–10 at the Taylor Street Methodist Episcopal Church in Portland. Courtesy Debra Shein's conference paper, "A Look at Portland's 1896 Congress of Women."

13. Myrick, Mss. 151, OHS.

14. This unsigned letter is in Mrs. Victor's scrapbook No. 234, OHS.

15. In the preface to his *A History of the Anmerican Fur Trade of the Far West*, p. xxxi, Chittenden noted: "Mrs. Frances Fuller Victor, the historian of Oregon and Washington, has woven around the biography of the trapper Joseph Meek a very complete account of the desultory operations of the mountain traders between 1830 and 1840. Her contributions to Bancroft's history of the Western states likewise contain a great deal relating to the fur trade." He added that "this extensive fund of information has been freely tendered through the medium of correspondence for use in the present work." On the same page, Chittenden acknowledged "the direct assistance received from Dr. Coues in the course of a

long and interesting correspondence." Evidently Chittenden put Mrs. Victor in touch with Dr. Coues.

16 Frances Fuller Victor—Oliver C. Applegate correspondence, letters no. 21, 22, OrU.

17. A copy of the 1896 *Christmas Souvenir* for the Women's Press Association is in the Frances Fuller Victor Collection, OHS

18. Chittenden's "Journal of a Journey to the Pacific Coast" in the Washington State Historical Society Library, courtesy of a letter from Gordon B. Dodds to Hazel E. Mills, dated July 11, 1959.

19. John Minto's correspondence in Oregon State Archives, Salem.

20. Filed in one of Mrs. Victor's scrapbooks, OHS.

21. "Horace S. Lyman," *Dictionary of Oregon History, op. cit.,* p. 154.

22. Mrs. Victor's Scrapbook, No. 20, OHS

23. Mrs. Victor's Scrapbook, No. 197, OHS.

24. Frances Fuller Victor's letters to Eva Emery Dye, No. 47, OHS.

25. "Frederic George Young," *Dictionary of Oregon History, op. cit.,* p. 278.

26. Frances Fuller Victor's letters to Professor Young, No. 45, OHS.

27. Salem *Oregon Statesman,* Jan. 6, 1898.

28. James Wickersham, "Life, Character, and Public Service of Elwood Evans, Pioneer, Lawyer, Governor, and Historian," *The Washington Historian,* Jan., 1900, No. 2, pp. 553–564.

29. "*Oregon* (Battleship)," *Dictionary of Oregon History, op. cit.,* p. 181.

30. Eells Collection, Penrose Memorial Library, Whitman College, Walla Walla, Wa.

31. Marshall Collection, University of Washington Library, Seattle, Wa.

32. Frances Fuller Victor's letters to Professor Young, No. 46, OHS.

33. "Oregon Historical Society," *Dictionary of Oregon History, op. cit.,* p. 184.

34. Native Sons Collection, OHS.

35. "William Gladstone Steel," *Dictionary of Oregon History, op. cit.,* p. 234.

36. Frances Fuller Victor's letters to Professor Young, No. 48, OHS.

37. *Ibid,* Nos, 49, 50, 51., OHS.

38. Frances Fuller Victor's letters to Oliver C. Applegate, No. 24, OrU.

39. Michael J. Brodhead, "A Dedication to the Memory of Elliott Coues 1842–1899), *Arizona and the West,* Spring, 1971, pp. 1–4.

40. Frances Fuller Victor's letters to Professor Young, No. 52, OHS.

More than a decade ago, another Oregon historian-journalist Jim Martin wrote also for *The Oregonian*, the Salem *Statesman-Journal* and the Eugene *Register-Guard*.

He also published a less comprehensive biography of his predecessor, *A Bit of a "Blue": The Life and Work of Frances Fuller Victor* (Deep Well Publishing Co., Salem, 1992). Professor Bordwell reviewed the study favorably in the *Oregon Historical Quarterly*, at a time when Mrs. Mills' mind had turned to other matters.

We are certain that both authors—Mills and Bordwell—would wish to give Mr. Martin's invigorating work prominent notice, which we do with special pleasure, and deep appreciation for its aim and contents.

INDEX